D1372808

KARL E. MUNDT LIBRARY
Dakota State University
Madison, SD 57042-1799

Semantic Web Services, Processes and Applications

KARL E. MUNDT LIBRARY
Dakota State University
Madison, SD 57042-1799

SEMANTIC WEB AND BEYOND
Computing for Human Experience

Series Editors:

Ramesh Jain
University of California, Irvine
http://ngs.ics.uci.edu/

Amit Sheth
University of Georgia
http://lsdis.cs.uga.edu/~amit

As computing becomes ubiquitous and pervasive, computing is increasingly becoming an extension of human, modifying or enhancing human experience. Today's car reacts to human perception of danger with a series of computers participating in how to handle the vehicle for human command and environmental conditions. Proliferating sensors help with observations, decision making as well as sensory modifications. The emergent semantic web will lead to machine understanding of data and help exploit heterogeneous, multi-source digital media. Emerging applications in situation monitoring and entertainment applications are resulting in development of experiential environments.

SEMANTIC WEB AND BEYOND
Computing for Human Experience
addresses the following goals:

➢ brings together forward looking research and technology that will shape our world more intimately than ever before as computing becomes an extension of human experience;

➢ covers all aspects of computing that is very closely tied to human perception, understanding and experience;

➢ brings together computing that deal with semantics, perception and experience;

➢ serves as the platform for exchange of both practical technologies and far reaching research.

Additional information about this series can be obtained from
http://www.springer.com

AdditionalTitles in the Series:
Canadian Semantic Web edited by Mamadou T. Koné., Daniel Lemire; ISBN 0-387-29815-0
Semantic Management of Middleware by Daniel Oberle; ISBN-10: 0-387-27630-0

Semantic Web Services, Processes and Applications

edited by

Jorge Cardoso
University of Madeira, Portugal

Amit P. Sheth
University of Georgia, USA

KARL E. MUNDT LIBRARY
Dakota State University
Madison, SD 57042-1799

Springer

Jorge Cardoso
Universidade da Madeira
Department de Matematica e
Engenharias
9000-390 FUNCHAL
PORTUGAL

Amit P. Sheth
Large Scale Distributed
 Information Systems (LSDIS) Lab
Department of Computer Science
University of Georgia
Athens, GA 30602
USA

Library of Congress Control Number: 2006926729

Edited by Jorge Cardoso and Amit P. Sheth

ISBN-10: 0-387- 30239-5
ISBN-13: 978-0-387-30239-3
e-ISBN-10: 0-387-34685-6
e-ISBN-13: 978-0-387-34685-4

Printed on acid-free paper.

© 2006 Springer Science+Business Media, LLC.
All rights reserved. This work may not be translated or copied in whole or
in part without the written permission of the publisher (Springer
Science+Business Media, LLC, 233 Spring Street, New York, NY 10013,
USA), except for brief excerpts in connection with reviews or scholarly
analysis. Use in connection with any form of information storage and
retrieval, electronic adaptation, computer software, or by similar or
dissimilar methodology now know or hereafter developed is forbidden.
The use in this publication of trade names, trademarks, service marks and
similar terms, even if the are not identified as such, is not to be taken as
an expression of opinion as to whether or not they are subject to
proprietary rights.

Printed in the United States of America.

9 8 7 6 5 4 3 2 1

springer.com

Dedication

To all researchers that devote weekends and evenings to take science always a step further.

Jorge Cardoso

To my parents, Professor Pravin Sheth and Surbhi Sheth. Their support and sacrifies for my education became the foundation of my career.

Amit Sheth

Contents

ß 14

Contributing Authors

Antonio Cau
Software Technology Research Laboratory, De Montfort University, Leicester, LE4 0GL, UK.

Adrian Mocan
Digital Enterprise Research Institute (DERI), National University of Ireland, Galway, Ireland.

Amit Sheth
Large Scale Distributed Information Systems (LSDIS) Lab, Department of Computer Science, University of Georgia, GA, USA.

Anca-Andreea Ivan
IBM Watson Research Center, 19 Skyline Drive, Hawthorne, NY, USA.

Daniela Barreiro Claro
ESEO, 4 rue Merlet de la Boulaye, Angers, France. LERIA, University of Angers, France.

Dean Allemang
TopQuadrant, Inc., USA

Jin-Kao Hao
LERIA, University of Angers, France.

John A. Miller
Large Scale Distributed Information Systems (LSDIS) Lab, Department of Computer Science, University of Georgia, GA, USA.

Jorge Cardoso
Department of Mathematics and Engineering, University of Madeira, 9000-390, Funchal, Portugal.

Hussein Zedan
Software Technology Research Laboratory, De Montfort University, Leicester, LE4 0GL, UK.

Karthik Gomadam
Large Scale Distributed Information Systems (LSDIS) Lab, Department of Computer Science, University of Georgia, GA, USA.

Ke Li
Large Scale Distributed Information Systems (LSDIS) Lab, Department of Computer Science, University of Georgia, GA, USA.

Kunal Verma
Large Scale Distributed Information Systems (LSDIS) Lab, Department of Computer Science, University of Georgia, GA, USA.

Matt Moran
Digital Enterprise Research Institute (DERI), National University of Ireland, Galway, Ireland.

Meenakshi Nagarajan
Large Scale Distributed Information Systems (LSDIS) Lab, Department of Computer Science, University of Georgia, GA, USA.

Michal Zaremba
Digital Enterprise Research Institute (DERI), National University of Ireland, Galway, Ireland.

Mick Kerrigan
Digital Enterprise Research Institute (DERI), National University of Ireland, Galway, Ireland.

Monika Solanki
Software Technology Research Laboratory, De Montfort University, Leicester, LE4 0GL, UK.

Patrick Albers
ESEO, 4 rue Merlet de la Boulaye, Angers, France.

Ralph Hodgson
TopQuadrant, Inc., USA

Rama Akkiraju
IBM Watson Research Center, 19 Skyline Drive, Hawthorne, NY, USA.

Ranjit Mulye
Large Scale Distributed Information Systems (LSDIS) Lab, Department of Computer Science, University of Georgia, GA, USA.

Reiman Rabbani
Large Scale Distributed Information Systems (LSDIS) Lab, Department of Computer Science, University of Georgia, GA, USA.

Richard Goodwin
IBM Watson Research Center, 19 Skyline Drive, Hawthorne, NY, USA.

Sanjay Chaudhary
Dhirubhai Ambani Institute of Information and Communication Technology, Gujarat, India.

Satya Sanket Sahoo
Large Scale Distributed Information Systems (LSDIS) Lab, Department of Computer Science, University of Georgia, GA, USA.

Sinuhe Arroyo
Digital Enterprise Research Institute (DERI), Innsbruck, Austria.

Tanveer Syeda-Mahmood
IBM Almaden Research Center, 650 Harry Road, San Jose, CA 95120, USA.

Vikram Sorathia
Dhirubhai Ambani Institute of Information and Communication Technology, Gujarat, India.

Zakir Laliwala
Dhirubhai Ambani Institute of Information and Communication
Technology, Gujarat, India.

Foreword

In order to stay competitive today, each company must be able to react fast to changes within its business environment. At the IT level this demands high flexibility of the application systems supporting the operation of the company and the cooperation with its partners. A key contributor to this high flexibility is "loose coupling" between these application systems as well as between the ingredients of each application system itself. Loose coupling basically means that interacting components make as few assumptions about each other as possible: the fewer assumptions made the easier it is to exchange one component by another without even noticing. Ultimately, a component providing certain required functionality can be discovered and used as late as when this functionality is actually needed. Such a component is said to behave like a "service".

The discipline of building systems based on such services is referred to as "service-oriented computing". The corresponding architectural style is called "service-oriented architecture": fundamentally, it describes how service requesters and service providers can be decoupled via discovery mechanisms resulting in loosely coupled systems. In practice, the various services reside in different environments, i.e. run on different machines, under different environments, are accessible via different transport protocols etc. Thus, implementing a service-oriented architecture means to deal with heterogeneity and interoperability concerns. These concerns must be addressed by appropriate standards and their implementation: both are subsumed by the term "Web services".

Consequently, the book at hand is concerned with topics from the area of building systems in a loosely coupled manner in order to support companies to stay competitive: this emphasizes the importance of the overall subject area the book is devoted to. The overarching theme addressed by each of its chapters is that of semantics, i.e. of "meaning": how can that what a service does be appropriately described, and how such a description can be exploited to build service-oriented systems – in order to significantly increase quality of discovery of appropriate services. These subjects will become more and more important as Web services become a mainstream in software construction.

Standards combining semantics and Web service technology will then play a key role, especially in heterogeneous environments. Recently, specifications for standards in this domain have been submitted to standard bodies. Key contributors to these specifications are amongst the authors of the book at hand. Thus, readers of the book will get first hand information about the details of the standards from the domain of "semantic Web services".

The book provides the basic background for various communities. Practitioners will enjoy the sections describing some applications of semantic Web services technologies and the impact of semantics on business processes. Researchers will find encouragements to consider semantic Web service technology in their areas of expertise. Lecturers will get a lot of material for teaching the subject area in advanced undergraduate as well as postgraduate courses. Students will be able to use the book as a textbook to get an overview of this new aspect of service-oriented computing. All readers will benefit from the questions closing each chapter to help readers to assess and deepen their comprehension of the subject area. Finally, I found the recommendations for further reading very helpful to quickly get information about special subjects of interest.

I wish that the book will get the attention it really deserves, and that readers of this book will enjoy reading it as much as I did.

Institute of Architecture of Application Systems
University of Stuttgart, Germany
February 2006

Frank Leymann

Preface

Chapter 1 discusses the evolution of the Web. The semantic Web is not a separate Web but an extension of the current one, in which information and services are given well-defined meaning, thereby better enabling computers and people to work in cooperation. To make possible the creation of the semantic Web the W3C (World Wide Web Consortium) has been actively working on the definition of open standards. These standards are important to define the information on the Web in a way that it can be used by computers not only for display purposes, but also for interoperability and integration between systems and applications resolving heterogeneity problems. Heterogeneity occurs when there are differences in syntax, representation, and semantics of data. Dealing with heterogeneity has continued to be a key challenge since the time it has been possible to exchange and share data between computers and applications. One approach to the problems of semantic heterogeneity is to rely on the technological foundations of the semantic Web. In this chapter we also present the state of the art of the applications that use semantics and ontologies. We describe various applications ranging from the use of semantic Web services, semantic integration of tourism information sources, and semantic digital libraries to the development of bioinformatics ontologies.

In **chapter 2**, we attempt to point the reader to existing work in the areas of semantic annotation. Creating semantic markup of Web services to realize the vision of Semantic Web services has received a lot of attention in the recent years. A direct offshoot has been the development of agent technologies that can utilize these annotations to support automated Web service discovery, composition and interoperability. The issues that need to be addressed in the context of annotation of Web services are quite different from traditional Web resource annotation frameworks and therefore deserve particular attention. This chapter covers different types of metadata, semantic annotation of Web resources and Web services in particular, types of semantics used in Web service annotation, current semantic web service efforts including OWL-S, WSMO and WSDL-S and some Semantic annotation tools and platforms.

Chapter 3 introduces and provides an overview of the Web Services Modeling Ontology (WSMO), a fully-fledged framework for Semantic Web Services (SWS), showing a reader practical examples aimed at explaining the application of WSMO concepts to a real world scenario. Existing Web Services specifications lack an appropriate semantic framework to allow for the automated execution of current business processes over the Web. SWS technology aims to add enough semantics to the specifications and implementations of Web Services to make possible the automatic integration of distributed autonomous systems, with independently designed data and behavior models. Defining data, behavior and system components in a machine understandable way using ontologies provides the basis for reducing the need for humans to be in the loop for system integration processes. The application of semantics to Web Services can be used to remove humans from the integration jigsaw and substitute them with machines. There are many problems which Semantic Web Services could be used to resolve. SWS will put in place an automated process for machine driven dynamic discovery, mediation and invocation. One of the major intentions of this chapter is to present the technological framework for SWS development around WSMO. We discuss and present some of the key technologies related to the conceptual framework of WSMO, especially the Web Services Modeling Execution Environment (WSMX), which is its reference implementation.

In **chapter 4**, we discuss the various discovery and publishing schemes available for Web Services. We present a detailed analysis of UDDI, the standard registry framework for publishing services. The API for publishing and discovering services using UDDI is discussed briefly. We present the best practices in using UDDI as discussed in the OASIS Best Practices document. The differences, advantages and disadvantages of keyword, port type and semantics based discovery are presented. The chapter also introduces the reader to the different flavors of semantics in Services life cycle. An approach to publish and discover semantic Web Services is presented. As an insight into the current research, we discuss registry federation towards the end.

In **chapter 5**, we propose a methodology to compositionally augment the semantic description of a reactive service, with temporal properties that provide the required support for reasoning about "ongoing" behavior. The properties are specified in Interval Temporal Logic, our underlying formalism for reasoning about service behavior over periods of time. These properties are specified only over observable behavior, and do not depend on any additional knowledge about the underlying execution mechanism of the services. We present "TeSCO-S", a framework for enriching Web service interface specifications, described as OWL ontologies with temporal assertions. TeSCO-S provides an OWL ontology for specifying properties in ITL, a pre-processor, "OntoITL" for transforming ontology instances into ITL formulae and an interpreter, "AnaTempura" that executes and validates temporal properties in "Tempura", an executable subset of ITL

Chapter 6 presents the main ideas and principles behind service choreography. Services need to interoperate with each other in order to realize the purposes of the software system they define by exchanging messages, which allow them to make or to respond to requests. Due to the heterogeneous technological, syntactic and semantic nature of services realizing semantic web processes, communication requirements become more complex, clearly necessitating a balance among interoperation and decoupling. In the context of providing support for *choreography* (i.e. the modeling of external, visible behavior of service interactions), a semantic layer could be supposed to provide the required convertibility between divergent specifications by the specification in machine-processable form of the message exchanging patterns (MEP). This chapter carefully reviews the main initiatives in the field pointing out their core characteristics and main drawbacks. Taking as starting point this analysis, the major driving principles and desire features, when it comes to modeling choreographies, are identified. Later, the most relevant challenges in the field, separation of models and support for semantic mediation are discussed. Based on this theoretical work, the core principles and architecture of a choreography engine that relies on the semantic description of MEPs to allow interoperation among heterogeneous services is presented. Finally, the concepts depicted on the framework as applied in the Assurance Integration Use case hosted by BT and part of the EU-funded project DIP are presented.

Chapter 7 focuses on the design of semantic web processes using WSDL-S. Many businesses are adopting Web Service technologies to provide greater access to their applications. Due to the fast-paced E-Commerce requirements, more and more businesses prefer to only creating their core applications, and outsourcing the non-critical applications, or making use of their partners' applications directly. There is a growing requirement to build complex processes which may include Web Services supplied by the different partners. However, there are two main difficulties in building such Web Processes: 1) the current syntactic search mechanism is ineffective to find out the highly suitable services and 2) there are not many process designing tools which allow dynamic binding of partner services. In this chapter, we present a solution for both the problems based on WSDL-S.

Chapter 8 discusses the composition of Web services based on non-functional properties. Web services are modular applications that can be described, located and invoked on the Internet. A user request may not only correspond to one specific service, but also to a set of Web services. Thus, it is necessary that a composition of services be done in order to obtain the expected result. Nonetheless, many services with the same goal but different characteristics can be discovered. Indeed, it is necessary to find non-functional criteria to distinguish them. In this chapter, we used the service quality variables as non-functional criteria in order to make an optimal service composition for a goal. Using multiobjective optimisation techniques, we proposed to find a set of optimal Pareto solutions from which a user can choose the most interesting tradeoff.

Chapter 9 motivates the need for semantic matching in different application domains and presents the generic matching framework. A semantic revolution is happening in the world of enterprise information integration. This is a new and emerging field that blurs the boundaries between the traditional fields of business process integration, data warehousing and enterprise application integration. Information integration is the process by which related items from disparate sources are integrated to achieve a stated purpose. There is a need for bridging the semantic gap between the descriptions in order to make true information integration feasible. The field of semantic matching and mapping has now emerged as a new and exciting field to address these problems of semantic mismatch of descriptions using automated relationship discovery techniques. Since the schemas arise from many applications, a generic framework for matching and mapping is needed. In this chapter, one such framework based on bipartite graph matching is described. This framework allows the best set of matching to be discovered using a variety of cues to determine semantic similarity of attributes ranging from name semantics to type and structural similarity. Related literature is reviewed.

Chapter 10 illustrated and describes the construction an ontology for e-tourism. Tourism is a data rich domain. Data is stored in many hundreds of data sources and many of these sources need to be used in concert during the development of tourism information systems. Our e-tourism ontology provides a way of viewing the world of tourism. It organizes tourism related information and concepts. The e-tourism ontology provides a way to achieve integration and interoperability through the use of a shared vocabulary and meanings for terms with respect to other terms. The e-tourism ontology was developed using OWL (Web Ontology Language). OWL was proposed by the W3C for publishing and sharing data, and automating data understanding by computers using ontologies on the Web. OWL is being planned and designed to provide a language that can be used for applications that need to understand the meaning of information instead of just parsing data for display purposes.

In **chapter 11** we give an account of one of the pilot projects that happened within the, now-called, Semantic Interoperability Community of Practice. In the last five years a number of significant developments have occurred that motivate the use of Semantic Technology in e-Government. In 2001, the US President announced 24 e-Government initiatives. In 2004 the Federal Enterprise Architecture (FEA) was first published. It is well-known that Semantic technology is an enabler for federation, mediation, aggregation and inferencing over information from diverse sources. Why then, not advocate its use for helping solve interoperability, integration, capability reuse, accountability and policy governance in agencies, across agencies and even across governments? With this vision, TopQuadrant set out in 2002 to bring Semantic Technology to the attention of the emerging technology work-groups of the US Government at their "Open Collaboration" Workshop meetings in Washington DC (Collaborative Expedition Workshops). What followed is a success story of growing awareness and advocacy of semantic technology in e-Government. In this chapter we describe the "eGOV FEA-Based Capabilities and Partnering Advisor", some coverage is also made of FEA-RMO, the Federal Enterprise Architecture Reference Model Ontology.

Chapter 12 discusses the application of Web services, Web processes and the role of semantics in the field of bioinformatics. Web services are being rapidly adopted as the technology of choice to share and integrate data and computational tools in life sciences. Web Services offers the life sciences research community the critical advantages of platform-independence and web-based access. Multi-step, complex processes characterize biological research. The automation of these processes is increasingly characterizing life sciences research and forms the framework for high-throughput experimental biology. In this scenario, it is nearly impossible for researchers to manually deal with extremely large and rapidly generated datasets. As the constituent stages of the experimental processes, are being implemented as Web Services, their integration into Web processes is a logical next step. The Semantic Web technology ensures that Web Services are implemented, published, searched and discovered in a standard and intuitive manner for researchers. Semantic Web also enables the seamless integration of Web Services into Web processes that will underpin a high-throughput experimental data management, analysis and retrieval framework. In this chapter, we discuss the use of Semantic Web technology in the field of bioinformatics. Specifically, we cover three areas of bioinformatics research namely computational genomics, computational proteomics and structural bioinformatics. An in-depth case study of implementation of a semantic Web Services based glycoproteomics workflow is also discussed.

Chapter 13 covers the design, development and deployment of semantic business services driven systems. Web Services is a proven effective approach for systems integration at a large scale, yet the prevailing diversity within a specific domain introduces many challenges. This chapter demonstrates how semantic Web Services based business process management system can be realized to address these challenges. The chapter explains the complexities of the business processes and introduces the issues involved to utilize the power of "Services" effectively. The semantics based approach is adopted with inclusion of an ontology development to cover all the concepts and their inter-relationship related to the problem domain. The development lifecycle contains other known building blocks like generation of Web Services, enabling service descriptions for semantic discovery, designing of a business process and finally the deployment of the business services. The objective is to provide a comprehensive experience of each building block to develop complete system that exhibit the required functionality.

In **chapter 14** we present several frameworks supporting the programmatic development of OWL ontologies. We will briefly discuss those most used by the developer community, namely Jena, Protégé-OWL API and the WonderWeb OWL API, which are all available for Java language. A more extensive description of the Jena framework will follow. The API of Jena is large and offers many possibilities. Since Jena supports several languages, there are interfaces for increasing levels of complexity: from simple RDF graphs to complex OWL ontologies. We further explain how OWL knowledge bases can be built up and modified programmatically, how Jena's query language (RDQL) is used and how reasoning and inference is carried out.

SUGGESTED COURSE STRUCTURE

This book is for people who want to learn about the main concepts behind semantic Web, semantic Web services and processes, current activities aimed towards future standardization and how they can be applied to develop real world applications. It brings together many of the main ideas of the semantic Web and Semantic Web services in one place. Although several researchers have contributed to elaborate this book, it has been designed so that it could be used as a textbook or a reference book for an advance undergraduate or graduate course. At the end of each chapter, questions for discussion and a list of suggested additional readings are provided.

The Web site for this book (a link to which you can find from the Web sites of book editors) lists the courses that have already adopted this book for graduate education. It also provides a variety of teaching aid including,

- presentations for majority of chapters prepared by book editors or chapter authors, compilation of answers to discussion questions,
- pointers to the fee tools that can be used for exercise related to techniques,
- technologies discussed in some of the chapters, and more.

The following list gives suggested contents for different courses at the undergraduate and graduate level:

- **Beginner** (generic, advanced undergraduate or graduate). Chapters 1, 10, and 14 provide the fundamental building blocks for developing semantic Web applications. Chapter 1 provides an overview on the technologies for building the semantic Web. A brief history of the Web and the concept of the semantic Web are explained. In order to have computers understand and automatically process Web contents, such contents cannot be within HTML or XML tags that are only human-understandable. Chapter 10 introduces the OWL language and serves as a good introduction before one reads the official OWL manual and OWL language guide. Chapter 14 introduces Jena, the Java toolkit for developing semantic Web applications based on W3C recommendations for RDF and OWL.

- **Intermediate** (undergraduate or graduate). Chapters 2, 3, 4, 6, 7, 11, and 13 introduce more advanced concepts and topics. Chapters 2, 3, 4, and 7 explain how semantics can be added to existing Web services standards, such as WSDL, and show how the Web Services Modeling Ontology (WSMO) provides ontological specifications for the main elements of semantic Web services using a conceptual model for developing and describing Web services and their composition based on the maximal de-coupling and scalable mediation service principles. Chapters 11 and 13 illustrate the role of semantics as an enabler for the interoperability, integration, mediation, and inferencing over information from diverse sources.

- **Advanced** (graduate or professional). An advanced student knows about semantics from past experience acquired while developing and implementing semantic Web applications involving Web services and processes. Chapter 5, 8, 9, and 12 introduce advanced topics where theory has an important role. For example, chapter 5 presents a formalism for reasoning about service behavior over periods of time is introduced. Chapter 8 and 9 discusses the composition of Web services based on non-functional properties using multi-objective optimization techniques and presents a generic framework for schema matching. Chapter 12 discusses the application of Web services, Web processes and the role of semantics in the field of bioinformatics to share and integrate data and computational tools in life sciences.

The following figure shows the suggested reading plans that are recommended for the different readers.

Beginner	Intermediate	Advanced
Chapter 1	Chapter 2	Chapter 5
Chapter 10	Chapter 3	Chapter 8
Chapter 14	Chapter 4	Chapter 9
	Chapter 6	Chapter 12
	Chapter 7	
	Chapter 11	
	Chapter 13	

PART I: SEMANTIC WEB SERVICES

Chapter 1

THE SEMANTIC WEB AND ITS APPLICATIONS

Jorge Cardoso[1] and Amit Sheth[2]

[1]*Department of Mathematics and Engineering, University of Madeira, 9000-390, Funchal, Portugal – jcardoso@uma.pt*

[2]*Large Scale Distributed Information Systems (LSDIS) Lab, Department of Computer Science, University of Georgia, GA, USA. – amit@cs.uga.edu*

1.   INTRODUCTION

Currently, the World Wide Web is primarily composed of documents written in HTML (Hyper Text Markup Language), a language that is useful for publishing information. HTML is a set of "markup" symbols contained in a Web page intended for display on a Web browser. During the first decade of its existence, most of the information on the Web is designed only for human consumption. Humans can read Web pages and understand them, but their inherent meaning is not shown in a way that allows their interpretation by computers

The information on the Web can be defined in a way that it can be used by computers not only for display purposes, but also for interoperability and integration between systems and applications. One way to enable machine-to-machine exchange and automated processing is to provide the information in such a way that computers can understand it. This is precisely the objective of the semantic Web – to make possible the processing of Web information by computers. "The Semantic Web is not a separate Web but an extension of the current one, in which information is given well-defined meaning, better enabling computers and people to work in cooperation." (Berners-Lee, Hendler et al. 2001). The next generation of the Web will combine existing Web technologies with knowledge representation formalisms (Grau 2004)

The Semantic Web was made through incremental changes, by bringing machine-readable descriptions to the data and documents already on the Web. As already stated, the Web was originally a vast set of static Web pages linked together. Currently the Web is in evolution, as illustrated in Figure 1-1, and different approaches are being sought to come up with the solutions to add semantics to Web resources. On the left side of Figure 1-1, a graph representation of the syntactic Web is given. Resources are linked together forming the Web. There is no distinction between resources or the links that connect resources. To give meaning to resources and links, new standards and languages are being investigated and developed. The rules and descriptive information made available by these languages allow to characterize individually and precisely the type of resources in the Web and the relationships between resources, as illustrated in the right side of Figure 1-1.

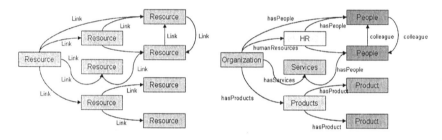

Figure 1-1. Evolution of the Web

Due to the widespread importance of integration and interoperability for intra- and inter-business processes, the research community has tackled this problem and developed semantic standards such as the Resource Description Framework (RDF) (RDF 2002) and the Web Ontology Language (OWL) (OWL 2004). RDF and OWL standards enable the Web to be a global infrastructure for sharing both documents and data, which make searching and reusing information easier and more reliable as well. RDF is the W3C standard for creating descriptions of information, describing their semantics and reasoning (Lassila and Swick 1999), especially information available on the World Wide Web. What XML is for syntax, RDF is for semantics. Both share a unified model and together provide a framework for developing Web applications that deal with data and semantics (Patel-Schneider and Siméon 2002). Relationships are at the heart of semantics (Sheth, Arpinar et al. 2002). Perhaps the most important characteristic of RDF is that it elevates relationships to first class object, providing the first representational basis for giving semantic description. RDF evolved from MCF designed by Guha, which was motivated for representing metadata. Hence RDF is also well suited for representing metadata for Web resources. OWL provides a language for defining structured Web-based ontologies which allows a richer integration and interoperability of data among communities and domains.

According to TopQuadrant (TopQuadrant 2005), a consulting firm that specializes in Semantic Web technologies, the market for semantic technologies will grow at an annual growth rate of between 60% and 70% until 2010. It will grow from its current size of US$2 billion to US$63 billion. According to William Ruh of CISCO, before the end of 2004, RDF was applied under the covers of well over 100 identified products and over 25 information service providers. Existing well known applications that add Semantic Web capabilities include Adobe's Extensible Metadata Platform, RDF of annotation of most of the product data that Amazon receives or digital media content a top mobile carrier receives, and well known infrastructure support include Creative Commons DF based annotations of license information and Oracle's support for RDF data.

Semantic software is being experimentally used by banks to help them to comply with the U.S. government's Patriot Act (the Patriot Act requires banks to track and account for the customers with whom they do transactions), by European police force to follow crime patterns, and by telephone service providers to create applications that provides information about pay-per-view movies (Lee 2005; Sheth 2005). In addition to investment banks, the Metropolitan Life Insurance Company, the U.S. Department of Defense and the Tennessee Valley Authority have also used Semantic software to integrate enterprise data to comply with federal regulations.

2.   SEMIOTICS – SYNTAX, SEMANTICS, AND PRAGMATICS

Semiotics is the general science of signs – such as icons, images, objects, tokens, and symbols – and how their meaning is transmitted and understood. A sign is generally defined as something that stands for something else.

The human language is a particular case of semiotics. A language is a system of conventional spoken or written symbols by means of which people communicate. Formal languages, such as logic, are also based on symbols and, therefore, are also studied by semiotics. Compared to the human language, formal languages have a precise construction rules for the syntax and semantics of programs. Semiotics is composed of three fundamental components: syntax, semantics, and pragmatics (Peirce 1960). These components are illustrated in Figure 1-2.

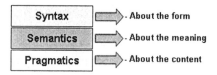

Figure 1-2. Semiotics and its components

Syntax. It deals with the formal or structural relations between signs (or tokens) and the production of new ones. For example, grammatical syntax is the study of which sequences of symbols are well formed according to the recursive rules of grammar. The set of allowed reserved words, their parameters, and the correct word order in an expression is called the syntax of a language. In computer science, if a program is syntactically correct according to its rules of syntax, then the compiler will validate the syntax and will not generate error messages. This, however, does not ensure that the program is semantically correct (i.e., return results as expected).

For example, when XML is used to achieve interoperability and integration of information systems, the data exchanged between systems must follow a precise syntax. If the rules of the syntax are not followed, a syntactical error occurs. For example, using a tag spelled <cust> instead of <customer>, omitting a closing tag, or not following the syntax of a XML Schema (XMLSchema 2004) will generate a syntactical error. It should be noticed, that syntax does not include the study of things such as "truth" and "meaning."

Semantics. It is the study of relations between the system of signs (such as words, phrases, and sentences) and their meanings. As it can be seen by this definition, the objective of semantics is totally different from the objective of syntax. The former concerns to what something means while the latter pertains to the formal structure/patterns in which something is expressed. Semantics are distinct from the concept of ontology (ontologies will be discusses later in this chapter). While the former is about the use of a word, the latter is related to the nature of the entity or domain referenced by the word. One important and interesting question in semantics research is if the meaning is established by looking at the neighborhood in the ontology that the word is part of or if the meaning is already contained in the word itself. Second important and interesting question is the formal representation language to capture the semantics such that it is machine processable with consistent interpretation. Third important question is the expressiveness of this representation language that balances computability versus capturing the true richness of the real world that is being modeled. Correspondingly, the following three forms of semantics have been defined in (Sheth, Ramakrishnan et al. 2005):

- **Implicit** semantics. "This type of semantics refers to the kind that is implicit in data and that is not represented explicitly in any machine processable syntax."
- **Formal** semantics. "Semantics that are represented in some well-formed syntactic form (governed by syntax rules) is referred to as formal semantics."
- **Powerful** (soft) semantics. "Usually, efforts related to formal semantics have involved limiting expressiveness to allow for acceptable computational characteristics. Since most KR mechanisms and the Relational Data Model are based on set theory, the ability to represent and utilize knowledge that is imprecise, uncertain, partially true, and approximate is lacking, at least in the base/standard models. Representing and utilizing these types of more powerful knowledge is, in our opinion, critical to the success of the Semantic Web. Soft computing has explored these types of powerful semantics. We deem these powerful (soft) semantics as distinguished, albeit not distinct from or orthogonal to formal and implicit semantics."

Pragmatics. It is the study of natural language understanding, and specifically the study of how context influences the interpretation of meaning. Pragmatics is interested predominantly in utterances, made up of sentences, and usually in the context of conversations (Wikipedia 2005). The context may include any social, environmental, and psychological factors. It includes the study or relations among signs, their meanings, and users of the signs, and the repercussions of sign interpretations for the interpreters in the environment. While semantics deals with the meaning of signs, pragmatics deals with the origin, uses, and effects of signs within the content, context, or behavior in which they occur.

3. SEMANTIC HETEROGENEITY ON THE WEB

Problems that might arise due to heterogeneity of the data in the Web are already well known within the distributed database systems community (e. g. (Kim and Seo 1991), (Kashyap and Sheth 1996)). Heterogeneity occurs when there is a disagreement about the meaning, interpretation, or intended use of the same or related data. As with distributed database systems, four types of information heterogeneity (Sheth 1998; Ouskel and Sheth 1999) may arise in the Web: system heterogeneity, syntactic heterogeneity, structural or schematic heterogeneity, and semantic heterogeneity.

- **System heterogeneity**: Applications and data may reside in different hardware platforms and operating systems.
- **Syntactic heterogeneity**: Information sources may use different representations and encodings for data. Syntactic interoperability can be achieved when compatible forms of encoding and access protocols are used to allow information systems to communicate.
- **Structural heterogeneity**: Different information systems store their data in different document layouts and formats, data models, data structures and schemas.
- **Semantic heterogeneity**: The meaning of the data can be expressed in different ways leading to heterogeneity. Semantic heterogeneity considers the content of an information item and its intended meaning.

Approaches to the problems of semantic heterogeneity should equip heterogeneous, autonomous, and distributed software systems with the ability to share and exchange information in a semantically consistent way (Sheth 1999). In the representation languages to support the Semantic Web approach, as recommended by the W3C, XML supports ability to deal with syntactic heterogeneity; XML, XPath, and XQuery provide ability to transcend certain structural heterogeneity, while RDF and OWL (or other ontology representation languages) provide a key approach to deal with semantic heterogeneity.

One solution is for developers to write code which translates between the terminologies of pairs of systems. When the requirement is for a small number of systems to interoperate, this may be a useful solution. However, this solution does not scale as the development costs increase as more systems are added and the degree of semantic heterogeneity increases. Assuming the development of bidirectional translators, i.e. translators that enable the interoperation of system A to system B and from system B to system A, to allow the interoperability of 'n' systems we need (n-1)+(n-2)+...+1 translators. Figure 1-3 shows the translators required to integrate 6 systems.

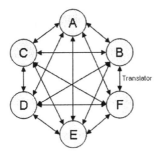

Figure 1-3. Using translators to resolve semantic heterogeneity

A more suitable solution to the problem of semantic heterogeneity is to rely on the technological foundations of the semantic Web. More precisely, to semantically define the meaning of the terminology of each distributed system data using the concepts present in a shared ontology to make clear the relationships and differences between concepts.

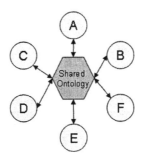

Figure 1-4. Using a shared ontology to resolve semantic heterogeneity

Figure 1-4 shows a possible architecture that achieves interoperability using the semantic Web and ontologies. This solution only requires the development of 'n' links to interconnect systems.

4.   METADATA

Metadata can be defined as "data about data." The goal of incorporating metadata into data sources is to enable the end-user to find items and contextually relevant information. Data sources are generally heterogeneous and can be unstructured, semi-structured, and structured. In the semantic Web, a data source is typically a document, such as a Web page, containing textual content or data. Of course, other types of resources may also include metadata information, such as records from a digital library.

Metadata can exist in several levels. These "levels of metadata" are not mutually exclusive; on the contrary, the accumulative combination of each type of metadata provides a multi-faceted representation of the data including information about its syntax, structure, and semantic context (Fisher and Sheth 2004).

The process of attaching semantic metadata to a document or any piece of content is called semantic. Metadata extraction is the process of identifying metadata for that document or content. This process could be manual, semiautomatic (e.g., (Handschuh, Staab et al. 2002)) or fully automatically (e.g., Semantic Enhancement Engine (Hammond, Sheth et al. 2002) or SemTag (Dill, Eiron et al. 2003)). Semantic applications are created by exploiting metadata and ontologies with associated knowledgebase (Sheth 2004). In essence, in the semantic Web, documents are marked up with semantic metadata which is machine-understandable about the human-readable content of documents. Other approaches, which are less expressive, consist on using purely syntactic or structural metadata.

4.1   Syntactic Metadata

The simplest form of metadata is syntactic metadata. It describes non-contextual information about content and provides very general information, such as the document's size, location, or date of creation. Syntactic metadata attaches labels or tags to data. The following example shows syntactic metadata describing a document:

```
<name> = "report.pdf"
<creation> = "30-09-2005"
<modified> = "15-10-2005"
<size> = 2048
```

Most documents have some degree of syntactic metadata. E-mail headers provide author, recipient, date, and subject information. While these headers provide very little or no contextual understanding of what the document says or implies (assuming value of author is treated as a string or ordered sets of words, rather than its full semantics involving modeling of author as a person authoring a document, etc.), this information is useful for certain applications. For example, a mail client may constantly monitor incoming e-mail to find documents, related to a particular subject, the user is interested in.

4.2   Structural Metadata

Structural metadata provides information regarding the structure of content. It describes how items are put together or arranged. The amount and type of such metadata will vary widely with the type of document. For example, an HTML document may have a set of predefined tags, but these exist primarily for rendering purposes. Therefore, they are not very helpful in providing contextual information for content. Nevertheless, positional or structural placement of information within a document can be used to further embellish metadata (e.g., terms or concepts appear in a title may be give higher weight to that appearing in the body). On the other hand, XML gives the ability to enclose content within more meaningful tags. This is clearly more useful in determining context and relevance when compared to the limitations of syntactic metadata for providing information about the document itself.

For example, a DTD or XSD outlines the structural metadata of a particular document. It lists the elements, attributes, and entities in a document and it defines the relationships between the different elements and attributes. A DTD declares a set of XML element names and how they can be used in a document. The following lines, extracted from a DTD, describe a set of valid XML documents:

```
<!ELEMENT contacts (contact*)>
<!ELEMENT contact (name, birthdate)>
<!ELEMENT name (#PCDATA)>
<!ELEMENT birthdate (#PCDATA)>
```

Structural metadata tell us how data are grouped and put in ordered arrangements with other data. This DTD sample indicates that a "contacts" element contains one or more "contact" elements. A "contact" element contains the elements "name" and "birthdate", and the "name" and "birthdate" elements contain data.

4.3   Semantic Metadata

Semantic metadata adds relationships, rules, and constraints to syntactic and structural metadata. This metadata describe contextually relevant or domain-specific information about content based on a domain specific metadata model or ontology, providing a context for interpretation. In a sense, they capture a meaning associated with the content. If a formal ontology is used for describing and interpreting this type of metadata, then it lends itself to machine processability and hence higher degrees of automation.

Semantic data provides a means for high-precision searching, and, perhaps most importantly, it enables interoperability among heterogeneous data sources. Semantic metadata is used to give meaning to the elements described by the syntactic and structural metadata. These metadata elements allow applications to "understand" the actual meaning of the data.

By creating a metadata model of data, information, and relationships, we are able to use reasoning capabilities such as inference engines to draw logical conclusions based on the metadata model, or path identification and ranking using graph based processing leading to mining and discovery. For instance, if we know that the ABC Company sends every year a gift to very good customers, and that John is a very good customer, then by inference, we know that the company will ship a gift to John next year. Or if we find a potential customer has a business partner with another person who is on the Bank of England list of people involved in money laundering, the potential customer is a suspect according to the government's anti-money regulations. Figure 1-5 (Sheth 2003) shows the types of metadata we have discussed.

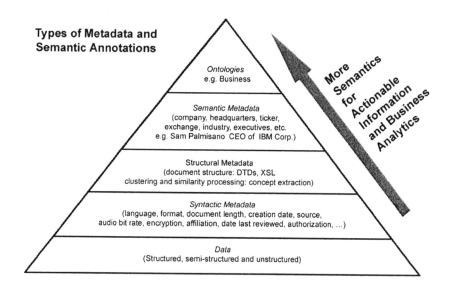

Figure 1-5. Types of metadata

4.4   Creating and Extracting Semantic Metadata

In order to extract optimal value from a document and make it usable, it needs to be effectively tagged by analyzing and extracting relevant information of semantic interest. Many techniques can be used to achieve this based on extracting syntactic and semantic metadata from documents (Sheth 2003). These include:

Semantic lexicons, nomenclatures, reference sets and thesauri: Match words, phrases or parts of speech with a static or periodically maintained dictionary and thesaurus. Semantic lexicon, such as WordNet (Voorhees 1998) which groups English words into sets of synonyms called synsets and records semantic relations between synonym sets, can be used to identify and match terms in different directions, finding words that mean the same or are more general or more specific. WordNet supports various types of relationships such as synonyms, hypernyms, hyponyms, holonym, and meronym which can de effectively used to find relationship between words and extract the meaning of words.

Document analysis: Look for patterns and co-occurrences, and apply predefined rules to find interesting patterns within and across documents. Regular expressions and relationships between words can be used to understand the meaning of documents.

Ontologies: Capturing domain-specific (application or industry) knowledge including entities and relationships, both at a definitional level (e.g., a company has a CEO), and capturing real-world facts or knowledge (e.g., Meg Witman is the CEO of eBay) at an instance or assertional level. If the ontology deployed is "one size fits all" and is not domain-specific, the full potential of this approach cannot be exploited.

The last option, also known as ontology-driven meta data extraction, is the most flexible (assuming the ontology is kept up to date to reflect changes in the real world) and comprehensive (since it allows modeling of fact-based domain-specific relationships between entities that are at the heart of semantic representations).

5.   EMPIRICAL CONSIDERATIONS ON THE USE OF SEMANTICS AND ONTOLOGIES

Semantics is arguably the single most important ingredient in propelling the Web to its next phase to provide standards to seamlessly enable interoperability of applications. Semantics is considered to be the best framework to deal with the heterogeneity, massive scale, and dynamic nature of the resources on the Web. Issues pertaining to semantics have been addressed in other fields like linguistics, knowledge representation, and AI. Based on the research on semantics, semantic Web, and real-world applications deployment, we present a set of empirical observations, considerations, and requirements for the construction of future applications, extended from the original set presented in (Sheth and Ramakrishnan 2003):

- It is the "ontological commitment" reflecting agreement among the experts defining the ontology and its uses that is a key basis for semantic integration. A good case in point is the Gene Ontology (GO) which despite its use of a representation with limited expressiveness has been extremely popular among the genomic scientists.
- Ontologies can capture human activities (e.g., modeling domains of travel or financial services) or natural phenomena and science (e.g., protein-protein interactions or glycan structures). Schemas modeling some domain, especially those modeling natural phenomena and science could be quite large and complex. For example, the Gycomics Ontology GlycO (http://lsdis.cs.uga.edu/projects/glycomics/) has over 600 classes, pushes the expressiveness of the OWL language in modeling the constraints, and is eleven levels deep.
- Ontology population which captures real world facts and trusted knowledge of a domain is critical. In the near future, it will not be uncommon to find ontology with millions of facts. Since it is obvious that this is the sort of scale Semantic Web applications are going to be dealing with, means of populating ontologies with instance data need to be automated.
- Semi-formal ontologies, possibly based on limited expressive power focusing on relationships but not constraints, can be very practical and useful. Ontologies represented in more expressive languages such as OWL (compared to RDF/S) have in practice yielded little value in industrial applications so far. One reasons for this could be that it is difficult to capture the knowledge that uses the more expressive constructs of a representation language. At the same time, when modeling more complex domains have required use of more expressive

languages and more intensive effort in schema design as well as population.

- Large scale metadata extraction and semantic annotation is possible, as exemplified by Semantic Enhancement Engine of Semagix Freedom (Hammond, Sheth et al. 2002) and SemTag/SemSeeker of IBM WebFountain (Dill, Eiron et al. 2003). Storage and manipulation of metadata for millions to hundreds of millions of content items requires best applications of known database techniques with challenge of improving upon them for performance and scale in presence of more complex structures.
- Support for heterogeneous data is key – it is too hard to deploy separate products within a single enterprise to deal with structured and unstructured data. New applications involve extensive types of heterogeneity in format, media and access/delivery mechanisms. Database researchers have long studied the issue of integrating heterogeneous data, and many of these come handy.
- A vast majority of the Semantic (Web) applications that have been developed rely on three crucial capabilities: ontology creation, semantic annotation, and querying/reasoning. A good percentage of reasoning used in real world applications is related to path finding and rule processing, rather than academically popular inferencing. All these capabilities must scale to millions of documents and concepts.

6.   APPLICATIONS OF SEMANTICS AND ONTOLOGIES

The intention of this section is to present the state of the art of the applications that use semantics and ontologies. We describe various applications ranging from the use of semantic Web services, semantic integration of tourism information sources, and semantic digital libraries to the development of bioinformatics ontologies.

6.1   Semantic Web Services

Web services are modular, self-describing, self-contained applications that are accessible over the Internet (Curbera, Nagy et al. 2001). Currently, Web services are described using the Web Services Description Language (Chinnici, Gudgin et al. 2003), which provide operational information. Although the Web Services Description Language (WSDL) does not contain semantic descriptions, it specifies the structure of message components using

XML Schema constructs. Semantic Web services are the result of the evolution of the syntactic definition of Web services and the semantic Web as shown in Figure 1-6.

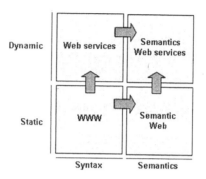

Figure 1-6. The nature of semantic Web services

One solution to create semantic Web services is by mapping concepts in a Web service description to ontological concepts. Using this approach, users can explicitly define the semantics of a Web service for a given domain.

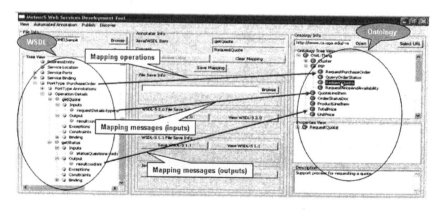

Figure 1-7. Annotating Web services with ontological concepts

Significantly different approaches to specifying semantic Web services are exemplified by four submissions to the World Wide Web consortium (W3C): OWL-S (OWL-S 2004), WSMO (WSMO 2004), FLOWS (SWSF 2005) and WSDL-S (Akkiraju, Farrell et al. 2005). WSDL-S is the most standard compliant and incremental approach that extends WSDL2.0, W3C's recommendation for Web service specification.

Figure 1-7 illustrates METEOR-S WSDL-S Annotator tool (Patil, Oundhakar et al. 2004) and the mapping that have been established between WSDL descriptions and ontological concepts.

Based on the analysis of WSDL descriptions, three types of elements can have their semantics increased by annotated them with ontological concepts: operations, messages, and preconditions and effects. All the elements are explicitly declared in a WSDL description.

Operations. Each WSDL description may have a number of operations with different functionalities. For example, a WSDL description can have operations for both booking and canceling flight tickets. In order to add semantics, the operations must be mapped to ontological concepts to describe their functionality.

Message. Message parts, which are input and output parameters of operations, are defined in WSDL using the XML Schema. Ontologies – which are more expressive than the XML Schema – can be used to annotate WSDL message parts. Using ontologies, not only brings user requirements and service advertisements to a common conceptual space, but also helps to use and apply reasoning mechanisms.

Preconditions and effects. Each WSDL operation may have a number of preconditions and effects. The preconditions are usually logical conditions, which must be evaluated to true in order to execute a specific operation. Effects are changes in the world that occur after the execution of an operation. After annotating services' operations, inputs, and outputs, preconditions and effects can also be annotated. The semantic annotation of preconditions and effects is important for Web services since it is possible for a number of operations to have the same functionality, as well as, the same inputs and outputs, but different effects.

6.2   Semantic Web Service Discovery

Given the dynamic nature of e-business environment, the ability to find best matching Web services that can also be easily integrated to create business processes is highly desirable. Discovery is the procedure of finding a set of appropriate Web services, select a specific service that meets user requirements, and bind it to a Web processes (Verma, Sivashanmugam et al. 2004). The search of Web services to model Web process applications differs from the search of tasks to model traditional processes, such as workflows. One of the main differences is in terms of the number of Web services available to the composition process. In the Web, potentially thousands of Web services are available. Therefore, one of the problems that need to be solved is how to efficiently discover Web services (Cardoso and Sheth 2003).

Currently, the industry standards available to register and discover Web services are based on the Universal Description Discovery and Integration specification (UDDI 2002). Unfortunately, discovering Web services using UDDI is relatively inefficient since the specification does not take into account the semantics of Web services, even though it provides an interface for keyword and taxonomy based searching as shown in Figure 1-8.

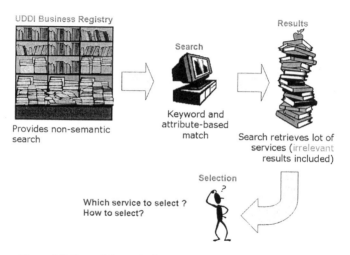

Figure 1-8. State of the art in discovery (Cardoso, Bussler et al. 2005)

The key to the discovery of Web services is having semantics in the description of services itself (Sheth and Meersman 2002) and then use semantic matching algorithms (e.g. (Smeaton and Quigley 1996; Klein and Bernstein 2001; Rodríguez and Egenhofer 2002; Cardoso and Sheth 2003), to find Web services. An approach for semantic Web service discovery is the ability to construct queries using concepts defined in a specific ontological domain. By having both the description and query explicitly declare their semantics, the results of discovery will be more relevant than keyword or attribute-based matching.

The semantic discovery of Web services has specific requirements and challenges compared to previous work on information retrieval systems and information integration systems. Several issues that need to be considered include:

- Precision of the discovery process. The search has to be based, not only on syntactic information, but also on data, functional, and non-functional/QoS semantics.
- Enable the automatic determination of the degree of integration of the discovered Web services and the Web process host.
- The integration and interoperation of Web services differs from previous work on schema integration due to the polarity of the schema that must be integrated (Cardoso and Sheth 2003).

Adding semantic annotations to WSDL specifications and UDDI registries allows improving the discovery of Web services. The general algorithm for semantic Web service discovery requires the users to enter Web service requirements as templates constructed using ontological concepts. There phases of the algorithm can be identified. In the first phase, the algorithm matches Web services based on the functionality (the functionality is specified using ontological concepts that map to WSDL operations) they provide. In the second phase, the result set from the first phase is ranked on the basis of semantic similarity (Cardoso and Sheth 2003) between the input and output concepts of the selected operations and the input and output concepts of the initial template, respectively. The optional third phase involves ranking the services based on the semantic similarity between the precondition and effect concepts of the selected operations and preconditions and effect concepts of the template.

6.3   Semantic Integration of Tourism Information Sources

Dynamic packaging technology helps online travel customers to build and book vacations. It can be described as the ability for a customer to put together elements of a (vacation) trip including flights, hotels, car rentals, local tours and tickets to theatre and sporting events. In the offline world, such packages used to be put together by tour operators in brochures. The new technology includes the ability to combine multiple travel components on demand to create a reservation. The package that is created is handled seamlessly as one transaction and requires only one payment from the consumer, hiding the pricing of individual components.

Current dynamic packaging applications are developed using a hard-coded approach to develop the interfaces among various systems to allow the interoperability of decentralized, autonomous, and heterogeneous tourism information systems. However, such an approach for integration does not comply with the highly dynamic and decentralized nature of the tourism industry. Most of the players are small or medium-sized enterprises with information systems with different scopes, technologies, architectures, and structures. This diversity makes the interoperability of information systems and technologies very complex and constitutes a major barrier for emerging e-marketplaces and dynamic packaging applications that particularly affects the smaller players (Fodor and Werthner 2004-5).

Two emerging technologies can enable the deployment of a more integrated solution to implement dynamic application (Cardoso 2005): Web services and semantics. As opposed to the hard-coded approach, Web services take a loosely coupled software components approach, which can be dynamically located and integrated on the Web. Web services are flexible to easily design processes that model dynamic packaging applications. Semantics are important to dynamic packaging applications because they provide a shared and common understanding of data and services of the tourism information systems to integrate. Semantics can be used to organize and share tourism information, which allow better interoperability and integration of inter- and intra-company travel information systems.

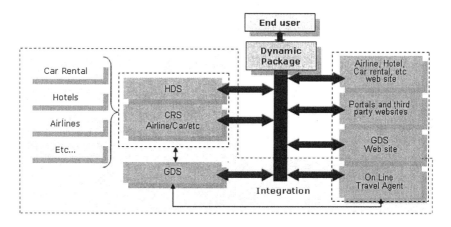

Figure 1-9. Integration of tourism information systems

Figure 1-9 illustrates the integration of various tourism information systems to support the concept of dynamic packaging. As it can be seen, new communication links are established among the various participant of the distribution model to integrate tourism products.

So far, the travel industry has concentrated its efforts on developing open specification messages, based on XML, to ensure that messages can flow between industry segments as easily as within. For example, the OpenTravel Alliance (OTA 2004) is an organization pioneering the development and use of specifications that support e-business among all segments of the travel industry. It has produced more than 140 XML-based specifications for the travel industry (Cardoso 2004).

The development of open specifications messages based on XML, such as OTA schema, to ensure the interoperability between trading partners and working groups is not sufficiently expressive to guarantee an automatic exchange and processing of information to develop dynamic applications. A more appropriate solution is the development of suitable ontologies for the tourism industry that can serve as a common language for tourism-related terminology and a mechanism for promoting the seamless exchange of information across all travel industry segments. Ontologies are the key elements enabling the shift from a purely syntactic to a semantic interoperability. An ontology can be defined as the explicit, formal descriptions of concepts and their relationships that exist in a certain universe of discourse, together with a shared vocabulary to refer to these concepts. With respect to an ontology a particular user group commits to, the semantics of data provided by the data sources to integrate can be made explicit. Ontologies can be applied to the area of dynamic packaging to explicitly connect data and information from tourism information systems to its definition and context in machine-processable form. Ontologies can be used to bring together heterogeneous Web services, Web processes, applications, data, and components residing in distributed environments. Semantic Web processes, managing dynamic package determine which Web services are used, what combinations of Web services are allowed or required and specific rules determine how the final retail price is computed (Cardoso, Miller et al. 2004).

6.4   Semantic Digital Libraries

Libraries are a key component of the information infrastructure indispensable for education. They provide an essential resource for students and researchers for reference and for research. Metadata has been used in libraries for centuries. For example, the two most common general classification systems, which use metadata, are the Dewey Decimal Classification (DDC) system and the Library of Congress Classification (LCC) system. In the United States, the DDC is used in 95% of all public and K-12 school libraries, in 25% of college and university libraries, and in 20% of special libraries. The DDC system has 10 major subjects, each with 10 secondary subjects (DDC 2005). The LCC system uses letters instead of numbers to organize materials into 21 general branches of knowledge. The

21 subject categories are further divided into more specific subject areas by adding one or two additional letters and numbers (LCCS 2005).

As traditional libraries are increasingly converting themselves to digital libraries, a new set of requirements has emerged. One important feature for digital libraries is the availability to efficiently browse electronic catalogues browsed. This requires the use of common metadata to describe the records of the catalogue (such as author, title, and publisher) and common controlled vocabularies to allow subject identifiers to be assigned to publications. The use of a common controlled vocabulary, thesauri, and taxonomy (Smrz, Sinopalnikova et al. 2003) allows search engines to ensure that the most relevant items of information are returned. Semantically annotating the contents of a digital library's database goes beyond the use of a controlled vocabulary, thesauri, or taxonomy. It allows retrieving books' records using meaningful information to the existing full text and bibliographic descriptions.

Semantic Web technologies, such as RDF and OWL, can be used as a common interchange format for catalogue metadata and shared vocabulary, which can be used by all libraries and search engines (Shum, Motta et al. 2000) across the Web. This is important since it is not uncommon to find library systems based on various metadata formats and built by different persons for their special purposes. By publishing ontologies, which can then be accessed by all users across the Web, library catalogues can use the same vocabularies for cataloguing, marking up items with the most relevant terms for the domain of interest. RDF and OWL provide a single and consistent encoding so implementers of digital library metadata systems will have their task simplified when interoperating with other digital library systems.

6.5   Semantic Grid

The concept of Grid (Foster and Kesselman 1999) has been proposed as a fundamental computing infrastructure to support the vision of e-Science. The Grid is a service for sharing computer power and data storage capacity over the Internet and goes well beyond simple communication providing functionalities that enable the rapid assembly and disassembly of services into temporary groups.

Recently, the Grid has been evolving towards the Semantic Grid to yield an intelligent platform which allows process automation, knowledge sharing and reuse, and collaboration within a community (Roure, Jennings et al. 2001). The Semantic Grid is about the use of semantic Web technologies in Grid computing; it is an extension of the current Grid. The objective is to describe information, computing resources, and services in standard ways that can be processed by computers. Resources and services are represented using the technologies of the semantic Web, such as RDF. The use of semantics to locate data has important implications for integrating computing resources. It implies a two-step access to resources. In step one, a search of metadata catalogues is used to find the resources containing the data or service required by an application. In the second step, the data or service is accessed or invoked.

6.6 Semantic Enterprise Information Integration

The challenges for today's enterprise information integration systems are well understood. In order to manage and use information effectively within the enterprise, three barriers that increase the complexity of managing information have to be overcome: the diverse formats of content, the disparate nature of content, and the need to derive "intelligence" from this content.

Current software tools that look at structuring content by leveraging syntactic search and even syntactic metadata are not sufficient to handle these problems. What is needed is actionable information from disparate sources that reveals non-obvious insights and allows timely decisions to be made. The new concept known as semantic metadata is paving the way to finally realize the full value of information. By annotating or enhancing documents with semantic metadata, software programs can automatically understand the full context and meaning of each document and can make correct decisions about who can use the documents and how these documents should be used.

Semantic is a key enabler for deriving business value via enterprise information integration and can enable the next generation of information integration and analysis software in the following areas (Sheth 2003):

- Extract, organize, and standardize information from many disparate and heterogeneous content sources (including structured, semi-structured, and unstructured sources) and formats (database tables, XML feeds, PDF files, streaming media, and internal documents)
- For a domain of choice, identify interesting and relevant knowledge (entities such as people's names, places, organizations, etc., and relationships between them) from heterogeneous sources and formats.
- Analyze and correlate extracted information to discover previously unknown or non-obvious relationships between documents and/or entities based on semantics (not syntax) that can help in making business decisions.

- Enable high levels of automation in the processes of extraction, normalization, and maintenance of knowledge and content for improved efficiencies of scale.
- Make efficient use of the extracted knowledge and content by providing tools that enable fast and high-quality (contextual) querying, browsing, and analysis of relevant and actionable information.

6.7   Semantic Web Search

Swoogle[1] is a crawler-based indexing and retrieval system for the semantic Web built on top of the Google API. It was developed in the context of a research project of the ebiquity research group at the Computer Science and Electrical Engineering Department of the University of Maryland.

In contrast to Google (Google 2005), Swoogle discovers, analyzes, and indexes Semantic Web Documents (SWD) written in RDF and OWL, rather than plain HTML documents. Documents are indexed using metadata about classes, properties, and individuals, as well as the relationships among them. Unlike traditional search engines, Swoogle aims to take advantage of the semantic metadata available in semantic Web documents. Metadata is extracted for each discovered document and relations (e.g. similarities) among documents are computed. Swoogle also defines an ontology ranking property for SWD which is similar to the pageRank (Brin and Page 1998) approach from Google and uses this information to sort search results. Swoogle provides query interfaces and services to Web users. It supports software agents, programs via service interfaces, and researchers working in the semantic Web area via the Web interface.

Swoogle's database does not stores all of the content of the SWD discovered. It only stores metadata about the documents, the terms, and the individuals they define and use. Currently, the database has information on more that 275 thousand semantic Web documents which contain more than 40 million triples and define more than 90 thousand classes, 50 thousand properties, and 6 million individuals.

A much earlier and commercial effort in building semantic search was Taalee's MediaAnywhere A/V search engine (Townley 2000; Sheth 2001). In this system, ontology driven metadata extraction automatically extracted and refreshed semantic metadata associated with audio/video content rich Web sites. It used ontologies in areas such as Sports, Entertainment,

---

[1] http://swoogle.umbc.edu/

Business and News. Ontology-driven forms based querying supported specification of semantic queries.

6.8   Semantic Web and AI

The merit of the semantic Web is that its concepts and vision are pragmatically oriented. This is a contrast to the speculative aims of Artificial Intelligence (AI). A sharp distinction between semantic Web and AI can be made between the relevance and understanding of data and programs. AI is concerned with highly complex programs being able to understand data, e.g. texts and common sense. The semantic Web is more concerned in making its data "smart" and giving them some machine-readable semantics. While, AI tends to replace human intelligence, semantic Web asks for human intelligence.

Inference mechanisms that can deal with the massive number of assertions that would be encountered by semantic Web applications are required. The claimed power behind many of the proposed applications of semantic Web technology is the ability to infer knowledge that is not explicitly expressed. Needless to say, this feature has attracted the attention from the AI community since they have been dealing with issues relating to inference mechanisms in the past. Inference mechanisms are applicable only in the context of formal ontologies. The idea is to use rules and facts to assert new facts that were not previously known. One of the most common knowledge representation languages has been Description Logic (Nardi and Brachman 2002) on which DAML, one of the earliest semantic Web languages is based.

6.9   Semantic Web and Databases

Although an ontology schema may resemble at a representational level a database schema, and instances may reflect database tuples, the fundamental difference is that ontology is supposed to capture some aspect of real-world or domain semantics, as well as represent ontological commitment forming the basis of semantic normalization. Nevertheless, many researchers in the database community continue to express significant reservations toward the semantic Web. The following list shows some examples of remarks about semantic Web technology (Sheth and Ramakrishnan 2003).

"As a constituent technology, ontology work of this sort is defensible. As the basis for programmatic research and implementation, it is a speculative and immature technology of uncertain promise."

"Users will be able to use programs that can understand semantics of the data to help them answer complex questions ... This sort of hyperbole is characteristic of much of the genre of semantic web conjectures, papers, and proposals thus far. It is reminiscent of the AI hype of a decade ago and practical systems based on these ideas are no more in evidence now than they were then."

"Such research is fashionable at the moment, due in part to support from defense agencies, in part because the Web offers the first distributed environment that makes even the dream seem tractable."

"It (proposed research in Semantic Web) pre-supposes the availability of semantic information extracted from the base documents -an unsolved problem of many years ..."

"Google has shown that huge improvements in search technology can be made without understanding semantics. Perhaps after a certain point, semantics are needed for further improvements, but a better argument is needed."

These reservations likely stem from a variety of reasons. First, this may be a product of the goals of the semantic Web as depicted in (Berners-Lee, Hendler et al. 2001). Specifically, database researchers may have reservations stemming from the overwhelming role of description logic in the W3C's Semantic Web Activity and related standards. The vision of the semantic Web proposed in several articles may seem, to many readers, like a proposed solution to the long standing AI problems. Lastly, one of the major reservations is related to the concern about the scalability of the three core capabilities for the semantic Web to be successful, namely the scalability of the (a) creation and maintenance of large ontologies, (b) semantic annotation, and (c) inference mechanisms or other computing approaches involving large, realistic ontologies, metadata, and heterogeneous data sets.

6.10   Bioinformatics Ontologies

The integration of information sources in the life sciences is one of the most challenging goals of bioinformatics (Kumar and Smith 2004). In this area, the Gene Ontology (GO) is one of the most significant accomplishments. The objective of GO is to supply a mechanism to guarantee the consistent descriptions of gene products in different databases. GO is rapidly acquiring the status of a *de facto* standard in the field of gene and gene product annotations (Kumar and Smith 2004). The GO effort includes the development of controlled vocabularies that describe gene products, establishing associations between the ontologies, the genes, and the gene products in the databases, and develop tools to create, maintain, and use ontologies (see http://www.geneontology.org/). GO has over 17,000 terms and it is organized in three hierarchies for molecular functions, cellular components, and biological processes (Bodenreider, Aubry et al. 2005).

Another well-known life science ontology is the Microarray Gene Expression Data (MGED) ontology. MGED provides standard terms in the form of an ontology organized into classes with properties for the annotation of microarray experiments (MGED 2005). These terms provide an unambiguous description of how experiments were performed and enable structured queries of elements of the experiments. The comparison between different experiments is only feasible if there is a standardization in the terminology for describing experimental setup, mathematical post-processing of raw measurements, genes, tissues, and samples. The adoption of common standards by the research community for describing data makes it possible to develop systems for the management, storage, transfer, mining, and sharing of microarray data (Stoeckert, Causton et al. 2002).

If data from every microarray experiment carried out by different research group were stored with the same structure, in the same type of database, the manipulation of data would be relatively easy. Unfortunately, in practice, different research group have very different requirements and, therefore, applications need mappings and translations between the different existing formats (Stoeckert, Causton et al. 2002).

Software programs utilizing the MGED ontology generate forms for annotation, populate databases directly, or generate files in an established format. The ontology can be used by researchers to annotate their experiments as well as by software developers to implement practical applications.

7.   CONCLUSIONS

Since its creation, the World Wide Web has allowed computers only to understand Web page layout for display purposes, without having access to their intended meaning. Now the Web has advanced to a lot more than a medium to publish data and documents; a Web resource can be a component of what is called deep web (such as a queryable database) or a service that wraps an application. The semantic Web aims to enrich this Web with a layer of machine-understandable metadata to enable the machine processing of information and services. The semantic Web is not a separate Web but an extension of the current one, in which information and services are given well-defined meaning, thereby better enabling computers and people to work in cooperation. To make possible the creation of the semantic Web the W3C (World Wide Web Consortium) has been actively working on the definition of open standards, such as the RDF (Resource Description Framework) and OWL (Web Ontology Language), and encourage their use by both the industry and academia. These standards are also important for e-commerce and e-science, involving sharing of services and the integration for intra- and inter-business processes that have become widespread due to the development of business-to-business and business-to-customer infrastructures.

To fully appreciate the objective of semantics and the semantic Web, it is essential to comprehend what is the place and role of semantics in science in general and computer science in particular. The heterogeneity of the data occurs when there are differences in syntax, representation (e.g. format or structure), and semantics of data. Dealing with heterogeneity has continued to be a key challenge since the time it has been possible to exchange and share data between computers and applications. Given the ease of publication and sharing of data and services on the Web, and the scale involved, the problem has assumed greater importance on the Web. From the various types of heterogeneity, the semantic heterogeneity is a particularly vexing problem. It arises due to a disagreement about the meaning, interpretation, or intended use of the same or related data. One approach to the problems of semantic heterogeneity is to rely on the technological foundations of the semantic Web. More precisely, to define the meaning of the terminology of data using the concepts present in an ontology to make clear the relationships and differences between concepts.

The theories, methodologies, algorithms, and technologies associated with semantic Web make this approach to application and data integration a strong candidate to solve many problems that current systems face. Currently, Web services, tourism information systems, digital libraries, and bioinformatics are some of the leading areas that are studying the potential brought by semantics and ontologies to solve the integration and interoperability problems they have been confronted for many years. For example, semantic Web services are the result of the evolution of the syntactic definition of Web services and the semantic Web. The idea behind Web services is to map concepts in a Web service description to ontological concepts. Using this approach, users can explicitly define the semantics of a Web service for a given domain. Afterwards, using the semantics added to Web services we are able to construct queries using concepts defined in an ontological domain to enable the discovery of service obtaining search results that are more relevant than keyword or attribute-based matching algorithms. Even more significant advantages can be realized when developing mappings for exchanging messages between services participating in a process.

8. QUESTIONS FOR DISCUSSION

Beginner:
1. Why is the search provided by Google, Yahoo! and MSN not semantic?
2. Why and how can metadata help in dealing with unstructured, semi-structured, and structured data?

Intermediate:
1. Why almost all of the semantic metadata efforts involve textual data? Does it make sense to have an ontology of icons or symbols?
2. What would it take to represent concepts found in the natural world, such as compounds and molecules?
3. Distinguish between database schemas and ontologies in terms of conceptual models or representation languages, intentions or uses, and development methodologies.
4. List various techniques used for metadata extraction from different computer science areas.
5. What are the differences in metadata for Web resources that are data versus services?
6. How would Amazon benefit from the use of a product ontology?

Advanced:
1. Discuss how would you define the quality of an ontology.
2. Distinguish between ontologies (representation, extraction/population, etc.) when modeling human activities (e.g., travel, financial services, sports, entertainment) versus natural phenomena and sciences (e.g., earthquakes, complex carbohydrates, protein-protein interactions, cancer research).

Practical Exercises:
1. Identify unstructured, semi-structured and structured documents on the same subject matter, such as a new on a football game (although actual content may be different). Develop a small ontology related to this subject matter. Annotate each of these documents.
2. Obtain at least one RDF(S) and one OWL ontology and load it using an ontology editor (e.g., Protégé).
3. Look up a tool or service on the Web for annotating Web pages and Web services.

4. Take a Web page on a news site. Design a small ontology related to the subject matter or domain of that page. Write syntactic, structural, and semantic metadata of that page.

9.   SUGGESTED ADDITIONAL READING

- Antoniou, G. and van Harmelen, F. *A semantic Web primer.* Cambridge, MA: MIT Press, 2004. 238 pp.: This book is a good introduction to Semantic Web languages.
- Pollock, J. and Hodgson, R. *Adaptive Information: Improving Business Through Semantic Interoperability, Grid Computing, and Enterprise Integration,* Wiley-Interscience, September 2004: Practitioners should find this book to be quite valuable companion.
- Gómez-Pérez, A., Fernandez-Lopez, M., and Corcho, O. *Ontological Engineering: With Examples from the Areas of Knowledge Management, E-Commerce and the Semantic Web* (Advanced Information and Knowledge Processing), Springer-Verlag, October 2003, 420 pp.: The book presents the practical aspects of selecting and applying methodologies, languages, and tools for building ontologies and describes the most outstanding ontologies that are currently available.

10.   REFERENCES

Akkiraju, R., J. Farrell, et al. (2005). Web Service Semantics - WSDL-S, http://lsdis.cs.uga.edu/projects/meteor-s/wsdl-s/.

Berners-Lee, T., J. Hendler, et al. (2001). The Semantic Web. Scientific American. **May 2001**.

Bodenreider, O., M. Aubry, et al. (2005). Non-Lexical Approaches to Identifying Associative Relations in the Gene Ontology. Pacific Symposium on Biocomputing, Hawaii, USA, World Scientific.

Brin, S. and L. Page (1998). The anatomy of a large-scale hypertextual Web search engine. Seventh World Wide Web Conference, Brisbane, Australia.

Cardoso, J. (2004). Issues of Dynamic Travel Packaging using Web Process Technology. International Conference e-Commerce 2004, Lisbon, Portugal.

Cardoso, J. (2005). E-Tourism: Creating Dynamic Packages using Semantic Web Processes. W3C Workshop on Frameworks for Semantics in Web Services, Innsbruck, Austria.

Cardoso, J., C. Bussler, et al. (2005). Tutorial: Lifecycle of Semantic Web Processes. The 17th Conference on Advanced Information Systems Engineering (CAiSE'05), Porto, Portugal.

Cardoso, J., J. Miller, et al. (2004). "Modeling Quality of Service for workflows and web service processes." Web Semantics: Science, Services and Agents on the World Wide Web Journal **1**(3): 281-308.

Cardoso, J. and A. Sheth (2003). "Semantic e-Workflow Composition." Journal of Intelligent Information Systems (JIIS). **21**(3): 191-225.

Chinnici, R., M. Gudgin, et al. (2003). Web Services Description Language (WSDL) Version 1.2, W3C Working Draft 24, http://www.w3.org/TR/2003/WD-wsdl12-20030124/.

Curbera, F., W. Nagy, et al. (2001). Web Services: Why and How. Workshop on Object-Oriented Web Services - OOPSLA 2001, Tampa, Florida, USA.

DDC (2005). Dewey Decimal Classification, OCLC Online Computer Library Center, http://www.oclc.org/dewey/.

Dill, S., N. Eiron, et al. (2003). SemTag and Seeker: Bootstrapping the Semantic Web via Automated Semantic Annotation. 12th international conference on World Wide Web, Budapest, Hungary, ACM Press, New York, NY, USA.

Fisher, M. and A. Sheth (2004). Semantic Enterprise Content Management. Practical Handbook of Internet Computing. C. Press.

Fodor, O. and H. Werthner (2004-5). "Harmonise: A Step Toward an Interoperable E-Tourism Marketplace." International Journal of Electronic Commerce **9**(2): 11-39.

Foster, I. and C. Kesselman (1999). The Grid: Blueprint for a New Computing Infrastructure, Morgan Kaufmann.

Google (2005). Google Search Engine, www.google.com.

Grau, B. C. (2004). A Possible Simplification of the Semantic Web Architecture. WWW 2004, New York, USA.

Hammond, B., A. Sheth, et al. (2002). Semantic Enhancement Engine: A Modular Document Enhancement Platform for Semantic Applications over Heterogeneous Content. Real World Semantic Web Applications. V. Kashyap and L. Shklar, IOS Press: 29-49.

Handschuh, S., S. Staab, et al. (2002). S-CREAM - Semi-automatic CREAtion of Metadata. LNCS - Proceedings of the 13th International Conference on Knowledge Engineering and Knowledge Management. Ontologies and the Semantic Web. London, UK, Springer-Verlag. **2473**: 358-372.

Kashyap, V. and A. Sheth (1996). Semantic heterogeneity in global information systems: The role of metadata, context and ontologies. Cooperative Information Systems: Current Trends and Applications. M. Papzoglou and G. Schlageter. London, UK, Academic Press: 139-178.

Kim, W. and J. Seo (1991). "Classifying schematic and data heterogeinity in multidatabase systems." IEEE Computer **24**(12): 12-18.

Klein, M. and A. Bernstein (2001). Searching for Services on the Semantic Web Using Process Ontologies. International Semantic Web Working Symposium (SWWS), Stanford University, California, USA.

Kumar, A. and B. Smith (2004). On Controlled Vocabularies in Bioinformatics: A Case Study in Gene Ontology. Drug Discovery Today: BIOSILICO. **2**: 246-252.

Lassila, O. and R. Swick (1999). Resource Description Framework (RDF) model and syntax specification., W3C Working Draft WD-rdf-syntax-19981008. http://www.w3.org/TR/WD-rdf-syntax.

LCCS (2005). The Library of Congress, Library of Congress Classification System, http://www.loc.gov/catdir/cpso/lcco/lcco.html.

Lee, Y. L. (2005). Apps Make Semantic Web a Reality (http://68.236.189.240/article/story-20050401-05.html). SDTimes.

MGED (2005). Microarray Gene Expression Data Society, http://www.mged.org/.

Nardi, D. and R. J. Brachman (2002). An Introduction to Description Logics. Description Logic Handbook. F. Baader, D. Calvanese, D. L. McGuinness, D. Nardi and P. F. Patel-Schneider, Cambridge University Press.: 5-44.

OTA (2004). OpenTravel Alliance.

Ouskel, A. M. and A. Sheth (1999). "Semantic Interoperability in Global Information Systems. A brief Introduction to the Research Area and the Special Section." SIGMOD Record **28**(1): 5-12.

OWL (2004). OWL Web Ontology Language Reference, W3C Recommendation, World Wide Web Consortium, http://www.w3.org/TR/owl-ref/. **2004**.

OWL-S (2004). OWL-based Web Service Ontology. **2004**.

Patel-Schneider, P. and J. Siméon (2002). The Yin/Yang web: XML syntax and RDF semantics. 11th international conference on World Wide Web, Honolulu, Hawaii, USA.

Patil, A., S. Oundhakar, et al. (2004). MWSAF - METEOR-S Web Service Annotation Framework. 13th Conference on World Wide Web, New York City, USA.

Peirce, C. (1960). Collected Papers of Ch. S. Peirce (1931-1935). Cambridge, Mass, Harvard University Press.

RDF (2002). Resource Description Framework (RDF), http://www.w3.org/RDF/.

Rodríguez, A. and M. Egenhofer (2002). "Determining Semantic Similarity Among Entity Classes from Different Ontologies." IEEE Transactions on Knowledge and Data Engineering (in press).

Roure, D., N. Jennings, et al. (2001). Research Agenda for the Future Semantic Grid: A Future e-Science Infrastructure http://www.semanticgrid.org/v1.9/semgrid.pdf.

Sheth, A. (1998). Changing Focus on Interoperability in Information Systems: From System, Syntax, Structure to Semantics. Interoperating Geographic Information Systems. M. F. Goodchild, M. J. Egenhofer, R. Fegeas and C. A. Kottman, Kluwer, Academic Publishers: 5-30.

Sheth, A. (2001). Semantic Web and Information Brokering: Opportunities, Early Commercialization, and Challenges. Workshop on Semantic Web: Models, Architectures and Management, Lisbon, Portugal.

Sheth, A. (2003). Semantic Meta Data For Enterprise Information Integration. DM Review Magazine. **July 2003**.

Sheth, A. (2004). From Semantic Search & Integration to Analytics. Dagstuhl Seminar on Semantic Interoperability and Integration, http://www.dagstuhl.de/04391/Materials.

Sheth, A. (2005). Enterprise Application of Semantic Web: the Sweet Spot of Risk and Compliance. IFIP International Conference on Industrial Applications of Semantic Web (IASW2005), Jyväskylä, Finland, Springer.

Sheth, A., B. Arpinar, et al. (2002). Relationships at the Heart of Semantic Web: Modeling, Discovering, and Exploiting Complex Semantic Relationships. Enhancing the Power of the Internet: Studies in Fuzziness and Soft Computing. M. Nikravesh, B. Azvin, R. Yager and L. A. Zadeh, Springer-Verlag.

Sheth, A. and R. Meersman (2002). "Amicalola Report: Database and Information Systems Research Challenges and Opportunities in Semantic Web and Enterprises." SIGMOD Record **31**(4): pp. 98-106.

Sheth, A. and C. Ramakrishnan (2003). "Semantic (Web) Technology In Action: Ontology Driven Information Systems for Search, Integration and Analysis." IEEE Data Engineering Bulletin, Special issue on Making the Semantic Web Real **26**(4): 40-48.

Sheth, A., C. Ramakrishnan, et al. (2005). "Semantics for the Semantic Web: The Implicit, the Formal and the Powerful." Intl. Journal on Semantic Web and Information Systems **1**(1): 1-18.

Sheth, A. P. (1999). Changing Focus on Interoperability in Information Systems: From System, Syntax, Structure to Semantics. Interoperating Geographic Information Systems. C. A. Kottman, Kluwer Academic Publisher: 5-29.

Shum, S. B., E. Motta, et al. (2000). "ScholOnto: an ontology-based digital library server for research documents and discourse." International Journal on Digital Libraries 3(3): 237-248.

Smeaton, A. and I. Quigley (1996). Experiment on Using Semantic Distance Between Words in Image Caption Retrieval. 19th International Conference on Research and Development in Information Retrifval SIGIR'96, Zurich, Switzerland.

Smrz, P., A. Sinopalnikova, et al. (2003). Thesauri and Ontologies for Digital Libraries. 5th Russian Conference on Digital Libraries (RCDL2003), St.-Petersburg, Russia.

Stoeckert, C. J., H. C. Causton, et al. (2002). "Microarray databases: standards and ontologies." Nature Genetics 32: 469 - 473.

SWSF (2005). Semantic Web Services Framework (SWSF) Overview, W3C Member Submission 9 September 2005, http://www.w3.org/Submission/SWSF/.

TopQuadrant (2005). TopQuadrant, http://www.topquadrant.com/. **2005**.

Townley, J. (2000). The Streaming Search Engine That Reads Your Mind, http://smw.internet.com/gen/reviews/searchassociation/.

UDDI (2002). Universal Description, Discovery, and Integration.

Verma, K., K. Sivashanmugam, et al. (2004). "METEOR-S WSDI: A Scalable Infrastructure of Registries for Semantic Publication and Discovery of Web Services." Journal of Information Technology and Management (in print).

Voorhees, E. (1998). Using WordNet for Text Retrieval. WordNet: An Electronic Lexical Database. C. Fellbaum. Cambridge, MA., The MIT Press: 285-303.

Wikipedia (2005). Wikipedia, the free encyclopedia, http://en.wikipedia.org/. **2005**.

WSMO (2004). Web Services Modeling Ontology (WSMO). **2004**.

XMLSchema (2004). XML Schema Part 2: Datatypes Second Edition, W3C Recommendation 28 October 2004.

Chapter 2

SEMANTIC ANNOTATIONS IN WEB SERVICES

Meenakshi Nagarajan
Large Scale Distributed Information Systems (LSDIS) Lab, Department of Computer Science, University of Georgia, GA, USA. – nbmeena@uga.edu

1. INTRODUCTION

"The Semantic Web is a vision: the idea of having data on the Web defined and linked in such a way that it can be used by machines not just for display purposes, but for automation, integration and reuse of data across various applications." (Semantic Web Activity Statement)

Meaningful use of any data requires knowledge about its organization and content. Contextual information that establishes relationships between the data and the real world aspects it applies to is called metadata. In other words, metadata is data that describes information about a piece of data, thereby creating a context in terms of the content and functionality of that data. Domain conceptualizations, ontologies or world models provide agreed upon and unambiguous models for capturing data and metadata to which applications, data providers and consumers can refer. Broadly speaking, there are two kinds of metadata – structural and syntactic metadata. Structural metadata provides information about the organization and structure of some data, e.g. format of the document. Semantic metadata on the other hand, provides information 'about' the data for example the meaning or what the data is about and the available semantic relationships from a domain model in which the data is defined.

The key aspect behind the realization of the Semantic Web vision is the provision of metadata and the association of metadata with web resources. The process of associating metadata with resources (audio, video, structured text, unstructured text, web pages, images etc) is called annotation and semantic annotation is the process of annotating resources with semantic metadata.

Semantic annotations can be coarsely classified as being formal or informal. Formal semantic annotations, unlike informal semantic annotations follow representation mechanisms, drawing on conceptual models represented using well-defined knowledge representation languages. Such machine processable formal annotations on web resources can result in vastly improved and automated search capabilities, unambiguous resource discoveries, information analytics etc. The annotation of web based resources like text files or digital content is very different from the annotation of Web services. In this chapter, we will explore the nature of semantics associated with the Web services and different aspects of semantic annotation of Web resources and Web services in particular.

1.1   Generic Semantic Annotation Architecture

Semantic annotation of resources supported by an existing world model (the ontology schema that provides an agreed upon and unambiguous model for capturing data and metadata) and knowledge base (ontology instances) follows three primary steps: entity identification, entity disambiguation and annotation. These three steps vary depending on the kind of resource one is trying to annotate.

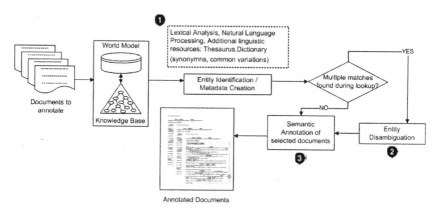

Figure 2-1. Semantic Annotation of documents

For example, the process of identifying entities that need to be annotated from a textual document is different from the process of identifying potential entities from experimental data. The underlying idea however remains the same. In this section, we will briefly cover the three steps involved in the semantic annotation of a resource. For the sake of simplicity, the resource considered for annotation is a text document and the semantics are brought in using a single ontology; although there is nothing that prevents the user from using multiple ontologies.

Figure 2-1 shows the process of semantically annotating a set of documents with the semantics provided by a world model (ontology schema) and a knowledge base (ontology instances).

1.1.1   Entity Identification

The process of entity identification (shown as step 1 in Figure 2-1), involves extracting useful information from a document with the help of rule-based grammars, natural language processing techniques, user-defined templates or wrappers, etc. In addition to the above technologies, ontology-driven extraction of entities also uses the populated ontology (instance level information, also called the knowledge base that is populated using the ontology schema) to extract specific instances of different classes. The approach shown in Figure 2-1 uses a combination of an existing ontology and knowledge base, lexicons and natural language processing techniques.

When an entity is identified in a document, a check is performed to see if the entity exists as an instance in the knowledge base. Variations of the entity like the presence of prefixes or suffixes (such as Jr., Dr., III), common abbreviations (such as US for United States), synonyms, similar strings (accounting for mis-spellings in the document) etc. are also taken into consideration while looking for corresponding instances in the knowledge base. Figure 2-2 shows identified entities in a CNN business article and the corresponding classes from a Stock ontology. Entities of interest are underlined (in blue) and the ontology classes they are associated with are shown in grey. For example, *New York* is an instance of class *City*; *Microsoft* is an instance of class *Company* etc.

In addition to making the process of entity identification more scalable and specialized to a domain, using a knowledge base also allows users to see relationships (already in knowledge base) between identified entities not present in the document itself. For example, the fact that Microsoft and Oracle (see Figure 2-2) are competitors is not in the document and is available to the user only because it was present in the knowledge base.

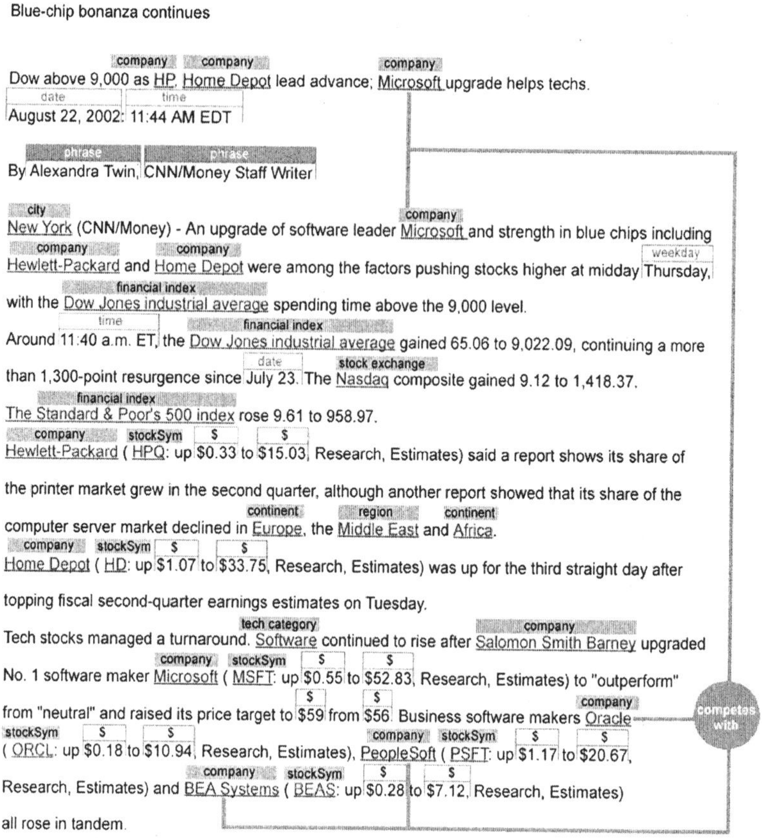

Blue-chip bonanza continues

Dow above 9,000 as HP, Home Depot lead advance; Microsoft upgrade helps techs.
August 22, 2002: 11:44 AM EDT

By Alexandra Twin, CNN/Money Staff Writer

New York (CNN/Money) - An upgrade of software leader Microsoft and strength in blue chips including Hewlett-Packard and Home Depot were among the factors pushing stocks higher at midday Thursday, with the Dow Jones industrial average spending time above the 9,000 level.
Around 11:40 a.m. ET, the Dow Jones industrial average gained 65.06 to 9,022.09, continuing a more than 1,300-point resurgence since July 23. The Nasdaq composite gained 9.12 to 1,418.37.
The Standard & Poor's 500 index rose 9.61 to 958.97.
Hewlett-Packard (HPQ: up $0.33 to $15.03, Research, Estimates) said a report shows its share of the printer market grew in the second quarter, although another report showed that its share of the computer server market declined in Europe, the Middle East and Africa.
Home Depot (HD: up $1.07 to $33.75, Research, Estimates) was up for the third straight day after topping fiscal second-quarter earnings estimates on Tuesday.
Tech stocks managed a turnaround. Software continued to rise after Salomon Smith Barney upgraded No. 1 software maker Microsoft (MSFT: up $0.55 to $52.83, Research, Estimates) to "outperform" from "neutral" and raised its price target to $59 from $56. Business software makers Oracle (ORCL: up $0.18 to $10.94, Research, Estimates), PeopleSoft (PSFT: up $1.17 to $20.67, Research, Estimates) and BEA Systems (BEAS: up $0.28 to $7.12, Research, Estimates) all rose in tandem.

Figure 2-2. Entity identification in an unstructured document (Hammond et al. 2002)

1.1.2   Entity Disambiguation

Very often it is possible that for an entity identified in the document, there are multiple references to it in the knowledge base. For example, for an instance John Smith identified in a document, there could be two instances of John Smith in the knowledge base, one a financial analyst and the other the CEO of a company. The information pertaining to the entity John Smith in the document might not exactly correspond to the information available for the same entity in the knowledge base. For example, the document might not explicitly mention John Smith as the CEO of the company but could be an article about the strategies of the company that John Smith is a CEO of. In such a case, sophisticated methods are required to glean the context in which John Smith is mentioned in the document. Different data sources have different ways of representing the same real world entity. Variations in representation usually arise due to incorrect spellings, use of abbreviations, different naming conventions, naming variations over time, etc. Entity disambiguation (shown as step 2 in Figure 2-1) is the process of identifying when different references correspond to the same real world entity. Entity disambiguation is crucial to basic functionalities like database/ontology integration, population, and to many information management system applications (Blume 2005). A multitude of approaches exist to disambiguate entities depending on the nature of the data source and the level of accuracy required; (Kalashnikov et al. 2005, Dong et al. 2005, Han et al. 2004) represents a small sample of the literature.

In this example setting, the need is to disambiguate the entity identified in the document and the multiple candidate references found in the ontology. Extensive use of context information provides the best evidence for reconciliation decisions. Context of an entity mentioned in a document could be defined in terms of the context of the document, the document's classification in a subject hierarchy etc. to glean what the document is talking about. Context of an entity in a knowledge base could be defined in terms of the values for attributes an entity has and the relationships it participates in. For example, if for the entity "BEAS" appearing in the document, there are two instances in the ontology appearing in the contexts "Bureau of Elder and Adult Services BEAS: an organization" and "BEAS: stock symbol for BEA Systems"; gleaning the context in which "BEAS" appears in the document i.e. associated with BEA Systems can help disambiguate the two references in the ontology. Entity disambiguation is a data and engineering intensive process and usually requires some amount of user involvement.

1.1.3   Annotation

After the entity disambiguation process (in the presence of ambiguities), the next step is to associate semantic metadata to the entities in the document through the process of annotation. Typically intended for use by humans and agents, these annotations are represented using W3C recommended standard representation languages like RDF (Resource Description Framework) / OWL (Web Ontology Language, OWL). Figure 2-3 shows sample metadata for a few entities in the document shown in Figure 2-2. The annotation made in XML (Extensible Markup Language (XML)) shows the entity *'Hewlett-Packard'* is an instance of class *'company'*, *'HPQ'* is a *'tickerSymbol'* etc.

<Entity id="494805" class="company">Hewlett-Packard</Entity> (*<Entity id="875349" class="tickerSymbol">HPQ</Entity>*: up *<Regexp type="money">$0.33</Regexp>* to *<Regexp type="money">$15.03</Regexp>*, Research, Estimates) said a report shows its share of the printer market grew in the second quarter, although another report showed that its share of the computer server market declined in *<Entity id="7852" class="continentRegion">Europe</Entity>*, the *<Entity id="7854" class="continentRegion">Middle East</Entity>*

Figure 2-3. Sample Semantic Annotation in XML

Metadata Enhancement: In the process of identifying entities in the document, it is possible that we find values for attributes or relationships that were not previously present in the knowledge base. Enhancing the existing metadata could be as simple as entering values for attributes, in which case they could be automated; or as complex as modifying the underlying schema, in which case some user involvement might be required.

1.2   Semantic Annotation Applications

Several efforts have been made towards building scalable, automatic semantic annotation platforms. Most of these systems focus on manual and semi-automatic tooling to improve the productivity of a human annotator rather than on fully automated methods. However, even with machine assistance, annotation of content is a difficult, time consuming and error-prone task.

Besides semantic tagging of content, a number of applications also provide storage of annotations and ontologies, user interfaces, access APIs, and features to fully support annotation usage. The most interesting aspect of these applications is the variety of information extraction techniques used. Rules, discovering patterns, machine learning and bootstrapping from taxonomies or ontologies are some techniques used. Examples of such efforts include SemTag (Dill et al. 2003), SHOE (The SHOE Knowledge Annotator), AeroDAML (Kogut et al. 2001), SEE (Hammond et al. 2002), OntoAnnotate (Staab et al. 2001), COHSE (Goble et al. 2001), CREAM (Handschuh et al. 2002), Annotea (Kahan et al. 2002), KIM (Popov et al. 2003) etc. The page on (Annotation Tools) also lists some available tools. Table 2-1 shows a comparison of some tools on the basis of the technology used. In this section, we will briefly describe some applications to give a general idea of the features of annotation frameworks. The reader should refer to Table 2-1 to relate different components of these applications to what has been presented earlier in this chapter.

SemTag is an application written on a platform for large-scale text analytics called Seeker. SemTag performs automated semantic tagging of large corpora using the TAP (Guha et al.) ontology. Also used is a disambiguation algorithm specialized to support ontological disambiguation of large-scale data. Annotations are represented using RDFS (RDF Vocabulary Description Language 1.0: RDF Schema).

SHOE, one the earliest systems for adding semantic annotations to web pages allows users to mark up pages in SHOE (Heflin et al. 1999) guided by ontologies available locally or via a URL. These marked up pages can also be reasoned about by SHOE-aware tools such as SHOE Search (Semantic Search - The SHOE Search Engine).

OntoAnnotate offers comprehensive support for the creation of semantically interlinked metadata by human annotators. In identifying entities in web pages, it uses a combination of the following techniques: wrapper generation, pattern matching and ontology based information extraction based on a shallow text processing engine. Also included in the framework is a document management system that stores annotated documents and their metadata represented in RDF.

Table 2-1. Semantic Annotation Platforms (Reeve et al. 2005)

Platform	Method	Machine Learning	Manual Rules	Bootstrap Ontology
AeroDAML	Rule	N	Y	WordNet
Armadillo	Pattern Discovery	N	Y	User
KIM	Rule	N	Y	KIMO
MnM	Wrapper Induction	Y	N	KMi
MUSE	Rule	N	Y	User
Ont-O-Mat: Amilcare	Wrapper Induction	Y	N	User
Ont-O-Mat: PANKOW	Pattern Discovery	N	N	User
SemTag	Rule	N	N	TAP

The KIM platform provides a novel Knowledge and Information Management (KIM) infrastructure and services for automatic semantic annotation, indexing, and retrieval of unstructured and semi-structured content. It analyzes texts and recognizes references to entities and tries to match the reference with a known entity. The reference in the document gets annotated with the URI of the entity. KIM is equipped with an upper-level ontology PROTON (PROTON Ontology) and a knowledge base KIM KB (KIM Knowledge Base). Other than automatic semantic annotation, KIM also allows one to perform content retrieval, based on semantic restrictions, as well as querying and modifying the underlying ontologies and knowledge bases.

The work in building ontologies and creating semantic annotations for resources is fundamental to the building of the Semantic Web and is gaining a lot of momentum (Berners-Lee et al. 2001). Besides textual and digital content, the most important Web resources are those that provide 'services'. Such services also called Web services are non-static in nature i.e. they allow one to effect some action or change in the world, such as the purchase of a product. The Semantic Web should enable users and agents to discover, use, compose, and monitor Web-based services automatically. The semantic annotation of Web services is however a completely different ball game than the annotation of other web resources. The semantics associated with Web services need to be formulated in a way that makes them useful to the application of Web services. In (Sheth 2003), four types of semantics are presented for the complete life cycle of a Web process. In the next few sections, we will see how the technology built for the Semantic Web is being applied to enhance Web service descriptions to make the aforementioned tasks possible.

2.   SEMANTIC ANNOTATION IN WEB SERVICES

There has been a recent proliferation of Web services as the technology for business process execution and application integration. Although Web services are based on widely accepted standards, the lack of a formal description of the meaning of their functionality and the data exchanged has been a significant roadblock in the realization of integration promises. As the number of Web services increase, it is important to have automated tools to discover and compose Web services. The extent of description available in the current WSDL standard leaves room for ambiguous interpretations of the functionality and data of a Web service. Ambiguity in interpretation hinders the automation of tasks like service discovery, composition, invocation etc. One of the ways the community is working to address these issues is by developing a semantic markup language for Web Services. This section of the chapter discusses different aspects of semantic annotation of Web service elements.

2.1 Annotating a Web Service

Semantically annotating a Web service implies explicating the exact semantics of the Web service data and functionality elements that are crucial towards the use of the Web service. This is done by annotating the Web service elements with concepts in domain models or ontologies. Since ontologies represent an agreed upon view of the modeled domain, any ambiguity in the interpretation of functionality or data of a Web service is eliminated. The purpose of annotating Web services is to enable unambiguous and automated service discovery and composition. For example, two Web services meant for completely different functionalities may use the same data types and names for their operations, inputs and outputs, thus making the interpretation of their functionality ambiguous. To understand what parts of a Web service need to be annotated, it is important to understand the interplay of semantics in the life cycle or their usage in a Web service.

While discovering or composing a Web service, a requestor describes his requirements in terms of the functionality i.e. operations of a Web service, and the data used by them i.e. inputs and outputs. Optional specifications include the preconditions and effects of the operation. Preconditions are requirements that must be met before a Web service operation is invoked and effects are the results of invoking an operation. Semantic annotations are therefore associated with the inputs, outputs, preconditions and effects of an operation element of a Web service. More advanced discovery mechanisms however, consider non-functional aspects of Web services and consumer requirements like quality metrics, reliability, security etc.

The benefits of adding semantics is pervasive in the entire life cycle of a Web process (see Figure 2-4). Developers can use semantic annotations to explicate the capabilities of their Web services (1). Once these Web services are published in the UDDI (Universal Description, Discovery and Integration) (2), a requestor can formulate his requirements in a semantic service template (3) (Sivashanmugam et al. 2003) to discover or compose Web services. A semantic service or process template is an abstract service or process description, where the control flow is created manually and the functionality required is described using terms from a domain model or ontology. Reasoning techniques can be used to compare the requirements in the service template with the capabilities of Web services available in the UDDI (4) to discover services (UDDI Technical White Paper 2000). During composition, the functional aspect of the annotations can be used to create useful service compositions.

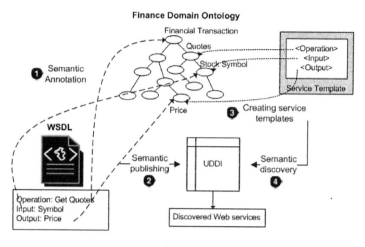

Figure 2-4. Semantics in the life cycle of a Web service

2.2   Four Types of Semantics in Web Services

Table 2-2 illustrates the four types of semantics; data, functional, non-functional and execution semantics associated with Web services and how they relate to the different stages shown in Figure 2-4. Chapter 4 of this book gives an example of how these semantics are modeled in Web services.

Table 2-2. Four types of semantics in Web processes

Type of Semantics	Description	Use
Data Semantics	Formal definition of data in input and output messages of a Web service	Service discovery and interoperabilit y between Web services
Functional Semantics	Formal definition of the capabilities of a Web service.	Discovery and composition of Web Services
Non-functional Semantics	Formal definition of quantitative or non-quantitative constraints like	Discovery, composition and interoperabilit

Service Profile in OWL-S

| | QoS (Quality of service) requirements like minimum cost and policy requirements like message encryption. | y of Web Services |
| Execution Semantics | Formal definition of the execution or flow of services in a process or of operations within a service. | Process verification and exception handling* |

* Process verification involves verifying the correctness (control and data flow) of a process composition. (Fu et al. 2004) The objective of exception-handling is to identify breakdown points in a Web process and define how to overcome from such breakdowns. (Verma et al. 2005)

Now that we understand why semantics are required in Web service descriptions and what kind of semantics is useful, we can proceed to explore how these semantic annotations are created.

3. CREATING SEMANTIC ANNOTATIONS

With the increasing number of Web services and independent domain models being created, a semi-automatic approach to annotating Web services is very crucial. The fundamental idea behind the association of semantics with Web service elements is to find the most appropriate semantic concept in an ontology for a WSDL element. This is done by matching a WSDL and a domain model schema. For the sake of simplicity let us assume that the domain models have been created using OWL, although they could well be represented in RDF, UML, etc.

Matching a WSDL (basically XML) and OWL schema introduces the problem of matching two heterogeneous models, each with its own expressiveness, capabilities and restrictions. The problem of matching two schemas dates back to the problem of data interoperability in the context of database schemas. The words matching and mapping have often been used interchangeably in the literature. In this chapter, the word schema matching refers to the process of finding semantic correspondences between elements of two schemas and mapping deals with the physical representation of the matches established by schema matching and the rules for transforming elements of one schema to that of the other. For example in Figure 7 that shows a WSDL element and an OWL concept, the result of schema matching is to identify that the POAddress object in the WSDL is semantically equivalent to the Address concept in the ontology. The mapping shown as XQuery (XQuery 1.0: An XML Query Language) and XSLT (XSL Transformations (XSLT)) scripts make the matching operational by specifying rules for transforming elements of one schema to that of the other. Sections 3.1 and 3.2 discuss matching and mapping in the context of Semantic Web services.

3.1   Matching

As far as the problem of schema matching goes, there has been significant work in the database community during 1980s and early 1990s on recognizing the need for data interoperability, schema mapping/merging/transformations, semantic heterogeneity, and use of ontology and description logics for schematic and semantic integration, etc. (e.g., see the discussion in (Sheth 2004)). This was followed by work on schema matching and mapping as part of the Model Management initiative (Model Management). There is ongoing work in the above areas especially in the context of new Web Service technologies and Semantic Web languages (XML, RDF/RDFS, OWL) (Patil et al. 2004, Kalfoglou et al. 2003, Stumme et al. 2001, F Hakimpour et al. 2005).

However, much of the past work in database integration has focused on matching homogeneous models, for example, two database schemas. Any difference in schema representation has been dealt with normalizing the disparate schemas before matching. In the case of matching a WSDL (XML schema) and OWL schema, we are really dealing with two different models. Transforming a less expressive model (XML) to a more expressive model (OWL) would usually require humans to supply additional semantics, while transformation in the other direction can be lossy at best.

Current work in the area of model management (Melnik 2004, Melnik 2005) has focused on developing a generic infrastructure that abstracts operations on models (i.e., schemas) and mappings between models as high level operations which are generic and independent of the data model and application of interest. In the area of Web services, (Patil et al. 2004) addresses the difference in expressiveness between OWL and WSDL (XML) by normalizing both the representations to a common graph format. The result of matching is to establish semantic correspondences which are then represented as annotations. The possible use of machine learning techniques to create metadata for Web services has been explored in ASSAM (Hess et al. 2004a). The annotator component of ASSAM (Hess et al. 2004b) casts the problem of classifying operations and data types in a Web Service as a text classification problems. The tool learns from Web Services with existing semantic annotations and given this training data, semantic labels for unseen Web Services are predicted. A similar attempt at using machine learning techniques is presented in (Oldham et al. 2004).

A semi-automated system for creating annotations on Web Service elements should therefore be able to match a WSDL schema and one or more domain model schemas and return the semantic correspondences with the degree of certainty in the matches. In case of ambiguity, user involvement could help refine the matches produced by the system. Although the need for schema matching is quite obvious (to generate semantic annotations), the need for providing mappings deserves more attention. In Section 3.2, we will discuss the motivation behind mappings, their common representation formats and uses in the context of Web service composition.

3.2   Mapping

As we have seen, semantic annotations on Web service elements facilitate unambiguous service discovery and composition. In the context of service composition, the ordering of services ensures a semantic compatibility between their inputs and outputs but does not necessarily ensure interoperability.

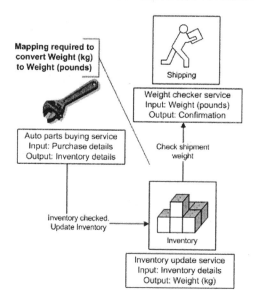

Figure 2-5. A Web process showing the need for mapping between Web service message elements

For example, the Web services shown in Figure 2-5 below make a meaningful process in terms of the semantics of their functionality and the data they exchange, but the format of the messages they exchange is incompatible. The output of the Inventory update service and the input of the Weight checker service are Weight elements and are semantically compatible but differ in their formats (kilograms and pounds), thus making the composition useless at runtime. A mapping between the two elements that converts one message format to another (from Weight in kilograms to Weight in pounds) is required to make this composition operational.

Table 2-3. Possible schematic / data conflicts between xml input/output messages (WSDL-S, Web Service Semantics)

Heterogeneities / Conflicts	Examples - conflicted elements shown in color	
Domain Incompatibilities – *attribute level differences that arise because of using different descriptions for semantically similar attributes*		
Naming conflicts Two attributes that are semantically alike might have different names (synonyms) Two attributes that are semantically unrelated might have the same names (homonyms)	*Web service 1* Student(Id#, Name) *Web service 1* Student(Id#, Name)	*Web service 2* Student(SSN, Name) *Web service 2* Book (Id#, Name)
Data representation conflicts Two attributes that are semantically similar might have different data types or representations	*Web service 1* Student(Id#, Name) Id# defined as a 4 digit number	*Web service 2* Student(Id#, Name) Id# defined as a 9 digit number
Data scaling conflicts Two attributes that are semantically similar might be represented using different precisions	*Web service 1* Marks 1-100	*Web service 2* Grades A-F
Entity Definition – *entity level differences that arise because of using different descriptions for semantically similar entities*		
Naming conflicts Semantically alike entities might have different names (synonyms) Semantically unrelated entities might have the same names (homonyms)	*Web service 1* EMPLOYEE (Id#, Name) *Web service 1* TICKET (TicketNo, MovieName)	*Web service 2* WORKER (Id#, Name) *Web service 2* TICKET(FlightNo. Arr. Airport, Dep. Airport)
Schema Isomorphism conflicts Semantically similar entities may have different number of attributes	*Web service 1* PERSON (Name, Address, HomePhone, WorkPhone)	*Web service 2* PERSON (Name, Address, Phone)
Abstraction Level Incompatibility – *Entity and attribute level differences that arise because two semantically similar entities or attributes are represented at different levels of abstraction*		
Generalization conflicts Semantically similar entities are represented at different levels of generalization in two Web services	*Web service 1* GRAD-STUDENT (ID, Name, Major)	*Web service 2* STUDENT(ID, Name, Major, Type)
Aggregation conflicts Semantically similar entities are represented at different levels of generalization in two Web services	*Web service 1* PROFESSOR (ID, Name, Dept)	*Web service 2* FACULTY (ID, ProfID, Dept)
Attribute Entity conflicts Semantically similar entity modeled as an attribute in one service and as an entity in the other	*Web service 1* COURSE (ID, Name, Semester)	*Web service 2* DEPT(Course, Sem, .., ..)

The generation of mappings like the one in Figure 2-5 is simple and can be automated. More complex mappings however are difficult to automate without human intervention. Table 2-3 illustrates some schema and data conflicts that make the generation of mappings a challenge.

Now that we have recognized the need for such mappings, how would one go about representing and associating these mappings with Web service elements? Clearly, creating mappings between the message elements of two Web services that need to interoperate is not an efficient proposal. Every time a new Web service is created, all existing interoperable Web services would have to create mappings with the new Web service's message elements in the presence of any heterogeneity. An alternative is to create mappings between the Web service element and the domain model or ontology concept with which the Web service element is semantically associated. The ontologies now become a vehicle through which Web services resolve their message level structural or syntactic heterogeneities. Once the mapping is defined and represented, Figure 2-6 shows how two Web services can interoperate using these mappings to ontology concepts. Steps (1), (2) and (3) facilitate message exchange between two communicating Web services. In the first step (1), the WS1 output message is transformed to the OWL concept to which it is mapped (upcast); the OWL concept is then transformed to the WS2 input message (3) (downcast). It is possible that two Web services are not annotated with or mapped to the same ontology. In this case mappings between ontology concepts have to be defined (2). Since mappings are always provided from the Web service element to the ontology concept, generating inverse mappings (to be able to do Step (3) in Figure 2-6) cannot always be automated and requires some user intervention.

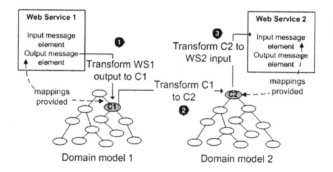

Figure 2-6. Domain models as the vehicle for inter-service communication

In addition to the process of automating the generation of mappings, another research focus has been the representation of the mappings. There have been several approaches to represent mappings in the database literature (Calvanese et al. 2001, Kementsietsidis et al. 2003, A Maedche et al. , Crub´ezy et al. 2003, S.B. Davidson et al. 1995). In the context of Web services, a popular representation for mappings has been the use of XQuery (XQuery 1.0: An XML Query Language) and XSLT (XSL Transformations (XSLT)). Both XQuery and XSLT work on XPATH (XML Linking Language (XLink) Version 1.0) to transform xml objects from one format to another. Figure 2-7 shows an example of a mapping between a WSDL message element and an OWL concept represented using XQuery and XSLT.

```
<complexType name="POAddress"
wssem:schemaMapping="http://www.ibm.com/
schemaMapping/POAddress.xsl#input-
doc=doc("POAddress.xml")">
<all>
<element name="streetAddr1" type="string" />
<element name="streetAdd2" type="string" />
<element name="poBox" type="string" />
<element name="city" type="string" />
<element name="zipCode" type="string" />
<element name="state" type="string" />
<element name="country" type="string" />
<element name="recipientInstName" type="string" />
</all>
</complexType>
WSDL complex type element
```

semantic match

mapping required

Address   has_ZipCode

has_StreetAddress

xsd:string   has_City   xsd:string

xsd:string

OWL ontology

Mapping using xquery

```
for $a in doc("POAddress.xml")/POAddress
return
<POOntology:Address rdf:ID="Address1">
<POOntology:has_StreetAddress rdf:datatype="xs:string">
    {fn:concat($a/streetAddr1 , " ", $a/streetAddr2 )}
</POOntology:has_StreetAddress>
<POOntology:has_City rdf:datatype="xs:string">
    { fn:string($a/city) }
</POOntology:has_City>
<POOntology:has_State rdf:datatype="xs:string">
    { fn:string($a/state) }
</POOntology:has_State>
<POOntology:has_Country rdf:datatype="xs:string">
    { fn:string($a/country) }
</POOntology:has_Country>
<POOntology:has_ZipCode rdf:datatype="xs:string">
    { fn:string($a/zipCode) }
</POOntology:has_ZipCode>
</POOntology:Address>
```

Mapping using XSLT

```
<xsl:template match="/">
<POOntology:Address rdf:ID="Address1">
<POOntology:has_StreetAddress rdf:datatype="xs:string">
    <xsl:value-of select="concat(POAddress/
    streetAddr1,POAddress/streetAddr2)"/>
</POOntology:has_StreetAddress >
<POOntology:has_City rdf:datatype="xs:string">
    <xsl:value-of select="POAddress/city"/>
</POOntology:has_City>
<POOntology:has_State rdf:datatype="xs:string">
    <xsl:value-of select="POAddress/state"/>
</POOntology:has_State>
<POOntology:has_Country rdf:datatype="xs:string">
    <xsl:value-of select="POAddress/country"/>
</POOntology:has_Country>
<POOntology:has_ZipCode rdf:datatype="xs:string">
    <xsl:value-of select="POAddress/zipCode"/>
</POOntology:has_ZipCode>
</POOntology:Address>
```

Figure 2-7. Representing mappings using XQuery and XSLT

4.   SEMANTIC ANNOTATION OF WEB SERVICES - EFFORTS

The most prominent efforts in the semantic markup of Web services have been OWL-S (OWL-S, OWL-based Web Service Ontology), WSMO (WSMO, Web Services Modeling Ontology) and WSDL-S (WSDL-S, Web Service Semantics). While WSMO and OWL-S define their own rich semantic models for Web services, WSDL-S works in a bottom up fashion by preserving the information already present in the WSDL. In this section, we will briefly discuss these initiatives.

4.1   OWL-S and WSMO

4.1.1   OWL-S

"OWL-S (OWL-S: Semantic Markup for Web Services - White Paper) supplies Web service providers with a core set of markup language constructs for describing the properties and capabilities of their Web services in unambiguous, computer-intepretable form. OWL-S markup of Web services facilitates the automation of Web service tasks including automated Web service discovery, execution, interoperation, composition and execution monitoring. Following the layered approach to markup language development, the current version of OWL-S builds on top of OWL."

OWL-S employs an upper level ontology to describe Web services. The ontology comprises of a service profile *(What does the service provide for prospective clients?)*, service model *(How is it used?)* and service grounding *(How does one interact with it?)*.

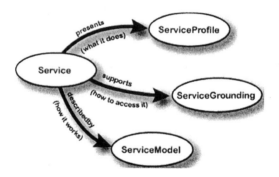

Figure 2-8. Top level of the OWL-S service ontology (OWL-S: Semantic Markup for Web Services - White Paper)

Every instance of a published Web service has an instance of the 'Service' class. The properties of the Service class, 'presents', 'describedBy' and 'supports' point to classes 'ServiceProfile', 'ServiceModel', and 'ServiceGrounding'. "Each instance of a Service will *present* a ServiceProfile description, be *describedBy* a ServiceModel description, and *support* a ServiceGrounding description." The ServiceProfile provides the information needed for an agent to discover a service, while the ServiceModel and ServiceGrounding together provide information for an agent to use the service. Figure 2-8 shows the upper level service ontology in OWL-S.

4.1.2 WSMO

Web Service Modelling Ontology WSMO, also a W3C submission, is a conceptual model for Semantic Web services. It comprises of an ontology of core elements for Semantic Web services, described in a formal description language (WSML) (WSML, Web Services Modeling Language) and also has a execution environment (WSMX) (WSMX, Web Service Execution Environment,). WSMO was derived and based on the Web Service Modelling Framework (WSMF) (D Fensel et al. 2002).

In WSMO, *Ontologies* provide the terminology used by other WSMO elements to describe the relevant aspects of the domains of discourse; *Goals* represent user desires which can be fulfilled by executing a Web service; and *Mediators* describe elements that overcome interoperability problems between different WSMO elements. WSMO considers three levels of mediation - Data Level (to mediate heterogeneous Data Sources), Protocol Level (to mediate heterogeneous Communication Patterns) and Process Level (to mediate heterogeneous Business Processes).

WSMO and OWL-S, both adopt the same view towards having service ontologies to build semantic Web services. OWL-S is based on OWL and represents rules using the Semantic Web Rule Language (SWRL). WSMO has it own family of languages WSML which is based on Description Logics (Description Logics) and Logic programming (Lloyd 1987).

4.2 WSDL-S

WSDL-S, very recently submitted to the W3C, provides a mechanism to annotate the capabilities and requirements of Web services (described using WSDL) with semantic concepts defined in an external domain model. Annotations are achieved using WSDL extensibility elements and attributes. Figure 2-9 shows how semantic annotations are associated with various elements of a WSDL document (including inputs, outputs and functional aspects like operations, preconditions and effects) by referencing the semantic concepts in an external domain semantic model. The domain model can consist of one or more ontologies.

WSDL **Domain Model**

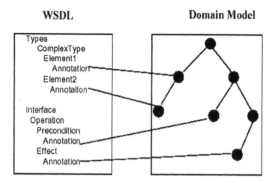

Figure 2-9. Externalized representation and association of semantics to WSDL elements
(WSDL-S, Web Service Semantics)

By building on existing Web service standards, something the community is already familiar with, WSDL-S shows good promise of acceptance and quick realization. Externalizing the domain models allows WSDL-S to take an agnostic view towards semantic representation languages. This allows developers to build domain models in any preferred language (not necessarily in OWL as required by OWL-S) or reuse existing domain models. This is a huge advantage since before OWL was popular, quite a few domain models were developed using RDF/S and UML. Table 2-4 below shows the basic extensibility elements and attributes used by WSDL-S and their purpose. The reader should notice that WSDL-S refers to what OWL-S calls the profile model. The OWL-S process model compares with BPEL4WS (Business Process Execution Language for Web Services version 1.1,) and is not a part of the WSDL-S specification.

Figure 2-10 shows an example of a WSDL-S document. In this WSDL-S, "processPurchaseOrder" is an operation whose output message element "processPurchaseOrderResponse" has been annotated using the *modelReference* and *schemaMapping* attributes. Also present are semantic annotations on the preconditions and effects of the operation and a category annotation on the interface element. Associating semantics with these Web service elements enables automation of service discovery, composition and invocation.

Table 2-4. WSDL-S Extensions (Gomadam et al. 2005)

Extension Element / Attribute	Description
modelReference *(Element: Input and Output Message types)*	Semantic annotation of WSDL input and output message types with concepts in a semantic model.
schemaMapping *(Element: Input and Output Message types)*	Association of structural and syntactic mappings between WSDL message types and concepts in a semantic model.
modelReference *(Element: Operation)*	Captures the semantics of the functional capabilities of an operation.
pre-conditions *(Parent Element: Operation)*	Set of semantic statements (or expressions represented using the concepts in a semantic model) that are required to be true before an operation can be successfully invoked
effects *(Parent Element: Operation)*	Set of semantic statements (or expressions represented using the concepts in a semantic model) that must be true after an operation completes execution.
category *(Parent Element: Operation)*	Service categorization information that could be used when publishing a service in a Web Services registry such as UDDI.

```
.....
<xs:element name= "processPurchaseOrderResponse" type="xs:string
wssem:modelReference="POOntology#OrderConfirmation"
wssem:schemaMapping="http://lsdis.cs.uga.edu/projects/meteor-s/wsdl-s/examples/
sample.xq"/>
</xs:schema>
</types>
<interface name="PurchaseOrder">
<wssem:category name="Electronics" taxonomyURI="http://www.naics.com/"
    taxonomyCode="443112">
<operation name="processPurchaseOrder" pattern=wsdl:in-out
modelReference = "rosetta:#RequestQuote" >
<input messageLabel = "processPurchaseOrderRequest"
element="tns:processPurchaseOrderRequest"/>
<output messageLabel ="processPurchaseOrderResponse"
element="processPurchaseOrderResponse"/>
<!—Precondition and effect are added as extensible elements on an operation>
<wssem:precondition name="ExistingAcctPrecond"
wssem:modelReference="POOntology#AccountExists">
<wssem:effect name="ItemReservedEffect"
wssem:modelReference="POOntology#ItemReserved"/>
</operation>
</interface>
```

Figure 2-10. Sample WSDL-S document

4.2.1   Radiant - WSDL-S Annotation Tool

The semi-automatic creation of a WSDL-S document depends on the automation of the matching and mapping process discussed in Section 3. Radiant (Gomadam et al. 2005), a manual WSDL-S annotation tool allows users to create WSDL-S files by providing a 'point and click' and 'drag and drop' interface to annotate an existing WSDL file using one or more ontologies. Figure 2-11 shows a snap shot of the tool. The tool offers tree representations of the source WSDL files (1) and OWL files ((3) and (4)) simultaneously to let the user choose the most appropriate semantic match. The WSDL-S file that is generated is shown in (2).

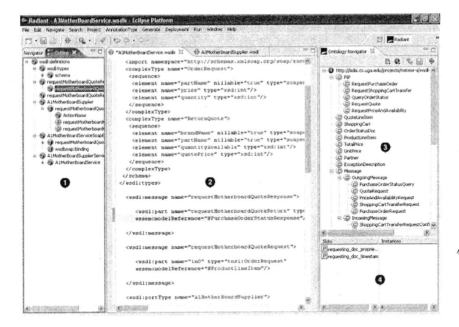

Figure 2-11. Radiant - WSDL-S Annotation tool (Gomadam et al. 2005)

5. CONCLUSIONS

Creating semantic markup of Web services to realize the vision of Semantic Web services has received a lot of attention in the recent years. A direct offshoot has been the development of agent technologies that can utilize these annotations to support automated Web service discovery, composition and interoperability. For the same reasons we recognize the value add that automated semantic annotation frameworks can bring to the Web service community. This chapter has therefore been an attempt to point the reader to existing work in the areas of semantic annotation of Web resources and Web services in particular. The issues that need to be addressed in the context of annotation of Web services are quite different from traditional Web resource annotation frameworks and therefore deserve attention. Challenges of automating (or reducing human involvement) the matching of heterogeneous schemas, representation and use of mappings for Web services are constantly being addressed.

The interested reader is encouraged to refer to resources mentioned in the Additional Readings section 7 below to gain an in-depth understanding of related topics. A Google Scholar search on topics like Semantic Heterogeneity that introduces the case for matching, Evaluation of metadata quality, Disambiguation etc. are possible resources to look at. Projects such as METEOR-S (METEOR-S: Semantic Web Services and Processes) focus on the use of semantics in the life cycle of Web services. Readers are encouraged to visit the web site of METEOR-S and that of similar projects to stay abreast with the state-of-the-art technology and research.

6.   QUESTIONS FOR DISCUSSION

Beginner:
1. Why is there a need for semantic markup of Web resources?
2. What is Entity Disambiguation?
3. What does the semantic markup of Web services offer or enable?
4. What are the four types of semantics that are useful in the life-cycle of a Web process?
5. Define semantic matching and mapping and give an example.
6. What is the fundamental difference between what WSDL-S advocates and the approach used by WSMO or OWL-S?

Intermediate:
1. Why do Semantic Web annotation tools need to disambiguation capability built into them?
2. Discuss how the annotation of Web services is different from annotation of a text document.
3. At what stages of the life-cycle of a Web process are the four semantics used?
4. Why is data integration a problem in Web services and how are ontologies used to facilitate this problem?

Advanced:
1. How can one measure the quality of annotations generated by semantic annotation tools?
2. Why is a semantic match between message elements not sufficient to make a service composition operational?
3. Compare and contrast WSDL-S with OWL-S and WSMO?

7.   SUGGESTED ADDITIONAL READING

Topic: Matching, Mapping, Disambiguation

- Semantic Heterogeneity in Global Information Systems - The Role of Metadata, Context and Ontologies (Kashyap et al. 1998)
- Semi-automatic Composition of Web Services using Semantic Descriptions (Sirin et al. 2002)
- Generic Model Management: Concepts and Algorithms (Melnik 2004)
- Reference reconciliation / Disambiguation (Dong and al 2005)

Topic: General
- Changing Focus on Interoperability in Information Systems: From System, Syntax, Structure to Semantics (Sheth 1998)
- Image Annotation (Hollink et al. 2003) (Wenyin et al. 2001)
- Evaluating the quality of metadata or annotations (Metadata Quality Evaluation)
- A Conceptual Architecture for Semantic Web Enabled Web Services (Bussler et al. 2002)

Projects and initiatives
- METEOR-S (METEOR-S: Semantic Web Services and Processes)
- Semantic Web Services Interest Group (Semantic Web Services Interest Group)
- Semantic tools for Web services (Semantic tools for Web services)
- Semantic Web Services Initiative (SWSI) (Semantic Web Services Initiative)
- Semantic Web Services Home Page (Semantic Web Services Home Page)

8. REFERENCES

A Maedche et al., MAFRA.

Annotation Tools http://annotation.semanticweb.org/tools

Berners-Lee T et al., The Semantic Web. Scientific American. 2001.

Blume M, Automatic Entity Disambiguation: Benefits to NER, Relation Extraction, Link Analysis, and Inference. International Conference on Intelligence Analysis, 2005.

Business Process Execution Language for Web Services version 1.1, http://www-128.ibm.com/developerworks/library/specification/ws-bpel/

Bussler C et al., A Conceptual Architecture for Semantic Web Enabled Web Services. 2002.

Calvanese D et al., Ontology of integration and integration of ontologies. In Description Logic Workshop 2001, 10-19.

Crub'ezy M et al. Ontologies in support of problem solving. Springer, 2003.

D Fensel et al., The Web Service Modeling Framework WSMF. 2002 Electronic Commerce Research and Applications, 1 (2).

Description Logics http://dl.kr.org/

Dill S et al., SemTag and seeker: bootstrapping the semantic web via automated semantic annotation. 2003.

Dong X et al., Reference Reconciliation in Complex Information Spaces. 2005.

Extensible Markup Language (XML) http://www.w3.org/XML/

F Hakimpour et al., Resolution of Semantic Heterogeneity in Database Schema Integration Using Formal Ontologies. 2005 Information Technology and Management.

Fu Xiang et al., Analysis of interacting BPEL web services. WWW, 2004, 621-630.

Goble CA et al., Conceptual Open Hypermedia = The Semantic Web? 2001.

Gomadam K et al., Radiant: A tool for semantic annotation of Web Services. The Proceedings of the 4th International Semantic Web Conference (ISWC 2005) 2005.

Guha R. et al., Tap: Towards a web of data. . http://tap.stanford.edu/.

Hammond et al., Semantic Enhancement Engine: A Modular Document Enhancement Platform for Semantic Applications over Heterogeneous Content. 2002.

Han H et al., Two supervised learning approaches for name disambiguation in author citations. Proceedings of the 4th ACM/IEEE-CS joint conference on Digital libraries, 2004.

Handschuh S et al., Authoring and annotation of web pages in CREAM. 2002.

Heflin J et al., SHOE: a knowledge representation language for Internet applications. 1999.

Hess A et al., Machine Learning for Annotating Semantic Web Services. 2004a.

Hess A et al., ASSAM: A Tool for Semi-Automatically Annotating Semantic Web Services. 2004b.

Hollink L et al., Semantic annotation of image collections. 2003.

Kahan J et al., Annotea: an open RDF infrastructure for shared Web annotations. 2002.

Kalashnikov DV et al., A probabilistic model for entity disambiguation using relationships. SIAM International Conference on Data Mining (SDM), 2005.

Kalfoglou Y. et al., Ontology mapping: the state of the art: The Knowledge Engineering Review. 2003, 18(1). 1--31.

Kashyap V et al., Semantic Heterogeneity in Global Information Systems: The Role of Metadata, Context and Ontologies. 1998.

Kementsietsidis A et al., Mapping Data in Peer-to-Peer Systems: Semantics and Algorithmic Issues. SIGMOD, 2003, 325-336.

KIM Knowledge Base http://www.ontotext.com/kim/KBStatistics.pdf

Kogut P et al., AeroDAML: Applying Information Extraction to Generate DAML Annotations from Web Pages. 2001.

Lloyd JW, Foundations of logic programming. 1987.

Melnik S. Model Management: First Steps and Beyond German Database Conference, 2005

Melnik S. Generic Model Management: Concepts and Algorithms, Ph.D. Dissertation, University of Leipzig, Springer LNCS 2967, 2004.

Metadata Quality Evaluation. SIG CR. http://www.asis.org/Conferences/AM05/abstracts/216.html

METEOR-S: Semantic Web Services and Processes http://lsdis.cs.uga.edu/projects/meteor-s/

Model Management http://research.microsoft.com/db/ModelMgt/

Oldham N et al., METEOR-S Web Service Annotation Framework with Machine Learning Classification. Proceedings of the 1st International Workshop on Semantic Web Services and Web Process Composition (SWSWPC'04), In Conjunction with the 2nd International Conference on Web Services (ICWS'04), 2004, 137 - 146.

OWL-S, OWL-based Web Service Ontology. http://www.daml.org/services/owl-s/

OWL-S: Semantic Markup for Web Services - White Paper. http://www.daml.org/services/owl-s/1.0/owl-s.html

Patil A et al., METEOR-S Web service Annotation Framework. The Proceedings of the Thirteenth International World Wide Web Conference, 2004, 553-562.

Popov B et al., KIM - Semantic Annotation Platform. 2003.

PROTON Ontology http://proton.semanticweb.org/

RDF Vocabulary Description Language 1.0: RDF Schema http://www.w3.org/TR/rdf-schema/

Reeve L et al., Survey of Semantic Annotation Platforms. 2005.

Resource Description Framework. http://www.w3.org/RDF/

S.B. Davidson et al., Semantics of Database Transformations: Semantics in Databases. 1995. 55-91.

Semantic   Search   -   The   SHOE   Search   Engine http://www.cs.umd.edu/projects/plus/SHOE/search/

Semantic tools for Web services http://www.alphaworks.ibm.com/tech/wssem

Semantic Web Activity Statement http://www.w3.org/2001/sw/Activity

Semantic Web Services Home Page http://www.daml.org/services/

Semantic Web Services Initiative http://www.swsi.org/

Semantic Web Services Interest Group http://www.w3.org/2002/ws/swsig/

Sheth A., Changing Focus on Interoperability in Information Systems: From System, Syntax, Structure to Semantics. 1998 Interoperating Geographic Information Systems. 5-30.

Sheth A. Early work in database research on schema mapping/merging/ transformation, semantic heterogeneity, and use of ontology and description logics for schematic and semantic integration Dagstuhl Seminar on Semantic Interoperability and Integration, 2004.

Sheth A.P. Semantic Web Process Lifecycle: Role of Semantics in Annotation, Discovery, Composition and Orchestration, Workshop on E-Services and the Semantic Web, 2003.

The   SHOE   Knowledge   Annotator http://www.cs.umd.edu/projects/plus/SHOE/KnowledgeAnnotator.html

Sirin E et al., Semi-automatic Composition of Web Services using Semantic Descriptions. 2002.

Sivashanmugam K. et al., Adding Semantics to Web Services Standards. Proceedings of the 1st International Conference on Web Services, 2003.

Staab S et al., An annotation framework for the semantic web. 2001.

Stumme G et al. FCA-Merge: Bottom-up merging of ontologies 7th Intl. Conf. on Artificial Intelligence, Seattle, WA, 2001.

UDDI   Technical   White   Paper http://www.uddi.org/pubs/Iru_UDDI_Technical_White_Paper.pdf

Universal Description, Discovery and Integration http://www.uddi.org/about.html

Verma Kunal et al. Optimal Adaptation in Autonomic Web Processes with Inter-Service Dependencies LSDIS Lab Technical Report, 2005.

Web Ontology Language, OWL http://www.w3.org/TR/owl-features/

Wenyin L et al., Semi-automatic image annotation. 2001.

WSDL-S, Web Service Semantics http://www.w3.org/Submission/WSDL-S/

WSML, Web Services Modeling Language. http://www.wsmo.org/wsml/

WSMO, Web Services Modeling Ontology. http://www.wsmo.org/

WSMX, Web Service Execution Environment, . http://www.wsmx.org/

XML Linking Language (XLink) Version 1.0 http://www.w3.org/TR/2001/REC-xlink-20010627/

XQuery 1.0: An XML Query Language http://www.w3.org/TR/xquery/

XSL Transformations (XSLT) http://www.w3.org/TR/xslt

Chapter 3

WEB SERVICES MODELING ONTOLOGY

Michal Zaremba, Mick Kerrigan, Adrian Mocan and Matt Moran
Digital Enterprise Research Institute (DERI), Ireland, National University of Ireland, Galway, Ireland – <firstname.lastname>@deri.org

1. INTRODUCTION

Existing technologies enabling the integration of enterprise systems, use very few of the capabilities of modern computers. For example, the activity of finding services, which should deliver expected enterprise functionality, has to be driven by humans. The process of assembling pieces of functionality into complex business processes also involves human interaction. Finally translating between different message formats, which are exchanged between enterprises systems, cannot be done automatically. Computers and computer networks are used mainly for storing and sending information, but the interpretation of this information is done by software engineers and domain experts. It is currently a manager's responsibility, not a computer's, to find services and to make decisions about their suitability. A software programmer has the responsibility of assembling these services into a complex process block. Finally a domain expert is responsible for defining mappings between the message formats sent by one system and the formats expected by the second.

Web Services have promised to solve some of these problems, but because of their syntactical nature[1], they have failed in most of these cases

---

[1] existing specifications cannot formally specify what services provide and how they should be used, so these descriptions can not be automatically processed by machines

and humans must still be kept in the loop. According to Tidwell (Tidwell), Web Services are self-contained, self-describing, modular applications that can be published, located, and invoked over the Web. This definition, like any of many such definitions describing Web Services, makes no comment on *who* should publish, locate and invoke them. The hidden answer is that these are the humans, who are involved in almost every step of Web Services usage process. The unquestionable success of existing Web Service specifications lies in their ability to separate service interface from its implementation, based on standards which were accepted by all the major players of the IT industry. However these standards lack an appropriate semantic framework allowing for automation of many of the processes which are currently handled manually.

The application of semantics to Web Services can be used to remove humans from the integration jigsaw and substitute them with machines. There are many problems which Semantic Web Services (SWS) could be used to resolve. SWS will put in place an automated process for machine driven dynamic discovery, mediation and invocation. Work that will be presented in this chapter does not question the enormous success of Web Services, but rather this chapter recognizes the need to extend the existing Web Service standards with semantics to enable their full automation. The purpose of this chapter is to introduce and provide an overview of the Web Services Modeling Ontology (WSMO), a fully-fledged framework for SWS, showing a reader practical examples aimed at explaining the application of WSMO concepts to a real world scenario. First we present a very simply use case from the e-banking domain, which is used in an overview of WSMO concepts. One of the major intentions of this chapter is to present the technological framework for SWS development around WSMO. We discuss and present some of the key technologies related to the conceptual framework of WSMO, especially the Web Services Modeling Execution Environment (WSMX), which is its reference implementation.

The chapter is structured as follows: Section 2 presents a motivational use case for Semantic Web Services, Section 3 introduces WSMO and its top level concepts, Section 4 discusses selected technologies for WSMO, Section 5 compares competitive approaches, and Section 6 concludes the chapter.

2. CASE STUDY – APPLICATION FOR SEMANTIC WEB SERVICES

In this section we introduce an application from the banking industry as an example of how Semantic Web Services can be used to provide an improved customer service. Our aim is to illustrate the benefits offered by Semantic Web Services in a familiar scenario. The application, for this use case, allows the comparison of the mortgage interest rates being offered by banks online. The emergence of internet banking has greatly increased the competitiveness of the market for services such as mortgage lending. Banks within the European Union (EU) can provide online banking facilities to any citizen of the EU. Many offer online tools allowing prospective bank customers to see, at a glance, current mortgage rates and the amount they could borrow. These tools are often constrained by being limited to the mortgage products offered by just one bank.

Third party websites are increasingly available that aggregate information from multiple banks allowing the comparison of the various mortgage products on offer. Different techniques can be used by these websites to retrieve data from the individual banks. In the next paragraphs, we describe three of the most common.

Manual population involves one or more humans researching the products offered by various banks based on telephone calls and investigation of marketing material – both print and internet based. This works best when interest rates are stable and the number of banks in the marketplace remains static. The reality is that neither of these conditions is likely to be true. Interest rates change and new online banks appear regularly.

Screen scraping is where a software application reads the HTML content of a Web page and extracts the required data. For example, the scraper may read the Web page used by a bank to publish details of the mortgage rates the bank is offering. The advantage is that, when it works, the information is always up-to-date. However, the technique tightly links the scraping application with the structure of the HTML page advertising the mortgage rates. These pages change frequently and each change requires the scraping application to be redesigned.

Web Services are where the banks themselves provide an online application using standard Web technology that allows their interest rates to be requested on demand. The advantage is that the interface to this application usually remains quite stable – requiring less ongoing maintenance at the client application side. Another advantage is that Web service technology is increasingly standards based. A drawback with Web Services is that the technology, by itself, does not help service requesters understand the meaning of the data or messages that they should exchange with the service. This must be determined by a human before the service is invoked for the first time.

Although Web Services provide the best solution of the three approaches described above, human intervention is still required to *find* services offered by banks online, *interpret* the data and the messages that the various banks' services can support, and know how to *invoke* those services. Semantic Web Services address these problems by providing machine-understandable descriptions of what the service can do (*capability*) and how to communicate with it (*interface*). The use of ontologies as the basis for the descriptions guarantees that they are unambiguous and machine-understandable. In our banking example, an application would automatically discover new Semantic Web Services offering mortgage rate information as they became available. When such a service is located, the description of the interface would be examined automatically to determine how the application and service should communicate. Once data mismatches have been resolved, the application retrieves the information about mortgages as required. The whole operation is transparent to the customer and is always up-to-date.

3.   THE WEB SERVICES MODELING ONTOLOGY

The Web Services Modelling Ontology (WSMO) initiative provides a complete framework enhancing syntactic description of Web Services with semantic metadata. The WSMO project[2] is an ongoing research and development initiative aiming to define a complete framework for SWS and consisting of three activities:

- WSMO, which provides formal specification of concepts for Semantic Web Services,
- WSML (Web Services Modelling Language), which defines the language for representing WSMO concepts;
- WSMX (Web Services Execution Environment), which defines and provides reference implementation allowing the execution of SWS

As depicted in Figure 3-1, there are four top level WSMO concepts: Ontologies, Goals, Web Services and Mediators.

In a nutshell, *Ontologies* provide formal terminologies which interweave human and machine understanding; *Goals* formally specify objectives, which clients would like to achieve by using Web Services; *Web Services* are the formal descriptions required to enable the automatic processing of Web Services, and finally *Mediators* enable handling any possible heterogeneity problems. More detailed explanation with the examples can be found in the following sections.

---

[2] http://www.wsmo.org

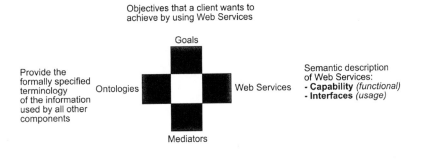

Figure 3-1. WSMO Top Level Concepts

3.1   Ontologies

The Web has revolutionised the publishing and sharing of information. The only obstacle to gaining access to this information is a communication link and simple software that can render and display HTML Web pages. The openness of the Web means the volume of published information is growing exponentially resulting in what is commonly termed 'information overload'. Finding specific data in this sea of information becomes increasingly difficult. Already, today's most valuable Web tools are search engines – the most popular of which accept keywords as input and get the results back fast. Each search engine uses its own proprietary, and usually secret, algorithm when determining what results to give back and in what order the results should be displayed.

It can often be difficult to extract relevant information from the retrieved search results. Sometimes, relevance can only be determined by sifting through the result, one by one. Although not difficult for a small number of search results this becomes impractical as the number of links increases. Ontologies provide a means to greatly help in querying for knowledge on the Web by enriching information with descriptions of its meaning. Significantly, these rich descriptions can be interpreted by computer systems allowing them to provide intelligently interpret the results of Web queries.

Ontology is a philosophical term meaning the study of things that actually exist. In the context of computer science, ontologies define formal shared descriptions of the things that exist in particular domains of interest as well as the relationships that exist between those things. Gruber (Gruber, 1993) defines an ontology as a formal specification of a shared conceptualization – formal because the descriptions it contains must have a precise provable meaning, and shared as an ontology is only valid if its definitions are accepted by a community of users.

Ontologies by themselves are static sources of knowledge but become very powerful instruments when combined with logic and reasoning. Knowledge can be represented formally, using logical languages, as facts that can be interpreted and reasoned about by machines. Reasoning allows implicit knowledge to be inferred from existing knowledge and form an extremely powerful tool when combined with ontologies. In the case of a search engine returning results based on logical reasoning, the engine could also provide the user with the logical proof of where the results came from, if this was necessary.

In WSMO, the basic building blocks of an ontology are *concepts*, *relations*, *functions*, *instances*, and *axioms*. Concepts are descriptions of things that exist in the domain of the ontology. For example, a banking ontology would probably include concept definitions for bank, account, customer, deposit, loan, and so on. Here is an example of a simplified WSMO concept definition for a bank account:

```
concept bank_account
    accountNumber   ofType validAccountNumber
    owner           ofType customer
    balance         ofType currency
    overdraftLimit  ofType currency
```

Concepts may contain attributes with names and types. Relations describe interdependencies between multiple concepts. The relation married-to describes an interdependency between a man and a woman. Functions are special relations that result in a single typed value. For example, a function might be defined to return the amount of a monthly loan repayment based on the amount of the loan, its duration and the interest rate.

Where ontologies describe the conceptual model for a particular domain, instances are the actual facts described using these concepts. For example the details of each individual customer would be used to populate instances of the customer concept. Axioms are the logical expressions used in WSMO for various purposes including the definition of constraints of data, the definition of relations.

3.2   Goals

A service requester uses Goals to represent the type of service that they are seeking by specifying what capability they would like that service to offer and what public interface they would like it to provide. Where Web

Service descriptions are intended to provide detailed descriptions of the mechanics of how a service provides its capability and behaviour, Goal descriptions describe what capability and behaviour the requester would like to find. Importantly, the Goal is described in terms of ontologies used by the requester. The ability to model both Goals and Web Services provide a distinct conceptual separation between the points of view of service requesters and providers. This allows more flexibility in how service requesters and providers are brought together than is possible with current Web Service technology.

For example, the following steps would be needed to search for a Web Service offering mortgage interest rate comparisons. First, a suitable service must be located in a UDDI repository. The requester might try looking for services with the name 'mortgage'. If no services were located, they might try a search on 'home loan' or 'banking services'. If a service is located, its textual description can be checked to see if it fits the requirements. However, as service descriptions provided in UDDI are informal, the requester must assume that their understanding is the same as that intended by the service provider. If the requester is satisfied with the Web Service, the associated WSDL document provides the syntactic description of what messages the service accepts and what transport protocol to use when interacting with the service. The input and output messages are described in XML, in terms of an XML schema. To make an invocation of the Web Service, the requester may have to adjust their data to fit the service description. This example would require the interaction between service requester and service provider to be tightly coupled together. If the requester wants to use another banking service later, they will have to repeat the entire process of finding and binding to a suitable service again.

Describing both Goals and Web Services separately using the Web Service Modelling Ontology shifts the responsibility of matching service requests to service descriptions from the requester to Semantic Execution Environments, such as WSMX, which can interpret the requester's Goal and carry out whatever discovery, mediation and invocation mechanisms are required to connect the service requester to the service provider at run-time. This is distinct from the design-time binding required in the WSDL example described in the last paragraph. WSMO Goals comprise of the following sub concepts: *Capability, Interface, Imported Ontologies* and *Used Mediators*.

3.3   Web Services

Informally, in terms of current specification, the term "Web Service" is usually understood as a composition of three major elements: (1) interface descriptions captured by WSDL documents, (2) the communication protocol,

SOAP using XML to exchange messages and (3) UDDI repositories allowing potential users to find services that are offered by providers. In WSMO the *Web Services* concept is not directly related to WSDL, SOAP and UDDI. In the WSMO context, a Web Service is a formal description required to enable the automatic processing of Web Services. With WSDL, SOAP and UDDI anybody can use a Web Service regardless of the programming language, which has been used to implement the functionality of the service. Similarly, WSMO focuses on the external interface of the Web Service, while its internal implementation remains out of the scope of WSMO. The Web Service description in WSMO provides rich descriptions enabling not only humans, but also software entities "understand" the capabilities and interfaces of the service. Such an unambiguous description of a Web Service with well-defined semantics can be processed and interpreted by software agents without human intervention. This enables the automation of the tasks involved in the Web Service usage process such as discovery, selection, mediation, composition, execution and monitoring. Having appropriate information, software agents can provide automatic matching between Goals received from bank clients and Web Services offered by banks. While the interest rates from a particular bank would not be directly included in a Web Service definition, the capabilities of the service would be defined in a way, that the software agent can "draw" conclusions about the service and its suitability for obtaining information about interest rates.

All the information, stored in the WSMO Web Service description, contains certain aspects of the functionality and behavior of the actual service. The functional aspects are described by the *Capability* of the service. The behavioral aspects are addressed by the *Interface* of the service, which contains both the *Choreography*, which expresses the interface for consumption and the *Orchestration*, which defines how functionality can be achieved by aggregating other Web Services.

The *Capability* describes the functionality of a Web Services from the black box perspective allowing for automated Web Services discovery. This functionality is captured by conditions that need to hold before the Web Service can be executed and by the results that have been achieved after its execution. Web Service Capabilities are defined by four notions:

- *Preconditions* – conditions on the information space that have to hold before execution; For the e-banking Web Service these can be inputs, which have to be provided by a client e.g. in the following example these could be two inputs: (1) an amount of money, which client would like to borrow and (2) repayment period for a requested mortgage.

```
capability aibBankWSCapability
    precondition
        definedBy
            ?interestRateRequest[
                borrowedAmount hasValue ?amount,
                repaymentPeriod hasValue ?period
            ] memberOf aib#interestRateRequest.
```

- *Assumptions* – conditions on the world that have to hold before execution e.g. the fact that a client is coming from a member country of European Union would be an assumption,
- *Postconditions* – conditions on the information space after execution. There are no postconditions for the simple example of e-banking use case. But if after checking interest rates, the client would decide to go ahead and request a mortgage from one particular bank, as a result of Web Service execution (its postconditions) the mortgage money would become available to the client.
- *Effects* – conditions on the world that hold after service execution. Again there are no effects for a simple example of requesting interest rates. But in a complex scenario, as a result of Web Service execution, money would be transferred to client account.

WSMO differentiates two parts of the Web Service *Interface* that are concerned with the interaction behavior of the Web Service. WSMO *Choreography* specifies how the service achieves its capability by means of interactions with its user i.e. the communication with the user of the service. WSMO *Orchestration* specifies how the service achieves its capability by making use of other services - i.e. the coordination of other services. We provide some more details on choreography and orchestration in upcoming sections. Anyway WSMO Choreography and Orchestration are complicated topics and the reader is advised to consult the WSMO specifications for more information and the WSMO deliverables for practical examples of choreography and orchestration interfaces.

3.4   Mediators

For decades, the attempt to make machines or applications work together, interoperate with each other, exchange data and share functionality has been a great challenge both from the technological and efficiency point of view. The Web has pushed these problems to the extreme by offering an environment which adds to the practically infinite quantity of information available. That is, business entities willing to interact bring with them completely independent applications with various ways of representing and structuring data. This drives the need for mediators[3], third-party systems able to deal with the potential mismatches that may appear both on the data and behaviour level between the interacting parties.

The techniques used in developing mediators have to be dynamic and scalable - hard-coded and one-scenario solutions are not feasible anymore. Mediators should be flexible systems and easy to extend, assuring loose coupling between various business entities.

WSMO provides the means of semantically describing mediator systems by introducing four classes of mediators able to cope with the heterogeneity problems that might occur between ontologies, web services and goals: *ontology-to-ontology mediators (ooMediators), goal-to-goal mediators (ggMediators), web services-to-goal mediators (wgMediators)* and *web service-to-web service mediators (wwMediators)*.

ooMediators describe the class of mediators able to solve the heterogeneity problems between ontologies. Indeed, the ontologies could represent very helpful tools in classifying and describing the huge amount of data available on the Web, but they could also be developed in isolation, by different parties. As a consequence, one can find ontologies describing the same domain in different terms and, without mediators, applications using these kinds of ontologies would not be able to exchange data. Also the reuse of external ontologies might not be possible if the heterogeneity problems are solved in advance. For example, in our banking scenario, the bank can use a specific ontology for modelling the details related to mortgages and interest rates. If the application that aggregates mortgage information from different sources uses a different ontology to represent its data, an ooMediator can be used to solve the potential mismatches and conflicts. Such a mediator points to a concrete mediation solution (as the one described in Section 4.2) able to actually solve the heterogeneity problems between the specified source and target ontologies (i.e. the ontology used by the bank and the ontology used by the application, respectively).

ggMediators are used for coping with the differences and for exploiting the similarities that may exist between different goals. Constructing goal ontologies, or explicitly expressing the differences/similarities between different goals, might facilitate the entire process of discovering a Web service, or even the process of invoking a particular goal. Any ggMediator may use the services of ooMediators, in case the goals, between which it

---

[3] One of the first definitions of mediator systems appears in (Wiederhold, 1992) in 1992: "A mediator is a software module that exploits encoded knowledge about some sets or subsets of data to create information for a higher layer of applications."

mediates, are expressed using different ontologies. If a client has as goal to find the mortgage interest rate and there is an already defined goal that asks for mortgage interest rate and the eligibility of the inquiring client for this mortgage, a *ggMediator* can be defined to link these two goals. The *ggMediator* assures that any web service that can satisfy the second goal can satisfy the first one as well.

wgMediators are the class of mediators that address the heterogeneity problems between a goal and a Web service at two different levels: *functionality* (can the Web service completely satisfy the goal?) and *communication* (how can the two partners communicate?). The first level can be addressed in two steps:

- find a goal that is completely satisfied by the Web service
- use the services of a ggMediator that defines the relation between the initial goal and the newly discovered one.

The communication problem addresses the interface heterogeneity – each partner in a communication defines its own way of communicating (communication pattern) with the other one. In case the two patterns do not exactly match (for example, at some point in time one of them may expect something that the other one intends to send later), a communication mediator, also known as process mediator will have to accommodate these mismatches. In the online banking scenario a *wgMediator* can link the goal that asks for mortgage interest rate directly with the web service offering both the mortgage rates and the eligibility details of the client.

wwMediators are the most complex class of mediators in WSMO, addressing the heterogeneity problems between different Web services. These problems may occur when a Web service is invoking one or many other Web services in order to achieve certain functionality, and implies three levels of mediation: *functionality*, *communication* and *cooperation*. The first level can be address in the similar way as for the wgMediators: find goals that can be completely satisfied by the given Web services, and use ggMediators for expressing functional relations; the second level can be address by using wgMediators; the third level, which represents the most complex one, deals with how multiple Web services can be combined (that is, in what order should the Web services be combined). Also known as a problem of composing Web services, this particular level is investigated by different well-known researchers (Milanovic and Malek, 2004), but no truly automatic solutions are discovered so far. In our example, if the web service described above, achieves its functionality by using two other web services, one for retrieving the mortgage interest rates and the other one to check the eligibility of a given client for a particular mortgage type, it is the task of a *wwMediator* to take care of how these two web services have to be combined.

4.   SELECTED TECHNOLOGIES FOR WSMO

Creating ontologies and semantic descriptions for Web Services is only useful if these descriptions can ultimately be applied. Infrastructure is vital for a technology to be applied. Web servers and web browsers are the infrastructure that has lead to the success of HTML on the web. An execution environment for Semantic Web Services is the infrastructure required to enable automated discover, mediation, selection and invocation of these services. This section presents the Web Service Execution Environment (WSMX), by introducing the technologies used and solutions provided by it. WSMX is an execution environment for finding and using Semantic Web Services that are described using WSMO. WSMX is a reference implementation of WSMO and takes the full conceptual model of WSMO into consideration. Considering current Web Service technologies there is a large amount of human effort required in the process of finding and using Web Services. Firstly the user must browse a repository of Web Services to find a service that meets their requirements. Once the Web Service has been found the user needs to understand the interface of the service, the inputs it requires and outputs it provides. Finally the user would write some code that can interact with the Web Service in order to use it. The aim of WSMX is to automate as much of this process as is possible. The user provides WSMX with a WSMO Goal that formally describes what they would like to achieve. WSMX then uses the Discovery component to find Web Services, which have semantic descriptions registered with WSMX that can fulfill this Goal. During the discovery process the users Goal and the Web Services description may use different ontologies. If this occurs Data Mediation is needed to resolve heterogeneity issues. Data Mediation in WSMX is a semi-automatic process that requires a domain expert to create mappings between two ontologies that have an overlap in the domain that they describe. Once these mappings have been registered with WSMX the runtime data Mediation component can perform automatic mediation between the two ontologies. Once this mediation has occurred and a given service has been chosen that can fulfill the users Goal WSMX can begin the process of invoking the service. Every Semantic Web Service has a specific choreography that describes they way in which the user should interact with it. This choreography describes semantically the control and data flow of messages the Web Service can exchange. In cases where the choreography of the user and the choreography of the Web Service do not match process mediation is required. The Process Mediation component in WSMX is responsible for resolving mismatches between the Choreographies (often referred to as public processes) of the user and Web Service. Running to the case study in section 2, an example of the sort of mismatches that the Process Mediator is likely to encounter is where the user wants to login to an online banking system using a Web Service, in this case the user may want to send the username and password together in one message where as the Web Service expects two messages, the first containing the username and the second containing the password. In this case the Process Mediator needs to take the message sent by the user and break it up into two messages, which are then sent in the correct order to the Web Service. At this point it is now possible to interact with the Web Service and the users Goal of logging into the system can be achieved.

More information on discovery can be found in section 4.1, mediation is described in section 4.2, choreographies of Web Services are presented in section 4.3 and a selection of front-end tools for use with WSMO and WSMX are shown in section 4.4.

4.1   Discovery

As already mentioned, with current Web Service technology the process of finding a Web Service is a manual one. The user must search by hand through a Web Service repository, which usually provides free-text descriptions of what the service does. This is a time consuming process and can be seen as a barrier to quick and efficient integration between potential business partners. With WSMX it is possible to perform automated discovery of Web Services on a semantic description of the service. When the user provides WSMX with a Goal that semantically describes what they want to achieve, WSMX can perform two types of discovery to find matching services. These two types of discovery will both return an ordered list of Web Services, ordered by how well they match the users Goal and are described in the following paragraphs.

Keyword Based Discovery. The keyword based discovery process involves matching keywords present in the user's Goal with keywords present in the Web Services semantic description. While this particular approach does not have well defined semantics and could suffer from natural language ambiguity issues it is useful to filter a large amount of Web Services down to a smaller more manageable set on which more advanced techniques can be used. There are a number of places that keywords can be found in the Web Service description, in the value sections of non-functional properties, for example title, subject and description, in the identifiers of the concepts used in the Web Service description and in the logical expressions defining the capability of the Web Service.

Semantic Based Discovery. Semantic based discovery is a more formal mechanism for determining if a given Web Service can fulfill a users Goal. As described in section 3.2 a Web Service description is made up of a formal description of the capability of the Web Service and the interface of the Web Service. Performing discovery based on a Web Service involves matching the capability of the Web Service with the requested capability in the users Goal, by comparing the pre-conditions, post-conditions, assumptions and effects of both. When performing this discovery the relationship between the Goal and Web Service can be a number of different types:

- *Exact match*: where the Web Service can provide exactly what the Goal requires.
- *Subsumption match*: where the Web Service can provide part of what the Goal requires.
- *Plug-in match*: where the Web Service can provide what the Goal requires and provides other functionality also.
- *Intersection match*: where the Web Service can provide part of what the Goal requires and provides other functionality also.
- *Non-Match*: where the Web Service does not provide what the Goal requires.

Different levels of semantics can be provided in this matching, the richer the semantics the more time consuming the operation.

4.2 Data Mediation

One of the most important principles of WSMO and of the Web in general implies that resources are developed in isolation by various parties and than made available over the internet. In this context, the semantics meant to disambiguate and to describe data, Web Services or Goals is expressed in different terms. That is, different ontologies are developed to model the same domains of activity, this fact adding an additional level of complexity to all the operations related to Semantic Web Services.

Data mediation has the role of coping with the heterogeneity problems that may appear at the data level, for example between the requester and a provider of a Web Service. These problems appear when the application existing on one side uses a data format or representation unknown to the other party. In the context of WSMO and WSMX, we assume that both parties have described their data in terms of ontologies and the solution we propose tries to resolve the potential mismatches at the semantic level and to apply the findings from this level to the actual data that is exchanged. The ontology mismatches are solved during design-time by an *Ontology Mapping Tool* and the results are applied during run-time by a *Runtime Mediation Component*. We describe each of these modules in more detail in the next subsections.

Ontology Mapping Tool. At this step of the mediation process, the mismatches existing between the ontologies used to describe the exchanged data have to be identified and captured in what it is called an *alignment* between these ontologies. In WSMX, the alignment consists of set of *mappings* that logically express the semantic relation between terms from one ontology and terms from the other ontology. As in most of the cases, the initial designers of one or both ontologies fails to completely capture the semantic of the domain in their model, the tool cannot determine the alignment in completely automatic and accurate manner[4]. As a consequence, the WSMX Ontology Mapping Tool is a design-time, graphical tool that provides support for semi-automatic mappings creation. The human user (i.e. the domain expert) is guided through the whole mapping process and they are asked to validate the suggestions offered by the tool.

The main advantage of this semi-automatic approach is that the tool transforms the mapping process from a laborious and error-prone task in to simple choices and validation using a graphical user interface. In particular, the mappings are expressed as logical rules and their manual editing would require domain experts with strong background in logics. With this approach the complexity of the mappings and the burdensome of logics are hidden under the system's hood: the domain expert places his inputs only through the graphical interfaces, while the underlying system automatically generates the corresponding mapping rules.

In the banking domain, the Ontology Mapping Tool can be used to create mappings between two ontologies that both model the mortgage concept. By such mappings it is stated that there is a semantic relationship between the two definitions of the concept; the mappings also describe what this semantic relationship means.

Runtime Mediation Component. The mappings created by using the Ontology Mapping Tool are saved in a persistent storage and made available to the Runtime Mediation Component for use during run-time. At this

---

[4] There are tools that automatically generate an alignment between two given ontologies, but they cannot guarantee the correctness and the accuracy of these alignments. As WSMX is a business oriented framework we consider these requirements a must.

second stage, the mappings are used for a specific mediation scenario, i.e. *instance transformation*[5]. This scenario requires that incoming data described in terms of one given ontology (i.e. source ontology) has to be transformed in order to comply with the definitions from another given ontology (i.e. target ontology). In other words, the source data represented as source ontology instances has to be transformed and expressed as target ontology instances.

In order to perform these transformations, the mapping rules generated during design-time are evaluated in a reasoner and applied on the source instances. The result consists of a set of target ontology instances, modelling exactly the same information as the source instances but conforming to the specifications in the target ontology.

It is worth mentioning that the run-time mediation process is a completely automatic one, no human intervention being necessary as long as the required mappings are available.

4.3   Choreography

An important part of Web Services interface is the *choreography*[6]. The choreography of a Web Service describes the way one can interact with the service in order to consume its functionality. In other words, the choreography defines the requester expected behaviour during the Web Service invocation. The requestors can also define their own choreographies as part of the goal they want to be accomplished – that is, the requested choreography, the behaviour they are able to comply with when invoking a Web Service.

WSMO choreography is expressed in terms of Abstract State Machine also formerly known as Evolving Algebra. This mechanism is used to describe systems in a precise manner using semantically well founded mathematical notations.

There are two main components in WSMX used to manage and to maintain the interaction between a requester and a provider of a Web Service

---

[5] Another well known mediation scenario (not required in WSMX) is *instance transformation*. By using a mediator that supports this scenario is possible to retrieve data expressed in terms of various ontologies by posting queries in terms of only one particular ontology.

[6] The other part of a WSMO Web Service's interface, not discussed in here, is the *Orchestration*. It describes the way that the web service functionality can be achieved by composing several other web services. It is very related as form of representation with choreography and it is strongly influenced the choreographies of the orchestrated web services.

in terms of their choreographies: the *Choreography Engine* and the *Process Mediator*.

Choreography Engine. The Choreography Engine has the role of managing all the operations regarding the choreographies of the two parties involved in a conversation: This implies:
- Identifying and loading the two choreographies;
- Creating a copy for each of the choreographies (i.e. choreography instances). These copies are used further as long as the communication session is maintained.
- Updating the choreography instances in respect with the incoming messages.

These messages might be sent by the communication partner provoking an update in the receiver's choreography instance. A response message could be generated and it will create in its turn an update in the target choreography instance.

Process Mediator. Choreography describes the behaviour of the service from the provider point of view, implying that all the requesters of that particular service should comply with that particular choreography. That is, the choreography of a requester should be compatible (but not necessarily equivalent) with the choreography of the service provider in order to enable communication. As one of the WSMO principles states that all entities involved in communication are equal partners, we should assume that none of them is willing to adjust its own choreography to match the other partner's choreography.

As a consequence there is a need for a Process Mediator, a component able to solve the communication mismatches that can appear during the conversation. It takes as inputs each party's choreography and analyses each incoming message to check if it is expected by the receiver choreography. If it is, it means that the message can be forwarded to the receiver; if it is not expected, the message can be transformed (as dictated by Data Mediator for example) or postponed for later stages of the conversation. The Process Mediator interacts directly with the Choreography Engine, acting as a middle layer between the choreographies of the requester and the provider. Such a process mediator (as well as the Data Mediator) is one of the technologies that can be used in realizing the types of mediators described by WSMO (i.e. ggMediators, wgMediators and wwMediators).

If we consider for example the service that checks the eligibility of an inquiring client for a particular type of mortgage, its choreography can specify that it expects first a message containing the incoming per year and than a message containing the type of mortgage the client is interested in. Unfortunately, the client application is designed to send first the requested type of mortgage, to expect for a confirmation and only then to send annual income of the client. It is the role of the process mediator to inverse the order of messages and to generate a dummy acknowledgement to enable the interaction.

4.4   Front-end Tools

As with any emergent technology it is important that end-users can actually use the technology. Providing high quality front-end tools is a good way to get a technology adopted. To this end a number of software projects have emerged attempting to create tools for modeling and using WSMO and Semantic Web Services. From the case study in section 2, banks providing Semantic Web Services for obtaining mortgage quotes would use these tools to create ontologies that model the banking domain and use these ontologies to semantically describe the Web Services capabilities and interfaces, while users would use these tools to describe their requirements in the form of a Goal. Each of these tools is available for download; links are available in section 9.

Web Services Modeling Toolkit (WSMT)

The Web Services Modeling Toolkit (WSMT) is a framework for the rapid creation and deployment of homogeneous tools for Semantic Web Services. A homogeneous toolkit improves the users experience while using the toolkit, as the tools have a common look and feel. Usability is also improved as the user does not need to relearn how to use the application when switching between tools. The WSMT was designed to be the front-end of the WSMX system and provides a number of tools to users:

WSML Editor. The WSML Editor is used to create and manage WSML documents. It can be used to edit WSMO Ontologies, Mediators, Web Services and Goals. The first versions of the WSML Editor focused on the creation of semantic descriptions in WSMO and reading and writing these semantic descriptions to and from the local machine using the WSML syntax. Subsequent versions have looked at mechanisms for visualizing ontologies using directed graphs. These ontology visualizations make it easier for the domain expert to understand the relationships between entities in the WSML document.

WSMX Data Mediation Mapping Tool. As described in section 4.2, data mediation in WSMX is a semi automatic process. Mappings are required where mediation between two ontologies is required. The WSMX Data Mediation Mapping Tool is used to create these mappings between two ontologies. These mappings can then be used by WSMX to transform instances of the source ontology into instances of the target ontology, thus resolving data mismatches between partners that use different ontologies to describe their web services.

WSMX Invoker. The WSMT contains a web service invocation component that can be used to send messages to and receive messages from web services. Messages can be received from the web services both synchronously (immediately following a sent message) and asynchronously (where the service calls the user back later with a response). The WSMX Invoker tool makes these components within the WSMT available to the end-user. The tool allows to user to send messages to a given service within the WSMX architecture, view the messages sent to services in the past and view responses received from these services.

Distributed Ontology Management Environment (DOME)

The DOME project aims to produce a suite of tools for the efficient and effective management of ontologies. DOME is implemented as a collection of Eclipse plug-ins that allows users to edit and manage WSMO Ontologies. These plugins include:

Editing and Browsing. The Editing and Browsing tool provides a tree structure for representing the concept and relation hierarchies within an ontology. Users can add new concepts and relations into these hierarchies as well as adding attributes and parameters to those already present. The tool also provides a real-time mechanism for switching between the graphical tree structure and the underlying file format. This allows users to make changes in one and see those changes reflected in the other.

Versioning and Evolution. The Versioning and Evolution tool allows users to mark the versions of a given ontologies. This is necessary as when an ontology reaches a stable position and individuals start using it, it becomes necessary to track which versions of a given ontology are being used by different individuals. Versions of a given ontology are tracked using the URI that identifies them; this URI is incrementally changed as the version of the ontology changes. This allows multiple versions of the same ontology to exist within the same knowledge base.

Mapping & Merging. The Mapping & Merging tool deals with cases where there are two ontologies that have an overlap in the domain that they describe. This tool is used to create mappings between these two ontologies so that execution environments, for example WSMX, can perform instance transformation, query rewriting and ontology merging. The mappings are created by opening two copies of the Editing and Browsing Tool and dragging items from one ontology to the other.

WSMO Studio

The aim of WSMO Studio is to create a collection of tools to assist potential users with ontology creation, service description, service discovery and service composition. These tools are implemented as a collection of plug-ins for the Eclipse framework. These tools include a WSMO Navigator for showing the entities in the WSMO description along with individual form-based editors for each of the WSMO entities. A syntax highlighting text editor is also available for editing the underlying WSML format for more advanced user. WSMO Studio also provides interfaces for interacting with WSMO repositories for storing and retrieving WSMO descriptions.

5.   RELATED WORK – RELATIONSHIPS WITH COMPETITIVE APPROCHES

In addition to WSMO there are two major research initiatives in Semantic Web Services. The first and largest of these is OWL-S (Martin), a joint effort by BBN Technologies, Carnegie Mellon University, Nokia, Stanford University, SRI International and Yale University. OWL-S is an ontology for semantic markup of Web Services based on the Web Ontology Language (OWL) (Dean and Schreiber, 2004). The second effort is WSDL-S (Web Service Semantics) from the LSDIS Laboratory at the University of Georgia in co-operation with IBM. The next subsections describe these approaches in more detail using a small set of criteria, followed by a matrix that summarizes the comparison.

5.1   OWL-S

OWL-S is an OWL ontology for describing Web Services by annotating them with semantic information described in OWL (a W3C Recommendation, http://www.w3.org/TR/owl-semantics/). The top-most concept is Service and this in turn consists of three sub-concepts – ServiceProfile, ServiceModel and ServiceGrounding.

The ServiceProfile describes what the service does at a high level and provides the means by which the service can be advertised. It also provides the means by which a service requester can advertise a service that is required. Within the ServiceProfile, the capability description allows for the definition of preconditions, inputs, outputs and effects. There are also slots available in the ServiceProfile description for security parameters, quality rating and for descriptions based on standard business taxonomies.

The ServiceModel describes how a service works and, as a result, how to interact with the service. This part of the OWL-S description is responsible for specifying the service interaction protocol in terms of the messages that should be exchanged with the service and the control flow of that exchange.

The ServiceGrounding is where the abstract description of the service process model is grounded to operations in a WSDL document. Through the ServiceGrounding the actual communication protocols, transport mechanism and the communication languages used by the service are specified. The grounding provides the bridge that links the implementation of a Web Service with its semantic description

Both WSMO and OWL-S address the same problem space. After identifying fundamental drawbacks with the OWL-S approach, the WSMO working group was formed to devise a more complete conceptual model for describing Web Services. Conceptually, unlike WSMO, OWL-S does not explicitly model separate concepts for Goals and Web Services. Additionally OWL-S does not explicitly model mediators; rather they are as considered specific types of services. A detailed discussion of this rationale is provided in (Lara et al., 2004).

5.2   WSDL-S

WSDL-S is a lightweight approach for adding semantics to Web Services. It allows semantic representation of inputs, outputs, preconditions and effects of Web Service operations, by adding extensions to WSDL. WSDL-S allows semantic annotations using domain models, which are agnostic to the ontology used to describe the Web Services or its representation language. It means that ontologies can be used in the annotation process and be directly included in the WSDL documents. The annotations of the inputs and outputs in WSDL will be represented as concepts in an ontology. Additionally, the preconditions and effects associated with WSDL operations will be defined by the preconditions and effects of a specific Semantic Web Service description.

5.3   Matrix of Features and Approaches

The comparison is based on the following features:
- Viewpoint – provider vs. requester
- Mediation – handling heterogeneity between data and process models
- Non-functional properties – additional information about aspects that may affect service usage
- Grounding – how service descriptions relate to Web Service standards
- Availability of execution environments – how do SWS get used

Table 3-1. Comparison of WSMO, OWL-S and WSDL-S

Approach	Supported Viewpoints	Mediation	Non-funct. props.	Grounding	Execution Environment
OWL-S	Single modeling element for both views	Does not treat heterogeneity as a modeling issue.	Restricted to the Service Profile	Grounding of behaviour to WSDL and data to XML	Described but details of impl. are unavailable.
WSDL-S	Service provider view – same as with WSDL	Adopts the behaviour of the ontology used to describe annotations	Agnostic	WSDL-S is a legal extension to WSDL and, as such is directly grounded	Any WSDL compliant execution engine could be extended for WSDL-S
WSMO		Supports mediation of data and processes	Available to all WSMO elements	Grounding of behaviour to WSDL and data to XML	Open source provided by WSMX

6.   CONCLUSIONS AND DISCUSSION

Web Services have become another milestone towards providing interoperability among distributed and independent software systems. But one major problem has remained unresolved. Although there is abundance of technologies which theoretically should enable interoperability for disperse systems, from the practical perspective the process of dynamic creation of ad-hoc interactions between companies, as envision by Web Services, is still a fiction. So it is the interoperability issue, not the communication, which has to be addressed next to enable dynamic collaboration of independent software entities on the Internet. Web Services specifications based on commonly agreed standards and implemented in .NET and J2EE frameworks, are struggling to overcome existing limitations of Web architecture. Data that is exchanged between Web servers and Web browsers remains solely dedicated for human consumption, and cannot be readily processed by automatic software agents. Similarly Web Services and their underlying XML technology still deal mainly with infrastructure, syntax and basic representational issues, but not with the meaning of data and processes that are used by particular systems. Adding semantics to the existing Web Services technologies is a fundamental requirement if we want to deliver workable integration solutions for the next Web generation.

Commercial successes of Semantic Web Services are not yet apparent because the underlying technologies such as presented in this chapter are still in their infancy. Available specifications and technologies will have to go through the lengthy standardization process and real effort of consequent prototype developments, before first commercial solutions are available to the market. There is widespread agreement and recognition that dynamic interoperability on the Internet is only possible if resources are semantically described. WSMO and its related specifications and technologies are principal candidates to become the backbone on the next Web generation, enabling software entities to dynamically interoperate over the Internet.

7. ACKNOWLEDGEMENT

This work is supported by the SFI (Science Foundation Ireland) under the DERI-Lion project and by the European Commission under the projects DIP, Knowledge Web and ASG. The authors thank all members of the WSMO (cf. http://www.wsmo.org/) and WSMX (cf. http://www.wsmx.org/) working groups for fruitful discussions on this chapter.

8. QUESTIONS FOR DISCUSSION

Beginners:
1. Discuss different techniques used by automatic agents to retrieve data from existing computer systems.
2. Why screen scraping cannot scale?
3. Install WSMT and WSMX on your machine. Create ontologies, Web Services, Goal and Mediators. Register them with WSMX.

Intermediate:

1. Explain why existing Web Services specifications are not suitable to enable automated collaboration between distributed software systems.
2. Discuss each of four building blocks of WSMO. Which of them is the most important?

Advanced:

1. Thinking about some real use case scenario (different than presented in this chapter), please explain which elements of automation are the more important from the others. Why?
2. Imagine an interaction scenario similar with the one exemplified in Section 4.3 on Choreography. In which case you would require the usage of both the data and process mediators?
3. Discuss which of the mediation techniques described in this chapter (i.e. data mediation and process mediation) can be used in creating the four types of WSMO mediators? Hint: An ooMediator relay on data mediation for solving the heterogeneity problems between two ontologies.

9.   SUGGESTED ADDITIONAL READING

Some key papers that provide more information on WSMO, WSML and WSMX are:

- D.Roman, U. Keller, H. Lausen, J. de Bruijn, R. Lara, M. Stollberg, A. Polleres, C. Feier, C. Bussler and D. Fensel: Web Service Modeling Ontology. Applied Ontology. Vol. 1, No. 1, 2005.
- H. Lausen, J. de Bruijn, A. Polleres, and D. Fensel: WSML - a Language Framework for Semantic Web Services. W3C Rules Workshop. In Proceedings of the W3C Workshop on Rule Languages for Interoperability, Washington DC, USA, April 2005. Position Paper: http://www.w3.org/2004/12/rules-ws/paper/44.
- M. Moran, M. Zaremba, A. Mocan and C. Bussler: Using WSMX to bind Requester & Provider at Runtime when Executing Semantic Web Services, In Proceedings of the 1st WSMO Implementation Workshop (WIW2004). Frankfurt, Germany, 2004.

For more information consider reading the following books:

- D. Fensel, Ontologies: A Silver Bullet for Knowledge Management and Electronic Commerce.
- H. Alesso and C. Smith, Developing Semantic Web Services.
- G. Antoniou and F. van Harmelen, A Semantic Web Primer.

10. ONLINE RESOURCES (INCLUDING OPEN SOURCE TOOLS)

Tool	URL
WSMX Execution Environment (WSMX)	http://www.wsmx.org
Web Services Modeling Toolkit (WSMT)	http://www.wsmx.org
Distributed Ontology Management Environment (DOME)	http://dome.sourceforge.net
WSMO Studio	http://www.wsmostudio.org

11. REFERENCES

Dean M. and Schreiber G. (eds.): OWL Web Ontology Language Reference. 2004. W3C Recommendation 10 February 2004

Gruber T. R., "A translation approach to portable ontology specifications, Knowledge," Knowledge Acquisition, vol. 5, pp. 199-220, 1993

Lara, R., Roman, D., Polleres, A. and Fensel, D., "A Conceptual Comparison of WSMO and OWL-S", Proceedings of The European Conference on Web Services, Erfurt, Germany, Sept 27-30, 2004, pp 254-269.

Martin D. (editor): OWL-S: Semantic Markup for Web Services, version 1.1 available at http://www.daml.org/services/owl-s/1.1/overview/

Milanovic N., Malek M., Current Solutions for Web Service Composition, IEEE Internet Computing, vol. 08, no. 6, pp. 51-59, November/December, 2004.

Tidwell D., "Web Services: the Web's next revolution", http://www-128.ibm.com/developerworks/edu/ws-dw-wsbasics-i.html

Web Service Semantics -- WSDL-S," A joint UGA-IBM Technical Note, version 1.0, April 18, 2005. http://lsdis.cs.uga.edu/library/download/WSDL-S-V1.pdf

Wiederhold G., Mediators in the architecture of future information systems, IEEE Computer, 25(3):38–49, March 1992

Chapter 4

KEYWORDS, PORT TYPES AND SEMANTICS: A JOURNEY IN THE LAND OF WEB SERVICE DISCOVERY

Karthik Gomadam, Kunal Verma, Amit Sheth and Ke Li.
Large Scale Distributed Information Systems (LSDIS) Lab, Department of Computer Science, University of Georgia, GA, USA. – {karthik,verma,amit}@cs.uga.edu

1.   INTRODUCTION

The evolution of Service Oriented Technology in the recent years has made SOA and Web Services the candidate technologies to realize application integration. Web Services are a set of protocols based on XML. The basic protocols are
1. SOAP: The Simple Object Access Protocol is the messaging protocol for request and response. SOAP is independent of platforms and network transport protocols.
2. WSDL: Web Services Description Language describes in a programmatic manner, the services capabilities and the end point to invoke a service.
3. UDDI: Universal Discovery, Description, Integration is a cross industry initiative to facilitate Web Service publication and discovery.

Figure 4-1 describes a basic architecture to realize Web Services using the above mentioned simple protocols.

In addition to the above mentioned basic protocols additional protocols have been specified to capture issues related to policies (WS-Policy and WS-Agreement), security (WS-Security), message reliability (WS-Reliable Messaging), transactions (WS-Transaction), etc.

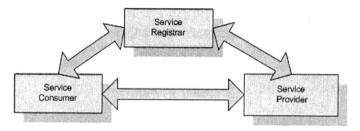

Figure 4-1. The basic Web Service Protocols in action

The growth in SOA has in turn also fueled a growth in the area of Web Processes, with WS-BPEL emerging as a de-facto specification to specify Web processes. Figure 4-2 is an illustration of the list of other protocols in the WS stack. A more comprehensive list can be found at (Wilkes. L).

Business Domain Specific extensions	Various	Business Domain
Distributed Management	WSDM, WS-Managebility	Management
Provisioning	WS-Provisioning	
Security	WS-Security	Security
Security Policy	WS-Security Policy	
Transaction	WS-Transaction, WS- Coordination	Transactions and business processes
Orchestration	WS-BPEL	
Routing/Addressing	WS-Addressing	Messaging
Message Packaging	SOAP	
Publication and Discovery	UDDI	Metadata
Service description	WSDL	

Figure 4-2. Partial view of current WS Stack

In this chapter we introduce the UDDI registry framework for Web Service discovery and publication. The UDDI data types and the different sections of the UDDI are introduced first. This is followed by a section introducing the UDDI4J API and using the API to discover and publish Web

Services. In this context the UDDI best practices for Web Service publication is also discussed.

The inadequacies of syntactic service publication and discovery are presented in the next section and the reader is introduced to the ideas of publishing and discovery of semantic Web Services. Web Service publication and discovery in the METEOR-S and WSMO frameworks is presented. Later in the chapter Registry federation is discussed in brief. This followed by a short discussion on UDDI version, suggested reading and questions for discussion.

2.   UDDI

UDDI (UDDI) stands for Universal Discovery, Description, and Integration. UDDI is a specification for creating a distributed Web based registry for Web Services. UDDI can be compared to that of a local phone book. In the same way a phone book has information about businesses and what they offer and how to reach them, the UDDI registry stores information about businesses, the services they offer and the technical information about those services. The End Point Reference (EPR) of a service can be thought of the phone number of a business in the phone book. UDDI provides three basic operations.

1. Publish : How service providers publish in the registry
2. Find : How service requestors find the service they want
3. Bind: How service requestors can connect to the service they want.

The rest of the section describes the how different kinds of registry data which UDDI supports, the data structures in UDDI, how WSDL maps onto UDDI, followed by publication and discovery (find) in UDDI.

2.1   UDDI Organization: White, Yellow and Green Pages

UDDI is organized into White, Yellow and Green pages.

a. White Pages:
    White pages contain information about businesses by organizing them by business names. The contain information on a business including the name and the contact details. In addition to these information, a publisher can also add other information like DUNS Identifier to uniquely identify himself.

In UDDI *BusinessEntity* is used to publish the white page information. *BusinessEntity* will be discussed with other UDDI data models.

b. Yellow Pages:
    Yellow pages contain categorized information about businesses. One or more taxonomies are assigned to businesses and users can search on the taxonomy categories to get all businesses that offer services in those categories. *BusinessEntity* is also used to publish the yellow pages information in UDDI.

c. Green Pages
    The technical information about services is stored in Green pages. All information that are needed to use a particular service can be found in the Green pages. Green page information can be used via the *BusinessEntity* and *BindingTemplate* data models of UDDI.

The next section introduces the different UDDI data models.

2.2   UDDI Data Models

Having looked at the different ways UDDI organizes its content, in this section we will look at how the various data models in UDDI are used in publication and discovery of Web services. UDDI has four different data structures to specify entry in the registry. The UDDI data structures are represented as XML documents. Figure 4-3 captures the relationships between the five data structures.

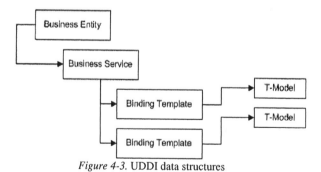

Figure 4-3. UDDI data structures

1. <businessEntity>
The *BusinessEntity* structure contains information about the business and all the services that it offers. It has all relevant publisher information like name, contact, relationships with other businesses and description of the business.

2. <businessService>
A categorized set of services offered by a business is represented using the *businessService* data structure. A *businessService* structure can be a part of one or more *businessElement* structures and in the same way a *businessElement* can have one or more *businessService* structures.

3. <bindingTemplate>
After a service is discovered, the binding information about the service is required to invoke the service. This information is captured using the *bindingTemplate* data structure. Each *bindingTemplate* belongs to one *businessService* element.

4. <tModel>
A *tModel* describes the specification, behavior, concept or a design to which the service complies. Specific information about interacting with a service is captured here. Each *tModel* element has a key, name and a URL from which more information can be found out about this service.

In addition to these four basic data structures, UDDI also has identifiers and categories for categorization of the published information. The two xml elements are specified in the UDDI, viz. <identifierBag> and <categoryBag>. Identifiers are key value pairs, which can be used to tag an entry in the registry with additional information like DUNS ID.

UDDI also has a <publisherAssertion> to capture relationship between various *businessEntities*. *publisherAssertion* contains a key for each of the two businesses whose relationship is being captured, a keyed reference which points to the asserted relationship in terms of a name-value pair within a *tModel*.

2.3   How Does WSDL Map to UDDI?

This section briefly outlines how WSDL maps onto UDDI. As shown in Figure 4-4, the WSDL types, messages, portType and binding information are bound to the tModel in UDDI. The EPR's in WSDL are published in bindingTemplate. The Service element in WSDL is published in Business Service.

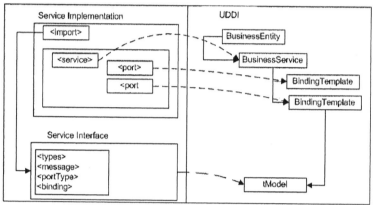

Figure 4-4. Mapping WSDL elements onto UDDI

2.4   Publishing in UDDI

In this section we will look at publishing services in UDDI.

2.4.1   Registry and API infrastructure:

For publication, it is best recommended to set up an UDDI registry. One can download an open source registry like jUDDI for this purpose. Once you have your registry up and running, it advised to make sure the permissions for publication. The relevance of it will become clear as we go on the road to publication in UDDI. Services can be published in the UDDI using the UDDI4J API. UDDI4J is an open source API for publishing and discovering services using an UDDI registry. UDDI4J can be downloaded from (UDDI4J).

2.4.2   Publishing using UDDI4J:

Figure 4-5 outlines publishing a service using UDDI4J. The steps give a brief outline of publishing a service in UDDI. However to get the exact methods of various data structures, the reader is advised to consult UDDI4J documentation before publishing.

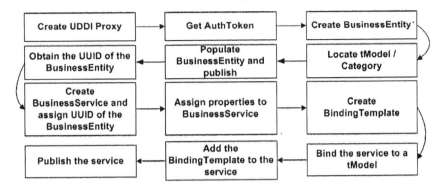

Figure 4-5. Publishing using UDDI4J

3.   UDDI BEST PRACTICES

In this section we will describe in brief the UDDI Best Practices (Curbera. F et al 2002). Although UDDI is not intended to be used only with WSDL, given the popularity of WSDL amongst service developers and publishers, OASIS has published a best practices docuement for usage of WSDL with UDDI. tModels and businessService data structures discussed in Section 2.2 are most relevant in the UDDI from the perspective of WSDL.

Every WSDL captures the service interface and service implementation. The key to realize useful synthesis between UDDI and WSDL is to separate the interface and the implementation. WSDL elements such as message formats, types, portTypes and bindings form the interface, whilst the service element that includes the EPR, is the implementation. Such a separation allows for publishing the various interfaces as tModels in UDDI. These tModels are referred to as "wsdlSpec tModels". The actual WSDL is referred to using the overviewDoc field in the tModel.

The main advantage is this practice allows standardization of interfaces. Service developers can search for suitable interfaces and create the implementations. Such implementations can then be deployed in the UDDI.

The impact of such a practice can best seen during discovery. Service Discovery can be done using:

1. Keywords based on Operation names. In operation name based discovery services are discovered based on operation names. The search is keyword drive.

2. Port Types based on published interfaces. In port type or interface driven discovery, services are discovered based on the wsdlSpec tModels that they implement.

The best practice document allows for services to be searched based on port types which are described using service interfaces. This makes searching for services more efficient than just searching using operation names. Operation names can in often cases mean nothing about what the operation does. For example a service might contain an operation named RequestPurchaseOrder, while that operation in reality might be adding two integers. However, if a service implements the wsdlSpec tModel for RequestPurchaseOrder, then there is more guarantee of discovering a service that meets the user requirements. In the next section we will discuss, why even portType or interface driven discovery is not sufficient enough.

4.   NEED FOR SEMANTICS IN WS-DISCOVERY

Although portType based discovery offers to standardize service interfaces to facilitate better discovery of services, it is insufficient because
1. It is very difficult to standardize all service interfaces
2. Standardization alone cannot guarantee interoperability at all times. Eg. A service might implement the RequestPurchaseOrder interface, but might still have different units for representing weight, money etc.
3. It is hard for machines to understand what an interface or an operation does, unless the semantics is sufficiently captured. This would make run time binding of services to processes almost impossible.
4. In the event of a data type mismatch, it would be very difficult to mediate between services to realize service execution.

Taking these limitations into consideration, we define four types of semantics for Web Services (A. Sheth, 2003). The semantics are defined based on the life cycle of Web Processes. Figure 4-6 illustrates the usage the different types of semantics during the various stages of Web process life cycle.

We now present the four types of semantics in detail with examples. The examples are created using WSDL-S. The reader is recommended to look into OWL-S and WSMO frameworks to understand in depth how they capture the semantics for Web services. WSDL 1.1 syntax is throughout to maintain consistency.

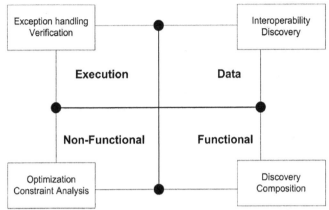

Figure 4-6. Semantics during the various stages of Web process life cycle

4.1 Data Semantics

Data semantics is the formal definition of data in input and output messages of a Web service. Data semantics is created to realize service discovery and interoperability. Data semantics can be added by annotating input/output data of Web services using ontologies. In WSDL-S Data Semantics can be added by using *modelReference* extensibility element on messages and types. Figure 4-7 illustrates Data Semantics in WSDL-S.

```
<wsdl:message name= "PurchaseOrderRequestMessage">
  <wsdl:part name="PORequest" type="tns:PORequest"
  wssem:modelReference="POOntology#PurchaseOrderRequest"/>
</wsdl:message"
```

Figure 4-7. Capturing Data semantics using WSDL-S

In the above figure, we capture the Data semantics by adding the ontology type PurchaseOrderRequest to the WSDL message PurchaseOrderRequestMessage. In the same way we add the ontology type PurchaseOrderConfirmation to the WSDL message PurchaseOrderResponse. The ontology used in the examples can be found at (RosettaOntolgy).

4.2   Functional Semantics

Functional semantics is used to formally capturing the capabilities of
Web service. This is used in discovery and composition of Web Services.
Functional semantics can be realized by annotating operations of Web
Services as well as provide preconditions and effects. In WSDL-S,
functional semantics can be captured by adding *ModelReference, Category,
Pre-Conditions and Effects*. Figure 4-8 illustrates an example of capturing
functional semantics using WSDL-S.

```
<operation name="GetOneQuote"
wssem:modelReference="Ontology1#FinancialTransaction">
<wssem:category categoryName="Stock quotation services"
taxonomyURI="http://www.census.gov/epcd/naics02/"
taxonomyCode="523999"/>

<input message="s0:GetOneQuoteSoapIn"/>
<wssem:precondition name="stockSymbol"
wssem:modelReference="Ontology0#stockSymbol"/>

<output message="s0:GetOneQuoteSoapOut"/>
<wssem:effect name="price"
wssem:modelReference="Ontology1#price"/>

</operation>
```

Figure 4-8. Capturing Functional Semantics for WSDL-S

The above example illustrates capturing the functional semantics of a
Web service using *modelReference* to the Ontology type Financial
Transaction. The *Category* is captured using NAICS classification. The
Preconditions and effects are captured using *modelReference* to ontology
types stockSymbol and price. The ontology used in the examples can be
found at (SUMO).

4.3 Non-Functional Semantics

Non-Functional semantics capture the QoS requirements/ constraints
(such as delivery time) and also policy requirements/ constraints (such as
reliable messaging). The QoS requirements could be both quantitative
constraints and non-quantitative constraints.

Feature	Scope	Goal	Value	Unit	Aggregation
Cost (Quantitative)	Process	Optimize		Dollars	Summation
Supply time (Quantitative)	Process	Satisfy	<7	Days	Maximum
Cost (Quantitative)	Process	Satisfy	<46000	Dollars	Summation
Preferred Logical Supplier (Logical)	Partner	Satisfy	True		
Compatible Suppliers (P1 and P2)	Process	Satisfy	True		

Figure 4-9. Capturing Non-Functional semantics

In Figure 4-9 we present an example of capturing QoS constraints using ILP and SWRL. The above example illustrates the constraints for a workflow that is being used to purchase various products. Quantitative constraints such as total cost must be less that USD 50,000 is represented as ILP constraints. Non-Quantitative constraints such as the partners must be preferred suppliers is captured using SWRL. QoS based process modeling is discussed in detail in (Cardoso. J 2002).

4.4 Execution Semantics

Execution semantics formally capture the execution or flow of services in a process or operations within a service. Execution semantics play a role in verification and exception handling. In the next section we will discuss using data and functional semantics in Web service publication and discovery.

5. PUBLISHING AND DISCOVERING SEMANTIC WEB SERVICES

Unlike publication using UDDI, publishing Semantic Web Services is still an area of active research. Various research groups like OWL-S, WSMO and METEOR-S have created frameworks for publishing and discovering semantic Web Services. We will present the METEOR-S Web Service Discovery and Publication framework (MWSDP).

MWSDP is based on WSDL-S (Akkiraju. R et al 2005). The data and functional semantics captured in WSDL-S services are used to publish the service in the UDDI registry. Semantic templates (discussed later in the section), created using WSDL-S, allow for template based discovery in MWSDP. The data and functional semantics of a Web service can be seen mapping to a tModel in UDDI. We will now in discuss the MWSDP interface for publishing and discovering WSDL-S services.

5.1   METEOR-S Framework

We will now discuss publishing WSDL-S services using METEOR-S publication framework. We will follow this with a discussion on template based service discovery.

5.1.1   Publishing WSDL-S Services

In order to create WSDL-S services, use the METEOR-S Radiant plugin (Gomadam. K et al 2005-A) or the WSDLS4J API. WSDLS4J API allows programmatic addition semantic annotations to WSDL. METEOR-S Radiant is an eclipse plug-in to annotate WSDL. METEOR-S Radiant plug-in also has discovery extensions that will publish WSDL-S files into registry. Alternatively, the METEOR-S Discovery and Publication Interface allows for publishing from within applications. The publication interface has wrappers which given the WSDL-S files, and registry category semantically publish the service into the registry.

5.1.2   Template based Discovery

In this section we describe a semantic template and propose a discovery mechanism based on semantic templates. Figure 4-10 conceptually illustrates a semantic template.

```
Semantic Template
IndustryCategory = NAICS:Electronics
ProductCategory = DUNS:RAM
Location = Athens, GA
Operation1 = Rosetta#requestPurchaseOrder
    Input = Rosetta#PurchaseOrderDetails
    Output = Rosetta#PurchaseConfirmation
    Non-Functional Requirements
        Encryption = RSA
        ResponseTime < 5 sec
Operation = Rosetta#QueryOrderStatus

 Input = Rosetta#  PurchaseOrderStatusQuery

 Output = Rosetta#  PurchaseOrderStatusResponse
```

Figure 4-10. Semantic Template illustration

A semantic template captures the requirements of service requestor using data, functional and non-functional semantics. In the example illustrated above in Fig 4-10, the data requirements are captured using Ontology types: *Rosetta#PurchaseOrderDetails* and Rosetta#PurchaseConfirmation. The functional requirement is captured using ontology type: *Rosetta#requestPurchaseOrder.* The non-functional quantitative requirement is captured as *ResponseTime < 5 sec.* The non-functional non-quantitative requirement is captured using *Encryption = RSA*.

6. REGISTRY FEDERATION

The increasing popularity of Web Services means that sooner or later more and more services are going to be published into registries. Thus the performance of the UDDI is essential to efficient service publication and discovery. An brief study of UDDI performance is presented in (Georgina Saez Et.Al 2004). Further, with the growth in semantic Web Services, there is also a need for some categorization at registry level. In this section we will take a brief look at registry federation using METEOR-S Web Service Discovery Infrastructure (MWSDI) (Verma. K, K. Sivashanmugam et al 2005).

MWSDI is a peer to peer registry framework. MWSDI addresses two fundamental issues related to service discovery: 1. locating the correct registry and 2. finding the correct service within the registry. The peer to peer framework of registries allows for creating a scalable distribution of registries and adding semantics at the registry level enables registries to be categorized based on various domains. This approach helps in discovering the most appropriate registry for a specific discovery request.

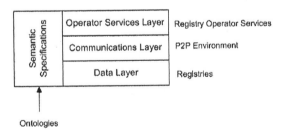

Figure 4-11. Layered Architecture of MWSDI (MWSDI)

The above Figure illustrates the layered architecture of the MWSDI framework. The data layer is composed of the registries. The P2P messaging is handled at the communications layer and the semantic discovery and publishing are handled at the Operation services layer.

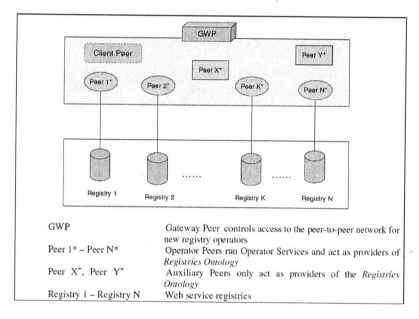

Figure 4-12. Peer and Registry architecture in MWSDI (MWSDI)

The semantic specifications such as registry ontologies and registry-registry relationships are given by the semantic specifications component across the three layers. The main advantage is that the architecture allows for registries to process non-semantic service discoveries as well as act in a standalone manner away from the P2P network.

The P2P framework of the peers in the registry collection is illustrated in Figure 4-12. The Gateway peer is not associated with any registry and is the entry point for new registries joining the registry collection. It is also responsible for propagating changes such as changes to the registries ontology to all peers. Operator peers controls a reigistry, provides the operator services to that registry and also acts as a provider of the registries ontology.

The auxiliary peers are simply providers of the registry ontology. The framework proposes two protocols:

1. Operator peer initiation protocol: This defines the process involved in adding new registries to the framework.

2. Client Peer interaction protocol: This defines the protocol for client communications in accessing the operator services.

In this section we have provided a brief overview of research towards scalability and performance of registries. In the recommended reading section we suggest research papers that will allow readers to get a more comprehensive picture about this area of research.

7.   CONCLUSIONS

Registries play a very important role in the Web Services stack. This chapter discusses the basics of UDDI which is the widely used and recommended registry architecture. We have covered the various data models of UDDI, their usage as well as using the UDDI4J API. The discussion also covered the role of semantics in service discovery, the different types of semantics for entire Web process lifecycle and using semantic Web Services in UDDI.

Keywords, portTypes and template based discovery approaches have been discussed and compared. We also provide a brief insight into some of the state-of-the-art research in the area of Web Services publication and discovery.

We would like readers to look at the recommended reading section to find more material for comprehensive understanding of Web Service discovery and publication.

Further readers are recommended to try and use the UDDI4J API along with open source implementations of UDDI (like jUDDI), to better understand the usage.

8.   QUESTIONS FOR DISCUSSION

Beginner:
1. What role does semantics play in enhancing service discovery and publication?
2. What are the main data structures of UDDI and how do they map to WSDL?

Intermediate:
1. "UDDI can be used for publishing any service. Not just Web Services". Is the validity of the above statement true?
2. From the perspective of database design discuss the efficiency of the UDDI schema.

Advanced:
1. "Relationships are the heart of Semantic Web". Discuss the importance of exploiting interesting relationships in a P2P registry environment.
2. How does having little semantics at registries help realize SOA go a long way?

Practical Questions:
1. Discover and publish registries using UDDI4J and an open source UDDI implementation (like jUDDI).
2. Create wrappers over UDDI4J to publish and discover any service.

9. SUGGESTED ADDITIONAL READING

- Abhijit Patil, Swapna Oundhakar, Amit Sheth, Kunal Verma, METEOR-S Web service Annotation Framework, The Proceedings of the Thirteenth International World Wide Web Conference, May, 2004 (WWW2004), pp. 553-562
- Liangzhao Zeng, Boualem Benatallah, Marlon Dumas, Jayant Kalagnanam, Quan Z. Sheng: Quality driven web services composition, Proceedings of WWW 2003, PP 411-421
- Rohit Aggarwal, Kunal Verma, John A. Miller and William Milnor, "Constraint Driven Web Service Composition in METEOR-S," Proceedings of the 2004 IEEE International Conference on Services Computing (SCC 2004), Shanghai, China, September 2004 , pp. 23-30
- UDDI V3 from http://uddi.org/pubs/uddi_v3.htm
- WSMX, http://www.wsmx.org/

10. REFERENCES

Sheth.A et al (2003), Semantic Web Process Lifecycle: Role of Semantics in Annotation, Discovery, Composition and Orchestration , invited talk at WWW 2003 Workshop on E-Services and the Semantic Web , Budapest, Hungary, May 20, 2003

Cardoso. J (2002). Quality of Service and Semantic Composition of Workflows . Ph.D. Dissertation. Department of Computer Science, University of Georgia, Athens, GA.

Curbera. F et al (2002), Using WSDL in a UDDI Registry, Version 1.07, UDDI Best Practice, http://www.uddi.org/pubs/wsdlbestpractices-V1.07-Open-20020521.pdf

Gomadam. K, K. Verma et al (2005-A), Radiant: A tool for semantic annotation of Web Services, International Semantic Web Conference (ISWC) 2005, Galway.

Gomadam. K, K. Verma et al (2005-B), Demonstrating Dynamic Configuration and Execution of Web Processes, International Conference on Service Computing (ICSOC), 2005, pp: 502 - 507

Verma. K, K. Sivashanmugam et al (2005), METEOR-S WSDI: A Scalable Infrastructure of Registries for Semantic Publication and Discovery of Web Services, Journal of Information Technology and Management, Special Issue on Universal Global Integration, Vol. 6, No. 1 (2005) pp. 17-39. Kluwer Academic Publishers.

Verma. K, K Gomadam et al (2005)"The METEOR-S Approach for Configuring and Executing Dynamic Web Processes", LSDIS Lab Technical Report

Wilkes. L, http://roadmap.cbdiforum.com/reports/protocols/

Akkiraju. R, J. Farrell, et al, (2005) "Web Service Semantics - WSDL-S,Position Paper for the W3C Workshop on Frameworks for Semantics in Web Services, Innsbruck, Austria, June 2005.

RossettaNet, http://www.rosettanet.org/RosettaNet/

RosettaOntolgy,http://lsdis.cs.uga.edu/projects/meteor-s/wsdl-s/ontologies/rosetta.owl

Saez. G, A.L. Sliva Et.Al (2004), Web Services-Based Data Management: Evaluating the Performance of UDDI Registries, Proceedings of the International Conference on Web Services (ICWS), 2004, pp 830-831.

SUMO, http://lsdis.cs.uga.edu/projects/meteor-s/wsdl-s/ontologies/SUMO-Finance.owl

UDDI4J, http://uddi4j.sourceforge.net/

UDDI: http://uddi.org

Chapter 5

TEMPORAL REASONING OF REACTIVE WEB SERVICES

Monika Solanki, Antonio Cau and Hussein Zedan.
Software Technology Research Laboratory, De Montfort University, Leicester, LE4 0GL, UK–
monika@dmu.ac.uk, acau@dmu.ac.uk, zedan@dmu.ac.uk

1. WEB SERVICES AS REACTIVE SYSTEMS

Computing systems can be conceptually partitioned into two primitive categories: **Transformational** and **Reactive**. Transformational systems, as shown in Figure 5-1 are generally modelled by abstracting away the computations and specifying the system as an input-output function. The non-termination of a transformational system is usually considered a failure. Compilers, assemblers and routines in a library of mathematical functions are examples of transformational systems. The objective of Reactive systems[1] (D. Harel and A. Pnueli 1985) on the other hand is not necessarily terminating after producing some result, but maintaining an ongoing interaction with their environment and responding with appropriate actions to the external stimuli. When designing, describing and reasoning (Kim Sunesen 1998) about reactive systems, the focus is not just on what is computed but equally on how and when it is computed, in terms of interaction capabilities over time. Conventional examples of reactive systems include flight control systems, nuclear reactors, web applications, electronic games and touch screens. Reactive systems as illustrated in Figure 5-2 cannot be specified by a relation between initial and final states.

---

[1] The term was coined by Harel and Pnueli (D. Harel and A. Pnueli 1985). A brief but useful discussion can be found in (Harel and M. Politi 1998).

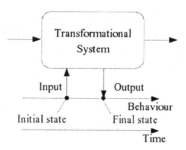

Figure 5-1 A simple transformational system

Although traditionally, Web services have been thought of as being information intensive, transformational programs, most useful Web services are in fact reactive systems. Examples include, web services deployed and composed as e-commerce applications, where an order once placed, can be cancelled, changed or put on hold because of unexpected conditions, anytime before its fulfillment. In certain cases a refund may also be requested later, if the service/product does not meet its specifications. In corporate e-business, it may not be a simple database query that generates a document, but an entire business process involving multiple partners. The final generation of the document may span several days. Web services deployed on wireless devices may take more than expected time to provide the requested service due to poor connection facilities.

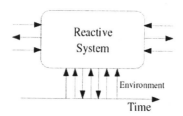

Figure 5-2. A Reactive system

Consider a typical example of a flight reservation service. The service provides results for a flight search and reserves tickets for the selected flight, thus changing the status of a seat from unbooked to booked i.e. transforming information by execution of a database query. However, the final selection of flight by a travel agent can span over an unlimited period of time, going through several rounds of selection. A typical interaction is shown in Figure 5-3. The service may also exert control over the environment by terminating the user session after pre-specified time limits of inactive sessions. In case of flight search the database server itself is reactive as it allows the environment i.e. service requesters to ask queries. Further, once a flight has been booked, the agent also has the option of cancelling the booking within a stipulated time period.

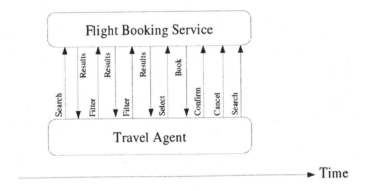

Figure 5-3. A Typical Flight Reservation Scenario

Further, service composition represent long running interactions between service requesters and providers that extend beyond single step execution of services. In order to correctly specify their behaviour, properties of services need to be expressed in a form that enables reasoning about their behaviour during such extended execution. Current XML-based and ontological specification standards for the description of service behaviour, do not have the capability to specify compositional properties. Languages like WSDL (Roberto Chinnic et al. 2005) and WSBPEL (Tony Andrews et al. 2003) provide an operational approach to service specification. They do not have the provision for specifying the conditions that restrict the execution of services to a limited set of valid behaviours. In other frameworks like OWL-S (The OWL-S Coalition 2004) and WSMO, specification of pre/post-conditions and effects contribute to some extent towards their behavioural specification. However they are limited to static behaviour descriptions in the sense that they are predicates required to hold only at the initial and final states.

The need for more expressive service specification also becomes evident, while reasoning about the composition of services and validation of the com-position at runtime. Model checking (E.M. Clarke et al 1999) and theorem proving are commonly used techniques for formal verification. In the context of analysing services and their composition at runtime, these techniques are not feasible due to the possible exponential growth in the number of reachable global states. In contrast to formal verification, practical validation techniques provide a mechanism to verify only properties which are of interest to the service requester or provider. Our notion of validation is different from the classical technique of "testing", generally associated with it. We believe, validation is a process of checking for inconsistent, redundant, incomplete or incorrect properties for a service. Properties are checked not for all possible behaviours (Shikun Zhou 2003) as in verification, but for a particular trace or execution of a service. As shown in our earlier work on service composition (M. Solanki et al, 2004), the objective of runtime validation is not to prove individual service implementation correct. It is to ensure that no undesirable behaviour emerges, when the service is composed with other services.

In this chapter, we propose a methodology to **compositionally** augment the semantic description of a reactive service, with **temporal** properties that provide the required support for reasoning about "ongoing" behaviour. The properties are specified in **Interval Temporal Logic** (ITL) (B. Moszkowski, 1986, 1994, 1996), our underlying formalism for reasoning about service behaviour over periods of time. These properties are specified only over observable behaviour, and do not depend on any additional knowledge about the underlying execution mechanism of the services. We present "TeSCO-S", a framework for enriching Web service interface specifications, described as OWL (Mike Dean and Guus Schreiber 2004) ontologies with temporal assertions. TeSCO-S provides an OWL ontology for specifying properties in ITL, a pre-processor, "OntoITL" for transforming ontology instances into ITL formulae and an interpreter, "AnaTempura" that executes and validates temporal properties in "Tempura", an executable subset of ITL.

2.   A MOTIVATING EXAMPLE: AN ONLINE BOOKSTORE

An Online Bookstore as shown in Figure 5-5 is a sequential composition of four services: Book search, Book buy, Payment validation and Book delivery. Each of these services is a reactive service, as they continuously interact with the customer as illustrated in Figure 5-4. The e-Bookshop requires the customer to be registered with the service, in order to search or buy a book. The customer sends the ISBN number of the book to the Book search service, which returns a message with the search results. The customer can continue searching for more books, always supplying the ISBN number or proceed to buy the book. The Book buying service, takes as input the list of books selected by the customer, the delivery address and the credit card details. The Card details and address are passed to the Payment validation service. If the card is validated, then depending on the amount paid and mode of delivery selected (standard or express), the book is arranged to be delivered to the customer. We informally define properties of the composition, some of which we formalise in the subsequent sections. We perceive Web services as black boxes and hence the properties strictly characterise the observable behaviour of services in the composition.

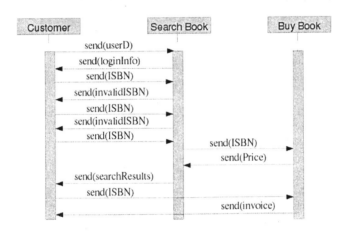

*Figure 5-4.*Interactions in an Online Bookstore

- At all times during the execution of the composed service, the customer is required to be a registered member of the e-Bookshop. This is a useful property to validate, when an inactive customer session is activated after a considerable period of time. Most services store customer registration details as session data, which is reset after a predefined period of inactivity.
- Once a customer starts searching for a book, the price of the book has to be constant till the search is over or if the customer buys the book, the price has to be constant till the book has been delivered to the customer.
- During the search, at any time if the customer sends an ISBN number, he gets back the search results, for the same ISBN number.

- Once a book or a list of books have been selected and ordered, the parameters of the book (title, language etc) should not change, till the book has been delivered to the customer.

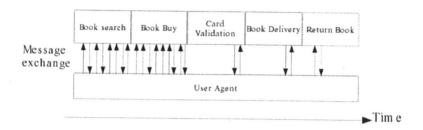

Figure 5-5. A Typical Book Buying Scenario

- In order to buy a book, the customer needs to have a valid credit card.
- Once the credit card has been validated, the e-Bookshop makes a commitment to deliver the book as per the delivery terms and conditions agreed with the customer.

We use the Online Bookstore as a running example throughout the chapter to explain various concepts

3.   INTERVAL TEMPORAL LOGIC

ITL is an important class of temporal logic which was initially devised by Ben Moszkowski in the 1980's in order to model digital circuits (B Moszkowski, 1983). Later it was designed particularly as a formalism for the specification and design of software systems (B Moszkowski, 1995, 1994, 1996). ITL is an extension of classical first order logic especially designed for representing time dependent behaviour. It has proved to be an efficient formalism for specifying and reasoning about concurrently executing, real time critical systems.

3.1   Model

ITL is a linear-time temporal logic with a discrete model of time for both finite and infinite intervals. The model of behaviour used in ITL is quite natural. The idea is to describe the system of interest by taking a number of "snapshots" at various points in time t_i, for $i \leq n$ and linking these snapshots together $(t_0 \ldots t_n)$. This link is the key notion in ITL and is called an "interval". Snap- shots define various relevant "states" for modelling the system and an interval is considered as an (in)finite, nonempty sequence of states $\sigma_0 \sigma_1 \cdots$

$$\sigma : \sigma_0 \sigma_1 \sigma_2 \cdots$$

Each state represents a mapping from the set of variables *Var* and their values *Val*.

$$State: Var \rightarrow Val$$

The length $|\sigma|$ of a finite interval σ is equal to the number of states in the interval minus one. An empty interval has exactly one state and its length is equal to 0. The notation $\sigma_{i:j}$ denotes the subinterval of length j-i with states $\sigma_i, \sigma_{i+1}, \cdots, \sigma_j$

3.2 Syntax

The syntax of ITL is defined in Figure 5-6, where μ is an integer value, a is a static variable (does not change within an interval), A is a state variable (can change within an interval), v a static or state variable, g is a function symbol, and p is a predicate symbol.

Expressions
$e ::= \quad \mu \mid a \mid A \mid g(exp_1, \ldots, exp_n)$
Formulae
$f ::= \quad p(e_1, \ldots, e_n) \mid \neg f \mid f_1 \wedge f_2 \mid \forall v \cdot f \mid \text{skip} \mid f_1 ; f_2 \mid f^*$

*Figure 5-6.*Syntax of ITL

1. Operators:

ITL contains conventional propositional connectives such as $\wedge, \neg$ and first order ones such as $\forall, \exists$ and =. Extending the logic to temporal reasoning are operators like "; (chop)", "* (*chopstar*)" and "*skip*". Additional temporal operators defined in ITL include $\bigcirc$ (next) and $\square$ (always).

2. Expressions:

Expressions are built inductively from variables, constants and functions as follows:

- Constant: μ
  A constant is denoted by a function without parameter. These are fixed

values

Examples: true, false, 2, 3, 5, [2, 3, 4, 5].

- Variables: A, B, C, . . . , a, b, c

  The value of a state variable can change within the interval, while the value of a static variable remains constant throughout the reference interval. Conventionally capital letters denote state variables, while small letters denote static variables. The letter v is used as a meta-variable in definitions to range over all variables.

- Function: $g(\exp_1, \cdots, \exp_n)$, where n $\geq$ 0

  The function symbols include arithmetic operators such as +,-, *mod* and * (multiplication). Constants such as 0 and 1 are treated as zero place functions.

  Examples: $A + B$, $a\text{-}b$, $A + a$, $v \bmod C$

- $ia : f$: An expression of the form $ia : f$ is called a *temporal expression*. It returns a value a for which the formula f holds in the reference interval. If there is no such an a then $ia : f$ takes an arbitrary value from a's range.

Some examples of syntactically legal expressions are given below:

- $I + (\bigcirc J) + 2$

  This expression adds the value of I in the current state, the value of J in the next state and the constant "2".

- $I + (\bigcirc J) - \bigcirc\bigcirc(I)$

  This expression adds the value of I in the current state to the value of J in the next state and subtracts the value of I in the next to next state from the result.

3. **Formulae**:

Formulae are built inductively from predicates and logical connectives as follows:

- Atomic formulae are constructed using relation symbols such as = and $\leq$.

  Examples: $e_0 \leq e_1$

- Logical connectives: $\neg f, f_1 \wedge f_2$ where f, f_1, f_2 are formulae.

- Universal Quantifier: $\forall v.f$

- Temporal Operators: skip, ";", "(chop) and "*" (*chopstar*) Examples:
  $$f_1; f_2, f *$$

Some examples of syntactically legal formulae are given below:

- $(J=2)\bigcirc(K=4)$
  This formula states that the value of J is "2" in the current state and the value of K is "4" in the next state.
- $\bigcirc(\Box[I=2] \wedge \bigcirc\Box[J=2])$
  The formula states that from the next state, the value of I would always be equal to "2" and the value of J in the next to next state will be equal to "2".

  Many more examples can be found in (B. Moszkowski 1986).

3.3   Informal Semantics

Expressions and Formulae in ITL are evaluated relative to the beginning of an interval. Formulae with no temporal operators are called "state" formulae. With respect to an interval, a state formula is required to hold only at the initial state of that interval.

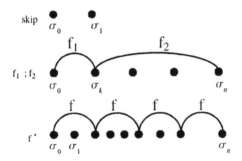

Figure 5-7. Pictorial illustration of ITL Semantics

The informal semantics of the most interesting temporal constructs are defined as follows:

- **skip**: unit interval (length 1).
  The formula **skip** has no operands and is true on an interval iff the interval has length 1 (i.e. exactly two states).

- $f_1; f_2$: A formula $f_1; f_2$ is true on an interval σ with states
  $\sigma_0 \cdots \sigma_{|\sigma|}$ iff the interval can be "chopped" into two sequential parts
  (i.e. a prefix and a suffix interval) sharing a single state σ_k for some
  $k \leq |\sigma|$ and in which the subformula f_1 is true on the left part
  $\sigma_0 \cdots \sigma_k$ and the subformula f_2 is true on the right part $\sigma_k \cdots \sigma_{|\sigma|}$.

- $f*$: A formula $f*$ is true over an interval iff the interval can be chopped into zero or more sequential parts and the subformula f is true on each.

Figure 5-7 pictorially represents the semantics of *skip, chop and chopstar*. Some ITL formulae together with intervals which satisfy them are shown in Figure 5-8

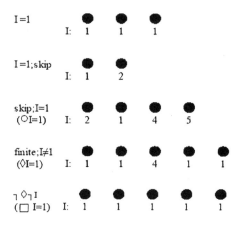

Figure 5-8. Some sample ITL formulae and satisfying intervals

true	$\hat{=} 0 = 0$	true value
false	$\hat{=} \neg true$	false value
$f_1 \vee f_2$	$\hat{=} \neg(\neg f_1 \wedge \neg f_2)$	or
$f_1 \supset f_2$	$\hat{=} \neg f_1 \vee f_2$	implies
$f_1 \equiv f_2$	$\hat{=} (f_1 \supset f_2) \wedge (f_2 \supset f_1)$	equivalent
if g then f_1 else f_2	$\hat{=} (g \wedge f_1) \vee (\neg g \wedge f_2)$	if-then-else
$\exists v \cdot f$	$\hat{=} \neg \forall v \cdot \neg f$	exists

Figure 5-9. Non-temporal constructs

3.4 Derived Constructs

The following constructs can be derived from primitives of the logic. Non-temporal constructs are presented in Figure 5-9. Frequently used temporal modalities are represented in Figure 5-10. The formula "f" is used as a reference formula for defining the constructs.

$\bigcirc f$	$\hat{=} \text{skip} ; f$	next
more	$\hat{=} \bigcirc true$	non-empty interval
empty	$\hat{=} \neg more$	empty interval
inf	$\hat{=} true ; false$	infinite interval
finite	$\hat{=} \neg inf$	finite interval
$\Diamond f$	$\hat{=} finite ; f$	sometimes
$\Box f$	$\hat{=} \neg \Diamond \neg f$	always
$\Diamond f$	$\hat{=} f ; true$	some initial subinterval
$\Box f$	$\hat{=} \neg(\Diamond \neg f)$	all initial subintervals
$\Diamond f$	$\hat{=} finite ; f ; true$	some subinterval
$\Box f$	$\hat{=} \neg(\Diamond \neg f)$	all subintervals
halt f	$\hat{=} \Box(\text{empty} \equiv f)$	terminate interval when
fin f	$\hat{=} \Box(\text{empty} \supset f)$	final state
fin exp	$\hat{=} \imath a : fin (exp = a)$	end value
keep f	$\hat{=} \Box(\text{skip} \supset f)$	all unit subintervals
$\bigcirc exp$	$\hat{=} \imath a : \bigcirc(exp = a)$	next value
$exp_1 \leftarrow exp_2$	$\hat{=} finite \wedge (fin \ exp_1) = exp_2$	temporal assignment
$exp_1 \ gets \ exp_2$	$\hat{=} keep (exp_1 \leftarrow exp_2)$	gets
stable exp	$\hat{=} exp \ gets \ exp$	stability
$len(exp)$	$\hat{=} \exists I \bullet (I = 0) \wedge (I \ gets \ I + 1) \wedge I \leftarrow exp$	interval length

Figure 5-10. Frequently used temporal abbreviations

3.5 Types in ITL

There are two basic inbuilt types in ITL. These are integers N and Boolean (true and false). In addition the executable subset of ITL (tempura) has basic types: integer, character, boolean, list and arrays. Further types can be built from these by means of X and the power set operator P (in a similar fashion as adopted in the specification language Z (M Imperato, 1991). For example the following introduces a variable x of type T.

$$(\exists x : T).f \stackrel{def}{=} \exists x.type(x,T) \wedge f$$

Here $type(x,T)$ denotes a formula that describes x to be of type T. Although this might seem to be a rather inexpressive type system, richer types can be added following that of (Spivey, 1996).

3.6 Formal Semantics

In this section we present the formal semantics of expressions (terms) and formulae in ITL. We define the data domain to be a set of integers denoted by Z. We assume "tt, ff" to represent the set of truth values. A state

(σ) is then a function mapping from variables Var to values in Z. We let Σ denote the set of all such functions,

$$\sigma_i \in \Sigma \triangleq Var \to Z$$

Each n-ary function symbol g is associated with a total function

$$\hat{g} \in Z^n \to Z$$

Interpretations of n-ary relational symbols ($\hat{p}$) are similar but map to truth values.

$$\hat{p} \in Z^n \to tt, ff$$

Function symbols, e.g. $+$ and $-$, and relation symbols, e.g. $\geq$ and $=$, are assumed to have their standard meanings. We define Σ^+ and Σ^ω to denote sets of finite and infinite intervals respectively. The relation

$$\sigma \sim_V \sigma'$$

is defined to be true iff the interval σ and σ', ($\sigma, \sigma' \in \Sigma^+ \cup \Sigma^\omega$) have the same length and agree on the behaviour of all variables except possibly the variable V.

3.6.1 Semantics of Expressions

The construct $\mathcal{E}_\sigma[\![exp]\!]$ denotes the function that defines the value in $\mathbb{Z}$ of the expression exp on the interval σ.

$$\mathcal{E}_\sigma[\![exp]\!] \in (\Sigma^+ \cup \Sigma^\omega) \to \mathbb{Z},$$

- $\mathcal{E}_\sigma[\![\mu]\!] = \sigma_0(\mu) = \mu.$

- $\mathcal{E}_\sigma[\![a]\!] = \sigma_0(a)$ and
  for all i s.t. $0 \leq i \leq |\sigma|, \sigma_i(a) = \sigma_0(a).$

- $\mathcal{E}_\sigma[\![A]\!] = \sigma_0(A).$

- $\mathcal{E}_\sigma[\![g(exp_1, \ldots, exp_n)]\!] = \hat{g}(\mathcal{E}_\sigma[\![exp_1]\!], \ldots, \mathcal{E}_\sigma[\![exp_n]\!]).$

- $\mathcal{E}_\sigma[\![\imath a\colon f]\!] = \begin{cases} \chi(u) & \text{if } u \neq \emptyset \\ \chi(Val_a) & \text{otherwise} \end{cases}$
  where $u = \{\sigma'(a) \mid \sigma \sim_a \sigma' \wedge \mathcal{E}_{\sigma'}[\![f]\!] = tt\}$

3.6.2. Semantics of Formulae

The construct $\mathcal{E}_\sigma[\![f]\!]$ denotes the function that defines the value in $\{tt, ff\}$ of the formula f on the interval σ.

$$\mathcal{E}_\sigma[\![f]\!] \in (\Sigma^+ \cup \Sigma^\omega) \to \{tt, ff\},$$

- $\mathcal{E}_\sigma[\![p(exp_1, \dots, exp_n)]\!] = tt$ iff $\hat{p}(\mathcal{E}_\sigma[\![exp_1]\!], \dots, \mathcal{E}_\sigma[\![exp_n]\!])$.

- $\mathcal{E}_\sigma[\![\neg f]\!] = tt$ iff $\mathcal{E}_\sigma[\![f]\!] = ff$.

- $\mathcal{E}_\sigma[\![f_1 \wedge f_2]\!] = tt$ iff $\mathcal{E}_\sigma[\![f_1]\!] = tt$ and $\mathcal{E}_\sigma[\![f_2]\!] = tt$.

- $\mathcal{E}_\sigma[\![\forall v \cdot f]\!] = tt$ iff for all σ' s.t. $\sigma \sim_v \sigma'$, $\mathcal{E}_{\sigma'}[\![f]\!] = tt$.

- $\mathcal{E}_\sigma[\![\mathsf{skip}]\!] = tt$ iff $|\sigma| = 1$.

- $\mathcal{E}_\sigma[\![f_1 ; f_2]\!] = tt$ iff
  (exists a k, s.t. $\mathcal{E}_{\sigma_0 \dots \sigma_k}[\![f_1]\!] = tt$ and
    ((σ is infinite and $\mathcal{E}_{\sigma_k \dots}[\![f_2]\!] = tt$) or
    (σ is finite and $k \le |\sigma|$ and $\mathcal{E}_{\sigma_k \dots \sigma_{|\sigma|}}[\![f_2]\!] = tt$)))
  or (σ is infinite and $\mathcal{E}_\sigma[\![f_1]\!]$).

- $\mathcal{E}_\sigma[\![f^*]\!] = tt$ iff
  if σ is infinite then
      (exist $l_0, \dots, l_n$ s.t. $l_0 = 0$ and $\mathcal{E}_{\sigma_{l_n} \dots}[\![f]\!] = tt$ and
          for all $0 \le i < n$, $l_i \le l_{i+1}$ and $\mathcal{E}_{\sigma_{l_i} \dots \sigma_{l_{i+1}}}[\![f]\!] = tt$.)
  or
      (exist an infinite number of l_i s.t. $l_0 = 0$ and
          for all $0 \le i$, $l_i \le l_{i+1}$ and $\mathcal{E}_{\sigma_{l_i} \dots \sigma_{l_{i+1}}}[\![f]\!] = tt$.)
  else
      (exist $l_0, \dots, l_n$ s.t. $l_0 = 0$ and $l_n = |\sigma|$ and

4. Compositional Reasoning for Web Services

Web services cannot exist in isolation. Most Web services interact with other services, users, devices or sensors to achieve a goal. The fundamental problem of composing specification of services, is to prove that a composite service satisfies its specification if all of the component services satisfy their specifications. For a compositional and modular specification of services, the description of interfaces between services and their environment is of utmost importance. The *interface* of a service provides the static/dynamic (logical) connection between the service and its environment. An interface description is a specification of those properties of a service that influences the overall behaviour of the composed system as well as those of the individual services. Interface specification of reactive services cannot simply be described in terms of functions or relation on states, a more expressive representation format is needed.

4.1   Compositionality

Compositionality refers to the technical property that enables reasoning about a composed system on the basis of its constituent parts without any additional need for information about the implementation of those parts. The notion of compositionality (W.P. de Roever, 1985, 2001, J. Zwiers, 1989) is very important in computer science as it facilitates modular design and maintenance of complex systems following the *verify-while-develop* paradigm. Compositional proof techniques have the advantage that they allow the systematic top-down development of systems from their specifications. Compositionality is also a desired criterion for verification methodologies particularly for the development and analysis of large scale systems. The idea was first suggested by E. W. Dijkstra (E. W. Dijkstra 1965) in where he discusses hierarchical decomposition and verification of a given program on the basis of its subprograms, and formalised by (Floyd, 1967) where properties of a sequential program are derived from the properties of its atomic actions. For reasoning satisfactorily about composed system, systems and their components are specified using **assertional** specifications i.e. *state predicates*, only over their observable behaviour.

4.2   Applying the Assumption-Commitment Paradigm to Web Services

For the development of a compositional framework that allows the specification and validation of services and their composition, we choose the Assumption-Commitment paradigm. The objective of an **Assumption-Commitment** style of specification is to specify a process within a network. In its most general form Assumption-Commitment (P. K. Pandya 1990, Qiwen Xu and Mohalik Swarup, 1998) reasoning, allows the verification of a service under the assumption that the environment behaves in a certain way. The Assumption-Commitment style of specification has been applied extensively as a proof technique to networks of processes executing concurrently via synchronous message passing in a seminal work by (J. Misra and K.M. Chandy 1981).

In our earlier work on service composition, we have shown the power of assumption-commitment style of specification for compositional reasoning of ongoing service behaviour. We have proposed a methodology (Solanki et al. 2004) to augment the specification of a service, with properties that are temporal and compositional, called *assumption* and *commitment*. Assumption-Commitment properties are specified only over observable behaviour, and do not depend on any additional knowledge about the underlying execution mechanism of the services. Interestingly, Interval Temporal Logic, our underlying formal framework can be used both for establishing the validity of the behaviour of a service and for proving the soundness of the compositional rules.

The assumption-commitment specification can be thought of as a pair of predicates (As, Co) where the assumption As specifies the environment in which the specified service is supposed to run, and the commitment Co states the requirement which any correct implementation of the service must fulfill whenever it is executed in an environment that satisfies the assumption. Since we are interested in the observable, ongoing behaviour of services, we model assumption-commitment as temporal properties defined over their interface specification.

4.3   An ITL Formalisation of Assumption-Commitment

A service, S, in ITL is expressed as a quadruple
$$(As, Co) : \{\omega\}S\{\omega'\}$$
where,

ω	: state formula about initial state
As	: a temporal formula specifying properties about the environment
Co	: a temporal formula specifying properties about the service
ω'	: state formula about final state

Figure 5-10. Frequently used temporal abbreviations

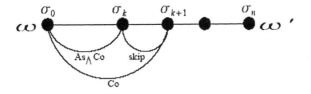

Figure 5-11. ITL representation of Assumption-Commitment

Formally in ITL, the validity of the Assumption-Commitment representation as illustrated in Figure 5-11 has the following form:

$$(As, Co) : \{\omega\}S\{\omega'\} \stackrel{\text{def}}{=} \omega \wedge S \supset (\square(\mathsf{empty} \vee ((As \wedge Co); \mathsf{skip}) \supset Co \wedge \mathit{fin}\ \omega'))$$

We have also proposed compositional proof rules based on assumption-commitment properties that allow validation of ongoing behaviour of services. Keeping in perspective the e-Bookshop service which is sequentially composed, we present the rules here for sequential composition.

We consider the sequential composition (ref. Figure 5-12) of two services, S_1 and S_2. For a detailed explanation of the rules and its proof obligations, the interested reader is referred to (Solanki et al. 2004).

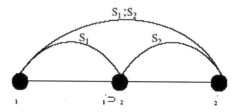

Figure 5-12 Sequential Composition

$$
\begin{array}{llll}
\vdash & (As, Co) & : & \{\omega_1\} S_1 \{\omega_1'\} & (1) \\
\vdash & (As, Co) & : & \{\omega_2\} S_2 \{\omega_2'\} & (2) \\
\vdash & \omega_1' & \supset & \omega_2 & (3) \\
\vdash & As & \equiv & \boxdot As & (4) \\
\vdash & Co & \equiv & Co^{\bullet} & (5) \\
\hline
\vdash & (As, Co) & : & \{\omega_1\} S_1; S_2 \{\omega_2'\} & (6)
\end{array}
$$

5.   Formalisation of the Online Bookstore

We now formalise some of the interesting properties of the e-Bookshop service from section 2.

- At all states ($\sigma_0 ... \sigma_l$) during the execution of the composed service, the customer is required to be a registered member of the e-Bookshop.

  $\square(isRegistered(userID))$

- Once a customer starts searching for a book, the price of any book returned as a result has to be constant till the search is over or if the customer buys the book, the price has to be constant till the book has been delivered to the customer i.e. the price of the book has to be constant at all states ($\sigma_0 ... \sigma_l$).

  $\square(isNotChanged(bookPrice))$

- During the search ($\sigma_0...\sigma_m$), at any state if the customer sends an ISBN number, he gets back the search results, for the same ISBN number in the next state.

$$\Box((searchBook(ISBN)) \supset (searchResults(ISBN)))$$

- Once a book or a list of books have been selected and ordered, the parameters of the book (title, language etc) should not change, till the book has been delivered to the customer ($\sigma_m...\sigma_l$).

$$\Box(isBook(selectedBook))$$

- In order to buy a book, the customer needs to have a valid credit card, that stays valid atleast till the book has been delivered to the customer ($\sigma_m...\sigma_l$).

$$\Box(validCard(userID, cardNumber))$$

- Once the credit card has been validated, the e-Bookshop makes a commitment to deliver the book as per the delivery terms and conditions agreed with the customer ($\sigma_n...\sigma_l$).

$$(finvalidCard(UserID, CardNumber))(DeliveryPeriod = CalculatedDays)$$

For sequential composition of services, the proof obligations require that we choose Assumption-Commitment properties of the form:

$$\vdash As \equiv \Box As$$
$$\vdash Co \equiv Co^*$$

We now define the assumption and commitment properties required to hold for the composition defined between states ($\sigma_0...\sigma_5$). Keeping in perspective the nature of properties, we informally define the assumption as,

At all states during the execution of the composed service, the customer is required to be a registered member of the e-Bookshop.

We define the corresponding commitment as

At all states during the execution, the e-Bookshop allows registered users to search and buy a book.

It is worth noting that these properties are specified as part of the behavourial specification of the e-Bookshop as well as the Customer. They are however required to be validated by the e-Bookshop. Formalising the above properties,

$$\Box(isRegistered(userID))$$
$$(validCustomer(userID))^*$$

For the composition between states σ_1 and σ_5, we define an additional commitment while keeping the assumption same,

Once a customer is returned the results of search, the price of book(s) selected should remain constant till the user finishes all transaction.

Formalising the above,

$$(unchangedPrice(userID, ISBN))^*$$

6.   SEMANTIC ANNOTATION OF TEMPORAL SPECIFICATION: TESCO-S

Web services are discovered and composed based on the declarative specification of their interfaces as exposed by service providers in service registries or repositories. Temporal properties for services, need to be made a part of this declarative specification. In the context of temporal properties and Web services, the notion of "Temporal" can be interpreted in terms of the following two intuitive contexts:

- **Time-related properties of Web services**: expressing facts about dates (calendar) of events ("Order placed on 4th July"), duration of activities ("Shipping the product takes 24 hrs once an order is received") and absolute time i.e. clock ("Confirmation of a Shipped good will be sent out at 9.00 a.m. IST"). The vocabulary to describe these concepts include time as a first class citizen as part of their syntactic and semantic representation.
- **Behaviour-related properties of Web services**: expressing facts about ordering of services ("Check the credentials of the supplier, **before** placing an order "), constraints during service execution ("Do not modify a submitted order **while** the transaction is in progress", "**As long as** the supplier continues proves the authenticity of his goods, we shall continue to place orders with him.").

When describing temporal properties of services at a declarative level, we focus on the second notion i.e. reasoning about behaviour of services relative to time. The objective of declarative representation of temporal properties and constraints is to enable their automated reasoning and further their runtime validation for automated discovery, composition and execution of services. In the case of services that are semantically described, an important part of this effort is the development of representative ontologies of the most commonly used domains.

TeSCO-S (<u>Te</u>mporal <u>S</u>emanti<u>C</u>s for <u>O</u>WL enabled <u>S</u>ervices) is a framework for semantically annotating and validating Web service specifications with temporal properties, defined using ITL and its executable subset "Tempura". The objective is:

- to provide an ontology for service providers to declaratively specify temporal properties in ITL.
- to provide a pre-processor for service requesters/composing middleware/software agents to process the declarative markup of properties and transform them into concrete ITL/Tempura formulae.
- to provide an execution engine for the generated tempura formulae, which can be used to validate properties about the service as well as perform runtime validation of assumption - commitment properties for service composition.

The semantics of the formulae and expressions modeled using TeSCO-S are the semantics as defined in ITL and implemented in its executable subset Tempura. TeSCO-S uses OWL as the ontology representation language. The choice of OWL as a representation format over XML is motivated by two objectives: (a) Our ultimate goal is to be able to automate reasoning about ITL formulae and expressions. (b) we want to be able to seamlessly use the ontology within standrads like OWL-S for services. Tools for reasoning about ITL-Tempura ontology, can be integrated with automated reasoning tools for services specified in OWL. For realising the objectives highlighted above, TeSCO-S includes the following components:

- An OWL ontology for first order formulae, expressions and temporal constructs as defined in ITL and Tempura.
- A pre-processor that transforms ontological representations of ITL and Tempura constructs defined in the ontology above to concrete formulae and expressions.
- An interpreter,"AnaTempura" that provides execution support for Tempura.

The following sections present a detailed discussion of each of these components.

6.1 The ITL-Tempura Ontology

The objective of the ITL-Tempura ontology is to express the syntactical framework of ITL and Tempura, as concepts and properties in OWL. ITL is very expressive and provides a number of primitive and derived constructs for the specification of a wide variety of temporal assertions. We have restricted the ontology to only a specific set, which we believe will be most useful and sufficient to express the kind of properties that most service providers would want to expose. On the other hand, the ontology itself is very modularly structured to enable future extensions. As discussed in section (3), the syntax of ITL is defined primarily by Expressions and Formulae. Expressions can be of various types for e.g. static and state variables, functions, and constants. Similarly formulae can be subclassed as being atomic: e.g. " ",composite: e.g. " $f_1 f_2$ " and predicates: e.g. "*isRegistered(userID)* " amongst others. Expressions and Formulae in the ontology are built incrementally. The root class of all Formulae is "Formula", while that of Expressions is "Expression". Formula has several subclasses such as "Atomic", "Composite" and "Prefixed" amongst others. "TempuraFormula", defines formulae specified in Tempura and which can be executed by AnaTempura. "Operator" denotes the kind of operators that can be used with formulae and expressions. Classes have properties and restrictions associated that define the kind of parameters that are required to build the expression or formula. Properties provide the link between expressions/formulae and operators. We follow an incremental approach to building ontology instances using the ITL-Tempura ontology as shown in the e-Bookshop example presented in secton 6.5. The modular approach to building ITL and Tempura formulae allows reusability of formulae and expression instances between ontologies. We use the Protege OWL plugin for modelling the ontology.

Figure 5-13 shows how formulae and expressions are structured. A complete description of the ontology is beyond the scope of the paper. A graphical and hierarchical representation of the classes in the ontology can be found at (Solanki 2005). The complete ontology itself can be found at (Solanki 2005).

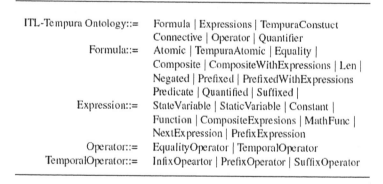

ITL-Tempura Ontology::=	Formula | Expressions | TempuraConstuct
	Connective | Operator | Quantifier
Formula::=	Atomic | TempuraAtomic | Equality |
	Composite | CompositeWithExpressions | Len |
	Negated | Prefixed | PrefixedWithExpressions
	Predicate | Quantified | Suffixed |
Expression::=	StateVariable | StaticVariable | Constant |
	Function | CompositeExpresions | MathFunc |
	NextExpression | PrefixExpression
Operator::=	EqualityOperator | TemporalOperator
TemporalOperator::=	InfixOpeartor | PrefixOperator | SuffixOperator

Figure 5-13 Primitives for the ITL-Tempura Ontology

6.2   OntoITL: A Pre-processor for Temporal Ontologies

So far, we have seen how ITL formulae and expressions can be modelled using the ITL-Tempura ontology. This enables service providers to specify temporal constraints as part of their service specification. In order to interpret this semantic markup of temporal properties, a utility is needed to generate concrete formulae and expressions from the OWL representation. The idea behind providing such a tool is to automate the process of generating, interpreting and analysing temporal properties of services. Service requestors and composers can use the tool to extract temporal properties that they would like to validate, while interacting with the service. At runtime, the properties are monitored against the behaviour of the interacting services.

OntoITL is a pre-processor that generates concrete ITL and executable Tempura formulae from instance ontologies built using the ITL-Tempura Ontology. The instances are defined using the core ontology as described in Section 6.1 or from ontologies that import these instances. It provides as output, complete information about instances of State and Static variables, Expressions, Formulae and Temporal Formulae modeled in the ontology. An output of the pre-processor for properties of the e-Bookshop, modeled using the ITL-Tempura Ontology and as explained in section 6.5 is shown in the Figure 5-16

OntoITL takes as input, the instance ontology in OWL for a formula or a set of formulae. It then generates ITL/Tempura formulae keeping the syntactical structure of the formula intact. OntoITL offers several options to store the generated ITL and Tempura formulae. It also provides the facility to directly pass the tempura formula to the AnaTempura interpreter, that executes the formulae and validates temporal properties. Alternatively, OntoITL stores the generated outputs in files that can be executed via the Tcl/Tk interface of AnaTempura as discussed in section 6.3.

6.3   AnaTempura: Validation of Tempura Specification

AnaTempura (available from (A. Cau, 2005)), which is built upon C-Tempura, is an integrated workbench for the runtime verification of systems using ITL and its executable subset Tempura. AnaTempura provides
- specification support
- verification and validation support in the form of simulation and runtime testing in conjunction with formal specification.

An overview of the run-time analysis process in AnaTempura is depicted in Figure 5-14.

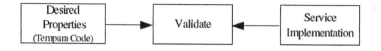

Figure 5-14 The Analysis Process

There are two ways of validating properties via AnaTempura:

- Concrete Tempura formulae generated by the OntoITL pre-processor are directly passed to AnaTempura. The results of the validation and execution are returned to OntoITL for display.
- Concrete Tempura formulae generated by the OntoITL pre-processor are stored in files for validation at a later stage. The results of the validation and execution can be displayed via the Tcl/Tk interface of AnaTempura.

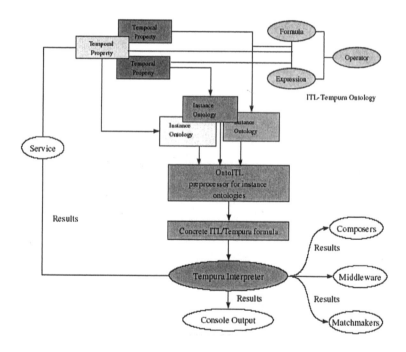

Figure 5-15 General Architecture for Web services

AnaTempura generates a state-by-state analysis of the system behaviour as the computation progresses. At various states of execution, values for variables of interest are passed from the system to AnaTempura. The Tempura properties are validated against the values received. If the properties are not satisfied AnaTempura indicates the errors by displaying what is expected and what the current system actually provides. The approach goes beyond a "keep tracking" approach, i.e. giving the running results of certain properties of the system, by not only capturing the execution results but also comparing them with formal properties. The general architecture that employs AnaTempura for validation of service properties is shown in Figure 5-15.

The validation results of the instance-ontology-formulae, generated from the TeSCO-S framework, can be returned to the composing agents, the middleware or to the service requestor depending on the design of the service composition.

6.4   Validating the Customer: e-Bookshop Composition

We have validated the assumption-commitment properties of the e-Bookshop as formalised in section 5.1.

We adopt the second approach to validating properties as mentioned in section 6.3. The property is extracted as a tempura formula, from its ontological representation using the OntoITL pre-processor and stored in a file. At the initial state, the customer registers using his login details[2]. The login details are set for the customer session and passed to AnaTempura. As illustrated in the Figure 5-16 for each phase of the composition (search, buy etc.) and for every interaction between the e-Bookshop and the customer, at all states, the property is validated.

Tempura interpreter validates the property against the values set in the session for that state. We have developed a minimalistic GUI for dislaying the results of the property validation. The blue circle indicates that a property holds for that state, while a red circle indicates that a property has been violated. In the example shown, a "1" indicates the first service in the composition i.e. the "Book Search", while a "2" indicates the second service i.e. the "Book Buy". If the values in the session are found to be reset and do not match the ones passed to the interpreter in the initial state, a warning message is sent to the e-Bookshop as indicated by the red circle. It is worth noting that the interpreter only validates the properties of interest. It does not define the behaviour of the service in case the properties are not satisfied.

---

[2]For practical purposes, we do not model the registration process over an interval, although this may well be the case if the user enters incorrect login details, and takes several attempts to correct login.

This is a design decision that has to be taken before the composition is realised.

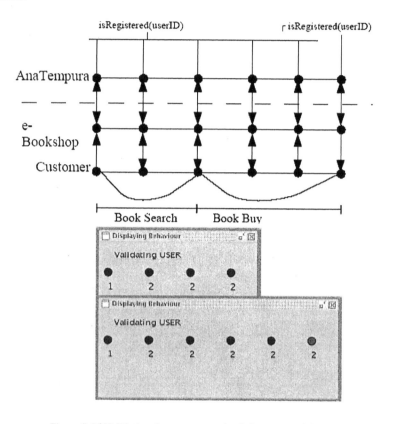

Figure 5-16 Validating the customer -e-bookshop composition

6.5   Specifying Properties in the ITL-Tempura Ontology

In this section, we model some interesting properties of the e-Bookshop service 5 using the ITL-Tempura ontology. For the sake of brevity in representation we model them as A-Box representations.

Recalling the definition of a composite formula,

Composite ô Formula ó (∀ hasPrefixedSubFormula.Formula) ó (∀ hasSuffixedSubFormula.Formula) ó (=1 hasInfixOperator.Operator) ó (=1 hasPrefixedSubFormula.Formula) ó (=1 hasSuffixedSubFormula.Formula)

We choose the following properties from the e-Bookshop example

Property (1): During the search, at any state if the user sends an ISBN number, he gets back the search results, for the same ISBN number in the next state.

$$((searchBook(ISBN)) \supset (searchResults(ISBN)))$$

We define the properties as assertional axioms (ABox) in Description Logic. We build the formula incrementally as shown below:

ABox representation of Property (1):

ISBN:StateVariable, P1:Predicate, P2:Predicate
(P1, searchNook):hasName, (P1, ISBN):hasExpressionList
(P2, searchResults):hasName, (P2, ISBN):hasExpressionList
PR1:Prefixed, (PR1, Next):hasPrefixOperator, (PR2, P2):hasSubFormula
C1:Composite, (C1, Imp):hasInfixOperator
(C1,P1):hasPrefixedSubFormula, (C1, PR1):hasSuffixedSubFormula
PR2:Prefixed, (PR2, Always): hasPrefixOperator, (PR2, C1):hasSubFormula

Property (2): Once the credit card has been validated, the e-Bookshop makes a commitment to deliver the book as per the delivery terms and conditions agreed with the user.

$$(finvalidCard(UserID, CardNumber))(DeliveryPeriod = CalculatedDays)$$

ABox representation of Property (2):

UserID:StateVariable, CardNumber:StateVariable
DeliveryPeriod:StateVariable, CalculatedDays:StateVariable
P1:Predicate, (P1, validCard):hasName, (P1,
UserID,CardNumber)):hasExpressionList
PR1:Prefixed, (PR1, fin):hasPrefixOperator, (PR2, P1):hasSubFormula
EQ1:Equality, (EQ1, Equals):hasEqualityOperator, (EQ1,
DeliveryPeriod):hasPrefixExpression
(EQ1, CalculatedDays):hasSuffixExpression
C1:Composite, (C1, Chop):hasInfixOperator
(C1,P1):hasPrefixedSubFormula, (C1, EQ1):hasSuffixedSubFormula

7.   CONCLUSIONS

From a historical perspective, research on Web services was initiated with a focus on automating business process composition within different enterprises. Such coordinations are long-lived processes and may last from a few minutes to a few months. An extensive review of state-of-the-art research in the domain of Web service composition reveals that current interface specification approaches do not provide capabilities to expose the reactive aspect of Web service behaviour. Based on service interfaces definitions (Roberto Chinnic et al 2005) and message exchange protocols (Martin Gudgin et al.2003), standards have been proposed for specifying composite services, by defining declaratively, their data and control flows. BPEL4WS (Tony Andrews et al. 2003) provides distinct constructs for specifying abstract and executable processes. BPEL, however does not prevent complex computation from being included in an abstract process, thus revealing implementation details.

Within the context of semantic Web services frameworks like OWL-S and WSMO, specification of pre/post-conditions and effects contribute to some extent towards their behavioural description. However they are limited to describing transformational behaviour. There is no support available for describing and reasoning about changes over time. This is due to the lack of explicit modelling of "states" in these languages. Rule languages for the web include RuleML and within the context of semantic web, initiatives such as SWRL (Ian Horrocks et al. 2003) and DRS (Drew McDermott and Dejing Dou 2002). These approaches are limited to describing only certain kinds of properties. The expressivity of the languages is restricted to specifying static rules and constraints. There are no constructs available for specifying ongoing behavioural semantics or temporal properties of services. Other related work in this area is mostly concerned with representation of time as a first-class citizen, (Feng Pan and Jerry R. Hobbs 2004, F. Bry and S. Spranger 2003) i.e. reasoning about time points, complex time intervals, calendars and durations.

For dynamic composition of services, compositional properties need to be abstracted at a level where service requesters, providers, composing engines and matchmakers can discover these properties of services. Assumption-Commitment properties can be suitably specified in any service description language, rich enough to capture the underlying expressiveness of these properties. In this chapter, we provide a modular approach, TeSCO-S, to building and executing temporal properties of services, with interfaces described as OWL ontologies. TeSCO-S is based on Interval Temporal Logic (ITL) and Tempura, its executable subset. Our pre-processor "OntoITL" enables transformation of the bulky XML representation of temporal properties into concrete ITL and Tempura formulae, that can be handled readily by AnaTempura. The ontology within the TeSCO-S framework can be used by service providers to describe temporal capabilities of services. Service requestors and composing agents can use "OntoITL" and AnaTempura for on-the-fly transformation and validation of these temporal properties. The ontology provides constructs not only for specifying temporal expressions and formulae, but general first order predicates and formulae as well. It can therefore, also be used to specify preconditions/post-conditions and effects in frameworks like OWL-S and WSMO. Ongoing work in TeSCO-S is providing reasoning support over temporal ontologies and tools for exploiting ITL formulae to build temporal ontologies. It is planned to have a protege plugin for defining temporal ontologies, that could be used along with the OWL-S editor for modelling OWL-S services.

8. QUESTIONS FOR DISCUSSIONS

Beginner:
1. What are the main categories under which computing systems can be partitioned?
2. What are the characteristics of reactive systems?
3. How does temporal logic help in formalising system behaviour?

Intermediate:
1. Discuss why Web services should be modelled as reactive systems.
2. What properties of a dynamically composed service can be formalised using temporal logic?
3. Discuss why the notion of Compositionality is important while defining composition of services.
4. Why should temporal properties of services be modelled as ontologies?
5. How does a service composition benefit from runtime validation of desired properties?

Advanced:
1. Discuss how properties of a holiday booking service can be formalised using Interval Temporal Logic.
2. How can properties of the holiday booking service be expressed using the ITL-Tempura ontology?
3. Identify assumption-commitment properties for the holiday booking services.

9. SUGGESTED ADDITIONAL READING

* Monika Solanki and Antonio Cau and Hussein Zedan. Introducing Compositionality in Web Service Descriptions. In Proceedings of the 10th International Workshop on Future Trends in Distributed Computing Systems - FTDCS 2004, Suzhou, China, May 26-28 2004. IEEE Computer Society Press.

- Antonio Cau. ITL and (Ana)Tempura Home page on the web. http://www.cse.dmu.ac.uk/˜cau/itlhomepage/itlhomepage.html.
- Z. Manna and A. Pnueli.The Temporal Logic of Reactive and Concurrent Systems: Specification. Springer-Verlag, New York, 1991.
- B. Moszkowski. Executing temporal Logic Programs. Cambridge University Press, Cambridge, England, 1986.

10.   REFERENCES

F. Bry and S. Spranger (2003). Temporal constructs for a web language.

A. Cau, (2005). ITL and (Ana)Tempura Home page on the web. http://www.cse.dmu.ac.uk/˜cau/itlhomepage/itlhomepage.html.

Antonio Cau and Hussein Zedan (1997). Refining interval temporal logic specifications. In ARTS, pages 79–94, 1997.

Roberto Chinnic, Hugo Haas, Amy Lewis, Jeans Jacque Moreau, David Orchard, and Sanjiva Weerawarana (2005). Web services description language (WSDL) version 2.0 part 1: Core language w3c working draft 3rd August, 2005. http://www.w3.org/TR/2005/WDwsdl20-20050803/.

W.P. de Roever (1985). The quest for compositionality a survey of assertion based proof systems for concurrent programs. In Neuhold EJ, editor, Proc of the IFIP conference: the role of abstract models in computer science,, Vienna. North Holland, Amsterdam.

W. P. de Roever et al (2001). Concurrency Verification: Introduction to Compositional and Noncompositional Methods. Cambridge University Press, Cambridge, England, 2001.

E. W. Dijkstra (1965). Solution of a problem in concurrent programming control. Commun. ACM, 8(9):569.

E. W. Dijkstra (1976). A Discipline of Programming. PrenticeHall.

Jurgen Dinge (2000). Systematic parallel programming. PhD thesis, Carnegie Mellon University.

Frank Leymann, IBM Software Group. Web Services Flow Language (WSFL) Version 1.0, 2001.

Drew McDermott and Dejing Dou (2002). Representing Disjunction and Quantifiers in RDF Embedding Logic in DAML/RDF. In ISWC2002. 1st International Semantic Web Conference, 2002.

E.M. Clarke and O. Grumberg, and D. A. Peled (1999). Model Checking. The MIT Press, Cambridge, Massachusetts.

R. W. Floyd. Assigning meaning to programs (1967). In Symposium in Applied Mathematics, volume 19, pages 19–31. American Mathematical Society, 1967.

Martin Gudgin, Marc Hadley, Noah Mendelsohn, JeanJacques Moreau, and Henrik Frystyk Nielsen (2003). SOAP Version 1.2 Part 1: Messaging Framework W3C Recommendation 24 June. http://www.w3.org/TR/soap12part1/.

D. Harel and A. Pnueli. (1985) On the development of reactive systems, pages 477–498. SpringerVerlag New York, Inc., New York, NY, USA .

D. Harel and M. Politi.(1998). Modeling Reactive Systems with Statecharts: The STATEMATE Approach. McGrawHill.

The Rule Markup Initiative. http://www.dfki.unikl.de/ruleml/.

C.A.R Hoare. An axiomatic basis for computer programming. Comm. ACM, 12 (1969) 576–580, 583, 1969.

Ian Horrocks, Peter F. PatelSchneider, Harold Boley, Said Tabet, Benjamin Grosof, Mike Dean (2003). SWRL: A Semantic Web Rule Language Combining OWL and RuleML . Technical report, University of Manchester, Version 0.5 of 19 November.

M Imperato (1991). An introduction to Z. ChartwellBratt, 1991.

Z. Manna and A. Pnueli (1991). The Temporal Logic of Reactive and Concurrent Systems: Specification. SpringerVerlag, New York.

Zohar Manna and Amir Pnueli .(1993) Models for reactivity. Acta Inf., 30(7):609–678.

Mike Dean and Guus Schreiber (eds.) 2004. OWL Web Ontology Language Reference, 10 February 2004. http://www.w3.org/TR/owlref/.

J. Misra and K.M. Chandy (1981). Proofs of networks of processes. In IEEE Transactions on Software Engineering, volume 7(7):417426.

Monika Solanki and Antonio Cau and Hussein Zedan (2003). Introducing compositionality in Webservice Descriptions. In Proceedings of the 3rd International Anwire Workshop on Adaptable Service Provision, Paris, France, 2003. SpringerVerlag.

Monika Solanki and Antonio Cau and Hussein Zedan (2004). Introducing Compositionality in Web Service Descriptions. In Proceedings of the 10th International Workshop on Future Trends in Distributed Computing Systems FTDCS 2004, Suzhou, China, May, 2004. IEEE Computer Society Press.

B Moszkowski (1983). Reasoning about Digital Circuits. PhD thesis, Department of Computer Science, Stanford University

B. Moszkowski (1986). Executing temporal Logic Programs. Cambridge University Press, Cambridge, England.

B. Moszkowski (1994). Programming Concepts, Methods and Calculi, IFIP Transactions, A-56., Some Very Compositional Temporal Properties, pages 307–326. Elsevier Science, B. V., NorthHolland, 1994.

B. Moszkowski (1995). Compositional reasoning about projected and infinite time. In Proceedings of the First IEEE Int'l Conf. on Engineering of Complex Computer Systems (ICECCS'95). In , pages 238245. IEEE Computer Society Press.

B. Moszkowski (1995). A temporal logic for multilevel reasoning about hardware. IEEE Computer, pages 10–19.

B. Moszkowski (1996). Compositionality: The Significant Difference, volume 1536 of LNCS, chapter Compositional reasoning using Interval Temporal Logic and Tempura, pages 439–464. Springer Verlag, Berlin, 1996.

B. Moszkowski (1996). Using temporal fixpoints to compositionally reason about liveness. In He Jifeng, John Cooke, and Peter Wallis, editors, BCSFACS 7th Refinement Workshop, electronic Workshops in Computing. "SpringerVerlag and British Computer Society", London.

Nickolas Kavantzas, David Burdett, Gregory Ritzinger, Tony Fletcher, Yves Lafon (2004). Web Services Choreography Description Language Version 1.0: W3C Working Draft 17 December.

Feng Pan and Jerry R. Hobbs (2004). Time in OWLS. In Proceedings of AAAI Spring Symposium Series on Semantic Web Services, 2004.

P. K. Pandya (1990). Some comments on the assumptioncommitment framework for compositional verification of distributed programs. In REX workshop: Proceedings on Stepwise refinement of distributed systems: models, formalisms, correctness, pages 622–640, New York, NY, USA. SpringerVerlag New York, Inc.

Satish Thatte. XLANG: Web Services for Business Process Design, 2002.

Amazon Web Service. www.amazon.com.

Monika Solanki. (2005) A Graphical representation of Class Hierarchies in the ITLTempura Ontology. http://www.cse.dmu.ac.uk/~monika/TeSCOS/OntoITL.jpg.

Monika Solanki. (2005) An Ontology for ITL and Tempura. http://www.cse.dmu.ac.uk/~monika/TeSCOS/OntoITL.owl.

Monika Solanki, Antonio Cau, and Hussein Zedan (2004). Augmenting semantic web service descriptions with compositional specification. In Proceedings of the 13th international conference on World Wide Web, pages 544–552. ACM Press.

J. Michael Spivey (1996). Richer types for Z. Formal Asp. Comput., 8(5):565–584, 1996.

The protege ontology editor and knowledge acquisition system. http://protege.stanford.edu/index.html.

Ketil Stölen (1990). Development of parallel programs on shared datastructures. Technical report, Department of Computer Science, University of Manchester.

Kim Sunesen (1998). Reasoning about Reactive Systems. PhD thesis, BRICS, Department of Computer Science University of Aarhus.

The OWL-S Coalition, (2004). OWLS 1.1 Release. http://www.daml.org/services/owls/1.0/.

Tony Andrews et al. (2003) Business Process Execution Language for Web Services, Version 1.1, 2003. http://www106.ibm.com/developerworks/library/wsbpel/.

Web Service Modelling Ontology, (2004). http://www.wsmo.org.

R. J. Wieringa (2003). Design Methods for Reactive Systems. MorganKaufmann: Elsevier Science, San Francisco.

Qiwen Xu and Mohalik Swarup, (1998). Compositional reasoning using the assumption-commitment paradigm. Lecture Notes in Computer Science, 1536:565–583.

Cau A. Xu Q. W. and Collette P (1994). On unifying assumptioncommitment style proof rules for concurrency. In B. Jonsson and Eds. J. Parrow, editors, In CONCUR'94, LNCS 836.

Shikun Zhou (2003). Compositional Framework for the Guided Evolution of TimeCritical Systems. PhD thesis, Software Technology Research Laboratory, De Montfort University UK.

J. Zwiers (1989). Compositionality, concurrency and partial correctness. SpringerVerlag New York, Inc., New York, NY, USA.

PART II: SEMANTIC WEB PROCESSES

Chapter 6

BASIC CONCEPTS IN CHOREOGRAPHY

Sinuhe Arroyo
Digital Enterprise Research Institute (DERI), Innsbruck, Austria – sinuhe.arroyo@deri.at

1. INTRODUCTION

Services constitute an emerging paradigm for the design of distributed software systems. Nonetheless, interoperability is a factor determining the adoption of innovation in business environments (DIP) so that interoperability must be carefully addressed as a critical element in SOA (Service Oriented Architecture) technology. Services need to interoperate with each other in order to realize the purposes of the software system they define by exchanging messages, which allow them to make or to respond to requests. Upon the reception of a message, services react by executing some internal invisible processes, and possibly, responding with other messages. Due to the heterogeneous technological and syntactic nature of services realizing semantic web processes, communication requirements become more complex, clearly defining a balance among interoperation and decoupling.

The concepts and ideas that underlie the so-called *Semantic Web* (Berners-Lee, Hendler et al. 2001) appear as a candidate solution for such complex compatibility problems (Brogi, Canal et al. 2004). Notably, formal ontology based on description logics (Baader, Calvanese et al. 2003) provides an appropriate formalism to deal with compatibility problems.

In the context of providing support for *choreography* (i.e. the modeling of external, visible behavior of service interactions), a semantic layer could be supposed to provide the required convertibility between divergent specifications by the specification in machine-processable form of the message exchanging patterns (MEP). Scalable and reliable service communication and integration beyond simple interchanges requires interoperable choreography as an essential service for business collaboration (Jung, Hur et al. 2004). This makes semantic compatibility between interchanges an important research objective, which has recently been stated in formal terms (Brogi, Canal et al. 2004).

The idea of overcoming the heterogeneity among messages using such semantic service-based mediation layer as choreography service(s) is thought to have a lot of potential (Watkins, Arroyo et al. 2005; Zaremba, Moran 2004). On the one hand, as the number of accessible services increases, so does the number of structural and behavioural styles, thus requiring the use of some intermediate layer to overcome heterogeneity. On the other hand, the development of new applications and integration of existing ones can be greatly decreased, as off-the-shelf services can be readily used to build bigger and more complex software systems minimizing integration efforts. In a nutshell, the design of modern applications requires a compromise among interoperation and decoupling that is sometimes hard to realize due to the heterogeneous nature of services. If services communicate by exchanging message, a choreography engine is a good mediation layer that could speed up the interoperation and development of new and existing software functionality.

A number of approaches exist, such as BPEL4WS (Andrews, Curbera et al. 2003), WS-CDL (Kavantzas, Burdett et al. 2004), WSCI (Zaremba, Moran 2004) or WSMO – Choreography (Roman, Scicluna, et al. 2005), which can be used to model the external visible behavior of services. However none of these approaches represents a complete solution to the problem due to:

- a lack of technological independence (BPEL4WS, WS-CDL)
- the lack of a clear model that separates structural, behavioral and operational aspects (BPEL4WS, WS-CDL, WSCI or WSMO-Choreography)
- the lack of proper support for semantics (BPEL4WS, WSCI, WS-CDL[1])
- an ad-hoc approach to solve heterogeneity among message exchanges (BPEL4WS, WS-CDL, WSCI or WSMO-Choreography)
- a central vs. decouple approach to model choreographies (BPEL4WS, WS-CDL, WSCI or WSMO-Choreography)

Thus, new initiatives are needed that overcome these limitations and provide interoperation mechanisms among services, which increase the degree of de-coupling and eliminate static dependencies.

---

[1] It supports the recording of semantics, but it does not use them at all.

In the following, the main ideas and concepts behind choreography are depicted. Section 2 carefully depicts related approaches and initiatives dealing with choreographies categorizing them and reviewing their main contributions and lacks. Section 3 details the main driving principles required to model and allow interoperation among heterogeneous message exchanges. Section 4, present the new challenges in choreography. Section 5 provides a detailed description of SOPHIE an initiative that aims to overcome the limitations of existing approaches. Section 6, exemplifies the concepts and ideas sketched so far by means of a use case centered in the telecommunications field. Finally, Section 7 draws the conclusion of the chapter.

2. LITERATURE REVIEW

In the following different technologies that are related to the definition of a conceptual framework for choreography are concisely reviewed. In doing so, their core characteristics are presented and main drawbacks identified.

Table 6-1 presents a preliminary classification based on a three dimension exam. The first dimension depicts the relation with the underlying communication framework, differentiating among tight and loose. The second one addresses the semantic support provided. Finally, the third one discriminates them depending on whether or not they follow a layered model. Based on these depiction four main categories of languages are distinguished:

- Technologies with a tight relation to the underlying communication framework, lacking of a layered model and no support for semantics, such as BPEL4WS
- Technologies with a tight relation to the underlying communication framework, that follow a layered model and no support for semantics, such as WS-CDL
- Technologies with a loose relation to the underlying communication framework, lacking of a layered model and no support for semantics, such as WSCI
- Technologies with a loose relation to the underlying communication framework, with support for semantics but lacking of a layered model, such as WSMO-Choreography

Table 6-1. A first cut in classifying related languages

		layered model		
		no		*yes*
relation with communication framework	*tight*	Business Process Languages	Choreography Languages	
	loose	Choreography Languages	Semantic-driven choreography initiatives	SOPHIE
		no	*yes*	
			semantic support	

2.1 Business Process Languages

Business Process Languages provide the means to specify business processes and interaction protocols, representing the first attempt to model the visible behavior of services. BPEL4WS is the main initiative classified in this group. It focuses on describing collaboration among processes through Web Service interfaces –orchestration–, rather than the sequence and cardinality of the messages exchanged –choreography–. Nevertheless, many of the concepts and ideas sketched in BPEL4WS have been adopted and improved in other choreography languages. BPEL4WS is characterized by a tight relation with the underlying communication framework, which seriously hampers its flexibility, a lack of support for semantics, which prevents the agile interoperation among Services and, a missing layered approach, which results in a confusing specification.

BPEL4WS. The Business Process Execution Language for Web Services (BPEL4WS) (Andrews, Curbera et al. 2003) is a model and a grammar for describing business work flow logic. In doing so, it represents interactions between processes and its partners through Web Service interfaces. BPEL4WS allows the creation of *abstract processes* that *describe business protocols* –public visible behavior–, as well as *executable processes* –private behavior–, that can be compiled into runtime scripts (Barros, Dumas et al. 2005).

The specification makes use of the following concepts. Business partners define groups of *partner links* that allow them to establish a number of conversational relations. A partner link models the services with which a business process interacts. Partner links are characterized by *partner link types*. A partner link type represents the conversational relationship between two services by defining the roles of each one of them and the port types that will be receiving each others messages. Correlation among messages within a conversation is provided by means of *correlation sets*. Correlation sets provide a declarative mechanism to define correlated groups of operations. Additionally, *variables* facilitate the means to hold messages that have been received or will be sent to partners, which constitute the state of a business process. The values of compatible variables can be copied among them by means of assignments.

BPEL4WS differentiates among two types of *activities*. *Basic activities* represent the invocation of an operation on a service as a synchronous or asynchronous request or response. Basic activities can be associated with other basic activities that act as its compensation action. *Structured activities* prescribe the order in which a collection of activities takes place, permitting to describe business processes by composing basic activities. The context where activities behave is called *scope*. A scope allows defining correlation sets and a number of *event handlers* for compensation, alarms and fault, among others. Event handlers define a set of actions that are invoked concurrently if a particular event occurs. A process definition is then made of one activity, a series of partners, some specific correlation sets, and the definition a number of handlers.

In practice, BPEL4WS focuses on the description of collaborative processes –orchestration–, rather than in the detailed description of the external visible behavior –choreography–. Also, it presents a tight relation with the underlying communication framework, which prevents the use of any technology other than WSDL and SOAP. Furthermore, even though roles might not hold through out the interaction, partners are tight to roles in conversations. Additionally, it lacks of a layered model and support for semantics. Finally, the use of variables and scopes has more to do with the private behavior of the process than with the external visible one, presenting, when assimilated to choreographies, a non-desirable centralized approach that goes against the decoupled nature of services.

2.2 Choreography Languages

Choreography languages deal with modeling the external visible behavior of Services as a number of message exchanges. The initiatives detailed in this group are WS-CDL and WSCI.

WS-CDL is the latest attempt of the W3C (WWW) to define an XML language for the description of the common and complementary behavior of services from a global point of view. Like in the case of BPEL4WS, WS-CDL has a tight relation to the underlying communication framework, and lacks of layered model. Additionally, it allows the recording of semantic description, even though the purpose of such feature is not clear.

WSCI is also an XML-based language aiming at describing the message interfaces of services. WSCI is not longer under development, as the W3C replaced with WS-CDL. WSCI does not count with any support for semantics, nor follows a layered model, establishing a loose relation with the underlying communication framework.

WS-CDL. The Web Service Choreography Description Language (WS-CDL) (Kavantzas, Burdett et al. 2004) is an XML-based language for the description of the observable behavior of Web Services defined under the auspices of the W3C. WS-CDL permits defining, from a global and common point of view, multiparty contracts, which describe the visible behavior of Web Services as a number of ordered message exchanges.

The specification makes use of the following concepts. *Participants* represent the consumers and producers of information. They identify a set of related roles. *Roles* enumerate the observable behavior of a participant with respect to another one. The association of two roles to fulfill a concrete purpose is called *relationship*. A relationship represents the possible ways in which two roles can interact. *Channels* specify where and how to exchange information, they define the links between WS-CDL choreographies and the operations described in the interfaces of services. *Variables* contain information about the objects partaking in the choreography that describe the information exchanged during an interaction.

Choreographies are described in WS-CDL *documents*. WS-CDL documents, describe, from a global point of view the rules agreed among participants that govern the message exchange. They are encapsulated in *packages*. Packages enclose information that is common to all the choreographies it contains. Additionally, packages enclose *activities*. Activities can be conducted by participants. The specification details three types of activities namely, *Ordering Structure*, *WorkUnit* and *Basic* activities. Ordering Structure activities are block-structure activities that enclose a number of sub-activities. WorkUnit activities describe the conditional and possibly repeated execution of an activity. Work activities are actual work performers.

To conclude, a WS-CDL choreography can specify one exception block and one finalizer block, which are respectively activated when an exception occurs or when the choreography has completed successfully.

In practice, the explicit association of roles to participants as modeled in relationships is a too constraining way of representing the interaction among services. Such relation should be transparent to the language and dependent only on the particular part of the message exchange conducted. Also, the use of channels further hampers flexibility, as it adds a new restriction to the interaction, which should be overcome by the addressing mechanism of the message exchange. In this direction, the specification is too tight to a particular technology. Furthermore, the use of variables to describe the context of the interaction and activities to model the functionality of parties helps to present a centralized approach which goes against the natural decoupling that services should follow. The state of each party should be private and transparent to other parties. Additionally, the interaction follows an asymmetric nature biased towards the receiver rather than the sender, refereeing to the operation performed when information is received, but not the action(s) (or operations) leading to the sending of information (Barros, Dumas et al. 2005). Moreover, the relation among the specification and the use of MEPs, understood as a key element that allows solving the heterogeneity among message exchanges is not explicitly addressed. As well, even though it allows the recording of semantic descriptions, their purpose is not clear. Besides, it lacks of any support to correlate messages and solve heterogeneities. Finally, the lack of a layered model differentiating among structural, behavioral and operational aspects helps portraying a confusing view of the language. It tries at the same time to define a model and a XML syntax, which does not discriminates among aspects.

WSCI. The Web Services Choreography Interface (WSCI) (Arkin, Askary et al. 2002) is an XML-based interface description language co-developed by a number of industrial partners. WSCI describes the flow of messages exchanged by Web Services in terms of dependencies among them, featuring sequencing rules, correlation, exception handling and transactions.

Interfaces describe how services are perceived to behave from a temporal and logical point of view within a *message exchange*. A service might have multiple interfaces for a given message exchange. A set of message exchange define a *conversation*. Conversations make use of *message correlation* in order to describe its structure and which *properties* must be exchanged to maintain the semantic consistency of a conversation. *Properties* are equivalent to variables and allow referencing a value or representing an abstraction for a message received. Such abstractions are conceptualized as *processes*. *Processes* are labeled with a name and represent a portion of behavior, such as receiving a message or calling a process. *Activities* represent the basic unit of behavior of a service. They are classified into *atomic* and *complex*. Atomic activities constitute a basic unit of behavior such as sending or receiving a message o waiting for an amount of time. Complex activities are recursively composed of other activities which defines a specific type of choreography for the activities it encloses. Ultimately complex activities are composed of *actions*. Activities are executed within the environment provided by a *context*. Context might be associated with *transactions* to describe from the interface perspective the transactional properties of a number of activities. In addition *exceptions* allow to model models exceptional behavior of a service in a conversation

WSCI does not take under consideration MEPs as a means to describe the behavior of parties and cornerstone to solve heterogeneities. Also, it lacks of any support for semantics. Furthermore, it leaves aside issues such as QoS and security. Additionally, it presents a global and centralized view of the choreography, which contradicts the decoupled nature of services. Moreover, the concept of transaction as presented seems to be more related to internal aspects than to internal ones. Finally, even though it sketches the concept of state to model behavior, the idea is not fully integrated, contributing to a confusing specification that lacks of a clear separation of models.

2.3   Semantic-driven Choreography Initiatives

Currently, only one initiative exists that tackles the choreography problem from a semantic perspective. The main advantages of this approach revolve around the dynamic generation of mappings among parties that allows them to interoperate in a more efficient and agile way.

WSMO Choreography represents the first attempt to model choreographies from a semantic perspective. It does not make any assumption about the underlying communication platform. The main draw back of WSMO Choreography is the lack of separation of models.

WSMO Choreography. The WSMO Choreography (Roman, Scicluna, et al. 2005) is an ontology-based approach that allows describing the behavior of services from the user point of view. WSMO-choreography is based on Abstract State Machines (ASMs), from which it inherits the core principles, namely, *state-based*, *state by and algebra* and *guarded transition rules*. The main building blocks of WSMO choreography are thus *states* and *guarded transitions*. States are described by a link to an instance of a WSMO ontology. Guarded transitions define transition rules that express changes of states by changing the set of instances of the ontology.

WSMO-chorography focuses only on the behavioral aspects of the choreography, leaving aside structural and operational considerations. Also, the behavioral model is based on the formalism presented by ASM from which it borrows an insufficient subset of concepts that can hardly model a complete choreography. Furthermore, it does not rely on the use of conversational patterns to define the order and cardinality of messages, thus complicating the mapping task among heterogeneous interaction styles.

Additionally, it does not specify how the message exchange mismatches should be identified, mapped and solved. Finally, the specification is too closed over WSMO and ASMs, leaving no room to accommodate other formalisms, such as Petri nets for the behavioral model, or OWL as underlying semantic language.

3.   DRIVING PRINCIPLES

When designing choreographies a number of driving principles need to be taken under consideration. In the following, such principles are enumerated and briefly discussed.

Conceptual framework
The first step in analyzing choreographies is to identify the different entities that partake in the interaction. A choreography service defines terms and roles for these entities.

Separation of models
The definition of a choreography service requires that the models that build it are clearly differentiated. As a result, a modular framework should be designed, where different formalism can be readily added, extended or replaced, in order to allocate the most suitable one, depending on the target application and application domain.

Semantic-driven and mediation
Due to the natural heterogeneity of the open environment where services reside, the interoperation of heterogeneous message exchanges requires the production of intermediate structures – mediators – that allow overcoming mismatches. By semantically describing the different entities that characterize the choreography service, such structures can be produced as a result of a mediation task. In doing so, mediation allows any party to speak with every other (Fensel, Bussler 2002), facilitating an intermediate layer that provides a generalized solution to resolve communication mismatches.

Technological independence
The design of a fully extensible choreography service should not make any assumptions about underlying technologies. In particular, the details regarding transport and communication frameworks should be left aside. In doing so, a choreography service should rely on such underlying technologies, defining a clear border, which allows separating the particular communication details from the conceptual model used. In addition, as new

ontological languages based on different logical formalisms are developed, independence from existing and emerging specifications should be obliged. In consequence the conceptual model is driven by the semantic description of its constituent entities, not making any constraint or assumption on the ontological language used to model such descriptions.

Separation of internal and external behavior

Choreographies deal with the externally visible behavior of parties. The internal details should be clearly separated from the external ones, allowing its independent definition. Deeply in this direction, the description of collaborative process is out of the scope of this work, same as orchestration in general.

Global view vs. decentralized approach

Many traditional models call for centralized approaches where the interaction among parties is controlled by a unique point. In contrast, the nature of ubiquitous systems is decentralized. While a decentralized approach is preferred due to its flexibility to adapt to different application domains, eventually, a global point of view is chosen to control the message exchange. A choreography service should take both approaches under consideration, allowing parties to choose the most suitable one at any time.

Pattern-driven

Particular types of interactions among services, such as, negotiation or interactive information gathering, follow well established and researched Message Exchange Patterns (MEPs). The choreography service should allow the usage of such conversational protocols as main building block that can be used to overcome heterogeneities among services.

SOA-based

A realization of all this basic principles, especially regarding semantic-driveness and technological independence, the choreography service should be realized as a SOA architecture with support for semantics.

4.   GOALS: SEPARATION OF MODELS AND MEDIATION

Services communicate with each other by exchanging messages, which allow them to make or to respond to requests. Upon the reception of a message, services react by executing some internal invisible processes, and possibly, responding with other messages. Choreography deals with describing such external visible behavior of services as message exchanges. In order to allow interoperation among services exposing different visible behaviors, the means to map heterogeneous messages exchanges is required. The problem is not trivial. On the one hand existing initiatives that tackle the choreography problem defined much interleaved conceptualizations, lacking of a clear separation of models that mix structural, behavioral and operational aspects. Furthermore, they portray choreographies from a global point of view, while services are characterized by their decentralized nature. On the other hand, such the approaches to solve heterogeneities are very much ad-hoc ones. Initiatives to overcome mismatches based on semantic descriptions should be envisioned as a core building block that provides the means to readily overcome heterogeneity by means of mediators. Still, the current state of the technology do not suffice for the degree of automation require, imposing human supported mediation techniques, which hamper the dynamism of the task.

The separation of models and support for semantic mediation are at the hearth of the challenges discussed above. Both characteristics are complementary and required in the design of a choreographies framework.

4.1   Separation of Models

The separation of models enables the definition of a flexible conceptual framework where the different abstract pieces are well decoupled from each other.

These are the most important requirements considered by the layered model:

- *Syntactic vs. Semantic*: Syntax and semantics should be clearly distinguished as in (Tsalgatidou, Pilioura 2002). While syntactic aspects identify core entities and interfaces, semantics cares for adding the machine understandable descriptions that allow the dynamic interoperation among the entities described in the syntax.
- *Separation of aspects*: Structural, behavioral and operational aspects should be clearly separated within the syntactic model.
  - *Structural* aspects deal with the provision of a reusable collection of entities following different levels of abstraction that provide the basis for the description of a conceptual model
  - *Behavioral* aspects care for the description of the dynamic interaction among the entities defined in the structural model
  - *Operational* aspects facilitate the means to allow interoperation among different operational models

A clear separation of aspects facilitates the addition, replacement and modification of the underlying paradigms without imposing the need to redesign the overall conceptual model and affecting the remaining aspects.

4.2   Mediation

Mediation refers to the ability to solve heterogeneities among heterogeneous entities. It allows parties to exchange messages, documents and the data they contain, disregard of the vocabulary and behavioral model used. Mediation by means of *mediators*, facilitates a generalized solution to resolve communication mismatches among heterogeneous parties.

Mediation is applied at two different levels:

- *Data and domain knowledge.* The interoperation of parties will require the mediation of data types and domain knowledge during the message exchange. Depending on the domain to which parties belong to different data types and domain knowledge might be used to encapsulate data and its meaning.
- *Message Exchange Patterns.* Parties follow well-defined heterogeneous message exchanges that model their external behavior. Patterns represent units of reference that allow formalizing such behavior.

By semantically describing data, domain knowledge and message exchange patterns, mappings that overcome the differences among heterogeneous behaviors and structures can be readily produced.

Elaborating on the previous statements, it can be easily derived that separation of models and mediation pose different degrees of complexity. The engineering of software systems is already driven by a differentiation of models, as a means to provide scalable and flexible systems. Likewise, the Semantic Web is trying to put in place the formalisms required to agilely solve heterogeneity at the ontological level. Additionally, there should not be any doubt about the close relation among separation of models and mediation, where later requires of the former. In fact the successful mediation necessitates a clear depiction and semantic description of the syntactical aspects.

5.   SOPHIE: SEMANTIC WEB SERVICES CHOREOGRAPHI ENGINE

SOPHIE (Arroyo 2006; Arroyo, López et al. 2005; Arroyo, Duke 2005; Arroyo, Sicilia et al. 2005; Arroyo, Kummenacher 2006; Arroyo, Sicilia 2005) is a conceptual framework and architecture for a choreography engine or service realized as a Semantic Service Oriented Architecture (SSOA). SOPHIE is especially suitable for supporting the fine grained interaction among services following different structural or behavioral models following precisely the principles detailed in Section 3. It elaborates on existing initiatives (Arkin, Askary et al. 2002; Andrews, Curbera et al. 2003; Kavantzas, Burdett et al. 2004; Roman, Scicluna, et al. 2005) trying to overcome their limitations with the addition of a layered syntactical model, support for semantics, technological independence as it does not make any assumptions about the underlying communication framework (WSDL, SOAP), ontological language (WSML, OWL, RDF, etc) or behavioral paradigm (Abstract State Machines (ASMs), Petri nets, temporal logic, etc). Furthermore, it relies on the use of MEPs as the core building block to semantically describe the skeleton of message exchanges.

5.1 Overall Architecture

Services that use SOPHIE fall into two categories, namely, *initiating parties* and *answering services*. Both parties produce and consume messages. Additionally, initiating parties indicate the choreography engine by means of any of its constituents *correlating services* that the infrastructure for the interoperation of heterogeneous message exchanges should be established.

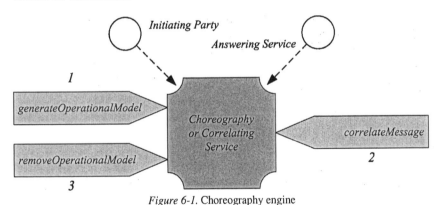

Figure 6-1. Choreography engine

Figure 6-1 shows a high level architecture of the conceptual framework realized as a single correlating service[2]. Informally, initiating parties indicate

---

[2] Notice that the choreography service itself is readily assimilated to one or more correlating service, in case a decentralized approach is preferred.

that want to communicate with an answering service by means of *"generateOperationalModel"* (1). Once an operational model that allows the interoperation among the heterogeneous message exchanges has been created, parties can start submitting messages by means of the *"correlateMessage"* (2) primitive. Messages will go through the designated operational model, forwarding the framework the message(s) to the receiving party according to its choreography.

Finally, when the conversation is finished, either party indicates that the operational model for a given conversation can be put off line, by means of the primitive *"removeOperationalModel"*.

5.2   Models

SOPHIE makes a clear distinction between semantic and syntactic models. The semantic model details the support for semantics, while the latter details the syntax of the framework. The syntactic model depicts three different complementary models: structural, behavioral and operational. The structural model provides the grounding pillars of the framework. The behavioral model permits to model the conduct of the structural model and, the operational model facilitates the means to allow the interoperation of different behavioral models. This layered approach enables a straight mechanism to extend the different models. The work presented here defines the behavioral model as Abstract State Machines (ASMs). Petri nets, temporal logic or transaction logic can however also be used instead of ASMs and easily plugged in. The semantic model is currently based on WSML. Nonetheless, the design allows to easily extending the grammar and ontology of SOPHIE to accommodate any other ontology language.

Structural model

A *conversation* represents the logical entity that permits a set of related message exchanges among parties to be grouped together. Conversations are composed of a set of building blocks. *Elements* represent units of data that build up *documents*. Documents are complete, self-contained groups of elements that are transmitted over the wire within *messages*. Messages characterize the primitive piece of data that can be exchanged among parties. As messages are exchanged, a variety of recurrent scenarios can be played out. *Message Exchange Patterns (MEP)*, identify placeholders for messages, that allow sequence and cardinality to be modeled, defining the order in which parties send and receive messages. A set of messages sent and received among parties optionally following a MEP that account for a well defined part of a conversation, are referred to as a *message exchange*. A conversation can be thus defined as a set of message exchanges among parties with the aim of fulfilling some goal. Every conversation is carried out over a communication facility, referred to as a communication network by parties. The specification differentiates among two type of parties, *initiating parties* and *answering services*. Both parties produce and consume messages, and additionally initiating parties take care of starting the message exchange.

Behavioural model

A *choreography* describes the behavior of the answering service from the initiating party's point of view (Roman, Scicluna, et al. 2005). It governs the message exchanges among parties in a conversation. Normally ASMs or Petri Nets are used to model the sequences of states the choreography goes through during its lifetime, together with its responses to events.

Operational model

The atomic building blocks that permit a number of mismatches among interacting parties to be resolved are *logic boxes*. A logic box facilitates the reorganization of the content of documents, its mapping to messages, and the order and cardinality of messages, thus enabling the interoperation among parties following different message exchange patterns. Additionally, and depending on the type of box, the differences in the vocabulary used to describe the application domain can be overcome. Currently the specification defines five different types of logic boxes, namely: *refiner box, merge box, split box, select box, add box.*

Semantic Model

Ontologies define the semantics of the engine. They provide a vocabulary that can be mediated for the understanding of interacting parties. *Domain ontologies* facilitate the general vocabulary to describe the application domain of the answering service and the initiating party. The *choreography ontology model* provides the conceptual framework and vocabulary required to describe choreographies. In doing so, it defines and allows reusing concepts for the definition of the structural and behavioral models of each party's choreography. Finally, *ontology mappings* put in place the mechanisms to link similar ontological concepts and instances and readily produce the operational model as a result of a reasoning task.

5.3   Interface Functions

SOPHIE exports the functions listed in Table 6-1.

Table 6-1. Interface functions of SOPHIE

---

generateOperationalModel (URI *choreographyOntology$_i$*,
                             URI *domainOntology$_i$*,
                             URI *choreographyOntology$_a$*,
                             URI *domainOntology$_i$*):
                                          operationalModel
removeOperationalModel (URI *operationalModel,*
                           URI *message,*
                           URI *choreographyOntology*): *void*

correlateMessage (URI *operationalModel,*
                      URI *message*): *operationalModel*

Intuitively, **generateOperationalModel** (*choreographyOntology$_i$,
domainOntology$_i$, choreographyOntology$_a$, domainOntology$_i$*) permits an
initiating party following the choreography "*choreography$_i$*" to indicate the
choreography service that wishes to establish a conversation with an
answering service following the choreography "*choreography$_a$*". As a
consequence, the operational model that will allow them to send and receive
messages according to the different message exchange patterns they are
using needs to be built. Additionally, the domain ontologies
"*domainOntology$_i$*", and "*domainOntology$_a$*" that describe the domain of
each one of the parties are also supplied. They allow the mediation of the
models used by the interacting parties. As a result, the choreography service
will generate and return the identifier of the operational model that will
govern the conversation.

removeOperationalModel (*operationalModel,   message,
choreographyOntology*) declares that the operational model
"*operationalModel*" is not any longer required by the parties taking part in
the conversation, and thus can be put off line.

The function **correlateMessage** (*operationalModel, message*) states that
the initiating party or the answering service desire their counterpart to
receive the message "*message*", which should go through the opertinal
model "*operationalModel*" in order to be adapted to the requirements of the
receiving choreography.

Initiating parties and answering services are not specified as part of the
parameters of the interface functions. It is important to do so because we
might want to allow parties to send messages to the framework on behalf of
others. In any case, the parameter *message*, specifies the sender and final

receiver of a concrete message. Also, for simplicity the concept of correlating party has been omitted in this section.

6.   CASE STUDY

SOPHIE is currently being trialed as part of the DIP (DIP) project B2B in Telecommunications case study, hosted by BT. SOPHIE has been applied to BT Wholesale's B2B Gateway which allows BT's ISP partners to integrate their Operation Support Systems with those of BT and, for example, carry out tests on BT's network as part of their broadband assurance activities. The B2B Gateway currently uses the Business Process Specifications of ebXML to represent the required choreography.

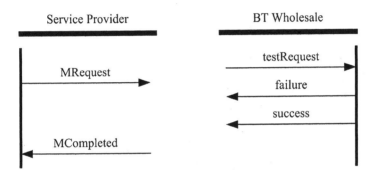

Figure 6-2. Request-Response and In-Multi-Out MEPs

The example applies the operational model of SOPHIE to the broadband test interface in order to illustrate how a partner's differing choreography could be integrated. Figure 6-2 shows the choreography of interacting parties following different MEPs as a realization of the same semantic web process. The Service Provider uses the message exchange *tPontTestRequest* following the MEP *request-response* while BT Wholesale makes use of the message exchange *eCoTestRequest* following the *In-Multi-Out* one. More concretely, the Service provider starts the message exchange with the *MRequest* message, while BT Wholesale expects the message *testRequest*. Additionally, BT provides two different response message (*failure* and *success*) indicating whether the test was accepted or rejected, and if accepted, the result of the test, while the *Service Provider* awaits the reception of a single message named *MCompleted* accounting for both of them.

Since both message exchanges are compatible, there exists a logic diagram which allows mapping the content, sequence and cardinality of both message exchanges.

Taking as input ontological mapping Ψ_X, that links the concepts that are similar in both choreography models the operational model that overcomes the heterogeneity ob both MEPs can be overcome a result of a reasoning task. Figure 6-3 details such model.

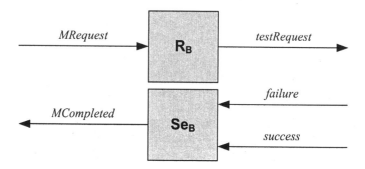

Figure 6-3. Resulting logic diagram

A refiner box is used to map the elements and documents within the message *"MRequest"* to the message *"testRequest"* as expected. Additionally, a select box was put in place to map the elements and documents used in the messages *"failure"* and *"success"* to the message *"MComplete"* containing the document *"DCompleted"*. Figure 6-3 shows the resulting logic diagram.

7.   CONCLUSIONS

This chapter has presented the main ideas and principles behind service choreography. In so doing it has carefully reviewed the main initiatives in the field with the aim of pointing out their drawbacks. Taking as starting point this analysis, the main driving principles and desire features, when it comes to modeling choreographies, were identified. Later, the most relevant challenges in the field, separation of models and support for semantic mediation were discussed. Based on this theoretical work, the core principles and architecture of a choreography engine that relies on the semantic description of MEPs to allow interoperation among heterogeneous services was presented. Finally, the concepts depicted on the framework as applied in the Assurance Integration Use case part of the DIP project (DIP) have been presented.

8. QUESTIONS FOR DISCUSSION

Beginner:
1. Usage and benefits of a centralized point of control vs. a decentralized one.
2. Benefits and extension of a layered model for choreography.

Intermediate:
1. Try to find real use cases where the support for transaction support within choreographies is required.
2. Discuss the benefits/drawbacks subsumed by a model that does not make any assumptions with respect to the underlying technology and one that is rigidly tight to a particular one.
3. Value added of using MEP to describe semantic business processes and their relation to choreography.

Advanced:
1. Discuss the main pros and cons of the different choreography-related initiatives paying special attention to their variable usage.

9. SUGGESTED READINGS

- Andrews, T., Curbera, F., Dholakia, H., Goland, Y., Klein, J., Leymann, F., Liu, K., Roller, D., Smith, D., Thatte, S., Trickovic, I., Weerawarana, S. *Business Process Execution Language for Web Services*, ftp://www6.software.ibm.com/software/developer/library/ws-bpel.pdf, 2003. Practitioners should find this specification to be quite valuable companion.
- Arkin, A., Askary, S., Fordin, S., Jekeli, W., Kawaguchi, K., Orchard, D., Pogliani, S., Riemer, K., Susan Struble S., Takacsi-Nagy, P., Trickovic, I. and Zimek, S. *Web Service Choreography Interface (WSCI) 1.0*, http://www.w3.org/TR/wsci/, 2002. This work provides a very consistent choreography specification.
- Arroyo, S. *SOPHIE - Semantic services chOreograPHi engInE*, PhD Thesis, To appear. The work provides a good insight to choreography from a semantic point of view.
- Kavantzas, N., Burdett, D., Ritzinger, G. *Web Services Choreography Description Language Version 1.0*, http://www.w3.org/TR/2004/WD-ws-cdl-10-20040427/, April 2004. This paper presents the WS-CDL specification.

- Barros, A., Dumas, M. and Oaks, P. *A Critical Overview of the Web Services Choreography Description Language (WS-CDL)*, BPTrends, March 2005. This paper presents a nice critical overview of WS-CDL.
- Roman, D., Scicluna, J., Feier, C., (eds.) Stollberg, M and Fensel, D. *D14v0.1. Ontology-based Choreography and Orchstration of WSMO Services*, http://www.wsmo.org/TR/d14/v0.1/, March, 2005. This deliverable is a good introduction to WSMO choreography.

10. REFERENCES

Arkin, A., Askary, S., et al. (2002). Web Service Choreography Interface (WSCI) Version 1.0, http://www.w3.org/TR/wsci/.

Arroyo, S. SOPHIE - Semantic services chOreograPHi engInE, PhD Thesis, To appear.

Arroyo, S., López Cobo, J.M. et al. (2005). Structural models of patterns of message interchange in decoupled hypermedia systems. International Workshop on Peer to Peer and Service Oriented Hypermedia: Techniques and Systems in conjunction with sixteenth ACM Conference on Hyertext and Hypermedia, (HT'05). Salzburg, Austria.

Arroyo, S. and Duke, A. (2005). SOPHIE - A Conceptual model for a Semantic Choreography Framework. Workshop on Semantic and Dynamic Web Process (SDWP'05) in conjunction with the International Conference on Web Services ICWS'05, Orlando, Florida, EEUU.

Arroyo, S., Sicilia, M. A. and López-Cobo, J. M. "Choreography Frameworks for Business Integration: Addressing Heterogeneous Semantics." Computers in Industry. Submitted.

Arroyo, S. and Kummenacher, R. A Choreographed Approach for Ubiquitous and Pervasive Learning. Ubiquitous and Pervasive Knowledge and Learning Management: Semantics, Social Networking and New Media to their full potential. Miltiadis D. Lytras and Ambjorn Naeve Editors. IDEA Group Inc. [to appear late 2006]

Arroyo, S. and Sicilia, M. A. (2005). SOPHIE – Architecture and Overall Algorithm of a Choreography Service. First Online Metadata and Semantics Research Conference.

Andrews, T., Curbera, F. et al. (2003). Business Process Execution Language for Web Services Version 1.1, ftp://www6.software.ibm.com/software/developer/library/ws-bpel.pdf.

Baader, F., Calvanese, D. et al. (2003). The Description Logic Handbook. Theory, Implementation and Applications. Cambridge, UK.

Barros, A., Dumas, M. et al. (2005). A Critical Overview of the Web Services Choreography Description Language (WS-CDL).BPTrends.

Berners-Lee, T., J. Hendler, et al. (2001). The Semantic Web. Scientific American. **May 2001**.

Booch, G., Rumbaugh, J. et al. (1999). The Unified Modelling Language User Guide. Addison-Wesley.

Brogi, A., Canal, C., et al. (2004). "Formalizing Web Services Choreographies." Electronic Notes in Theoretical Computer Science **105**, 73-94.

DIP-Data, Information, and Process with Semantic Web Services, http://dip.semanticweb.org/.

Chen, M. (2003). "Factors affecting the adoption and diffusion of XML and Web services standards for E-business systems." International Journal of Human-Computer Studies **58**(3), 259-279.

Erl, T. (2004). Service-Oriented Architecture – A Field Guide to Integrating XML and Web Services, Prentice Hall.

Fensel, D. and Bussler, C. (2002). "The Web Service Modeling Framework (WSMF)." Electronic Commerce: Research and Applications **1**:113-137.

Jung, J., Hur, W. et al. (2004). "Business process choreography for B2B collaboration." IEEE Internet Computing **8**(1), 37 – 45.

Kavantzas, N., Burdett et al. (2004). Web Services Choreography Description Language Version 1.0,
http://www.w3.org/TR/2004/WD-ws-cdl-10-20040427/

Roman, D., Scicluna, J., Feier, C. et al. (2005). D14v0.1. Ontology-based Choreography and Orchstration of WSMO Services,
http://www.wsmo.org/TR/d14/v0.1/

Tsalgatidou, A. and Pilioura, T. (2002). "An Overview of Standards and Related Technology." Web Services Distributed and Parallel Databases **12**:135–162.

World Wide Web Consortium,
http://www.w3.org/

Watkins, S., Arroyo, et al. (2005). D8.3: Prototype Platform Design" Case Study B2B in Telecommunications. DIP (Data, Information and Processes). **June 2005**.

XML Schema Part 2: Datatypes Second Edition, (2004)
http://www.w3.org/TR/xmlschema-2/.

Zaremba, M. and Moran M. (2004). D13.4v0.1 WSMX Architecture,
http://www.wsmo.org/2004/d13/d13.4/v0.1/20040622/.

Chapter 7

DESIGNING SEMANTIC WEB PROCESSES: THE WSDL-S APPROACH

Ke Li, Kunal Verma, Ranjit Mulye, Reiman Rabbani, John A. Miller, and Amit P. Sheth.
Large Scale Distributed Information Systems (LSDIS) Lab, Department of Computer Science, University of Georgia, GA, USA. – (ke,reiman,verma,jam,amit}@cs.uga.edu

1. INTRODUCTION

Many businesses are adopting Web Service technology to expose their business applications, enabling them to have business collaboration, both within their organization and with business partners outside. The adoption of the Service Oriented Architecture (SOA) helps businesses contract-out their non-critical functions. Web Services, based on the SOA, are inherently designed for interaction in a loosely coupled environment, and hence an ideal choice for companies seeking inter- or intra-business interactions that span heterogeneous platforms and systems. Growing wide acceptance of Web Services is largely due to the fact that they are built on XML based standards like SOAP, WSDL and UDDI. Simple Object Access Protocol (SOAP) is a lightweight protocol for exchange of information among Web Services. Web Service Description Language (WSDL) describes a Web service similar as an interface. The Universal Description, Discovery and Integration (UDDI) protocol creates a service lookup platform that enables a service provider to register Web Services, and enables a service consumer to quickly, easily, and dynamically find and locate Web Services over the Internet. The need arisen to interconnect the various services offered by different businesses to create a complex business process or workflow that spans wider boundaries than ever before. The Web Service Business Process

Execution Language (WS-BPEL) provides an XML-based language for the formal specification of business processes and business interaction protocols (OASIS).

The idea of building complex business processes has brought importance for tools that can model a business process. Though languages like WS-BPEL offer solutions for integrating Web Services into a business process, they are difficult to learn, involve understanding detailed language syntax and are only part of the solution for designing fully-functional Web processes. Tools that aid developers in easily building Web processes are becoming available; however, they do not alleviate several inherent limitations of current Web service technologies that make developing a process overly complicated or error-prone. Currently there are no Web Service composition tools that include discovery in a seamless fashion. The developer usually needs go to public, semi-public or local registries to look for partner services. Most UDDI registries supply Business Entity, Business Service and TModel as the searching format and adopt the syntactic searching mechanism. Users without enough knowledge about the partner services may spend much time searching for the suitable services, and they are likely to miss some highly suitable services. To solve this problem, we employ Semantic technology not only for the Web process designing task, but also for the whole Web Service lifecycle. A lightweight extension to the WSDL specification – WSDL-S (WSDL-S) is being jointly proposed by the LSDIS lab and IBM research. The WSDL-S specification allows annotating services and operations by mapping certain key elements to ontological concepts. These enhanced semantic services are published to a UDDI registry and can be dynamically discovered using some ontological concepts. This work enables users to find highly suitable and appropriate partner services in much less time than by manual discovery using a non-semantic, syntactic based UDDI searching mechanism. It also features the ability of partner services to be bound at design-time, deployment-time or execution-time (run-time) to further optimize the process and add greater dynamism, as opposed to the static-binding of partners.

In this work, we present a practical approach for designing Semantic Web Process using WSDL-S as a foundation. There are three tools used to accomplish this:

Radiant: Enables the service provider to annotate a WSDL file using ontological concepts and publish it to a UDDI registry.

Lumina: Allows the service requester to discover services with the required ontological concepts.

Saros: Helps the process developer to design a Semantic Web Service Process.

2.   BACKGROUND

Different approaches have been proposed for modeling a WS-BPEL process. These approaches aid in designing the process model and later converting it to a WS-BPEL format.

UML Activity Diagrams are candidates, but they are unable to model all patterns supported by WS-BPEL (Arkin, Askary, et al. 2005; Wohed, Aalst et al. 2002). To maximize compatibility with the standards, Saros uses its own abstraction model that resembles the WS-BPEL specification.

There are two ways to design a Web process using today's available tools; the first way is to use a text-editor and type in the BPEL syntax and expressions, and the second is to use a process designer tool.

Several tools are emerging as the need for a streamlined and efficient process development is growing. Some prominent tools in current usage are: IBM WSADIE Designer, Oracle BPEL Designer, CapeScience Orchestrator and Active Webflow. While most of the aforementioned tools have similar features to Saros, e.g., GUI, graphical design, auto-generate BPEL etc., we focused on Saros as it supports semantics in process design via the use of WSDL-S-based Semantic Template.

3.   DESIGN SEMANTIC WEB PROCESS USING WSDL-S

Before designing a Semantic Web Process, the Web services have to be annotated with ontological concepts using the extensibility elements and attributes provided with WSDL-S. The annotated files must then be published to an enhanced UDDI registry. This preparatory work supplies the possibility to carry out the partner services discovery at process design time / deployment time/execution time. The following three sections present the WSDL-S tool suite with an emphasis on how they can be used together to conveniently create Semantic Web Processes.

3.1   Service Annotation and Publish using Radiant

WSDL-S supplies an effective approach for describing Web Services by annotating WSDL elements with ontological concepts. Radiant was developed by the METEOR-S group to facilitate this annotation. This tool provides an easy-to-use GUI for a Web Service developer to do the following: 1. Add WSDL-S namespace and other namespaces for all the ontologies used; 2. Drag and drop ontological concepts to the suitable

WSDL elements (element, operation, input, output); 3. Add precondition/effect as a child element of operation. Furthermore, it also provides the ability to annotate a Java file with semantic concepts using source code annotations. Figure 7-1 is a screen shot of the METEOR-S Radiant Tool for Semantic Annotation which used to annotate WSDL elements with ontological concepts.

Figure 7-1. Screen Shot of METEOR-S Radiant Tool

As mentioned in Chapter 2, UDDI currently does not support publication or discovery of Semantic Web Services. To enhance UDDI to support semantics, we define an infrastructure to map WSDL-S to UDDI, shown in Figure 7-2, and the mapping details are given in Table 7-1. This is loosely based on UDDI Best Practice (Colgrave and Anuszewski, 2003), which defines a mapping from WSDL to UDDI. As shown in the figure, a WSDL-S service is captured using Business Service entity in UDDI, while portType and each operation within the WSDL-S service is captured using Technical Model.

After annotating a WSDL file to produce a WSDL-S file, the Radiant tool supplies the functionality to publish the service to a UDDI registry. Moreover, during publication using Radiant, users can publish service provider information as a Business Entity and publish services based on WSDL files, see Figure 7-3.

Table 7-1. WSDL-S to UDDI Mapping Detail

WSDL-S	UDDI
Service	**Business Service**
Local name	Name
Service description	Description
Namespace, wsdl location	CategoryBag
portType	**TModel**
Local name	Name
Wsdl location	OverviewDoc
Namespace	CategoryBag
Operation	**TModel**
Local name	Name
Wsdl location	OverviewDoc
Namespace,domain,inputs, outputs,ontological concepts for operation, inputsand outputs, service name,business name	CategoryBag

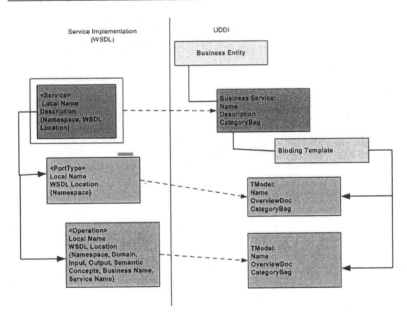

Figure 7-2. Mapping WSDL-S to UDDI

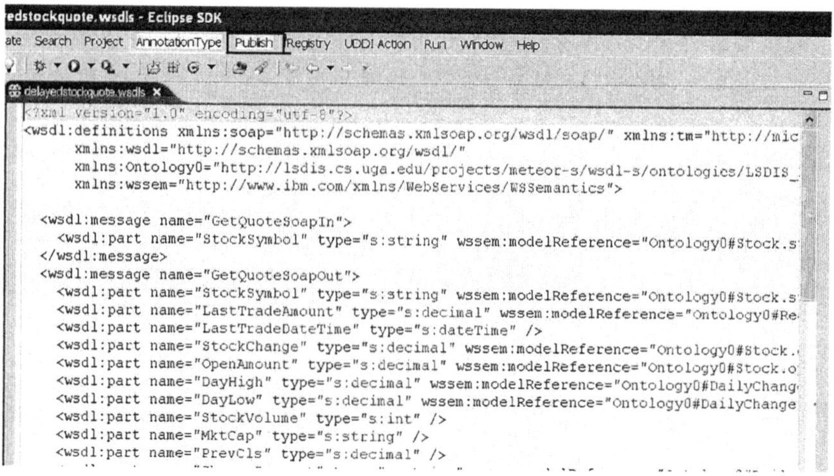

```
edstockquote.wsdls - Eclipse SDK
ate  Search  Project  AnnotationType  Publish  Registry  UDDI Action  Run  Window  Help

  delayedstockquote.wsdls  ×

<?xml version="1.0" encoding="utf-8"?>
<wsdl:definitions xmlns:soap="http://schemas.xmlsoap.org/wsdl/soap/" xmlns:tm="http://mic
    xmlns:wsdl="http://schemas.xmlsoap.org/wsdl/"
    xmlns:Ontology0="http://lsdis.cs.uga.edu/projects/meteor-s/wsdl-s/ontologies/LSDIS_
    xmlns:wssem="http://www.ibm.com/xmlns/WebServices/WSSemantics">

  <wsdl:message name="GetQuoteSoapIn">
    <wsdl:part name="StockSymbol" type="s:string" wssem:modelReference="Ontology0#Stock.s
  </wsdl:message>
  <wsdl:message name="GetQuoteSoapOut">
    <wsdl:part name="StockSymbol" type="s:string" wssem:modelReference="Ontology0#Stock.s
    <wsdl:part name="LastTradeAmount" type="s:decimal" wssem:modelReference="Ontology0#Re
    <wsdl:part name="LastTradeDateTime" type="s:dateTime" />
    <wsdl:part name="StockChange" type="s:decimal" wssem:modelReference="Ontology0#Stock.
    <wsdl:part name="OpenAmount" type="s:decimal" wssem:modelReference="Ontology0#Stock.o
    <wsdl:part name="DayHigh" type="s:decimal" wssem:modelReference="Ontology0#DailyChang
    <wsdl:part name="DayLow" type="s:decimal" wssem:modelReference="Ontology0#DailyChange
    <wsdl:part name="StockVolume" type="s:int" />
    <wsdl:part name="MktCap" type="s:string" />
    <wsdl:part name="PrevCls" type="s:decimal" />
```

Figure 7-3. Publish Web Services using Radiant

3.2   Semantic Discovery using Lumina

Based upon the WSDL-S to UDDI mapping structure, the Lumina GUI tool was developed to facilitate Semantic Web Service discovery during process design time or deployment time. The requirements of the user are captured using a semantic template, which captures the abstract functionality of a Web service. The information captured includes a list of abstract operations whose functionality, inputs and outputs are defined using ontological concepts. The discovery engine returns services that are annotated with ontological concepts that are the same or semantically related to concepts in the template.

When discovering a service based on the WSDL-S description, the user can add one or more ontology URLs in the discovery panel and input the ontological concepts to represent input, outputs and operations. After discovery, the result will be shown in the result panel. The result gives not only the operation's detail information, but also the related service and the service provider's information. See Figure 7-4 which shows the annotation of the operation and the result of the discovered services.

Many services have multiple operations within them. With the consideration of economic and connection convenience, the process developers usually would likely to invoke as many operations as possible from one partner service. To deal with this problem, Lumina enables the user to find services that hold more than one required operations. Figure 7-5 shows this by listing two operations in one service.

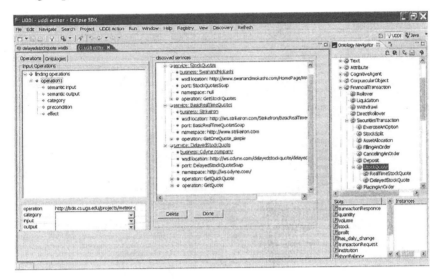

Figure 7-4. WSDL-S Discovery

Moreover, to complement today's non-semantic discovery and give more flexibility for the users to search in different UDDI registries, Lumina provides general UDDI discovery. Using the same mapping structure as WSDL-S to UDDI, Radiant can publish a WSDL file to a UDDI registry directly. This enables Lumina to discover the services described in WSDL based on the keyword searching mechanism. Figure 7-6 shows the general UDDI Discovery format, which has a familiar style to the current UDDI users.

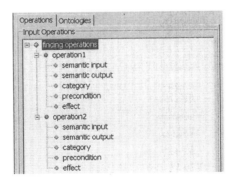

Figure 7-5. Searching Service with Multiple Operations

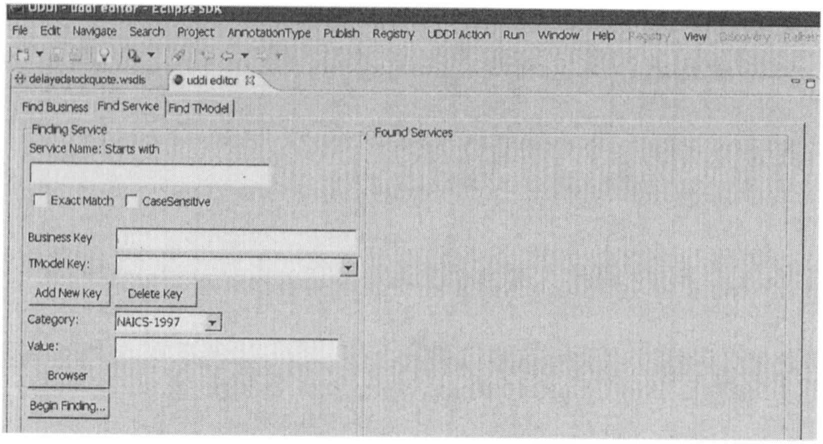

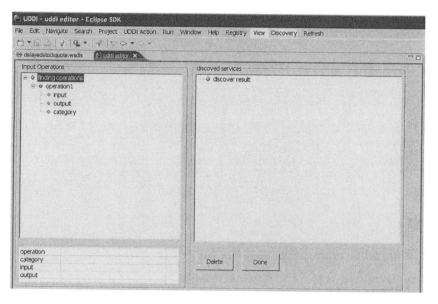

Figure 7-6. General UDDI Discovery Panel

Figure 7-7 shows the WSDL Discovery panel. To support the users who wish to use different UDDI registries, Lumina allows the user to add new UDDI registries to the environment and use a uniform searching style to do the discovery.

Figure 7-7. WSDL Discovery Panel

Figure 7-8 shows the registry control panel, which holds the different registries' information and allows users to add or edit a registry

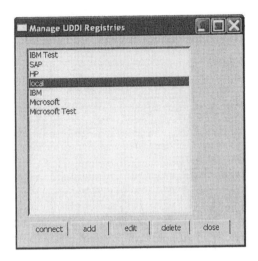

Figure 7-8. Registry Control Panel

3.3 Process Design using Saros

3.3.1 Methodology

To support capabilities for dynamic partner selections, the Saros tool makes use of Semantic Template technology. A semantic template can be used to insert a virtual partner into the Web Process. The selection process can be thought of as being constituted of two phases, which are elaborated below.

In the first phase, the process developer generates a semantic template by using the Semantic Template Viewer, which can graphically capture the ontological concepts of the desired virtual partner Web Services, allowing constraints, policies and operational conditions to be added. The developer can add operations to the template and specify the input and output messages for each operation. Each of these entities is annotated by the ontological concepts. The developer can either create a new template or s/he has a choice to load an existing template.

Phase two utilizes the core searching mechanism for dynamic partner discovery.

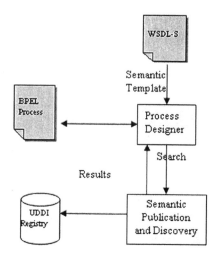

Figure 7-9. Phase II - Dynamic Partner Discovery

In the second, once the semantic template has been generated, Lumina then processes it for partner discovery. Lumina extracts the semantic information from the template using the METEOR-S WSDLS4J Java implementation and passes it to the discovery module. The discovery module performs semantic search and returns a set of matching ranked results. To further find better matched Web Services, the returned set may be passed through a constraint analyzer module that was developed by the METOER-S lab (Verma, Gomadam, et.al. 2005). An example of some constraints could be TurnAroundTime <= 7 days or Cost<=$5000 or Virtual Partner A, B and C must be compatible with each other. Therefore the process developer can use the semantic template for dynamic partner discovery while s/he is designing the process, so the exact Web Service instance is known beforehand. This phase is explained in Figure 7-9. Alternatively, the semantic template can be used to create a Virtual Partner in the Web Process and the discovery can be deferred until run-time/execution. Both options are available using the Saros and Lumina tools.

There are three types of service binding in a Web Process supported by the WSDL-S tool suite as outlined below:

1. Design-time: The set of partners are permanently bound to the Web Process during the design phase.
2. Deployment-time: Uses a virtual partner at design-time, but during deployment the partners are bound to the discovered Web Services. This happens before execution of the process.

3. Run-time: After process instances have started executing, the partners are (re-) discovered and bound.

3.3.2   Architecture of Saros

This section presents an overview of the METEOR-S Process Design Tool – SAROS. The UI of the Process design and development tool consists mainly of three components: Element Palette, Process Canvas, and Element Property Sheet, as illustrated in Figure 7-10. The process designer uses the Model View Controller (MVC) (Reenskaug, 2003) pattern as the underlying architecture. To realize this architecture it uses the Graphical Editing Framework (GEF) toolkit, which is part of the Eclipse tool integration platform. This tool is integrated with Eclipse as an Eclipse plug-in or can be run as an Eclipse application. Figure 7-11 shows a diagram of the tool architecture using the MVC pattern.

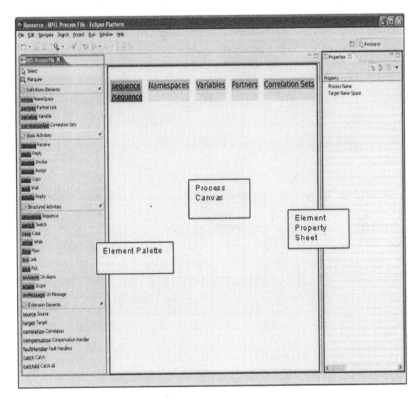

Figure 7-10. METEOR-S Process Design and Development Tool

1. MODEL VIEW CONTROLLER (MCV) ARCHITECTURE

The MVC architecture is a commonly used and effective architecture to build GUI-based systems because it separates the code from the model and view. The "Model" defines the behavior of the application logic, representing the in-memory model of the entire process. The "View" handles the graphical rendering of the model to the UI. The "Controller" is the code that forms the link between the model and the view; it is responsible for handling the editing of BPEL element properties.

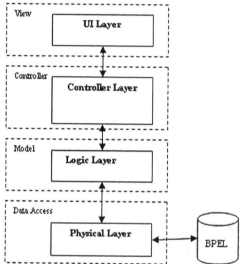

Figure 7-11. METEOR-S Semantic Process Design and Development Tool Architecture

2. GRAPHICAL EDITING FRAMEWORK (GEF)

GEF enables developers to create a rich graphical editor for an existing application model (Graphical Editing Framework). The process designer uses the GEF framework to build its graphical user interface because both use the MVC pattern. GEF is fully written in Java and works on all operating systems officially supported by the Eclipse platform (Open platform for tool integration), thereby eliminating any porting issues. GEF depends on Draw2d which is a lightweight toolkit built · with the Standard Widget Toolkit (SWT) and offers optimized layout and painting along with providing a native look and feel for the GUI.

USABILITY FEATURES

Saros offers an easy to use GUI for process developers to rapidly build Web processes. Process developers are offered support for dragging and dropping of process elements on a process "canvas". This, combined with ease of element selection and deletion, offers a simple to use GUI. Selecting a particular element opens up a property sheet that allows the user to modify element properties. This approach helps in hiding the unnecessary syntactic details from the developer. Other usability features are outlined below.

• Color coded process activities

The activities have been categorized by functionality so that the developer can quickly understand the canvas visually and intuitively.

• Definition lookup

Many of the basic activities of the business process have properties that refer to definition elements (Variables, Partnerlinks or XML namespaces). To avoid typographical errors, the Process designer tool offers a drop-down box of available choices for the entries. Figure 7-12 provides a sample illustration of this feature.

Property	Value	
⊟ Misc		
Create Instance	No	
Name	Receive1	
Operation		
Partner Link		
Supress Join Failure	No	
Variable		▾
⊟ Port Type		
PortType Local Part	processRequest	
PortType Namespace P...	processReply	
	serviceReply	
	serviceRequest	

Figure 7-12. Definition Lookup

• Avoiding ambiguous process designs

Before allowing addition of a new element to a container type element, Saros validates the insertion. This prevents the process from being in an ambiguous state. For example, the only valid addition to an activity of "Switch" is a case activity, others are not allowed.

• Designing complex processes

Container elements such as sequence, flow, etc. can be nested to any depth. This helps in generating a process with arbitrary complexity but intuitive visualization.

• Intuitive help messages

The tool provides descriptive messages for many of the editable properties of process elements in the status bar. Figure 7-13 shows an illustration of such a help message.

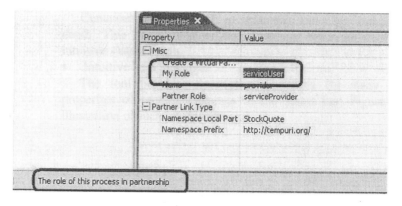

Figure 7-13. Status bar Helper Message

4.   SAMPLE USE CASE

In this section, we present a use case in the finance field. Consider this scenario, an investment company provides a service that helps their customers analyze the feasibility of buying some stocks. This service gives the evaluation result based on the following stock ticker information: current price, volume, bid quantity, the highest price in the past one year, earnings per share, and how much money the customer wants to invest. The customer tells the service which stocks s/he is interested in and how much money s/he may invest. The remaining information should depend on other partner services. Following our the WSDL-S approach, we give an outline of 8 steps to present how to use the BPEL Designer tool – Saros – to design such a composite service. These steps also make use of the Lumina discovery tool.

1. **Analyze the business requirement and build a UML diagram**. In this use case, the investment company will use an evaluation service. This service can either belong to the company or belong to the other investment companies. Such an evaluation service needs the stock quote information and the corresponding company financial profile of the past one year. We need two partner services to fill in the above requirements, respectively. Moreover, the two partner services can run simultaneously because they do not depend on each other. The UML diagram is shown in Figure 7-14 according to this use case.

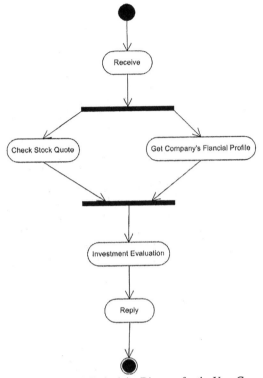

Figure 7-14. UML Activity Diagram for the User Case

2. **Fill in the process skeleton:** Map the process sequence in the activity diagram to the sequence element of WS-BPEL, shown in Figure 7-15.

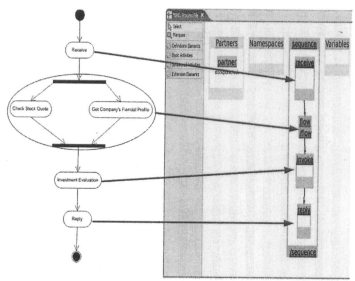

Figure 7-15. Process Skeleton

3. **Fill in the nested constructs/structured activities**: such as Flow, Switch, While, etc. We insert two "Invoke" in the "Flow" for invoking the corresponding two simultaneous partner services, shown in Figure 7-16.

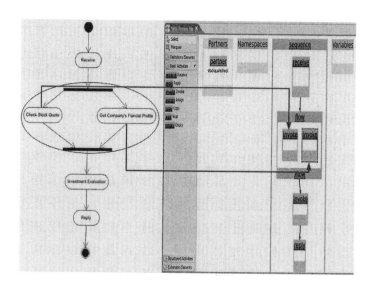

Figure 7-16. Fill in Nested Constructs

4. Identify Partners by using either one of the following methods:

- Binding the real partners: Based on the business requirements, Lumina can help the developer find highly suitable partner services. It provides two GUIs to accomplish the partner services discovery: UDDI Editor and Semantic Template View. Although their discovery functionalities are the same, they focus on different design aspects. The UDDI Editor provides the flexibility for the developer to do the discovery using both the WSDL-S approach and the general UDDI discovery approach by using Business Entity, Business Service and TModel. The Semantic Template View focuses on building a discovery template based on the business requirements, and its "easy to drag" property enables it to be used with Saros. Because we focus on the WSDL-S approach, here we use the Semantic Template View in our example.

In this use case, the investment company needs an investment evaluation service. The developer can use the company's own service or search for a more suitable one. The only knowledge about this service is that it can perform investment evaluation. We use the SUMO Finance ontology as the domain knowledge base. Here we choose ontologyNS#investing to annotate the service's operation. Two services are found and the discovered service provides the detailed information at both the service level and the operation level, shown in Figure 7-17.

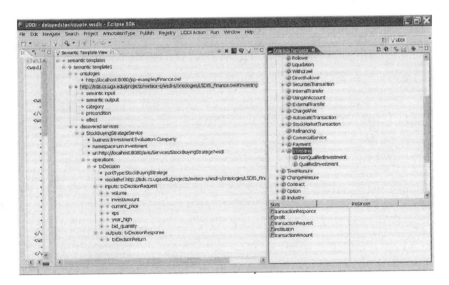

Figure 7-17. Discovery the Basic Service Using Operation's Domain Concept

In the next step, we can use the operation information of the discovered service to search for the other two services: the "stock quote" service and the "company profile" service. There are six attributes in the discovered operation's input message. The current_price, bid_quantity and volume belong to "stock quote" service; the eps (earning per share) and year_high belong to "company profile" service; the investAmount is provided by the customer. We build the other two semantic templates and add the corresponding output concepts to them respectively.

- Binding the virtual partners: Shown in Figure 7-18, there are eight Web services discovered for the "stock quote" service. The developer can pick the most suitable one and insert it to the process if s/he wants to build an executable BPEL process. Alternatively, s/he can make the chosen decision later and build an abstract BPEL process by adding a virtual partner based on the semantic template. The advantages of using the semantic template technology to build an abstract BPEL process fall in two aspects: i) After partner selection has been finalized in the BPEL process, it is possible that more optimal services become available (in regards to various pre-defined quality properties, e.g., cost, time, reliability, accuracy, etc.). ii) The partner functionalities or the user terms change, or a partner becomes unavailable unbeknownst to the process. These problems would render the Web process prone to errors. The Semantic Template View in Lumina enables the developer to design the semantic template graphically with the help of Radiant. Moreover, it can generate the semantic template files or load the semantic template files built previously. Saros can link these semantic template files as the virtual partners. Appendix A shows one semantic template file and Figure 7-19 shows in the box how Saros adds a virtual partner using the file.

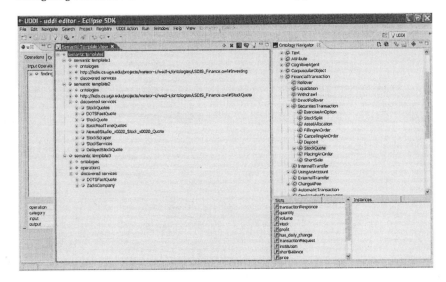

Figure 7-18. Discovery Partner Services Using Input and Output Attributes' Domain Concepts

5. **Add Namespaces, Variables and Correlation Sets constructs (for executable BPEL process)**: Add the namespace for each partner service. Create all the variables for the message exchange between the services. All the information in this design phase can be found in the discovered services shown by Lumina.

6. **Link Partners to Invoke, Receive and Reply constructs (for executable BPEL process)**: Link the partner to the corresponding activity element by clicking on the element objects property view from a drop down list.

7. **Add the supplementary elements and fill in details**: Add "assign", "copy", "link" etc to accomplish the process.

8. **Generate BPEL process**: The BPEL process file and the corresponding process WSDL file are generated by clicking on the save button. The complete BPEL and WSDL files for our scenario are in Appendix B and Appendix C. The completed process view is at Figure 7-20 and Figure 7-21.

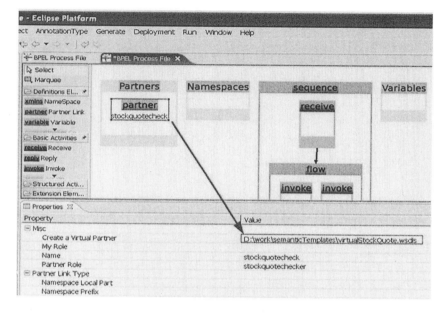

Figure 7-19. Add a Virtual Partner

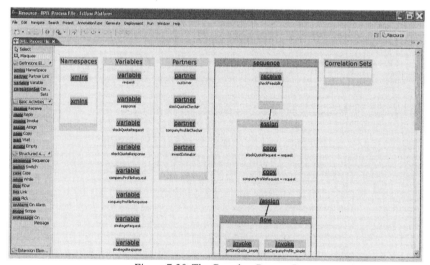

Figure 7-20. The Complete Process I

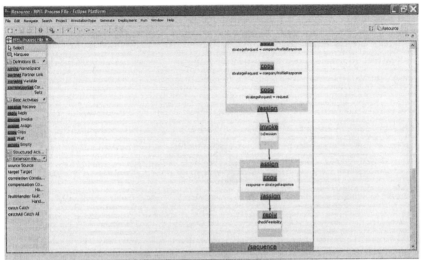

Figure 7-21. The Complete Process II

5. RELATED WORK

The methodologies of automatic Web Services composition are mainly separated into two categories: workflow composition and AI planning. To achieve automatic Web Service composition, there are two tasks that should be done. One is to generate an abstract process model by analyzing the process requirements; the other is to dynamically discover and bind the concrete services for the abstract process. The methods to solve the first task are usually related to AI planning and deductive theorem proving.

The workflow composition approach can be further divided into two levels: static workflow composition and dynamic workflow composition. In static workflow composition, the abstract process model is designed by the process developer and the concrete services are discovered, located and combined automatically. EFlow (Casati, Ilnicki, et al. 2000) adopts a graph oriented approach to implement a static workflow composition. There are three types of nodes in the graph: service, decision and event. Arcs represent the dependency relationships between two nodes. The service node gives the service's requirements which are used to discover and bind a concrete service to the process model either at process instantiation time, or at process execution time. Composite Service Definition Language (CSDL) (Casati, Sayal, et al, 2001) is another approach for static workflow composition. It pays attention not only to service level, but also to the operation level.

Polymorphic Process Model (PPM) (Schuster, Georgakopoulos, et al. 2000) adopts a state machine to implement service based dynamic composition, while the sub services still follow the static workflow composition approach.

The AI planning problem in Web Service composition can be described using five attributes: the initial state, the final goal, all the available services, the state change functions and all the possible states. Golog is a logic programming language built on top of the situation calculus (a logical language for reasoning about the state change according to actions). Several papers (McIlraith, Son, et al. 2001; Narayanan and McIlraith, 2002; McIraith and Son, 2002) have extended Golog for automatic Web Service composition. The Planning Domain Definition Language (PDDL) (Schuster, Georgakopoulos, et al., 2000) is a language designed specifically to support AI planning. McDermott (McDermott, 2002) presented Web Service composition based on PDDL. The author introduced a new value – value of an action – to deal with the closed world assumption in the AI planning. In the closed world assumption, the literal's value is false if it does not exist in the current world. However, this assumption may fail in the automatic Web Service composition procedure, because a new Web Service can be dynamically created, changing the state of the knowledgebase. SWORD (Ponnekanti and Fox, 2002) is another toolkit for Web Service composition based on rule-based plan generation. It adopts the Entity Relationship Model (ER) to describe the set of preconditions and postconditions of a service. SHOP2 (Wu, Sirin, et al. 2003) is a Hierarchical Task Network (HTN) based planner and adopts OWL-S as its description language. A detailed survey of different approaches for workflow composition and AI planning that can be found in (Rao and Su, 2004).

6. CONCLUSION

In this work, we presented the current research and development in the area of Semantic Web Processes. We discussed the importance of Web Services discovery for designing a Web Process, and pointed out that the current non-semantic Web Service technologies do not support automatic Web Service discovery well. WSDL-S jointly proposed by the LSDIS lab and IBM research, is a Semantic Web Service standard candidate which intends to solve the problems of non-semantic Web Service technologies. To indicate the functionalities of WSDL-S in Semantic Web Process design, we applied our WSDL-S based tools – Radiant, Lumina, Saros – to the whole Web Service lifecycle. Following our WSDL-S based approach, the Web Process developer can find the partner services efficiently and effectively. Moreover, by cooperating with the Semantic Template technique in Lumina,

Saros enables the developer to design an abstract Web Process by inserting virtual partners. This property facilitates partner search at design time or deployment time, and is helpful to adapt to the Web Service environments which change dynamically. Furthermore, this work highlights some key usability features of the WSDL-S based tool suite that assist process developers in easily designing complex business processes.

The potential of the WSDL-S approach is much more than what we showed in the current tool suite. For example, we do not take "preconditions" and "effects" into consideration. As demonstrated in pervious chapters, the search result can be more accurate by using non-functional constrains, such as cost, reliability, quality, etc. The project of adding WS-Policy to Web Service discovery is on going in the METEOR-S group.

In this work, we used the WSDL-based tool suite to design a Web Process semi-automatically. In some cases, the discovered partner services can not be inserted automatically, because we have yet to complete the data mapping part of this work.

7. QUESTIONS FOR DISCUSSION

Beginner:
1. What are the major entities in UDDI?
2. What is the usage of UDDI for the Web Service Composition?

Intermediate:
1. How is the Semantic Template helpful to build an abstract Web Process?
2. What are the advantages of allowing the developer to put multiple operations within one Semantic Template?
3. Give the mapping structure between WSDL-S and UDDI.

Advanced:
1. What is the usage of a Virtual Partner?

Practical Exercises:
1. Download the three tools - Radiant, Lumina and Saros - from LSDIS web site from http://lsdis.cs.uga.edu/projects/meteor-s/downloads/. Use the Sumo-Finance ontology (same URL as above) to annotate several WSDL files and publish them to an enhanced UDDI registry.
2. Discover the services by using the ontology concepts.
3. Design a Web Process.

8. SUGGESTED ADDITIONAL READING

- Narayanan S., and McIlraith S., "Simulation, Verification and Automated Composition of Web Services" Proceedings of the eleventh international conference on World Wide Web, May 2002, pp. 77 – 88.
- Verma K., Akkiraju R., Goodwin R., Doshi P., and Lee J., "On Accommodating Inter Service Dependencies in Web Process Flow Composition", 2004 AAAI Spring Symposium Series, March 2004, pp. 37-43.
- Rajasekaran P., Miller J., Verma K., Sheth A., "Enhancing Web Services Description and Discovery to Facilitate Composition", Proceedings of the 1st International Workshop on Semantic Web Services and Web Process Composition, July 2004, pp. 55-68.
- Ranjit Mulye, John A. Miller, Kunal Verma, Karthik Gomadam and Amit P. Sheth, "A Semantic Template Based Designer for Semantic Web Processes," Proceedings of the 3rd International Conference on Web Services (ICWS'05), Orlando, Florida (July 2005).
- Rama Akkiraju, Joel Farell, John A. Miller, Meena Nagarajan, Amit Sheth and Kunal Verma, "Web Service Semantics - WSDL-S," Proceedings of the W3C Workshop on Frameworks for Semantics in Web Service (*W3CW'05*), Innsbruck, Austria (June 2005)
- Rohit Aggarwal, Kunal Verma, John A. Miller and William Milnor, "Constraint Driven Web Service Composition in METEOR-S," Proceedings of the 2004 IEEE International Conference on Services Computing (SCC'04), Shanghai, China (September 2004) pp. 23-32
- Sivashanmugam K., Verma K., Sheth A., and Miller J., "Adding Semantics to Web Services Standards", 1st International Conference on Web Services, June 2003, pp. 395-401
- Kunal Verma, Kaarthik Sivashanmugam, Amit P. Sheth, Abhijit Patil, Swapna Oundhakar and John A. Miller, "METEOR-S WSDI: A Scalable P2P Infrastructure of Registries for Semantic Publication and Discovery of Web Services," *Journal of Information Technology and Management* (*ITM*), Special Issue on Universal Global Integration, Vol. 6, No. 1 (2005) pp. 17-39. Kluwer Academic Publishers.

9. REFERENCES

Universal Description, Discovery and Integration (UDDI), *http://www.uddi.org/*
Web Services Business Process Execution Language (WS-BPEL), *http://www.oasis-open.org/committees/tc_home.php?wg_abbrev=WS-BPEL*

METEOR-S: Semantic Web Services and Processes, *http://lsdis.cs.uga.edu/projects/METEOR-S/*

Narayanan S., and McIlraith S., "Simulation, Verification and Automated Composition of Web Services" Proceedings of the eleventh international conference on World Wide Web, May 2002, Pages: 77 - 88

Traverso P., and Pistore M., "Automated Composition of Semantic Web Services into Executable Processes", Proceedings of the 3rd International Semantic Web Conference (ISWC2004), pp. 380-394

W.M.P. van der Aalst and A.H.M. ter Hofstede. YAWL: Yet Another Workflow Language. QUT Technical report, FIT-TR-2002-06, Queensland University of Technology, Brisbane, 2002

Rajasekaran P., Miller J., Verma K., Sheth A., "Enhancing Web Services Description and Discovery to Facilitate Composition", Proceedings of the 1st International Workshop on Semantic Web Services and Web Process Composition, July 2004, pp. 55-68

J. Miller, D. Palaniswami, A. Sheth, K. Kochut, H. Singh, "WebWork: METEOR's Web-based Workflow Management System", Journal of Intelligence Information Management Systems, 1997, pp. 185-215

Nau D., Cao Y.,Lotem A.,and Muñoz-Avila H, "SHOP: Simple Hierarchical Ordered Planner", Proceedings of the Sixteenth International Joint Conference on Artificial Intelligence, 1999, Pages 968 - 975

GEF: Graphical Editing Framework, *http://www.eclipse.org/gef/*

Verma K., Akkiraju R., Goodwin R., Doshi P., and Lee J., "On Accommodating Inter Service Dependencies in Web Process Flow Composition", 2004 AAAI Spring Symposium Series, March 2004, pp 37-43

Berners-Lee, T., Hendler, J., Lassila, O., "The Semantic Web", Scientific American, May 2001, pp. 34-43

WSDL: Web Service Description Language, *http://www.w3.org/TR/wsdl*

Zarras A., Vassiliadis P., and Issarny V., "Model-Driven Dependability Analysis of Web Services", International Symposium on Distributed Objects and Applications, October 2004, pp. 69-79

Ponnekanti S., and Fox A., "SWORD: A Developer Toolkit for Web Service Composition", In Eleventh World Wide Web Conference (WWW2002, Web Engineering Track), Honolulu, Hawaii, May 2002.

Dogac A., "Exploiting Semantic of Web Services through ebXML Registries", Keynote Talk, 14th International Workshop on Research Issues on Data Engineering, Boston, 2004, *ttp://www.srdc.metu.edu.tr/~asuman/Dogac_RIDE_04_KeynoteAddress.ppt*

Dong X., Halevy A., Madhavan J., Nemes E., and Zhang J., "Similarity Search for Web Services", 30th VLDB Conference, August - September 2004, pp. 372-383

UML: Unified Modeling Language, Object Management Group, *http://www.uml.org/*

Paolucci M., Sycara K., and Kawamura T., "Delivering Semantic Web Services" In Proceedings WWW2003, May 2003, pp. 829

Sivashanmugam K., Verma K., Sheth A., and Miller J., "Adding Semantics to Web Services Standards", 1st International Conference on Web Services, June 2003, pp. 395-401.

Web Service Semantics – WSDL-S, W3C member submission, Version 1.0, 7 November 2005

Aggarwal R., Verma K., Miller J., and Milnor W., "Constraint Driven Web Service Composition in METEOR-S" Proceedings of the 2004 IEEE International Conference on Services Computing (SCC 2004), Shanghai, China (September 2004) pp. 23-32.

Verma K., Sivashanmugam K., Sheth A., Patil A., Oundhakar S., and Miller J., "METEOR-S WSDI: A Scalable Infrastructure of Registries for Semantic Publication and Discovery of

Web Services", Journal of Information Technology and Management, Special Issue on Universal Global Integration, Vol. 6, No. 1 (2005) pp. 17-39. Kluwer Academic Publishers

Aggarwal R., Verma K., Miller J., and Milnor W., "Dynamic Web Service Composition in METEOR-S", Technical Report, LSDIS Lab, Computer Science Dept., UGA, May 2004.

Sirin E., Parsia B., and Hendler J., "Composition-driven filtering and selection of semantic Web services", AAAI Spring Symposium on Semantic Web Services, 2004, pp. 129-138

Sivashanmugam K., Miller J., Sheth A., and Verma K., "Framework for Semantic Web Process Composition", International Journal of Electronic Commerce (IJEC), Special Issue on Semantic Web Services and Their Role in Enterprise Application Integration and E-Commerce, Vol. 9, No. 2 (Winter 2004-5) pp. 71-106. M.E. Sharpe, Inc.

Reenskaug T., "The Model-View-Controller (MVC) Its Past and Present", http://heim.ifi.uio.no/~trygver/2003/javazone-jaoo/MVC_pattern.pdf

OWL-S: Semantic Markup for Web Services, *http://www.daml.org/services/owl-s/1.0/owl-s.html*

Eclipse: Open platform for tool integration, *http://www.eclipse.org/*

Oracle BPEL Process Manager, http://www.oracle.com/technology/products/ias/bpel/index.html

IBM WebSphere: *http://www-306.ibm.com/software/websphere/*

A. Sheth, "Semantic Web Process Lifecycle: Role of Semantics in Annotation, Discovery, Composition and Orchestration", Invited Talk WWW 2003 Workshop on E-Services and the Semantic Web, Budapest, Hungary, May 2003, http://www.ics.forth.gr/isl/essw2003/talks/seth_essw_semanticwebprocess.htm

K. Sivashanmugam, A. Sheth, J. Miller, K.Verma, R. Aggarwal, P. Rajasekaran, "Metadata and Semantics for Web Services and Processes", 2003, Book Chapter, Datenbanken und Informationssysteme: Festschrift zum 60- Geburtstag von Gunter Schlageter, Benn et al Eds, Praktische Informatik I, Hagen, pp. 245-272.

A. Patil, S. Oundhakar, A. Sheth and K. Verma, "METEOR-S Web service Annotation Framework", World Wide Conference, In the Proceedings of the 13th W3C Confernece, New York, USA, 2004, pp. 553-563.

K. Sivashanmugam, K. Verma and A. Sheth, "Discovery of Web Services in a Federated Registry Environment", 2004, Proceedings of IEEE Second International Conference on Web Services, San Diego, California, USA, pp. 270-278.

Dumas M., and ter Hofstede A. H. M, "UML Activity Diagrams as a Workow Speci_cation Language", *Lecture Notes in Computer Science*, vol. 2185, pp. 76–90, 2001

WS-Policy: Web Services Policy Framework, http://www-128.ibm.com/developerworks/library/specification/ws-polfram/

SWT: The Standard Widget Toolkit, http://www.eclipse.org/swt/

BPWS4J: The IBM Business Process Execution Language for Web Services Java™ Run Time, *http://www.alphaworks.ibm.com/tech/bpws4j*

ActiveBPEL, Open Source BPEL Server, http://www.activebpel.org/

Kochut K., Sheth A., and Miller J., "ORBWork: A COBRA-Based Fully Distributed Scalable and Dynamic Workflow Enactment Service for METEOR", Technical Report #UGA-CS-TR-98-006, Department of Computer Science, University of Georgia, 1998

METEOR: Managing End-To-End OpeRations, http://lsdis.cs.uga.edu/Projects/past/METEOR/

Simple Object Access Protocol (SOAP) 1.1, http://www.w3.org/TR/soap/

Peltz C, "Web Services Orchestration and Choreography", Web Services Journal, Volume 03 Issue 07, July 2003, pages 30-35

Doshi P., Goodwin R., Akkiraju R., and Verma K., "Dynamic Workflow Composition using Markov Decision Processes", International Journal of Web Services Research, 2005, pp. 1-17

RosettaNet: *http://www.rosettanet.org*

Azami M., RosettaNet Ontology, *http://lsdis.cs.uga.edu/~azami/pips.html*

Kitamura Y., and Mizoguchi R.,"Functional Ontology for Functional Understanding", Twelfth International Workshop on Qualitative Reasoning (QR-98), Cape Cod, USA, AAAI Press, 1998, pp.77-87

Gardner D., Knuth K.H., Abato M., Erde S.M., White T., DeBellis R., and Gardner, Common data model for neuroscience data and data model interchange. J. Am. Med. Informatics Assoc. 8(1): 17-33, 2001

Kunal Verma, Karthik Gomadam, Amit P. Sheth, John A. Miller, Zixin Wu, "The METEOR-S Approach for Configuring and Executing Dynamic Web Processes", LSDIS METEOR-S project Technical Report . Date: 6-24-05

Ranjit Mulye, John A. Miller, Kunal Verma, Karthik Gomadam and Amit P. Sheth, "A Semantic Template Based Designer for Semantic Web Processes," Proceedings of the 3rd International Conference on Web Services (ICWS'05), Orlando, Florida (July 2005)

Rama Akkiraju, Joel Farell, John A. Miller, Meena Nagarajan, Amit Sheth and Kunal Verma, "Web Service Semantics - WSDL-S," *Proceedings of the W3C Workshop on Frameworks for Semantics in Web Service* (W3CW'05), Innsbruck, Austria (June 2005)

Kunal Verma, Kaarthik Sivashanmugam, Amit P. Sheth, Abhijit Patil, Swapna Oundhakar and John A. Miller, "METEOR-S WSDI: A Scalable P2P Infrastructure of Registries for Semantic Publication and Discovery of Web Services," *Journal of Information Technology and Management* (ITM), Special Issue on Universal Global Integration, Vol. 6, No. 1 (2005) pp. 17-39. Kluwer Academic Publishers

X. Su and J. Rao. A Survey of Automated Web Service Composition Methods. In Proceedings of First International Workshop on Semantic Web Services and Web Process Composition, July 2004

D. McDermott. Estimated-regression planning for interactions with Web services. In Proceedings of the 6th International Conference on AI Planning and Scheduling, Toulouse, France, 2002. AAAI Press

S. McIlraith and T. C. Son. Adapting Golog for composition of Semantic Web services. In Proceedings of the 8th International Conference on Knowledge Representation and Reasoning(KR2002), Toulouse, France, April 2002.

S. McIlraith, T. C. Son, and H. Zeng. Semantic Web services. IEEE Intelligent Systems, 16(2):46–53, March/April 2001

B. Medjahed, A. Bouguettaya, and A. K. Elmagarmid. Composing Web services on the Semantic Web. The VLDB Journal, 12(4), November 2003

S. Narayanan and S. McIlraith. Simulation, verification and automated composition of Web service. In Proceedings of the 11th International World Wide Web Conference, Honolulu, Hawaii, USA, May 2002. ACM. presentation available at http://www2002.org/presentations/narayanan.pdf

D. Wu, E. Sirin, J. Hendler, D. Nau, and B. Parsia. Automatic Web services composition using SHOP2. In Workshop on Planning for Web Services, Trento, Italy, June 2003.

Technical Note Using WSDL in a UDDI Registry, Version 2.0.2

John Colgrave and Karsten Januszewski, Technical Note Using WSDL in a UDDI Registry, Version 2.0.2, 2003

Assaf Arkin, Sid Askary, Ben Bloch, Francisco Curbera, Yaron Goland, Neelakantan Kartha, Canyang Kevin Liu, Satish Thatte, Prasad Yendluri, Alex Yiu, Web Service

Business Execution Process Language Version 2.0 (WS-BPEL), http://www.oasis-open.org/committees/download.php/14616/wsbpel-specification-draft.htm

Petia Wohed1, Wil M.P. van der Aalst Marlon Dumas, Arthur H.M. ter Hofstede, "Pattern Based Analysis of BPEL4WS", http://is.tm.tue.nl/staff/wvdaalst/publications/p175.pdf, QUT Technical report, FIT-TR-2002-04, Queensland University of Technology, Brisbane, 2002

F. Casati, S. Sayal, M. Shan. Developing e-services for composing e-services. 2001. Submitted for publication andavailable on request

10. APPENDIX

10.1 Appendix A: Semantic Template for the "Stock Quote" Service

```xml
<?xml version="1.0" encoding="UTF-8"?>
<wsdl:definitions
    xmlns:targetNamespace="semantic template2"
    xmlns:wssem="http://www.ibm.com/xmlns/
                    WebServices/WSSemantics"
    xmlns:wsdl="http://schemas.xmlsoap.org/wsdl/"
    xmlns:ontology0="http://lsdis.cs.uga.edu/projects/meteor-
                    s/wsdl-s/ontologies/LSDIS_Finance.owl"
    xmlns:location0="http://localhost:8080/jsp-
                    examples/Finance.owl">
  <wsdl:message name="input1">
  </wsdl:message>
  <wsdl:message name="output1">
   <wsdl:part name="part0"
            wssem:modelReference=
                    "ontology0#StockQuote.price"/>
   <wsdl:part name="part1"
            wssem:modelReference=
                    "ontology0#StockQuote.volume"/>
  </wsdl:message>
  <wsdl:portType name="portType">
   <wsdl:operation wssem:modelReference=
                            "ontology0#StockQuote">
    <wsdl:input message="input1"/>
    <wsdl:output message="output1"/>
   </wsdl:operation>
  </wsdl:portType>
```

```
<wsdl:service>
</wsdl:service>
</wsdl:definitions>
```

10.2   Appendix B: The BPEL File for the User Case

```
<process xmlns="http://schemas.xmlsoap.org/ws/2003/03/business-
process/"
        name="simpleStockStratege"
        targetNamespace="urn:simpleStockStratege"
        xmlns:tns="urn:simpleStockStratege">
    <partnerLinks>
     <partnerLink name="customer" partnerLinkType=
       "tns:checkStockTrasactionFeasibilityPLT" myRole="caller"/>
     <partnerLink name="stockQuoteChecker"
                  xmlns:ns1="http://www.strikeiron.com"
                  partnerLinkType="ns1:stockQuoteCheckPTL"
                  myRole="stockQuoteChecker" />
     <partnerLink name="companyProfileChecker"
                  partnerLinkType="tns:companyProfileCheckerPTL"
                  partnerRole="companyProfileChecker"/>
     <partnerLink name="investEstimator"
                  xmlns:ns2="urn:investment"
                  partnerLinkType="ns2:investEstimationPTL"
                  partnerRole="investEstimator"/>
    </partnerLinks>
    <variables>
     <variable name="request" messageType="tns:input"/>
     <variable name="response" messageType="tns:output"/>
     <variable name="stockQuoteRequest"
                  xmlns:ns3="http://www.strikeiron.com"
                  messageType="ns3:GetOneQuoteSoapIn"/>
     <variable name="stockQuoteResponse"
                  xmlns:ns4="http://www.strikeiron.com"
                  messageType="ns4:GetOneQuoteSoapOut"/>
     <variable name="companyProfileRequest"
                  xmlns:ns5="http://www.strikeiron.com"
                  messageType="ns5:GetCompanyProfileSoapIn"/>
     <variable name="companyProfileResponse"
                  xmlns:ns6="http://www.strikeiron.com"
                  messageType="ns6:GetCompanyProfileSoapOut"/>
     <variable name="strategeRequest" xmlns:ns7="urn:investment"
```

```
                  messageType="ns7:txDecisionRequest"/>
    <variable name="strategeResponse"
           xmlns:ns8="urn:investment"
           messageType="ns8:txDecisionResponse"/>
</variables>


<sequence>
 <receive name="receive"
       partnerLink="customer"
       portType="tns:CheckStockTransactionFeasibility"
       operation="checkFeasibility"
       variable="request" createInstance="yes">
 </receive>
 <assign >
  <copy>
   <from variable="request" part="symbol"/>
   <to variable="stockQuoteRequest" part="TickerSymbol"/>
  </copy>
  <copy>
   <from variable="request" part="symbol"/>
   <to variable="companyProfileRequest" part="ticker"/>
  </copy>
 </assign>
 <flow>
   <invoke name="invokeStockQuote"
        partnerLink="stockQuoteChecker"
        xmlns:ns9="http://www.strikeiron.com"
        portType="ns9:BasicRealTimeQuotesSoap"
        operation="getOneQuote_simple"
        inputVariable="stockQuoteRequest"
        outputVariable="stockQuoteResponse">
   </invoke>

   <invoke name="invokeCompanyProfileCheck"
        partnerLink="companyProfileChecker"
        xmlns:ns10="http://www.strikeiron.com"
        portType="ns10:ZacksCompanySoap"
        operation="GetCompanyProfile_simple"
        inputVariable="companyProfileRequest"
        outputVariable="companyProfileResponse">
   </invoke>
```

```
</flow>
<assign >
 <copy>
  <from variable="stockQuoteResponse" part="Last"/>
  <to variable="strategeRequest" part="current_price"/>
 </copy>
 <copy>
  <from variable="stockQuoteResponse" part="BidQuantity"/>
  <to variable="strategeRequest" part="bid_quantity"/>
 </copy>
 <copy>
  <from variable="stockQuoteResponse" part="Volume"/>
  <to variable="strategeRequest" part="volume"/>
 </copy>
 <copy>
  <from variable="companyProfileResponse"
        part="Est_EPS_F1"/>
  <to variable="strategeRequest" part="eps"/>
 </copy>
 <copy>
  <from variable="companyProfileResponse"
        part="W52_High_Price"/>
  <to variable="strategeRequest" part="year_high"/>
 </copy>
 <copy>
  <from variable="request" part="investAmount"/>
  <to variable="strategeRequest" part="investAmount"/>
 </copy>
</assign>

<invoke name="invokeStratege"
        partnerLink="investEstimator"
        xmlns:ns11="urn:investment"
        portType="ns11:StockBuyingStratege"
        operation="txDecision"
        inputVariable="strategeRequest"
        outputVariable="strategeResponse">
</invoke>

<assign >
 <copy>
```

```
   <from variable="strategeResponse"
         part="txDecisionReturn"/>
   <to variable="response" part="result"/>
 </copy>
</assign>
<reply name="reply"
       partnerLink="customer"
       portType="tns:CheckStockTransactionFeasibility"
       operation="checkFeasibility"
     variable="response">
</reply>

 </sequence>
</process>
```

10.3   Appendix C: The Process WSDL File for the User Case

```
<?xml version="1.0" encoding="UTF-8"?>
<wsdl:definitions targetNamespace="urn:simpleStockStratege"
         xmlns:tns="urn:simpleStockStratege"
         xmlns:plnk=
         "http://schemas.xmlsoap.org/ws/2003/05/partner-link/"
         xmlns:xsd="http://www.w3.org/2001/XMLSchema"
         xmlns:wsdl="http://schemas.xmlsoap.org/wsdl/">
  <wsdl:message name="output">
   <wsdl:part name="result" type="xsd:boolean"/>
  </wsdl:message>
  <wsdl:message name="input">
   <wsdl:part name="symbol" type="xsd:string"/>
   <wsdl:part name="investAmount" type="xsd:double"/>

  </wsdl:message>
  <wsdl:portType name="CheckStockTransactionFeasibility">
   <wsdl:operation name="checkFeasibility">
    <wsdl:input message="tns:input"/>
    <wsdl:output message="tns:output"/>
   </wsdl:operation>
  </wsdl:portType>

  <wsdl:service name="simpleStockStrategeBP">
```

```
  </wsdl:service>
  <plnk:partnerLinkType
        name="checkStockTrasactionFeasibilityPLT">
    <plnk:role name="caller">
     <plnk:portType name="CheckStockTransactionFeasibility"/>
    </plnk:role>
  </plnk:partnerLinkType>

  <plnk:partnerLinkType name="stockQuoteCheckPTL">
    <plnk:role name="stockQuoteChecker">
     <plnk:portType xmlns:n1="http://www.strikeiron.com"
                    name="n1:BasicRealTimeQuotesSoap"/>
    </plnk:role>
  </plnk:partnerLinkType>

  <plnk:partnerLinkType name="companyProfileCheckerPTL">
    <plnk:role>
     <plnk:portType xmlns:n2="http://www.strikeiron.com"
                    name="n2:ZacksCompanySoap"/>
    </plnk:role>
  </plnk:partnerLinkType>

  <plnk:partnerLinkType name="investEstimationPTL">
    <plnk:role>
     <plnk:portType xmlns:n3="urn:investment"
                    name="n3:StockBuyingStratege"/>
    </plnk:role>
  </plnk:partnerLinkType>
</wsdl:definitions>
```

Chapter 8

WEB SERVICES COMPOSITION

Daniela Barreiro Claro[1,2] and Patrick Albers[1] and Jin-Kao Hao[2]

[1]*ESEO, 4 rue Merlet de la Boulaye, BP 30926 49009 Angers cedex 01 France.*
daniela.claro@eseo.fr, patrick.albers@eseo.fr

[2]*LERIA, University of Angers, 2 Boulevard Lavoisier, 49045, Angers cedex 01 France.*
jin-kao.hao@univ-angers.fr

1. INTRODUCTION

Nowadays many enterprises publish their applications functionalities on the Internet. This new generation of applications allows greater efficiency and availability for business. In fact, more and more applications make functionalities available using a web service format.

However there are many services around the web, each one, taken alone, has a limited functionality. In many cases, a single service is not sufficient to respond to the user's request and often services should be combined through services composition to achieve a specific goal. For example, if a user wants to travel, it is not sufficient to book a flight, but she should also take care of reserving a hotel, renting a car, getting entertained, and so on. Such composition is carried out manually today, it means that the user needs to execute all these services one by one and these tasks can be time and effort consuming.

For that reason, the notion of composite services is starting to be used as a collection of services combined to achieve a user's request. In other words, from a user perspective, this composition will continue to be considered as a simple service, even though it is composed of several web services.

Nevertheless, prior to composing web services, candidate services should first be discovered and then selected. One difficulty is that many functionally similar services are available and thus, the number of discovered services by search mechanisms increases as a consequence. The discovery process returns a set of candidate services from which the subset of those belonging to the composition should be extracted according to non-functional criteria (i.e. cost, availability, reputation). In fact, discovery is a prerequisite for selection, but selection is the main problem (Sreenath and Singh 2004). The non-functional criteria are here characterized by the QoS model presented in each web service. The QoS model has more than one criterion to be evaluated. Thus, services composition can be considered as a multiobjective optimization problem.

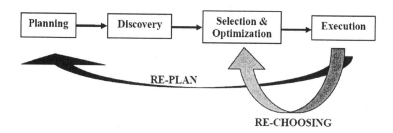

Figure 8-1. SPOC Architecture

As depicted in Figure 8-1, we propose SPOC (**S**emantic based **P**lanning for **O**ptimal web services **C**omposition), an architecture to compose web services. In our point of view, the problem of composing web services can be reduced into four fundamental phases: the first one is planning, which determines the execution order of the tasks, we consider here a task as being a service functionality or a service activity. The second one is discovery that aims at finding candidate services for each task in the plan. The third phase aims at optimizing services composition and is the point treated in this chapter, and, finally, the fourth concerns execution. This fourth phase is characterized as a problem because, even during the execution process, the services may not be found and another tradeoff composition needs to be used or other plan needs to be envisioned.

The composition of web services starts by creating the initial plan based on tasks definition. All the definitions of existing tasks should be located in a repository that the planner can consult for obtaining tasks interfaces. This repository can be represented as an ontology and for us, it can be an improvement over UDDI registries. Hence, we propose a UDDI (Universal Description, Discovery and Integration) that is actually an ontology which describes the services and their providers in an unambiguous way. The name we give to this new UDDI is UDDI-O, standing for ontology. Thus, prior to knowing task interfaces, it is necessary to find a plan that satisfies the users' request. After creating the initial plan, the discovery process will take place. The discovery process aims at matching service descriptions with task definitions that belong to the plan. The present work will not cover the matchmaking problem concerning web services discovery. The optimization phase is the main topic of this chapter and will be explained in detail in the next sections. As a result of this phase we obtain a set of Pareto optimal solutions to execute services composition. In the execution phase, if some service is not available such as an invalid URL or changed location, the environment proposes another Pareto optimal solution to be executed (this corresponds to "re-choosing" in figure 8-1. If after some predefined time the problem continues, the environment will propose to construct another plan, for example, by reordering the tasks (this corresponds to re-plan in Figure 8-1.

This work proposes an analysis of quality criteria in order to select from a set of services those that will belong to the composition. It is organized as follows: the next section describes the selection process and the QoS model. Here, we reinforced the concepts of reputation, because the original concept (Zeng et al. 2003) did not measure the pertinence of the rank given to a service by a user. Thus, in our model, rankings from users with good knowledge of the service domain are considered more accurate. For this purpose, we use fuzzy numbers to measure this criterion. The third section describes web services composition emphasizing its structure and the models that exist to compose web services. The fourth section explains the problem model with its objectives and constraints. In the fifth section we explain the multiobjective approach emphasizing the Pareto and Non-Pareto approach. The sixth section presents existing works related to ours and the seventh highlights our experimentations. We conclude in the last section.

2. WEB SERVICES SELECTION

The current web service architecture and semantic web efforts address the problem of web service discovery but not of web services selection. Discovery deals with finding a set of services that corresponds to a predetermined user request while selection deals with choosing a service between those that are discovered. Moreover, selection seems to be the main problem. In fact, if the discovery process is exhaustive, a very large number of services may be found. Due to the number of services, and consequently the number of candidate services, the selection process will be harder (Sreenath and Singh 2004).

Discovering services mean matching a user request with service functionalities. Works have been undergone concerning service architecture (Sreenath and Singh 2004) in order to better describe web services. Even though more functionalities are incorporated into service descriptions, it still remains difficult for selection to find the subset of services that will be part of the composition (Sreenath and Singh 2004).

Despite the fact that functional attributes have been incorporated by web services architecture, selection should consider more than functional criteria to make a distinction between discovered services. As a result, a quality of service (QoS) model composed of time, cost, availability and reputation is proposed as non-functional criteria. Since non-functional criteria have been incorporated by each service, selection can use these QoS variables in order to choose the optimal subset from all the discovered services.

2.1   QoS (Non-functional) Model

The aim of the selection process is to choose among services discovered according to their functionalities, those that will belong to the composition. The set of discovered services can be subdivided into the subsets of services that are all candidates for a given task. Therefore, in the discovered set, there are subsets of services that execute a determined task and other subsets that execute another kind of tasks. As mentioned earlier, we consider here a task as being a service functionality or a service activity. Thus, in the selection process we should determine a set of candidate services s_i, $i \in [1..n]$ that can execute a set of tasks t_j, $j \in [1..m]$. Our main goal, considering that there is a set of candidate services for each task, is to determine which service fulfills each task, thus finding services composition.

The QoS model that we propose is composed of four criteria as parameters for the quality model: cost, time, availability and reputation. Each of the candidate services will receive a value for representing these quality criteria. Each of these criteria is presented below.

Cost. (Zeng et al. 2003) (Cardoso et al. 2004)(Liu et al. 2004) The cost quality c_{ij} is the amount that a service requester needs to pay to execute service i using task j:

$$c_{ij}, i \in [1..n], j \in [1..m]$$

We consider that c_{ij} is undetermined when service i cannot execute task t.

Time. (Zeng et al. 2003) (Cardoso et al. 2004) (Liu et al. 2004) The time quality t_{ij} measures the execution time between the moment the request is sent and the moment the results are received:

$$t_{ij}, i \in [1..n], j \in [1..m]$$

Availability. (Zeng et al. 2003) The availability quality a_{ij} is the probability that the service can be accessed and used. It is a function of the number of times the service responds to a request and of the number of total requests made to the service. We can express by:

$$a_{ij} = \frac{req_{ij}}{tot_{ij}}, tot_{ij} \neq 0, i \in [1..n], j \in [1..m]$$

where req_{ij} is the number of successful requests to service i using task j, and tot_{ij} is the total number of invocations.

Reputation. The reputation quality r_{ij} is the measure of its trustworthiness. It depends on the user's experience using the service. Different end users can have different opinions about the same service.

For many authors (Zeng et al. 2003) (Liu et al. 2004), reputation can be defined as the average ranking given to the service by end users. The reputation of a given service is usually defined as:

$$q_{rep} = \frac{\sum_{b=1}^{N} k_b}{N}$$

where k_b is the bth ranking given to the service and N is the number of times the service has been ranked.

However, there is no consensus concerning measuring reputation. Here, we propose a new way of measuring reputation. We tried to translate a real world judgment into our example. Thus, in real world, when something is judged for example, a paper in a conference, the reviewers have to give their knowledge domain, prior to giving their judgment. In the case where a reviewer receives a paper that she classifies as belonging only 60% to her area (knowledge domain), the grade that is given must be moderated based on 60% of knowledge. If the same grade is given by a reviewer with 90% of know-how on the domain, for sure her grade will be more accurate. Translating this real scenario into our reputation quality, we must have another way to measure reputation, including the knowledge domain of end users. After service execution, the user ranks the service, and gives a percentage about her knowledge on the service's domain. It will be, for instance, a simple question as "how much do I know about this area".

In order to measure this criterion, we used fuzzy logic to represent an imprecise quantity, as "nearly 8" or "practically 15" (Moura 2001). We used the notion of fuzzy number which is represented as

$$\tilde{a} = [\underline{a}, a, \overline{a}]$$

where $\tilde{a}$ is the fuzzy number with minimal limit, modal value and maximal limit respectively. The *linguistic variables* that represent our reputation values are: bad, average and good, as shown in Figure 8-2.

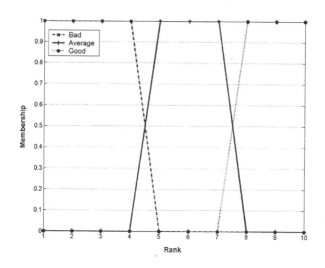

Figure 8-2. Fuzzy set representation

Figure 8-2 shows that until 4, all grades are considered *bad*, from 5 to 7, grades are *average*, and after 8, all grades are *good*. The measure between 4 and 5, for example, depends on membership values. The membership or degree of pertinence means how much a value is inside a set, for example the *bad* set or inside the *average* set. Thus, if a service has a rank of 4.8 we need to analyze its membership $\mu(d1)$. If its membership has the value 0.33, it means that it belongs to the *bad* set. On the other hand, if it has 0.66 as membership value, it belongs to the *average* set. Each service will be ranked several times and thus we will have a set of fuzzy numbers. However, at the end, what we need is a crisp number that characterizes the reputation value, and for that we need to convert fuzzy sets to a crisp number. Defuzzification is the final phase that does this conversion. There are several defuzzification methods, but we use the CENTROID method that calculates the hypothetical center of gravity for the output fuzzy set (Löstedt et al. 2000) (Fuzzy 2005). Thus, our reputation criterion is characterized as:

$$r_{ij} = \frac{\sum_{b=1}^{N} d_{bi}\mu(d_{bi})}{\sum_{b=1}^{N} \mu(d_{bi})}; \, d_{bi} \in [0,10], \mu(d_{bi}) \in [0,1], i \in [1..n], j \in [1..m]$$

where d_{bi} represents the domain value (ranking) of service s_i for task t_j and $\mu(d_{bi})$ is the membership value for that domain point. Using this model, reputation ranking is more precise and trustworthy.

We showed above that non-functional quality criteria such as cost, time, availability and reputation, could be defined to better describe services. In the next sections, we will present web services composition and how these criteria can help in obtaining optimal compositions.

3.   WEB SERVICES COMPOSITION

Web service composition originated from the necessity to achieve a predetermined goal that cannot be realized by a standalone service. Internally, in a composition, services can interact with each other to exchange parameters, for example a service's result could be another service's input parameter.

3.1   Problem Description

As an illustrative example, we will consider in this work a Travel problem. This scenario is a typical web services composition problem (Narayanam and McIlraith 2002) (OWL-S 2005). As far as creating the Travel service, we can use three atomic services (which are not composed) that will internally execute the travel; each one independently executes a task. A task can be described as an activity that applies to a specific domain. In this work, we treat activities and tasks identically. In our problem we will consider 3 tasks (BookFlight, BookHotel and RentCar) executed by 3 services (Airplane service, Hotel service and CarRental service). As explained in section 1 the planner will determine the execution order of these tasks. All the services resulting from the discovery process for a given task are candidate to execute this task. The aim of composition is to determine, out of all these candidate services, which one will belong to the composition.

3.2   **Structure of Web Services Composition**

The problem of composing web services can be characterized as a combinatory problem. As explained earlier, in the composition we have a set of services s_i, $i \in [1..n]$ that can execute a set of tasks t_j, $j \in [1..m]$. However, it is necessary to consider that one service can be dependent of other services. The main goal is to find the trade-off services composition, considering that there is a set of candidate services for each task.

In a composition, each service s_i is allocated to one task t_j. This association can be represented by a matrix (x_{ij}) where s_i represents the services and t_j represents the tasks. The matrix χ thus represents the services allocated to a composition.

$$\chi = \begin{pmatrix} x_{11} & x_{12} & \cdots & x_{1n} \\ x_{21} & x_{22} & \cdots & x_{2n} \\ \vdots & \vdots & \ddots & \vdots \\ x_{m1} & x_{m2} & \cdots & x_{mn} \end{pmatrix}$$

In our scenario the number of tasks and of services, m and n, are both limited to 3.

Actually, we can consider that a composition is a set of atomic web services or a set of composed web services. For instance, in the case of atomic services, if service s_1 is allocated to task t_2, it cannot be allocated to another task, because its domain is restricted to execution of task t_2. If we consider our Travel problem, a Hotel service cannot execute the bookFlight task, since it only deals with hotel reservations. On the other hand, considering that the composition may also have composed (non atomic) services, it means that one service can execute several tasks in the same composition. In our experimentations, we only consider atomic web services; this means that the sum of lines and that of columns in matrix χ should be 1.

$$\forall i \in [1..n], \forall j \in [1..m]$$

$$x_{ij} = \begin{cases} 1, \text{ if service } i \text{ is allocated to task } j \\ 0, \text{ otherwise} \end{cases}$$

The equation above determines whether a service belongs to a composition or not. It actually gives the result of our composition, since it defines, in the previous matrix whether service i is allocated to task j.

For instance, matrix χ' below represents one of the possible combinations in which service s_3 will execute task t_1, service s_1 will execute task t_2 and task t_3 will be executed by service s_2. As a result, this composition will be formed by services s_3, s_1 and s_2 respectively.

$$\chi' = \begin{pmatrix} 0 & 0 & 1 \\ 1 & 0 & 0 \\ 0 & 1 & 0 \end{pmatrix}$$

An undetermined number of tasks, m, can be used to compose a service and an unlimited number of services, n, for each task t_j can be found. In fact, these possible combinations are considered for a predefined plan, which determines exactly in which order the tasks should be composed. However, concerning our architecture, the plan can also be changed, and so other possible combinations might be overseen. Moreover, if it is considered that p plans using m tasks can be created, the problem becomes even harder.

3.3   Models to Compose Web Services

The Web Service community is dealing with composition, interoperability between services, automated discovery and composition. Efforts have already been made by industrials and researches in order to achieve this goal. There are two main languages created in order to compose web services: BPEL4WS and OWL-S. Both languages are created focusing on activity-based models. In this way, BPEL4WS provides the basis for manually specifying composite web services. On the other hand, OWL-S is more ambitious and it provides a machine-readable description of web services which will enable automated discovery and composition (Hull and Su 2004). Indeed, there are other models to compose services such as: workflows, graphs, Petri nets and also currently programming languages as Java and C. Depending on each choice, composing web services can be harder and time consuming. Here we will focus on the two specific languages mentioned above: BPEL4WS and OWL-S. We will then illustrate some works using different models to compose web services.

3.3.1   Composing using BPEL4WS

Web services composition using BPEL4WS allows the manipulation of services as activities and processes. Actually, BPEL4WS language is a merge between Microsoft's XLang and IBM's WSFL, but all of them are considered as a web service flow language (van der Aalst 2003). As an executable process implementation language, the role of BPEL4WS is to define a new web service by composing a set of existing ones. The interface of the composite service is described as a collection of WSDL PortTypes.

A BPEL4WS process defines the roles involved in a composition as abstract processes. A buyer and a seller are examples of two roles. They are expressed using partner link definitions. We can have a role for each web service that is composed and does some activity. In order to integrate services, they are treated as partners that fill roles (Mandel and McIlraith 2003). BPEL4WS depends directly on the WSDL of the service. A business process defines how to coordinate the interactions between a process instance and its partners. Thus, a BPEL4WS process provides one or more WSDL services. The BPEL4WS process is defined only in an abstract manner, allowing only references to service portTypes in the partnerLink (Andrews et al. 2003). Each partner is characterized by a partner link and a role name. In summary, the main idea of business process is to create an organizer that point to each service endpoint that will be actually executed.

Characteristics. The distinction between roles and partners in a business process is an important characteristic of BPEL4WS. This allows more simple and intuitive integration between enterprises. Another important characteristic of BPEL4WS is the fault handlers. Faults handlers have the ability to catch errors in BPEL4WS. Another characteristic from BPEL4WS is message correlation that allows processes to participate in stateful conversations. It can be used to match returning or known customers to long-running business process. Furthermore, correlation mechanisms allow interaction between a service instance and a partner. BPEL4WS addresses correlations scenarios by providing a declarative mechanism to specify correlated groups of operations within a service instance (Andrews et al. 2002).

In a BPEL4WS process we define the interactions between these activities that compose the service. Thus, there are some types of interaction like sequence, flow, switch, pick, moreover, each one can be combined.

Implementation. We developed a prototype using BPEL4WS. We created our composition based on our simple Travel. Our composition has three services: Airplane, Hotel and CarRental. In BPEL4WS we define a composed service, such as Travel by describing which others services it contains. Figure 8-3, adapted from (Khalaf 2004), shows the relation between the Travel service and the others that compose it.

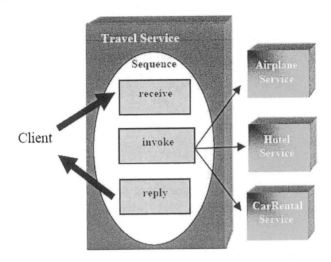

Figure 8-3. Internal view of Travel Service (BPEL4WS)

We put these three services in sequence, using the *sequence* structure. The *receive* structure indicates the location of the input variables in the sequence. The *invoke* structure is actually the service invocation. The *reply* is the response given by the sequence that here is the total cost of the travel. Between each structure, we can add an *assign* structure that is responsible for passing values between invoked services. See below our example using BPEL4WS:

```
<sequence name="TravelSequence">
    <receive partnerLink="client"
            portType="tns:travelPT"
            operation="trip"
            variable="request"
            createInstance="yes"/>
    <invoke name="invokeAirplane"
            partnerLink="airplane"
            portType="sairplane:Airplane"
            operation="bookAirplane"
            inputVariable="request"
            outputVariable="airplaneReturn">
    </invoke>
    <invoke name="invokeHotel"
            partnerLink="hotel"
            portType="shot:Hotel"
```

```
                        operation="bookHotel"
                        inputVariable="request"
                        outputVariable="hotelReturn">
            </invoke>
            <invoke name="invokeCar"
                        partnerLink="car"
                        portType="scar:Car"
                        operation="rentcar"
                        inputVariable="request"
                        outputVariable="totalReturn">
            </invoke>
            <reply partnerLink="client"
                        portType="tns:travelPT"
                        operation="trip"
                        variable="carReturn"/>
        </sequence>
```

After constructing the composition, we need to deploy our composite Travel service, making it available for execution. At this moment, the deployment engine will require the WSDL files that were related to partner's links. As we have an interaction with each service developed, we must have a WSDL for each one. We have to mention in each WSDL the grounding tag in order to actually find the service. Additionally, we invoke the composition using an API created by IBM called BPWS4J1.1 (BPWS4J 2004). Using this API to execute our composite service, we call a broker and we use the endpoint given by the Travel deployment to do the connection between the client and services' providers. Using the endpoint, the broker can find the service, and then it can pass the first parameters that are sent by the client.

3.3.2   Composing using OWL-S

The process of composing services using a semantic web language like OWL-S increases the automatic discovery and composition. In fact, OWL-S is based on ontology and OWL. This means that OWL-S is also based and constructed using resources and hierarchical concepts. With such a language, software agents can find services based on their computer-interpretable description.

The main motivating task for OWL-S was the ability to automatically discover web services. Other motivating tasks are automatic invocation of a service, with which a software agent can interpret markup to understand what input is necessary for the service call, what information will be returned and how to execute the service.

Additionally, the composed web service is actually an abstract service. In fact, the composition file has only the service calls. In OWL-S each service that is part of composition has the same structure as the composed one.

Characteristics. OWL-S is composed of three other structures called: service Profile, service Model and service Grounding, used to describe different aspects of the service (OWL-S 2005). The service Profile is responsible for presenting the service to other services or agents that want to use it. It describes the service in order to facilitate the search process, specifying what organization provides the service and what functions the service provides. See below a Profile example:

```
<profile:Profile rdf:ID="TravelProfile">
   <service:isPresentedBy
                 rdf:resource="#TravelService"/>
     <profile:serviceName xml:lang="en"> Travel
     </profile:serviceName>
          <profile:textDescription xml:lang="en">
             Return travel: book flight, hotel, car rental.
          </profile:textDescription> ...
```

The service Model describes the service with regards to its inputs, outputs, effects and preconditions parameters. Furthermore, the process model is the core of OWL-S architecture; it defines how the process will be executed. Services can be composed using a combination of atomic or composite services. This implies that a composition can have services that are themselves composed. Additionally, in the service model we can say how the services will be executed: sequentially (*sequence*) or in parallel (*split/split+join*) or some other way (OWL-S 2005).

The service grounding is responsible for giving the endpoint of a service. A service grounding can be thought of as a mapping between an abstract and a concrete specification (OWL-S 2005). It is also in the grounding that we put the reference to each WSDL document.

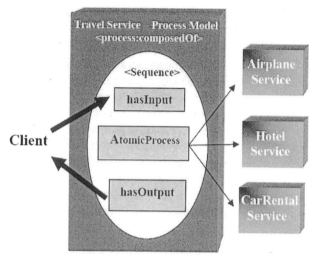

Figure 8-4. Internal view of Travel service (OWL-S)

Implementation. In our implementation using OWL-S composition, we defined the Travel service as being composed of three atomic services called Airplane, Hotel and CarRental services. We must define the OWL file for each atomic service. Furthermore, in these files we must put the grounding reference positioning exactly where the service is running. The Travel.owl file is only an abstract service where we define the input/output parameters and which service will be called. Figure 8-4 shows the internal view of Travel service.

After creating the OWL-S file containing the three services above, we can invoke the Travel service, sending it the parameters: *date_arrival*, *date_departure* and *destination_city*. As a result we will obtain the total amount for traveling. We also used a sequence structure in order to compose our services. In OWL-S we can pass values between services using *process:sameValues* structure.

```
<process:ProcessModel rdf:ID="TravelProcessModel">
  <service:describes
                rdf:resource="#TravelService"/>
  <process:hasProcess
                rdf:resource="#TravelProcess"/>
</process:ProcessModel>
<process:CompositeProcess rdf:ID="TravelProcess">
  <process:hasInput rdf:resource="#dt_arrival"/>
  <process:hasInput rdf:resource="#dt_departure"/>
```

```
<process:hasInput
                rdf:resource="#destination_city"/>
<process:hasOutput rdf:resource="#total"/>
<process:composedOf>
  <process:Sequence>
    <process:components
                      rdf:parseType="Collection">
      <process:AtomicProcess
       rdf:about="Airplane.owl#AirplaneProcess"/>
      <process:AtomicProcess
              rdf:about="Hotel.owl#HotelProcess"/>
      <process:AtomicProcess
       rdf:about="CarRental.owl#CarRentalProcess"/>
    </process:components>
  </process:Sequence>
</process:composedOf>
</process:CompositeProcess>
```

In order to execute the travel service, we have used OWL-S API (Mindswap 2004). For a client side, we defined an endpoint called Travel as the name of our service. Continue the execution, we invoke the Travel service and the OWL-S works on executing the others services that belongs to this composition.

It is important to highlight that these two examples were done in a statically way. In other words, we knew in advance which services would be part of the composition.

3.3.3 Other Web Service Composition Models

Many works opted for neither using BPEL4WS nor OWL-S. They modeled web services composition using other types of procedures.

In (Grigori and Bouzeghoub 2005) they propose modeling web services composition as graphs. In their work, even though they were worried about services match, the user requirements and the published service are graph based. The service retrieval approach is based on process graphs. Thus, a process is represented as a directed graph, whose nodes are activities. Edges have associated transition conditions expressing the control flow dependencies between activities.

In (Cardoso et al. 2004), they model web services composition using a workflow. In this work, a web service is considered as being a part of the workflow and it is argued that tasks and web services are treated with no difference. Between workflow and web services, both require tasks to have a structure which includes information such as task name, formal parameters, etc. Concerning web processes and workflows, in the authors' opinion, web processes can be viewed as workflows that manage web services instead of tasks. Thus, a workflow is composed of tasks and these tasks are actually web services.

In the work presented in (Narayanam and McIlraith 2002), web services compositions are modeled as Petri nets. In fact, all approaches mentioned above use graph representations. For instance, a Petri net is a bipartite graph containing places (drawn as circles) and transitions (drawn as rectangles).

Summarizing, several different manners exist for modeling web services composition; using various types of graphs, specific languages, etc.

4.   PROBLEM MODEL

Many authors have studied the problem of web services composition, but only a few have worried about how complex this composition could be. Concerning our Travel problem, consider that we can now have more than ten tasks to be executed and over a hundred candidate services; with the daily growth of the Internet, these figures may soon be realistic. Thus, combining each task, respecting their restrictions and respectively finding the service to execute the tasks can be considered as a combinatory problem. Since we treat our services composition as a combinatory problem it requires optimization, so our Travel problem can be treated as an optimization problem.

Optimization problems require basically two elements: a search space composed of potential solutions and an objective function to be optimized. The search space may be restricted by a set of constraints. In our example, prior to execute the services, it is necessary to find optimal composition. In order to achieve optimal compositions we defined four main objectives that should be optimized: cost, time, reputation and availability. In addition to these objectives, we restricted the search space using constraints stating, for example, that one service can only be allocated to one task. Actually these objectives are our QoS model explained earlier. Since each QoS variable will be described inside a service, our optimization problem will retrieve these values in order to make possible combinations. The QoS (non-functional criteria) model was used as the objectives to be optimized because we need to differentiate candidate services with identical functionalities. In the next subsections we explain our objectives and the constraints we used in detail.

4.1   Objectives

Our problem consists of four objectives. The first one is cost minimization:

$$Min \sum_{i=1}^{n} \sum_{j=1}^{m} c_{ij} p_{ij} x_{ij}$$

In this problem, c_{ij} represents the cost criterion in the quality model. It defines the cost of using service s_i for executing task t_j. p_{ij} indicates the service's ability to execute a given task. Since we can have atomic or composed services belonging to the composition, not all of the discovered services will be able to execute all the tasks. Thus, p_{ij} is a binary variable informing whether service s_i is able to execute a task t_j or not. The binary variable x_{ij} is responsible for expressing if a service belongs or not to the composition. This is represented in matrix χ.

Another objective concerns time. As explained in the QoS model, time is the elapsed time between the request and the response. The time objective also needs to be minimized:

$$Min \sum_{i=1}^{n} \sum_{j=1}^{m} t_{ij} p_{ij} x_{ij}$$

In our model, t_{ij} concerns the time taken by service s_i to execute task t_j. The other variables p_{ij} and x_{ij} are those explained above.

The availability objective shows the probability that a service can be accessed and used. In our case, it should be maximized, because it is preferable that this probability is as high as possible.

$$Max \sum_{i=1}^{n} \sum_{j=1}^{m} a_{ij} p_{ij} x_{ij}$$

Variable a_{ij} should belong to [0,1].

The last objective is related to the reputation a service has in a determined field.

$$Max \sum_{i=1}^{n} \sum_{j=1}^{m} r_{ij} p_{ij} x_{ij}$$

r_{ij} stands for the reputation service s_i has when executing task t_j. This objective needs to be maximized because the higher the reputation the better the service is judged.

Using our objectives, we can now reconsider our Travel problem. Cost represents the price of a service execution and Time is the execution time of a service. Moreover, Availability is the probability a service is "alive" and

Reputation is the trustworthiness of the service in a determined field. We can easily understand that some clients do not give any preference to cost and prefer spending more money on travel, provided it is on a reliable airline company. In fact, we want to consider the four objectives simultaneously for travel.

In fact, even if the four objectives are contradictory with each other, we do not give any preference to any one of them. This means that we do not need to give them a weight. For instance, we do not want to give any preference to cost over time. Thus, the service with the smallest cost will not necessarily be part of our composition, since its other measures of quality must be considered. We will explain how one can treat this kind of problem in section 5.

4.2   Constraints

In our model the solutions of our problem must also satisfy two constraints. The first one states that only one service in a composition is allocated to each task. It can be represented by:

$$\sum_{i=1}^{n} x_{ij} p_{ij} = 1, \forall j \in [1..m], x_{ij} \in \{0,1\}$$

where x_{ij} specifies whether or not a service belongs to a composition. Variable p_{ij} represents the capacity of service s_i to execute task t_j. Thus, this first constraint specifies that each task in the composition must be executed by exactly one service.

The second constraint concerns the user's budget.

$$\sum_{i=1}^{n}\sum_{j=1}^{m} c_{ij} x_{ij} \leq W, W > 0, x_{ij} \in \{0,1\}$$

This constraint states that the cost of using the resulting composition should not exceed a given value W.

5.   MULTIOBJECTIVE OPTIMIZATION

As explained in section 4 we have four objectives that we want to minimize and maximize. However, neither a preference nor a weight should be given to any one of them. We want to treat all of them together and simultaneously. Although single-objective optimization problems may have a unique optimal solution, Multiobjective Optimization Problems (MOP) present a possibly uncountable set of solutions, which when evaluated, produce vectors whose components represent tradeoffs in objective space. A decision maker then implicitly chooses an acceptable solution by selecting one or more of these vectors (Coello et al. 2002;Tan et al. 2005;Deb 2001;Collette and Siarry 2003).

Multiobjective optimization allows the co-existence between two or more objectives that are normally contradictory. Two objectives are contradictory if the decrease of one of them implies the increase of the other. Another important feature is that in a multiobjective problem we do not have only one optimal solution but a set of solutions. These solutions are called *Pareto solutions* (Tan et al. 2005).

Thus, MOP can be defined as finding (Osyczka 1985): "a vector of decision variables which satisfies constraints and optimizes a vector of function whose elements represent the objective functions." This is formally defined in (Coello et al. 2002) as:

Find the vector $\vec{x} = [x_1, x_2, ..., x_n]^T$ which satisfies the m inequality constraint s :

$$g_i(\vec{x}) \geq 0, \, i = 1,2,...,m$$

and optimize the vector function

$$\vec{f}(\vec{x}) = [f_1(\vec{x}), f_2(\vec{x}), ..., f_k(\vec{x})]^T$$

The constraints define the feasible region and any point in $\vec{x}$ defines a feasible solution. T stands for vector transposition. Thus, the points inside the feasible region satisfy all defined constraints.

A large number of approaches exist to resolve multiobjective optimization problems. Some of them use the knowledge they have about the problem to give preferences to some objectives, thus bypassing the multiobjective aspect. Others give all objectives the same level of importance, etc. Among these approaches, we should distinguish between two categories: non-Pareto and Pareto approaches. Non-Pareto approaches do not actually treat the problem as a multiobjective problem. They try to convert it into a mono-objective problem. On the other hand, Pareto approaches do not transform the problem's objectives, but try to optimize them simultaneously.

5.1 Non-Pareto Approach

There are many non-Pareto approaches; however, we focus here on two of them used in multiobjective problems.

5.1.1   Objective aggregation method

This method is the most commonly used in multiobjective optimization problems. The goal is to transform the multiobjective problem into a mono-objective problem. Hence, they use a weight mechanism to aggregate all objectives into a unique objective. This approach has the advantage of being able to reuse all classic algorithms used for solving mono-objective optimization problems. However, the weights must be given with attention because it impacts directly into the solutions.

5.1.2   ε-Constraint

This is another manner of transforming a multiobjective problem into a mono-objective one. When confronted with a problem consisting of *m* objectives, we convert *m-1* of them into constraints. Thus, the idea is to optimize the preferred objective, considering all the others as constraints. This method is also known as the trade-off method.

5.2   Pareto Approach

Having several objective functions, the notion of "optimum" changes, because in MOP, the aim is to find good compromises ("tradeoffs") rather than a single solution. We can say that $\vec{x}$ is Pareto optimal if there exists no feasible vector $\vec{y}$ which decreases some criterion without causing a simultaneous increase in at least one other criterion (Coello et al. 2002).

5.2.1   The Relation of Dominance

Despite the fact that we have obtained many solutions resolving our multiobjective problem, only a restricted number of them will actually be relevant. Thus, in multiobjective problems, in order to consider an interesting solution, we need to have a means of determining the most relevant solutions. In order to determine these solutions, a relation of dominance is defined as follows:

Definition: The relation of dominance in a minimization problem is defined in (Coello et al. 2002) as:

Vector $\vec{v}$ dominates vector $\vec{\tau}$ ($\vec{v} \preceq \vec{\tau}$) if, and only if:

$\vec{v}$ *is partially   less than* $\vec{\tau}$

i.e. $\forall i \in \{1,...,k\}, v_i \leq \tau_i \land \exists i \in \{1,...,k\}: v_i < \tau_i$

Solutions that dominate other solutions but which do not dominate each other are called optimal solutions in the sense of Pareto (or nondominated solution).

5.2.2   MultiObjective Evolutionary Algorithms

The use of Evolutionary Algorithms (EA) to solve Multiobjective problems has been motivated mainly because of the population-based nature of EAs which allows the generation of several elements of the Pareto optimal set in a single run. The Multiobjective Evolutionary Algorithms (MOEA) are among the most powerful resolution methods for multiobjective optimization (Coello et al. 2002). MOEA take into account contradictory objectives and allow finding a set of nondominated solutions. An evolutionary algorithm is composed of three fundamental elements:

- Population: it is composed of individuals that represent potential solutions
- Evaluation: it is a mechanism that allows individual evaluations in order to measure the individual adaptation into an environment.
- Evolution: it is the mechanism that allows the population evolution. Evolution is ensured by selection, crossover and mutation.

The selection mechanism determines the individuals that can reproduce its characteristics in future generations. The crossover is the mechanism responsible to create new individuals based on parents' characteristics. The mutation mechanism introduces limited changes in the individuals.

Genetic Algorithm to MOP (NSGA-II). The NSGA-II (Nondominated Sorting Genetic Algorithm) (Deb el al. 2002) used in this work is one variation of Goldberg's Pareto ranking (Goldberg 1989), though any other MOEA such as SPEA(Zitizler and Thiele 1998), PAES (Knowles and Corne 1999) and PICPA (Barichard and Hao 2003) could have been used.

In NSGA-II, the tournament selection, crossover and mutation operators are used to create a child population that will be added to a result population given by the later generation. The new population is sorted based on non-domination. In this step, elitism is ensured because the best nondominated sets will be chosen for the next population. Using constraints, the relation of domination between two individuals can be characterized as a feasible or unfeasible solution. Thus, the ranking will be done based also on feasible solutions.

Applying NSGA-II to our Travel problem, a chromosome corresponds to a services composition which is defined by a 0/1 string. Each binary variable that represents a gene indicates whether the service belongs to the optimal composition or not. The example below shows a chromosome representing a solution of a services composition problem using 15 services and 3 tasks (each of them having 5 candidate services):

0	0	0	1	0	1	0	0	0	0	0	0	1	0	0
genes: 1-5					genes: 6-10					genes: 11-15				

Each service is represented in the above chromosome by a binary variable (a gene) and the binary variables (genes) are grouped according to the task they are candidate for (genes 1-5: task 1, genes 6-10: task 2, genes 11-15: task 3). For each group of 5 binary variables, only one service will belong to our composition. This chromosome corresponds exactly to our matrix χ and means that service s_4 is allocated to task t_1. Task t_2 will be executed by service s_6 and task t_3 by service s_{13}.

6.   RELATED WORK

Many authors have proposed quality of service models for selecting web services. Some authors applied their QoS model to agents based architectures, others to centralized registries or to individual services.

In (Ran 2003) the main idea is to include a QoS model into UDDI registries so that QoS parameters can be included as search criteria. In fact, they propose to use a QoS model as non-functional requirements to enable a service search based on functional and non-functional (QoS) parameters. They also explain that the current UDDI model limits the service discovery to functional requirements. Due to this limitation, they propose to incorporate a QoS model into UDDI registries. The proposed model will coexist with the current UDDI. If no services are found with these qualities, feed-back is returned to clients and so they can reduce their quality values.

In (Sreenath and Singh 2004) the authors propose a mutual evaluation process between agents to select a web service. It selects the best service based on rates given to providers by agents. A provider is ranked by an agent and the agent's evaluations are, themselves, evaluated by other agents. Thus, selecting a service provider involves getting a list of rated service providers and choosing the best based on a weighted average calculation. The result of the execution of the chosen service is then feedback into the service provider rating mechanism.

The main idea in (Cardoso et al. 2004) is an adaptation of Workflow Quality of Services and its transposition to web service technologies. First of all, they propose to characterize workflows based on their QoS in order to better fulfill customers' expectations. The QoS model is composed of: time, cost, fidelity and reliability. Fidelity means how well workflows, instances and tasks are meeting user specifications. Concerning reliability, it is the measure of the likelihood that the component performs a task demanded by a user. These QoS constraints are implemented into METEOR workflow management systems for Genomic Projects.

Ideas in (Zeng et al. 2003) are very close to our proposition regarding the QoS model and also to the resolution method. This work treats the services selection during the execution process and so it takes into account multiple criteria. Thus, the idea is that services are selected by the composite service execution engine based on a set of criteria. This paper presents a quality model that is characterized by non-functional properties: price, duration, reputation and availability. Service selection is then formulated as an optimization problem and a linear programming method is used to compute optimal services execution plans to compose services. This work is an example of objective aggregation approach. In other words, they weight the objectives and then sum them all in order to create a single aggregate objective. The transformed problem is solved using linear programming. Notice that this approach cannot lead to alternative solutions and is not able to handle automatically non-linear constraints. The most important difference between our work and Zeng et al's work (Zeng et al. 2003) is that, as opposed to their work, we do not give any weight to any objective. We treat all objectives with the same importance using a multiobjective optimization approach. Even though our objectives are contradictory, they are taken into account simultaneously by our resolution algorithm.

In (Liu et al. 2004), in order to improve the work of (Zeng et al. 2003), the authors propose specific domain criteria for each service that will be selected. Thus, QoS information is collected from the properties of services as they are published by providers. The main idea is that some users want to select services based on time while others only want to consider cost. Thus this paper proposes a QoS model based on user preferences.

In (Canfora et al. 2005), the authors propose a QoS-aware composition based on run-time values. They argue that QoS values based on estimation may differ from those at runtime. Thus they prefer to use runtime QoS value when composing services in order not to go against SLA accords. An example is that, at runtime, some services may not be available when, according to estimations, they should be. Thus, this framework needs to reconsider services composition in order to change the bindings between abstract and concrete services.

Ideas in (Jaeger et al. 2005) discuss how the selection can consider different QoS categories to determine the most suitable candidates for the composition. If more than one category is used for optimization, a multi-dimensional optimization problem arises. On the other hand, if exactly one category is relevant, an algorithm chooses the candidate that offers the optimal value. For each task the candidate that offers the best QoS constraint category is assigned. Thus, if a combination which respects the constraints exists, it is found.

In (Bonatti and Festa 2005) the authors consider optimal services selection based on a given set of service requests (i.e. activities occurring in a workflow), a set of available services (offered services), result of the matchmaking process (association of the request and the offer) and a numeric preference measure. Their selection is based on cost and two different QoS-like criteria. These criteria are ordered and static.

7.   CASE STUDY

One of the main contributions of this work concerns the multiobjective optimization approach. As explained earlier, we consider that objectives and solutions should be searched considering these four criteria simultaneously. To achieve this, we use the multiobjective evolutionary algorithm NSGA-II. The next sections describe our experimentation using the NSGA-II for composing web services.

7.1   Experimentation

Applying this algorithm to our problem, several experiments using our composition model were done in order to find optimal compositions.

7.1.1   Tests set

The main objective of our tests was to find a set of Pareto optimal compositions from which a user can select her preferred solution. The first test that we did was to analyze the same number of services and tasks, changing the number of generations and populations. The number of services was set to 30 and the number of tasks to 3. We chose to allocate the same number of candidate services to each task. The aim of this experimentation was to analyze how the algorithm treats services composition.

The next test that we did was aimed at studying the scalability of the services composition algorithm with respects to the number of candidate services and to the number of tasks. Population and generation were kept constant in all experiments, but the number of services and tasks was changed. In fact, we increased candidate services for each tasks. The population was fixed to 200 individuals and the generations were fixed to 500. These values were taken considering other experiments using the NSGA-II algorithm.

As for the previous experiment, we also consider that the numbers of candidate services for each task are equal. The number of services is thus equal to the number of variables, because each service is represented as a variable in our model.

7.1.2 Algorithm Parameters

In the first experiment we used population ranges from 10 to 200 and generation ranges from 10 to 500. The crossover probability was 0.9 and the mutation was $1/l$ where l is the number of binary variables. In our case, we used 30 binary variables because we have 30 services. These 30 binary variables represent 3 tasks and each task can be executed by 10 candidate services. The crossover used was single-point. We used 4 objective functions and 2 constraints as previously defined in our model. The first constraint determines the candidate services and the other one represents the maximal budget given by the user. This value was fixed for all compositions. The QoS values were given randomly to each service.

In the second test, the population size was set to 200 and generation to 500. We did these experiments using 30 and 60 services with 3 and 5 tasks. It means that, for example, using 60 services and 3 tasks, we have 20 candidate services equally distributed for each task. The crossover mutation and probability was maintained (of course they changed according to the number of variables). In both experiments, all constraints must be satisfied in all generations and thus only feasible solutions were selected for the next generation.

7.1.3 Results

The results of our experiments consist of a set of chromosomes; each one representing a services composition. Since we defined a population size of 200, the maximum number of solutions found was also 200. However, out of these solutions we only highlighted the distinct Pareto optimal solutions.

In Figure 8-5, we show the evolution of our model based on the number of distinct Pareto optimal solutions found for 30 services and 3 tasks. We can see that 70 distinct solutions are found for a population size of 200 and a generation size of 500. The tradeoff solutions do not violate any constraints.

Using 30 services for 3 tasks, the algorithm gives 70 distinct nondominated solutions in approximately 18 seconds.

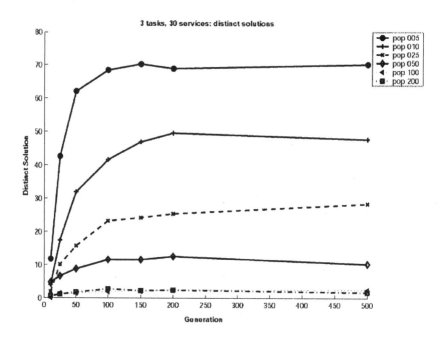

Figure 8-5. Distinct Pareto solutions

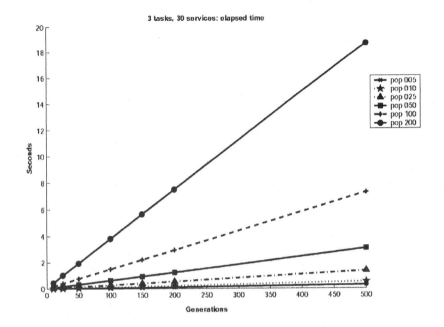

Figure 8-6. Elapsed Time

We notice, in Figure 8-6, that it is not necessary to use large Distinct Pareto solutions populations since for a population size of 100, the 47 distinct solutions are obtained in 7 seconds.

The next experiment consisted in changing the number of services and the number of tasks. In Figure 8-6 we observe that as the number of services increases, more solutions are found. In addition, as the number of candidate services increases, the elapsed time to find the solutions also increases.

For example, using 60 services for 3 tasks means that there are 20 candidate services. However using 60 services for 5 tasks, there are only 12 candidate services. The difficulty in finding tradeoff solutions increases with the number of candidate services. Augmenting the number of tasks also means increasing the number of constraints and so facilitating the achievement of Pareto optimal compositions, as shown in Figure 8-7.

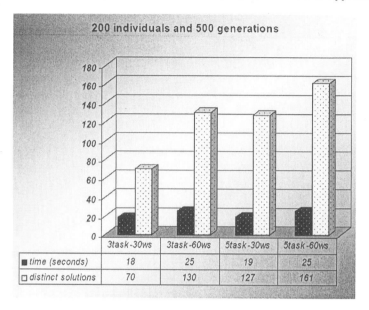

Figure 8-7. Services and Tasks

8.   CONCLUSIONS

In this paper we have explained how services could be selected in order to make optimized compositions. We proposed some improvement on quality models, highlighting the reputation criterion. We based the calculation of reputation on fuzzy numbers. Using non-functional features (QoS) for the optimization of composite services may lead to contradictory objectives. However, we do not wish to give any preference (weight) to any of these objectives. Thus we chose to treat services composition as a multiobjective problem. We used the multiobjective evolutionary algorithm called NSGA-II and obtained a set of optimized compositions representing different tradeoffs. The experimentations carried out validate our approach and show its feasibility in solving the Travel problem.

9.   QUESTIONS FOR DISCUSSION

Beginner:
1. Why do we need to compose web services?

2. What is the difference between static composition and automatic composition?
3. List different techniques used for composing automatically web services.

Intermediate:
1. Should QoS values be assigned to web services or should they be associated to service providers?
2. List other possible approaches to solve the multiobjective model for the optimization of web services composition?
3. Could the availability criterion be a continuous measure? Why?
4. Why is it necessary to optimize the composition?

Advanced:
1. In our problem, what happens if the number of services and tasks is increased?
2. What are the benefits of using multiobjective approaches?

Practical Exercises:
1. Choose an example to compose statically using three services. Develop it using OWL-S or BPEL4WS.
2. Take a composition example, enumerate all possible compositions, choose a quality criterion and try to optimize using a linear programming approach.

10. SUGGESTED ADDITIONAL READING

- Coello Carlos A., van Veldhuizen D.A., Lamont G.B.; *Evolutionary Algorithms for Solving Multi-Objective Problems.* Kluwer Academic/Plenum Publishers, New York, 2002: This book is a reference in the domain of Evolutionary Multiobjective Optimization.

11. ACKNOWLEDGMENT

Daniela Barreiro Claro is supported by a research scholarship given by the Région du Pays de La Loire (2003-2006).

12. REFERENCES

Andrews T., Curbera F., Dholakia H., Goland Y., Klein J., Leymann F., Liu K., Roller D., Smith D., Thatte S., Trickovic I. and Weerawarana S. Specification: BPEL4WS - Business Process Execution Language for Web Services - Version 1.1. Retrieved May 30, 2005, from ftp://www6.software.ibm.com/software/ developer/library/ws-bpel.pdf, May (2003).

Barichard H., Hao J-K. A population and Interval Constraint Propagation Algorithm. In Second International Conference Evolutionary Multi-Criterion Optimization (EMO). Lecture Notes in Computer Science 2632:88-101(2003).

Bonatti P., Festa P. On Optimal Service Selection. In International World Wide Web Conference (WWW'2005), May 10-14, Chiba, Japan (2005).

BPWS4J API. Retrieved November 26, 2004, from http://www.alphaworks.ibm.com/tech/bpws4j.

Canfora G., di Penta M., Esposito R., Villani M.L. QoS-Aware Replanning of Composite Web Services. In International Conference of Web Services (ICWS'2005), July 11-17, Orlando (2005).

Cardoso J., Sheth A., Miller J., Arnold J., Kochut K. Quality of Service for Workflows and Web Service Processes. In Web Semantics: Sciences, Services and Agents on the World Wide Web 281-308, 1 (2004).

Collette Y., Siarry P. Multiobjective Optimization: Principles and Case Studies, Springer, NY, Berlin (2003).

Coello C.C.A., Van Veldhuizen D.A, Lamont G.B. Evolutionary Algorithms for Solving Multi-objective Problems. Kluwer Academic Publishers, New York (2002).

Deb K. Multi-Objective Optimization using Evolutionary Algorithms. John Wiley \& Sons, ISBN 0-471-87339-X, Chichester, UK (2001).

Deb K., Pratap A., Agarwal S., Meyarivan T. A Fast and Elitist Multi-Objective Genetic Algorithm: NSGA-II. IEEE Trans Evol Computat, Volume 6, pp. 182-197, April, (2002).

Fuzzy Logic Fundamentals, Chapter 3, pg 61-103. Retrieved February 8, 2005. Available on http://www.informit.com/content/images/0135705991/ samplechapter/0135705991.pdf (2005).

Goldberg D.E. Genetic Algorithms in Search, Optimization and Machine Learning. Addison-Wesley Publishing Company, Reading, Massachusetts (1989).

Grigori D., Bouzeghoub M. Service retrieval based on behavioral specification. In International Conference of Web Services (ICWS'05), July 11-17, Orlando (2005).

Hull R., Su J. Tools for Design of Composite Web Services. In SIGMOD 2004, June 13-18, Paris (2004).

Jaeger M.C., Mühl G., Golze S. QoS-aware Composition of Web Services: A Look at Selection Algorithms. In International Conference of Web Services (ICWS'2005), July 11-17, Orlando (2005).

Khalaf R. Business Process with BPEL4WS, Part 2. Retrieved October 27, 2004. Available on http://www-128.ibm.com/developerworks/webservices/library/ws-bpelcol2/

Knowles J., Corne D. The Pareto archived evolution strategy: A new baseline algorithm for multiobjective optimization. In Congress of Evolutionary Computation, Piscataway, New Jersey: IEEE Service Center, 98-105 (1999)

Liu Y., Ngu A.H.H., Zeng L. QoS Computation and Policing in Dynamic Web Service. In Thirteenth International Conference of WWW 2004, May 17-22, New York, New York (2004).

Löstedt J., Svensson M. Baltazar - A Fuzzy Expert for Driving Situation Detection. Master Diss., Department of Sciences, Lund University (2000).

Mandel D.J., McIlraith S.A. Adapting BPEL4WS for the Semantic Web Bottom-up Approach to Web Services Interoperation. In Second International Semantic Web Conference (ISWC), Sanibel Island, Florida (2003).

Mindswap G. Maryland Information and Network dynamics lab semantic web agents projects. Retrieved October 28, 2004. Available on http://www.mindswap.org/ 2004/owl-s/api/index.shtml (2004).

Moura L. A Genetic algorithm to fuzzy multiobjective optimization. Master diss. Department of Electric Engineer, Campinas University (2001).

Narayanan S., McIlraith S.A. Simulation, Verification and Automated Composition of Web Services. In Eleventh International World Wide Web Conference (WWW 2002), Honolulu, May 7-10 (2002).

Osyczka A. Multicriteria optimization for engineering design. In Gero, J.S., editor Design Optimization, pg.193-227. Academic Press (1985).

OWL-S Coalition. OWL-S: Semantic Markup for Web Services. Retrieved April 12, 2005. Available on http://www.daml.org/services/owl-s/1.1/ (2005).

Ran S. A Model for Web Services Discovery with QoS. In ACM SIGecom Exchanges, Volume 4, Issue 1, Spring, pp. 1-10, ACM Press, New York, NY (2003)

Sreenath R.M., Singh M.P. Agent-based service selection. In Web Semantics: Science, Service and Agents on the World Wide Web, 261-279 (2004).

Tan K.C., Khor E.F., Lee T.H. Multiobjective Evolutionary Algorithms and Applications. Springer-Verlag, ISBN 1-85233-836-9, London (2005).

van der Aalst W.M.P. Don't Go with the Flow: Web Services Composition Standards Exposed. IEEE Inteligent Systems, 18(1):72-76 (2003).

Zeng L., Benatallah B., Dumas M., Kalagnanam J., Sheng Q.Z. Quality Driven Web Services Composition. In Twelfth International Conference of WWW, May 20-24, Budapest (2003).

Zitizler E., Thiele L. Multiobjective Optimization using Evolutionary Algorithms - A Comparative Case Study. Parallel Problem Solving from Nature V, A.E.Eiben, T.Bäck, M.Schoenauer and H-P. Schwefel Eds. Berlin, Germany: Springer, 292-301 (1998).

Chapter 9

MATCHING AND MAPPING FOR SEMANTIC WEB PROCESSES

Tanveer Syeda-Mahmood[1], Richard Goodwin[2], Rama Akkiraju[2], Anca-Andreea Ivan[2]

[1]*IBM Almaden Research Center, 650 Harry Road, San Jose, CA 95120 -.*
stf@almaden.ibm.com

[2]*IBM Watson Research Center, 19 Skyline Drive, Hawthorne, NY-*
rgoodwin,akkiraju,ivananca@us.ibm.com

1. INTRODUCTION

A semantic revolution is happening in the world of enterprise information integration. This is a new and emerging field that blurs the boundaries between the traditional fields of business process integration, data warehousing and enterprise application integration. By information integration, we mean the process by which related items from disparate sources are integrated to achieve a stated purpose. For example, in data warehousing, data from two separate databases may need to be merged into a single database. This is particularly needed during mergers and acquisitions, where the respective company information from two separate databases may need to be merged into a single database. The terminology used to describe the same information in two disparate sources is hardly identical, subject to the vagaries of human use. Figure 9-1 illustrates two schemas from two databases that need to be reconciled during a data warehousing task. The two tables are called PurchaseOrder and POrder, respectively. They consist of 4 columns with names as shown. To properly merge such schemas, we need to reconcile the two terminologies and find their semantic relationships. Ordinarily, this is the job of a data warehousing specialist, who manually identifies the relationships using an application's user interface. Recent research is trying to make this process semi-automated by performing candidate matching between the names automatically, and having people verify the mappings.

POrder			
Sale Price	ItemID	ItemNumber	UnitOfMesaure

PurchaseOrder			
BrandID	Price	Qty	UoM

Figure 9-1. Illustration of schema matching in a data warehousing scenario.

Consider another scenario, now in the context of business process integration. Here a typical task may be a business flow that routes the data between suppliers and their associated applications. Typically, such flows are composed by business analysts who have limited programming skills, and work with user-interfaces that aid in the creation of business flows. They work with an abstraction of data being routed through schemas called business objects. Examples include generic business objects and application specific business objects made popular by CrossWorld (CrossWorld (2002)) a company that was later absorbed by IBM. These business objects are often encoded in XML syntax but are really structured data as illustrated in Figure 9-2. Here two business objects are depicted that come from two separate business applications, say, SAP (SAP (2005)) and Oracle e-Business Suite (Oracle (2002)) that both describe the concept 'Inventory'. The interface descriptions are shown here in the form of a tree for purpose of illustration here. In order to transform the output of one application into the next in a business flow, mapping of attributes from source to target schema is again needed. One such mapping is shown in Figure 9-2. The closely related terms shown by the arrows include some obvious cases such as terms (OrganizationID, OrgID) as well as non-obvious ones such as (InventoryType, StockType).

Our final example comes from the domain of web services. Service-oriented architecture is the latest trend in distributed computing where the need-to-know abstraction of object-oriented programming is again deployed. In service-oriented architecture, the capability of a code component anywhere on a network is described through an interface language called Web Service Definition Language (WSDL) (Chinnici, R., M. Gudgin, et al. (2003)). A WSDL describes a service as a collection of operational interfaces and their type specification, together with deployment information. Let's look at an extract of a WSDL description of an inventory checking service of an electronics company XYZ as depicted in Figure 9-3a.

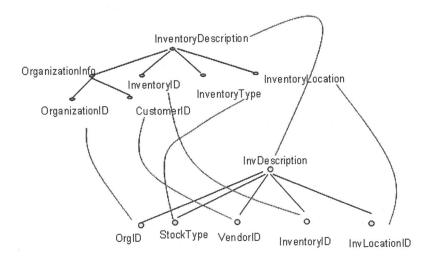

Figure 9-2. Illustration of semantic schema matching in a business process modeling scenario.

We can observe that the WSDL document follows the XML syntax. A set of operations supported by a service are encapsulated in a description using the PortType tag. The PortType in turn lists the operations supported by the service. Each operation lists the inputs and outputs the service takes in the form of messages. In this example, the actual inputs and outputs are expanded in QueryAvailabilityServiceRequest and QueryAvailabilityServiceResponse message tags. Inside each message declaration are the name and type declarations of the inputs and outputs. Here the message shows that it takes the requested item's part number, delivery date and the requested quantity as inputs, and returns the quantity available to be delivered on the requested date as output.

Despite the advancement in service abstraction, the WSDL specification does not prescribe the use of consistent terminology to express the capabilities and requirements of services. Thus two services that accomplish the same task may use different terms to describe similar operations. In some cases, the similarlity between the terms could be spotted through lexical similarity of names, while in other cases, such similarity can only be discovered through the use of domain-specific information. To illustrate this, let's consider a service related to the one depicted in Figure 9-3a. This web service is offered by ABC Inc. and also checks inventory. Its description is shown in Figure 9-3b. We notice first that ABC calls it CheckInventoryService and its inputs and outputs are different from the ones offered by XYZ company's QueryAvailabilityService. ABC's service requires a Universal Product Code instead of a manufacture's part number. The term dueDate is used rather than DeliveryDate and NumberOfItems is used rather than Quantity. Also, ABC's service just returns an ItemAvailabilityConfirmation, which is true if the requested quantity is available and false otherwise. On the other hand, XYZ's service indicates when a request can be partially filled, by returning the number of available items.

As can be seen, there are differences in the interfaces of the services. However, if the objective is to find a service that gives information about the availability of a given part, both services could be semantically similar. In order to chain a sequences of services such as the one above, or to select a similar service from a pool based on a desired interface such as the one shown in Figure 9-3a, we need to find the semantic match between the input or output descriptions present in these WSDL schemas.

This last example also illustrates that finding semantic relationship may require the use of both domain-independent and domain-specific information. A domain independent source of clues gives us a breadth of coverage for common terms, while a domain specific ontology can give a depth of coverage by providing clues based on industry and application specific terms and relationships.

```
<message name="QueryAvailabilityServiceRequest">
    <part name="partNumber_in" type="xsd:string" />
        <part name="deliveryDate_in" type="xsd:string" />
    <part name="quantityRequested_in" type="xsd:string"/>
</message>
<message name="QueryAvailabilityServiceResponse">
    <part name="quantityAvailable_out" type="xsd:string" />
</message>

<portType name="QueryAvailabilityService">
    <operation name="queryAvailabilityService" >
        <input message="tns:queryAvailabilityServiceRequest"
name="queryAvailabilityServiceRequest"/>
        <output message="tns:queryAvailabilityServiceResponse"
name="queryAvailabilityServiceResponse"/>

    </operation>
    </portType>
... ... . .
```

(a)

```
... ..
<message name="CheckInventoryService ">
    <part name="UPC_in" type="xsd:string"/>
        <part name="duedate_in" type="xsd:string"/>
    <part name="numberOfItems_in" type="xsd:string"/>
</message>
<message name="CheckInventoryServiceResponse">
    <part name="itemAvailabilityConfirmation_out" type="xsd:string"/>
</message>
<portType name="CheckInventoryService">
    <operation name="checkINventoryService" >
        <input message="tns:checkInventoryServiceRequest"
name="checkInventoryServiceRequest"/>
        <output message="tns:checkInventoryServiceResponse"
name="checkInventoryServiceResponse"/>
    </operation>
    </portType>
... ... . .
```

(b)

Figure 9-3. Illustration of the schema matching in a web service scenario.

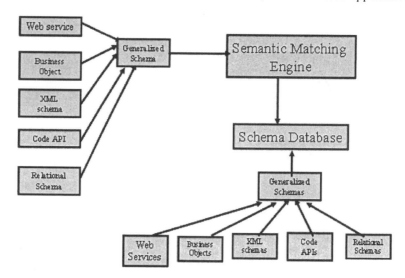

Figure 9-4. Generalized schema matching by normalizing schemas of different origin.

2.   SEMANTIC MATCHING AND MAPPING

As we saw from the above scenarios, matching and mapping of schemas is a problem that is applicable in different contexts and would need to be independent of the nature of schemas used in the semantic web process. Further, we saw that there is a need for bridging the semantic gap between the descriptions in order to make true information integration feasible. The field of semantic matching and mapping has now emerged as a new and exciting field to address these problems of semantic mismatch of descriptions using automated relationship discovery techniques.

We can now define the semantic schema matching problem as follows. Given a source and a target schema defined it terms of its attributes and relationships, find a way to semantically match the schema attributes in a way that is independent of the schema origin. Since different schema origins have different nuances, the schema matching techniques would have to be agnostic to the details of the schema format, but at the same time, capture the underlying name, type and structure relationships described therein. One way to achieve this is to develop a generic schema representation that captures the essential information across different schema formats, and then use this general schema representation as the basis for matching. This approach is illustrated in Figure 9-4. Here schemas arising from different application domains are reduced to a normalized format called the generalized schema. The semantic schema matching is then performed between a pair of source and target generalized schemas.

2.1 Generalized Schema

Schemas of different origin such as code APIs, Web services, XSD (XMLSchema (2004) can be reduced to a normalized format called the Generalized Schema using the following simple grammar.

$$Gs->NaCtTyRsUdOjGs* \qquad (1)$$

Where Na stands for the name of the schema, Ct stands for its category (eg. Its origin as WSDL, XSD, etc.), Ty stands for its type (eg. A complexType or simpleType), Rs stands for any restrictions on its values (eg. Range of values supported), Ud stands for a simple user-friendly name for the schema (as exposed through user interfaces), and Oj stands for the original schema object from which the normalized schema is derived. The Generalized schema can be recursively expanded to describe the structure in its full detail. The type expansions of each of the symbols in the above grammar are given below:

Na->a String
Ct-> a String
Ty->primitive type|language-defined type
Rs->language-defined restrictions
Ud->User-friendly name
Oj->Language-defined object instance
Primitive type --> int|char|String|double|Boolean|Byte|Char|Short|Integer|Long|Float|Double

The above normalized format for schemas has been used earlier for representing code objects (D. Caragea et al. (2004)) and for web services (Syeda-Mahmood et al. (2005)). It can be shown that many abstract data types supported in schemas can be modeled by the above generalized schema. In fact, automatic conversion programs can be written to transform incoming schemas from any of the formats described in Figure 9-4 into Generalized Schema.

3. A FRAMEWORK FOR SCHEMA MATCHING

Let us now consider the problem of semantic schema matching using the generalized schema representation. As defined in Section 2, this is the problem of matching the attributes of the source and target schemas. Ideally, we would like the matching to be 'best' in some objective sense. In other words, we seek a 'best' correspondence of source and target schema attributes. A general way to model such correspondence is to treat the source and target schema attributes as two sets of nodes of a bipartite graph as shown in Figure 9-5. An edge can then be drawn between a source and target node, if the corresponding attributes are semantically similar. Finding the best set of matching attributes then reduces to the problem of finding the maximum matching in the bipartite graph, i.e. with the largest pair of nodes matching. A matching in a bipartite graph is formally defined as a subset of edges of the bipartite graph such that there is a unique assignment for the selected source and target attributes.

Thus the problem of determining an optimal correspondence between the source and target schemas can be expressed as the problem of finding a maximum matching in the bipartite graph. Figure 9-5 illustrates such a maximum matching. On the left is the original bipartite graph formed from the attributes in the pair of source and target schemas. Here we see that multiple edges emanate from source and target attributes indicating there is more than one possible match for an attribute. In the maximum matching, selected attributes are paired with unique matches. The size of the matching is 5 indicating that at most 5 attributes find a match in this arrangement.

In practice, the semantic similarity between attributes is actually reflected through a similarity score which can be treated as a weighted edge. The optimal matching desired in that case is then a matching of maximum cardinality and maximum weight as well. Well-known algorithms are available in literature to obtain such a matching using variants of the maximum flow algorithm (A. Goldberg and Kennedy (1993), J.E. Hopcroft, R.M. Karp (1973)). In these algorithms, the matching is computed by setting up a flow network, with weights such that the maximum flow corresponds to a maximum matching.

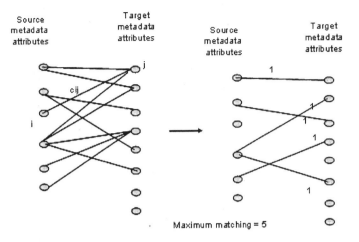

Figure 9-5. Bipartite graph matching framework for schema matching.

Algorithms for finding the maximum matching involve compute-intensive operations as they solve the network flow optimization problem. Often, a good lower bound on the size of the matching can be quickly obtained using a greedy matching algorithm in which the edges are sorted in cost and picked in descending order starting with the highest scoring edge and deleting all edges emanating from the selected pair of attributes.

Notice we have not yet described how the similarity between attributes can be determined. But assuming that such a similarity score can be developed, we now have a general way of picking the best possible subset of edges, and hence a best matching of the attributes of the respective schemas using the above framework for bipartite graph matching.

4.   FINDING SEMANTIC SIMILARITIES BETWEEN ATTRIBUTES

Several cues can be exploited to define the cost of edges in the above framework. In particular, we can exploit the similarity in name, type, or structure to define a semantic similarity score. In this section, we describe some of the popular approaches to capturing semantic similarity between attributes.

4.1   Lexical Comparison of Terms

The simplest one is to do a lexical comparison of their names using a variant of string matching algorithms. A popular approach is to take the longest common subsequence of the two names of attributes being considered (Cormen et al, (1994)). For example, the longest common subsequence between pair *'customer'* and *'custmr'* is *'custmr'* of length 6. A popular formula for finding the similarity between terms on a lexical basis is:

$$Lex(A,B)= |LCS(A,B)|/|A|+|B| \qquad (2)$$

Where LCS(A,B) is the longest common subsequence between strings A and B and the | | stands for the length of the strings. The LCS measure is good for capturing obvious similarities in name of the type above, and also when terms differ by numeric values, or are abbreviations. Examples include, (Address1, Address2), (Num, Number), etc. However, a score value has to be sufficiently high to be a meaningful similarity to avoid false positives. It is very easy for a sequence of symbols to be common without any basis of semantic similarity. Examples include (Address, Adroit), (summary, summon), etc.

4.2   Semantic Similarity of Terms

Next, we address cases where the terms are not syntactically similar but semantically related. A thesaurus is usually employed for this purpose. Among the popular ones are WordNet, a free thesaurus (G.A. Miller (1995)), and SureWord (SureWord (2005)), a commercial thesaurus software for English language.

To determine the semantic similarity of terms we have to first tokenize the multi-word term. Part-of-speech tagging and stop-word filtering has to be performed. Abbreviation expansion may have to be done for the retained words. A thesaurus can then be used to find the similarity of the tokens based on synonyms. The resulting synonyms are assembled back to determine matches to candidate multi-term word attributes, after taking into account the tags associated with the attributes. The details of these operations are described below.

4.2.1 Work Tokenization

To tokenize words, common naming conventions used by programmer analysts, DBAs and business analysts may have to be exploited. In particular, word boundaries in a multi-term word attribute can be found using changes in font, presence of delimiters, such as underscore, spaces, and numeric to alphanumeric transitions. Thus words such as CustomerPurchase can be separated into Customer and Purchase. Address_1, Address_2 would be separated into Address, 1 and Address, 2 respectively.

4.2.2 Part-of-speech tagging and filtering

Simple grammar rules can be used to detect noun phrases and adjectives. Stop-word filtering when performed using a pre-supplied list can help further pruning. Common stop words in the English language similar to those used in search engines include words such as and, or, the, etc.

4.2.3 Abbreviation expansion

The abbreviation expansion operation can exploit domain-independent as well as domain-specific vocabularies. It is possible to have multiple expansions for a candidate words. All such words and their synonyms can be retained for later processing. Thus, a word such as CustPurch can be expanded into CustomerPurchase, CustomaryPurchase, etc.

4.2.4 Synonym search

A language thesaurus such as SureWord or WordNet can be used to find matching synonyms to words. Using SureWord, it is possible to assign to each synonym, a similarity score based on the sense index, and the order of the synonym in the matches returned.

4.2.5 Semantic similarity scores

Given a pair of candidate matching multi-term attributes (A, B) from the source and destination schemas, we can generate a similarity score between the attributes by combining the match scores returned by a thesaurus for their word tokens as follows.

Let A and B have m and n valid tokens respectively, and let S_x and S_y be their expanded synonym lists based on semantic processing. We consider each token i in source attribute A to match a token j in destination attribute B where i ε S_x and j ε S_y. The semantic similarity between attributes A and B is then given by

$$Sem(A, B) = 2*Match(A,B)/(m + n) \qquad\qquad (3)$$

where Match(A, B) are the matching tokens based on the definition above.

Using the similarity scoring such as above, we can determine semantically similar attributes such as (state, province) for the single token case, to (CustomerIdentification, ClientID), (CustomerClass, ClientCategory), for the multi-term attributes.

4.3   Ontological Similarity of Terms

In addition to domain-independent thesaurus, schema matching can be aided by domain-specific terminology. In fact, each organization usually has a glossary of terms compiled that are specific to their domains, such as a banking glossary, electronics parts glossary, etc. With the newly developed standards, it is now possible to represent complete ontologies in formats such as OWL (OWL, (2004)).

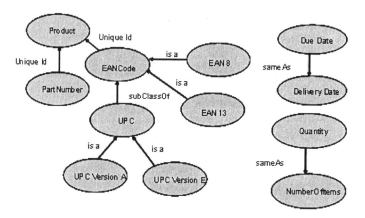

Figure 9-6. Illustration of a simple domain ontology.

To discover similarities between attributes by consulting ontologies, they would first have to be loaded into an ontology management system. An example of such a system is SNOBASE (Lee et al. (2003)), that can reason with concepts and supply similar concepts by derivation from the defined concepts in the ontology. A simple domain-specific ontology that models the relationships between electronic parts is indicated in Figure 9-6. As can be seen, four different types of relationships between two concepts A and B are modeled, namely, subClassOf, superClassOf, instanceOf, and equivalenceClass. Larger ontologies may model many more relationships.

4.3.1 Finding related terms in an ontology

Given a domain-specific ontology and a term from the source schema, how can we find a matching term in the destination schema? Using rule-based inference in the ontology, we can recover all potential similar terms that are in one of the specified relationships, such as subclass, superclass, etc. The matches returned are a set of related concepts along with distance scores representing distance between them. A simple scoring scheme to compute distance between related concepts in the ontology could be as shown in Table 9-1. The discretization of the score into three values (0, 0.5, 1.0) gives a coarse idea of semantic separation between ontological concepts. For example, in the electronics domain ontology shown in Figure 9-6, concepts DueDate and DeliveryDate have a distance of 0 while EANCode and UPC have a distance of 0.5. More refined scoring schemes are possible, but a simple choice such as the one in Table 9-1 works well in practice, without causing a deep semantic bias. Thus given a source attribute DueDate, we can retrieve ontologically matching concepts as the terms DeliveryDate, while a source term "UPC" will return as related concepts (EAC code, Part Number, EAN8, EAN13,UPCversion A, and UPC version E using inference in the ontology of Figure 9-6. In practice, we can choose a suitable threshold T so that all related concepts with distance scores above T can be ignored.

Once the related concepts are found, we can search for these terms in the destination schema and record them as matching attributes to the given attributes from the source schema. Instead of finding ontologically similar terms directly from the attributes of the source schema, it often makes sense to invoke such similarity on annotations associated with the source and destination schemas. Such annotations are usually manually attached by domain experts and are likely to be well-defined terms rather than the cryptic abbreviated multi-term phrases that technical personnel used to name attributes of database and other schemas. As for the inference itself, several rule-based engines are available for reasoning with ontologies including the ABLE (Bigus et al. (2001)) system that uses Boolean and fuzzy logic, forward chaining, backward chaining etc. Rule sets created using the ABLE Rule Language can be used by any of the provided inference engines, which range from simple if-then scripting to light-weight inference to heavy-weight AI algorithms using pattern matching and unification.

Table 9-1. Illustration of a Ont(A,B) for different relationships in the ontology.

Concept Pair	Relationship	Distance Score Ont(A,B)
(A,B)	EquivalentClass	0
(A,B)	RDFType	0
(B,A)	SubClassOf	0.5
(A,B)	SubClassOf	0.5
(A,B)	Other	1

4.4 Type and Structural Similarity of Attributes

So far, we have considered each attribute on an individual basis. However, there are inter-relationships between attributes that need to be respected such as their associated types and positions in schema structure. We now discuss how type and structural information can be taken into account during similarity computations.

4.4.1 Type similarity

For schemas that correspond to code APIs the type of attributes is a strong cue in matching. Specifically, unless the type can be properly cast, the destination component cannot be launched even if the schema matching says otherwise. One way to capture the type similarity is to take the help of the reference type hierarchy defined for the language specification such as XSD, Java, etc. If the conversion is possible but will cause a loss of data (eg. *float* to *int* conversion), then we attach a lower weight. Lossless type conversion (eg. *int* to *float*) and other equivalent subclass type inheritance and polymorphism can be given higher weights. If the similarity cannot be inferred using the reference type hierarchy, explicit user-defined data type conversion functions may exist. For example, a 2D to 1D data type conversion, such as an array to vector conversion is not allowed in the reference type hierarchy but can be achieved through an explicitly written conversion function.

A simple reference type similarity measure can be given by

$$\text{Type(A,B)} = \begin{cases} 1.0 \text{ for lossless type conversion or if type conversion function exists} \\ 0.5 \text{ for lossy type conversion} \\ 0.0 \text{ otherwise} \end{cases} \quad (4)$$

4.4.2   Structural similarity

The structural similarity of schemas can be captured in many ways. A simple way is to consider each level in the schema as representing a grouping of related concepts. For example, all related aspects of a data structure are grouped under an abstract data type by programmers. These in turn may be composed of substructures which are suitable abstract data types formed from lower level type structures. The leaf level attributes in such cases are usually attributes with type primitives such as int, float, etc. Thus structural similarity in the attributes can be measured by the difference in the tree depth at which the attribute occurs. If we record the depth of the attribute from the root node of the schema, the structural similarity between two attributes A and B from source and destination schemas respectively can be given by

$$\text{Struct(A,B)} = 1 - \frac{(|D(A) - D(B)|)}{\max\{D(G_A), D(G_B)\}} \qquad (5)$$

where $D(A)$ and $D(B)$ are the depths of the attributes in their respective schema trees G_A and G_B .

4.5   Combining Similarity of Attributes

As we saw in the above sections, there are many cues that can be used to compute the similarity of attributes. To use these measures in the graph matching framework of Section 3, we need to combine them into an overall similarity measure. Here again, several choices are possible, including linear combination, probabilistic fusion (Kahler et al., (2004)), etc. Here we describe a simple weighted linear combination, where the relative contributions of each cue can be tuned based on the origin of the schemas. For example, the type cue may be more important for API schemas, while the name may be more important for business objects. The overall similarity of a pair of attributes A, B from source and destination schemas respectively can then be given by.

$$Sim(A, B) = \alpha_1 Lex(A, B) + \alpha_2 Sem(A, B) + \alpha_3 Ont(A, B) + \alpha_4 Type(A, B) + \alpha_5 Struct(A, B) \qquad (6)$$

The above similarity score can be used as the edge score in the graph matching framework and a maximum matching can be derived used network flow optimization methods as described in Section 3.

5.   SUMMARY

In this chapter the matching and mapping problem for web processes has been introduced. We have seen that the matching of schemas is a general problem for schemas derived from a variety of application domains. A graph matching framework has been described for addressing the mapping and matching of semantic web process. Multiple cues for determining the similarity of attributes has been defined based on name semantics, type and structural information. The emergence of a general paradigm for accommodating the matching and mapping problem from several different domains ranging from business process modeling to schema integration, is a significant advancement in the development of semantic web processes.

6.   RELATED WORK

The schema matching problem has been addressed by a number of researchers from both database and web service communities. Recently, clustering and classification techniques from machine learning are being applied to the problem of web service matching and classification at either the whole web service level (Hess et al. (2003)) or at the operation level (Dong, (2004)). In (Hess et al. (2003)) for example, all terms from portTypes, operations and messages in a WSDL document are treated as a bag of words and multi-dimensional vectors created from these bag of words are used for web service classification. The paper by Dong et al. addresses this aspect by focusing on matching of operations in web services. Specifically, it clusters parameters present in input and outputs of operations (i.e. messages) based on their co-occurrence into parameter concept clusters. This information is exploited at the parameter, the inputs and output, and operation levels to determine similarity of operations in web services. The notion of elemental and structural level schema matching has been present in the METEOR-S project (Patil et al. (2004)), where the engine can perform both element and structure level schema matching for Web services. The element level matching is based on a combination of Porter-Stemmer (Porter , (1980)) for root word selection, WordNet dictionary for synonyms (Miller (1995)), abbreviation dictionary to handle acronyms and NGram algorithm for linguistic similarity of the names of the two concepts. The schema matching examines the structural similarity between two concepts. Both element match score and schema match score are then used to determine the final match score.

The problem of automatically finding semantic relationships between schemas has also been addressed by a number of database researchers lately

(Madhavan et al., (2003)), (Rahm and Bernstein, (2001)), (Madhavan et al. (2001)). Thus algorithms are available for XML schema matching such as Clio (Miller et al. 2001), Cupid (Madhavan et al. (2001)), and similarity flooding (Melnik et al. (2002)). In the case of database schema matching both schema content (i.e. data) and names of attributes are exploited for schema matching.

The use of ontology match making engines for semantic matching has also been explored by a number of researchers. One of the earliest ontology-based semantic matchmaking engines is Sycara et al MatchMaker (Sycara, (1999)) that is available on the Web as a service. In addition to utilizing a capability-based semantic match, the engine also uses various other IR-based filters. Another related effort is Racer (Li and Horrocks, (2003)), that focuses solely on a service capability-based semantic match for application in e-commerce systems. In a recent work, both ontological and semantic similarity cues were combined to address the larger problem of semantic search which embeds semantic schema matching (Syeda-Mahmood et al, (2005)).

7.   QUESTIONS FOR DISCUSSION

Beginner:
1. Name some real-world problems that have been solved by maximum matching in bipartite graphs.
2. What is the difference between schema matching and schema mapping?

Intermediate:
1. If both domain-specific and domain-independent ontologies had to be used, how would you prioritize the matches to attributes?
2. Suggest other combination schemes for cues besides the linear combination described in text.
3. Think of other cues that can be used for capturing similarity of attributes. Describe how they can be measured.

Advanced:
1. Can the service composition problem by addressed by the bipartite graph matching framework? If not, suggest modifications to the framework to model composition.
2. In practice, a combination of source attributes may map to a single target attribute (eg. A database join) and vice versa. Can such mappings be handled in the graph matching framework? If not, show how the framework can be adapted to handle such combination mappings.

Practical Exercises:
1. Go to xmlmethods.com. Hand-simulate the schema matching on a pair of web services and postulate what the mappings would be.
2. Now write a program to generate the candidate mappings for an arbitrary pair of web services selected from xmlmethods.com.

8. SUGGESTED ADDITIONAL READING

- R. Fagin and P. Kolaitis and L. Popa and W. Tan (2004), "Composing schema mappings: Second-order dependencies to the rescue", in Proc. of PODS, 2004.
- P. Bernstein et al. (2004): "Industrial-strength schema matching," in SIGMOD Record, Vol. 33, No. 4, pp.38-43, December 2004.

9. REFERENCES

CrossWorlds (2002), http://www306.ibm.com/software/info1/websphere/cw011402.jsp.
SAP (2005), http://www.sap.com.
Oracle (2005), http://www.oracle.com.
Chinnici, R., M. Gudgin, et al. (2003). Web Services Description Language (WSDL) Version 1.2, W3C Working Draft 24, http://www.w3.org/TR/2003/WD-wsdl12-20030124/.
XMLSchema (2004). XML Schema Part 2: Datatypes Second Edition, W3C Recommendation 28 October 2004.
D. Caragea and T. Syeda-Mahmood (2004), "Semantic API matching for web service composition" in Proc. ACM WWW 2004 conference, New York, NY.,pp., 436-439, June '04.
T. Syeda-Mahmood et al. (2005): Semantic search of schema repositories. IEEE Int. Conference on World-Wide Web (WWW), 1126-112.
A. Goldberg and Kennedy (1993) : An efficient cost-scaling algorithm for the assignment problem. SIAM Journal on Discrete Mathematics, 6(3):443-459, 1993.
J.E. Hopcroft, R.M. Karp (1973): An n 5=2 algorithm for maximum matching in bipartite graphs, SIAM Journal on Computing 2, 225-231, 1973.
T.H. Cormen, C.E. Lieserson, and R.L. Rivest (1990): Introduction to Algorithms. New York: McGraw Hill, Cambridge: MIT Press, 1990.
G.A. Miller (1995): Wordnet: A lexical database for English. Communications of the ACM, 38(11):39-41, 1995.
SureWord (2005): http://www.patternsoft.com/sureword.htm.
OWL (2004). OWL Web Ontology Language Reference, W3C Recommendation, World Wide Web Consortium, http://www.w3.org/TR/owl-ref/. **2004**.
Lee J., Goodwin R. T., Akkiraju R., Doshi P., Ye Y.(2003): SNoBASE: A Semantic Network-based Ontology Ontology Management. http://alphaWorks.ibm.com/tech/snobase.

Bigus J., and Schlosnagle D. 2001. Agent Building and Learning Environment Project: ABLE. http://www.research.ibm.com/able/

Olaf Kähler, Joachim Denzler, and Jochen Triesch (2004) : Hierarchical Sensor Data Fusion by Probabilistic Cue Integration for Object Tracking, Image Analysis and Interpretation, 2004. 6th IEEE Southwest Symposium on Object Tracking, pages 216–220.

UDDI Technical Committee. "Universal Description, Discovery and Integration (UDDI)". http://www.oasis-open.org/committees/uddi-spec/

X. Dong et al (2004): "Similarity search for web services," in Proc. VLDB, pp.372-283, Toronto, CA, 2004.

A.Hess and N. Kushmerick (2003): "Learning to attach metadata to web services," in Proc. Intl. Semantic web conference, 2003.

E. Rahm and P. Bernstein (2001): A survey of approaches to automatic schema matching, in VLDB Journal 10:334-350, 2001.

J. Madhavan et al (2001), "Generic schema matching with cupid," in Proc. VLDB 2001.

S. Melnik et al, "Similarity flooding: A versatile graph matching algorithm and its application to schema matching," in Proc. ICDE, 2002.

A.Patil et al. (2004): "Meteor-s web service annotation framework", in Proc. WWW conference, pp. 553-562, 2004.

Porter, M. F. (1980): "An Algorithm for Suffix Stripping." Program 14, 1980, 130-137.

S. Melnik et al. (2002): Similarity flooding: A versatile graph matching algorithm and its application to schema matching. In Proc. ICDE, 2002.

Renee J. Miller et al. (2001): The Clio project: managing heterogeneity. SIGMOD Record (ACM Special Interest Group on Management of Data), 30(1):78-83, 2001.

K. Sycara et al. (1999): "Dynamic service match making among agents in open information environments," in Jl. ACM SIGMOD Record, 1999.

L. Li and I. Horrocks, (2003): " A software framework for matchmaking based on semantic web terminology," in Proc. WWW Conference, 2003.

T. Syeda-Mahmood et al. (2005): "Searching schema repositories by combining semantic and ontological matching," in Proc. IEEE Intl. Conf. on Web Services, (ICWS), pp.13-20, 2005.

J. Madhavan et al. (2003). Corpus-based Schema Matching. In Workshop on Information Integration on the Web at IJCAI, 2003.

PART III: REAL-WORLD APPLICATIONS

Chapter 10

DEVELOPING AN OWL ONTOLOGY FOR E-TOURISM

Jorge Cardoso
Department of Mathematics and Engineering, University of Madeira, 9000-390, Funchal, Portugal – jcardoso@uma.pt

1. INTRODUCTION

Currently, the World Wide Web is mainly composed of documents written in Hyper Text Markup Language (HTML). HTML is a language that is useful for visual presentation and for direct human processing (reading, searching, browsing, querying, filling in forms, etc). HTML documents are often handwritten or machine generated and often active HTML pages. Most of the information on the Web is designed only for human consumption. Humans can read HTML documents and understand them, but their inherent meaning is not shown to allow their interpretation by computers.

To surpass this limitation, the W3C (World Wide Web Consortium, www.w3.org) has been working on approaches to define the information on the Web in a way that it can be used by computers not only for display purposes, but also for automation, interoperability, and integration between systems and applications. One way to enable machine-to-machine understanding, exchange, and automated processing is to make Web resources more readily accessible by adding meta-data annotations that describe their content in such a way that computers can understand it. This is precisely the objective of the semantic Web – to make the information on the Web understandable and useful to computer applications in addition to humans. "The semantic Web is not a separate Web but an extension of the current one, in which information is given well-defined meaning, better enabling computers and people to work in cooperation." (Berners-Lee, Hendler et al. 2001).

The W3C has proposed a language designed for publishing and sharing data, and automating data understanding by computers using ontologies on the Web. The language, called OWL (Web Ontology Language), will transform the current Web to the concept of Semantic Web. OWL is being planned and designed to provide a language that can be used for applications that need to understand the meaning of information instead of just parsing data for display purposes.

2.   OWL AND THE SEMANTIC WEB STACK

The semantic Web identifies a set of technologies, tools, and standards which form the basic building blocks of an infrastructure to support the vision of the Web associated with meaning. The semantic Web architecture is composed of a series of standards organized into a structure that is an expression of their interrelationships. This architecture is often represented using a diagram first proposed by Tim Berners-Lee (Berners-Lee, Hendler et al. 2001). Figure 10-1 illustrates the different parts of the semantic Web architecture. It starts with the foundation of URIs and Unicode. On top of that we can find the syntactic interoperability layer in the form of XML, which in turn underlies RDF and RDF Schema (RDFS). Web ontology languages are built on top of RDF and RDFS. The last three layers are logic, proof, and trust, which have not been significantly explored. Some of the layers rely on the digital signature component to ensure security.

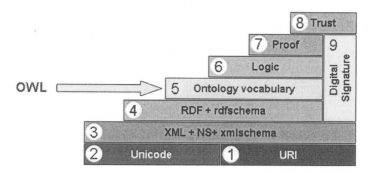

Figure 10-1. Semantic Web layered architecture (Berners-Lee, Hendler et al. 2001)

In the following sections we briefly describe these layers. While the notions presented have been simplified, they give a reasonable conceptualization of the various components of the semantic Web.

2.1   URI and Unicode

A Universal Resource Identifier (URI) is a formatted string that serves as a way for identifying abstract or physical resource. Uniform Resource Locator (URL) refers to the subset of URI that identify resources via a representation of their primary access mechanism. A Uniform Resource Name (URN) refers to the subset of URI that are required to remain globally unique and persistent even when the resource ceases to exist or becomes unavailable. For example,

- The URL http://dme.uma.pt/jcardoso/index.htm identifies the location where a Web page can be retrieved from
- The URN urn:isbn:3-540-24328-3 identifies a book using its ISBN

Unicode provides a unique number for every character, independently of the underlying platform, program, or language. Before the creation of unicode, there were various different encoding systems that made the manipulation of data too complex. Any given computer needed to support many different encodings. There was always the risk of encoding conflict, since two encodings could use the same number for two different characters, or use different numbers for the same character.

2.2   XML

XML is accepted as a standard for data interchange on the Web allowing the structuring of data but without communicating its meaning. It is a language for semi-structured data and has been proposed as a solution to solve integration problems, because it allows a flexible coding and display of data.

While XML has gained much of the world's attention it is important to recognize that XML is simply a way to standardize data formats. But, from the point of view of semantic interoperability, XML has limitations. One significant aspect is that there is no way to recognize the semantics from a particular domain because XML aims at document structure and imposes no common interpretation of the data (Decker, Melnik et al. 2000). Another problem is that XML has a weak data model incapable of capturing relationships or constraints. While it is possible to extend XML to incorporate rich metadata, XML does not allow supporting automated interoperability of systems without human involvement. Even though XML is simply a data-format standard, it is part of the set of technologies that constitute the foundations of the semantic Web.

2.3   RDF

On the top of XML, the W3C has developed the Resource Description Framework (RDF) (RDF 2002) language to standardize the definition and use of metadata. Therefore, XML and RDF each have their merits as a foundation for the semantic Web, but RDF provides more suitable mechanisms for developing ontology representation languages like OIL (Horrocks, Harmelen et al. 2001) or OWL (OWL 2004).

RDF uses XML and it is at the base of the semantic Web, so that all the other languages corresponding to the upper layers are built on top of it. RDF is a formal data model for machine understandable metadata used to provide standard descriptions of Web resources. By providing a standard way of referring to metadata elements, specific metadata element names, and actual metadata content, RDF builds standards for applications so that they can interoperate and intercommunicate more easily, facilitating data and system integration and interoperability. In a first approach it may seen that RDF is very similar to XML, but a closer analysis reveals that they are conceptually different. If we model the information present in a RDF model using XML, human readers would probably be able to infer the underlying semantic structure, but applications would not.

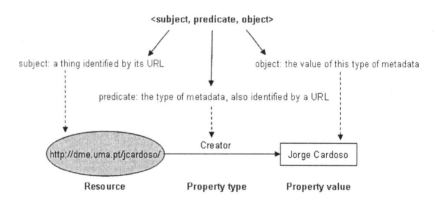

Figure 10-2. An RDF statement

RDF is a simple general purpose metadata language for representing information in the Web and provides a model for describing and creating relationships between resources. A resource can be a thing, such as a person, a song, or a Web page. With RDF it is possible to add pre-defined modeling primitives for expressing semantics of data to a document without making any assumptions about the structure of the document. RDF defines a resource as any object that is uniquely identifiable by a URI (Universal

Resource Identifier). Resources have properties associated to them. Properties are identified by property-types, and property-types have corresponding values. Property-types express the relationships of values associated with resources. The basic structure of RDF is very simple and basically uses RDF triples of the form <subject, predicate, object> as illustrated in Figure 10-2.

2.4   RDF Schema

The RDF Schema (RDFS 2004) provides a type system for RDF. The RDFS is technologically advanced compared to RDF since it provides a way to build an object model from which the actual data is referenced and which tells what things really mean.

Briefly, the RDF Schema (RDFS) allows users to define resources with classes, properties, and values. The concept of RDF class is similar to the concept of class in object-oriented programming languages such as Java and C++. A class is a structure of similar things and inheritance is allowed. This allows resources to be defined as instances of classes and subclasses of classes allowing classes to be organized in a hierarchical fashion. For example, the class First_Line_Manager might be defined as a subclass of Manager which is a subclass of Staff, meaning that any resource which is in class Staff is also implicitly in class First_Line_Manager as well.

An RDFS property can be viewed as an attribute of a class. RDFS properties may inherit from other properties, and domain and range constraints can be applied to focus their use. For example, a domain constraint is used to limit what class or classes a specific property may have and a range constraint is used to limit its possible values. With these extensions, RDFS comes closer to existing ontology languages. As with RDF, the XML namespace mechanism serves to identify RDFS.

2.5   Ontologies

An ontology is an agreed vocabulary that provides a set of well-founded constructs to build meaningful higher level knowledge for specifying the semantics of terminology systems in a well defined and unambiguous manner. For a particular domain, an ontology represents a richer language for providing complex constraints on the types of resources and their properties. Compared to a taxonomy, ontologies enhances the semantics by providing richer relationships between the terms of a vocabulary. Ontologies are usually expressed in a logic-based language, so that detailed and meaningful distinctions can be made among the classes, properties, and relations.

Ontologies can be used to increase communication both between humans and computers. The three major uses of ontologies (Jasper and Uschold 1999) are:

- To assist in communication between humans.
- To achieve interoperability and communication among software systems.
- To improve the design and the quality of software systems.

Currently, the most prominent ontology language is OWL (OWL 2004), the language we will cover in this chapter. OWL is a vocabulary extension of RDF and is derived from the DAML+OIL language (DAML 2001), with the objective of facilitating a better machine interpretability of Web content than the one supported by XML and RDF. This evolution of semantic Web languages is illustrated in Figure 10-3.

OWL evolution

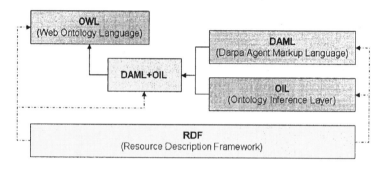

Figure 10-3. Evolution of Semantic Web Languages

DAML+OIL resulted from the integration of the DAML and OIL languages. DAML (DARPA Agent Markup Language) was created as part of a research program (www.daml.org) started in August 2000 by DARPA, a US governmental research organization. OIL (Ontology Inference Layer) is an initiative funded by the European Union programme for Information Society Technologies. OIL was intended to support e-commerce and enable knowledge management. OIL and DAML were merged originating DAML+OIL, which later evolved into OWL.

3.   LIMITATIONS OF RDFS

RDF Schema is a semantic extension of RDF and it is used for describing vocabularies in RDF. It provides mechanisms for describing groups of related resources and the relationships between resources. These resources are used to determine characteristics of other resources, such as the domains and ranges of properties.

However, RDFS is a very primitive language and a more expressive solution is advantageous to describe resources in more detail. In order to fully understand the potentialities of OWL, it is important to identify the limitations that RDFS suffers from. It is the recognition of the limitations of RDFS that led to the development of OWL.

Let's analyze some of the limitations of RDFS to identify the extensions that are needed:

1. RDFS cannot express equivalence between concepts. This is important to be able to express the equivalence of ontological concepts developed by separate working groups.

2. RDFS does not have the capability of expressing the uniqueness and the cardinality of properties. In some cases, it may be necessary to express that a particular property value may have only one value in a particular class instance. For example, a sedan car has exactly four wheels and a book is written by at least one author.

3. RDFS can express the values of a particular property but cannot express that this is a closed set by enumeration. . For example, the gender of a person should have only two values: male and female.

4. RDFS cannot express disjointedness. For example, the gender of a person can be male and female. While it is possible in RDFS to express that John is a male and Julie a female, there is no way of saying that John is not a female and Julie is not a male.

5. RDFS cannot build new classes by combining other classes using union, intersection, and complement. For example, the class "staff" might be the union of the classes "CEO", "manager" and "clerk". The class "staff" may also be described as the intersection of the classes "person" and "organization employee". Another example is the ability to express that a person is the disjoint union of the classes male and female.

6. RDFS cannot declare range restrictions that apply to some classes only. The element rdfs:range defines the range of a property for all classes. For example, for the property "eats", it is not possible to express that cows eat only plants, while other animals may eat meat, too.

7. RDFS cannot express special characteristics of properties such as transitive property (e.g. "more complex than"), unique property (e.g. "is mother of"), and that a property is the inverse of another property (e.g. "writes" and "is written by")

4. THREE TYPES OF OWL

Ontology is a term borrowed from philosophy that refers to the science of describing the kinds of entities in the world and how they are related. In OWL, an ontology is a set of definitions of classes and properties, and constraints on the way those classes and properties can be employed.

In the previous sections, we have established that RDFS was one of the base models for the semantic Web, but that it suffered from several limitations. At the top of the RDFS layer it is possible to define more powerful languages to describe semantics. The most prominent markup language for publishing and sharing data using ontologies on the Internet is the Web Ontology Language (OWL). OWL adds a layer of expressive power to RDFS, providing powerful mechanisms for defining complex conceptual structures, and formally describes the semantics of classes and properties using a logical formalism.

OWL has been designed to meet the need for a Web ontology language. As already mentioned, XML gives a syntax for semi-structured documents but does not associate an XML tag with semantics. Therefore, XML tags do not carry out any meaning, at least for computers. XML Schema gives a schema to XML documents and extends XML with a broad set of data types. RDF is a simple data model represented using the XML syntax for resources and the relations between them. The RDF Schema provides a type system for RDF which allows users to define resources with classes, properties, and values. It provides a vocabulary for describing properties and classes of RDF resources. The RDFS is technologically advanced compared to RDF since it provides a way to build an object model from which the actual data is referenced and which tells what things really mean. OWL goes a step further and allows for describing properties and classes, such as property type restrictions, equality, property characteristics, class intersection, and restricted cardinality.

OWL is the proposed standard for Web ontologies. It builds upon RDF and RDF Schema. XML-based RDF syntax is used, instances are defined using RDF descriptions, and most RDFS modeling primitives are also used. The W3C's Web Ontology Working Group defined OWL as three different sublanguages:

- OWL Lite
- OWL DL
- OWL Full

Each sublanguage fulfils different requirements. OWL Lite supports those users primarily needing a classification hierarchy and simple constraint features. The advantage of OWL Lite is that it is a language that is easier for users to understand and it is also easier for developers to implement tools and applications than the more complicated and wide-ranging DL and Full versions. The main disadvantage is that it has a restricted expressivity. For example, it does not support the concept of disjunction, excludes enumerated classes, and cardinality is restricted to only 0 or 1.

OWL DL supports those users who want maximum expressiveness. OWL DL is more expressive but still ensures completeness and decidability, i.e. all the calculations will compute and terminate. OWL DL (DL for description logics) corresponds to a field of research concerning a particular fragment of decidable first order logic.

OWL Full has maximum expressivity and the syntactic freedom of RDF but does not guarantee computation. It uses all the OWL language primitives and the combination of these primitives in arbitrary ways with RDF and RDF Schema. One major problem is that OWL Full is so expressive that it is undecidable.

Figure 10-4. OWL sublanguages

According to Figure 10-4, every OWL Lite ontology or conclusion is a legal OWL DL ontology or conclusion, but not the inverse, and so on for OWL DL and OWL Full.

5. OWL ONTOLOGY DEVELOPMENT

Tourism is a data rich domain. Data is stored in many hundreds of data sources and many of these sources need to be used in concert during the development of tourism information systems. Our e-tourism ontology provides a way of viewing the world of tourism. It organizes tourism related information and concepts. The e-tourism ontology provides a way to achieve integration and interoperability through the use of a shared vocabulary and meanings for terms with respect to other terms.

Figure 10-5. What, Where, and When

The e-tourism ontology was built to answer three main questions (Figure 10-5) that can be asked when developing tourism applications: What, Where, and When.

- **What**. What can a tourist see, visit and what can he do while staying at a tourism destination?
- **Where**. Where are the interesting places to see and visit located? Where can a tourist carry out a specific activity, such as playing golf or tennis.
- **When**. When can the tourist visit a particular place? This includes not only the day of the week and the hours of the day, but also the atmospheric conditions of the weather. Some activities cannot be undertaken if it is raining for example.

Constructing an ontology is a time-consuming task since it is necessary to find out information about real tourism activities and infrastructures and feed them into the knowledge base.

In the next section, we will be construction an OWL ontology for e-tourism. Since RDFS and OWL are compatible, the ontology developed will contain RDFS elements within the OWL syntax. For those who dislike writing ontologies by hand, a few ontology editors are available. We recommend using one of the most well-know ontology editors, Protégé, which is illustrated in Figure 10-6, to develop the ontology presented in the next section.

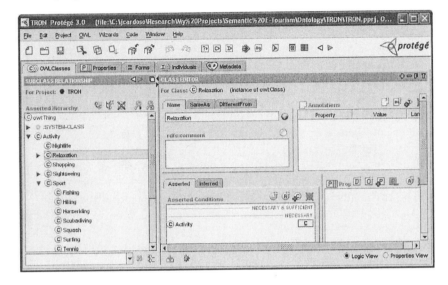

Figure 10-6. Creating the e-tourism ontology using Protégé editor

5.1   Header

An OWL ontology starts with a set of XML namespace declarations enclosed in an opening rdf:RDF tag. XML namespaces allow a means to unambiguously interpret identifiers and make the rest of the ontology presentation much more readable. A namespace is declared using three elements: the reserved XML attribute xmlns, a short prefix to identify the namespace, and the value which must be a URI (Uniform Resource Identifier) reference. An example of a namespace for our e-tourism ontology is:

```
<rdf:RDF
...
  xmlns:weather="http://dme.uma.pt/owl/weather#"
...
>
```

Our initial set of XML namespace declarations which is enclosed in an opening rdf:RDF tag is the following:

```
<rdf:RDF
  xmlns:owl ="http://www.w3.org/2002/07/owl#"
```

```
xmlns:rdf  ="http://www.w3.org/1999/02/22-rdf-syntax-
ns#"
  xmlns:rdfs="http://www.w3.org/2000/01/rdf-schema#"
  xmlns:xsd ="http://www.w3.org/2001/XMLSchema#">
  xmlns =" http://dme.uma.pt/jcardoso/owl/e-tourism#"
  xml:base="http://dme.uma.pt/jcardoso/owl/e-
tourism#">
  xmlns:weather="http://dme.uma.pt/owl/weather#"
```

The first four namespace declarations are conventional declarations. They are used to introduce the OWL (xmlns:owl), RDF (xmlns:rdf), and RDFS (xmlns:rdfs) vocabularies, and XML Schema (xmlns:xsd) datatypes.

The following three declarations identify the namespace associated with our ontology. The first makes it the default namespace, stating that unprefixed qualified names refer to the current ontology. The second identifies the base URI for our ontology. The third declaration identifies the namespace of the supporting weather ontology with the prefix weather. The URI for an identifier is the concatenation of the xml:base value (or the document URL if there is no xml:base) with "#" and the identifier. Thus, the complete URI for an OWL class named ABC is http://dme.uma.pt/owl/e-tourism#ABC.

Once the namespaces are specified, an OWL ontology specifies a set of assertions grouped under the owl:Ontology element. The assertions include the version information which assumes that different versions of the ontology may possibly be developed. The main assertions that can be made about the versioning are:

- owl:versionInfo – a statement which generally contains a string giving information about the version of the ontology.
- owl:priorVersion – a statement that makes reference to another ontology indicating earlier versions of the current ontology. This statement can be used by ontology management tools and applications.
- owl:backwardCompatibleWith – contains a reference to another ontology and indicates that all identifiers from the previous version have the same intended interpretations in the new version.
- owl:incompatibleWith – a statement contains a reference to another ontology indicating that the ontology is a newest version of the referenced ontology but is not backward compatible with it.
- owl:imports – provides support for integrating definitions specified in another OWL ontology published on the Web and identified by a URI. The meaning of the imported ontology is considered to be part of the meaning of the importing ontology.

For example:

```
<rdf:RDF
...
<owl:Ontology rdf:about="">
  <rdfs:comment>E-Tourism OWL Ontology
  </rdfs:comment>
  <owl:versionInfo> v.1 2005-10-25
  </owl:versionInfo>
  <owl:priorVersion>
    <owl:Ontology rdf:about=
  "http://dme.uma.pt/jcardoso/owl/tourism.owl"/>
  </owl:priorVersion>
  <owl:backwardCompatibleWith
      rdf:resource="http://dme.uma.pt/owl/tourism"/>
  <owl:imports
        rdf:resource="http://math.uma.pt/owl/places"/>
  <rdfs:label>E-Tourism Ontology</rdfs:label>
...
</owl:Ontology>
...
</rdf:RDF>
```

Between the header and the closing rdf:RDF tag is the definition of the ontology itself.

5.2   Classes

The main components of the tourism ontology are concepts, relations, instances, and axioms. A concept represents a set or class of entities within the tourism domain.

Each class defined by an ontology describes common characteristics of individuals. OWL classes permit much greater expressiveness than RDF Schema classes. Consequently, OWL has created their own classes, owl:Class. owl:Thing is a predefined OWL class. All instances are members of owl:Thing. The owl:Nothing is also a predefined class and represents the empty class. Each defined class is of type owl:Class. What, Where, and When are examples of classes used in our e-tourism ontology. These concepts are represented in OWL in the following way:

```
<owl:Class rdf:ID="What"/>
```

```
<owl:Class rdf:ID="Where"/>
<owl:Class rdf:ID="When"/>
<owl:Class rdf:ID="Tourist">
  <rdfs:comment> Describes a tourist </rdfs:comment>
</owl:Class>
```

The class What refers to activities that tourists can carry out, such as golf, sightseeing, shopping, or visiting a theatre. The class Where refers to the places where a tourist can stay (such as a Hotel) and places where he can carry out an activity. Examples of infrastructures that provide the means for exerting an activity include restaurants, cinemas, or museums. The class When refers to the time when a tourist can carry out an activity at a certain place.

The ontology also includes relations which describe the interactions between classes or properties. A class hierarchy may be defined by stating that a class is a subclass (owl:subClassOf) of another class. For example, in the tourism domain, the class Squash, Paintball, and Golf are subclasses of the class What. These three classes and their relationship are defined using the OWL vocabulary:

```
. . .
<owl:Class rdf:ID="Squash">
  <rdfs:comment> Squash is an activity a tourist
                 can carry out
  </rdfs:comment>
  <rdfs:subClassOf>
    <owl:Class rdf:about="#What"/>
  </rdfs:subClassOf>
</owl:Class>

<owl:Class rdf:ID="Paintball">
  <rdfs:subClassOf rdf:resource="#What"/>
</owl:Class>

<owl:Class rdf:ID="Golf">
  <rdfs:subClassOf rdf:resource="#What"/>
. . .
</owl:Class>
```

The first statement states that in order to be an instance of the class Squash, an individual must also be an instance of the class What. However, there may be instances of the class What that are not instances of Squash. Thus being a What is a necessary condition for Squash, but is not sufficient.

In our example, we have defined the three subclasses using two different notations. The semantics of the two notations are the same. Nevertheless, we prefer the second one, since it is easier to read.

Two classes can be made equivalent using the assertion owl:equivalentClass. This property, when applied to two classes, A and B, is to be interpreted as "classes A and B contain exactly the same set of individuals." This property is especially useful to be able to indicate that a particular class in an ontology is equivalent to a class defined in a second ontology. For example, the class What can be defined equivalent to the class Activity:

```
<owl:Class rdf:ID="Activity"/>
<owl:Class rdf:ID="What">
  <rdfs:comment> Describes an activity a tourist
                can carry out
  </rdfs:comment>
  <owl:equivalentClass rdf:resource="#Activity"/>
</owl:Class>
```

It is also possible to state that two classes are disjoint using the owl:disjointWith statement. This statement guarantees that an individual that is a member of one class cannot simultaneously be an instance of another class. For example, we can express that the activity Golf is disjoint with the activities Squash and Paintball.

```
<owl:Class rdf:ID="Golf">
  <rdfs:comment> Golf is an activity a tourist
                can carry out
  </rdfs:comment>
  <rdfs:subClassOf rdf:resource="#What"/>
  <owl:disjointWith rdf:resource="#Squash"/>
  <owl:disjointWith rdf:resource="#Paintball"/>
</owl:Class>
```

This example expresses that instances belonging to one subclass, e.g. Golf, cannot belong to another subclass, e.g. Squash or Paintball. A reasoning engine could identify an inconsistency when an individual of the class Golf is stated to be an instance of the class Squash. The reasoning engine could also deduce that if G is an instance of Golf, then G is not an instance of Squash or Paintball.

5.3   Complex Classes

The OWL language provides a set of statements for building complex class descriptions from simpler ones by allowing the specification of the Boolean combination of classes. Boolean connectives (owl:complementOf, owl:intersectionOf, and owl:unionOf) combine class descriptions using logical connectives. For example, two classes, A and B, can be intersected yielding a new class C. Additional set operators include the union and the complement. With OWL Lite only the intersection of classes is allowed.

The owl:complementOf element is applied to a single class and describes the set of all individuals which are known not to be instances of the class. For example, we can state that tourists from the European Union are not tourists from the non-European Union countries.

```
<owl:Class rdf:ID="EUTourist">
  <rdfs:subClassOf rdf:resource="#Tourist"/>
</owl:Class>


<owl:Class rdf:ID="NonEUTourist">
  <rdfs:subClassOf rdf:resource="#Tourist"/>
  <owl:complementOf rdf:resource="#EUTourist" />
</owl:Class>
```

In this example, the class NonEUTourist refers to a very large set of individuals. The class has as its members all individuals that do not belong to the EUTourist class. This means that an individual of any class, such as Locals, Countries, and SiteSeeingPackage, other than the class EUTourist, belongs to the class NonEUTourist.

As the name suggests, the owl:intersectionOf, can be used to intersect two classes, A and B. The new class includes the individuals that were both in class A and in class B.

This element is often used with the owl:Restriction element. For example, taking the intersection of the class of tourist with the anonymous class of people that are senior citizens describes the class of senior tourists.

```
<owl:Class rdf:ID="seniorTourists">
  <owl:intersectionOf rdf:parseType="Collection">
    <owl:Class rdf:about="#Tourist"/>
    <owl:Restriction>
      <owl:onProperty rdf:resource="#category"/>
      <owl:hasValue rdf:resource="#Senior"/>
    </owl:Restriction>
```

```
    </owl:intersectionOf>
  </owl:Class>
```

The individuals who are members of the seniorTourists class are precisely those individuals who are members of both the class #Tourist and the anonymous class created by the restriction on the property #category. While not shown in this example, the category of a tourist is divided into Junior, Young, and Senior. Restrictions will be discussed later.

The element owl:unionOf when applied to two classes, A and B, works in a similar way to the owl:intersectionOf element, but creates a new class which has as its members all individuals that are in class A or in class B. The new class is equal to the union of the two initial classes. For example, the individuals of the class OutdoorSport are the union of all the individuals that belong to the class Golf or to the class Paintball.

```
<owl:Class rdf:ID="OutdoorSport">
  <owl:unionOf rdf:parseType="Collection">
    <owl:Class rdf:about="#Golf"/>
    <owl:Class rdf:about="#Paintball"/>
  </owl:unionOf>
</owl:Class>
```

In other words, the individuals who are members of the class OutdoorSport are those individuals who are either members of the class Golf or the class Paintball.

5.4 Enumeration

An OWL class can be described by enumeration of the individuals that belong to the class. The members of the class are exactly the set of enumerated individuals. This is achieve using the element owl:oneOf and enables a class to be described by exhaustively enumerating its individuals. This element is not allowed with OWL Lite. For example, the class of HotelRoomView can be described by enumerating it individuals: Sea, Mountain, and City.

```
<owl:Class rdf:ID="HotelRoomView"/>
  <owl:oneOf rdf:parseType="Collection">
    <owl:Thing rdf:ID="#Sea"/>
    <owl:Thing rdf:ID="#Mountain"/>
    <owl:Thing rdf:ID="#City"/>
  </owl:oneOf>
```

```
</owl:Class>
```

5.5   Properties

5.5.1   Simple Properties

OWL can define the properties of classes. The OWL property is not very different from a RDFS property. They both use the rdfs:domain and rdfs:range elements. Simple properties can be defined using: owl:ObjectProperty and owl:DatatypeProperty.

Object properties link individuals to individuals. They relate an instance of a class to an instance of another class. The other class can actually be the same class.

For example, the object property hasActivity related the class Where with the class What. This means that a place (i.e., an individual of the class Where) may supply a kind of activity (i.e., an individual of the class What) to its customer, such as Golf and Paintball. The first related class is called the domain, while the second is called the range:

```
<owl:ObjectProperty rdf:ID="hasActivity">
  <rdfs:domain rdf:resource="#Where"/>
  <rdfs:range rdf:resource="#What"/>
</owl:ObjectProperty>
```

Datatype properties link individuals to data values and can be used to restrict an individual member of a class to RDF literals and XML Schema datatypes. Since OWL does not include any data types, it allows the XML Schema data types to be used. All OWL reasoners are required to support the xsd:integer and xsd:string datatypes. In the following example, the year a tourist was born is specified using the &xsd;positiveInteger data type from the XML Schema.

```
<owl:DatatypeProperty rdf:ID="ageYear">
  <rdfs:comment> The year a tourist was born
  </rdfs:comment>
  <rdfs:range rdf:resource= "&xsd;positiveInteger"/>
  <rdfs:domain rdf:resource="#Tourist"/>
</owl:DatatypeProperty>
```

5.5.2   Property Characteristics

Property characteristics allow data to be made more expressive in such a way that reasoning engines can carry out powerful inference. They enhance reasoning by extending the meaning behind relationships. In OWL, it is possible to define relations from one property to other properties. Two examples are the elements owl:equivalentProperty and owl:inverseOf.

The equivalence of properties is defined using the owl:equivalentProperty element. Property equivalence is not the same as property equality. Equivalent properties have the same property extension, but may have different meanings. The following example expresses that stating that "a Person plays a sport" is equivalent to stating that "a Person engages in a sport".

```
<owl:ObjectProperty rdf:ID="plays">
  <rdfs:domain rdf:resource="#Person"/>
...
  <owl:equivalentProperty rdf:resource="#engages"/>
</owl:ObjectProperty>
```

The owl:inverseOf construct can be used to define inverse relation between properties. If the property P' is stated to be the inverse of the property P'', then if X'' is related to Y'' by the P'' property, then Y'' is related to X'' by the P' property. For example, "a tourist plays an activity" and "an activity isPlayedBy a tourist" are cases of an inverse relation between properties. In such a scenario, if the tourist John plays the activity Golf, then a reasoner may infer that Golf isPlayedBy John. This can be expressed formally in OWL as:

```
<owl:ObjectProperty rdf:ID="isPlayedBy">
  <owl:inverseOf rdf:resource="#plays"/>
</owl:ObjectProperty>
```

Functional properties (owl:FunctionalProperty) express the fact that a property may have no more than one value for each instance. Functional properties have a unique value or no values, i.e. the property's minimum cardinality is zero and its maximum cardinality is 1. If an individual instance of Tourist has the PassportID property, then that individual may not have more than one ID. However, this does not state that every Tourist must have at least one passport ID. This is illustrated in the following example with the hasPassportID property, which ensures that a Tourist has only one passport ID:

```
<owl:ObjectProperty rdf:ID="hasPassportID">
  <rdf:type rdf:resource="&owl;FunctionalProperty"/>
  <rdfs:domain rdf:resource="#Tourist"/>
  <rdfs:range rdf:resource="#PassportID"/>
</owl:ObjectProperty>
```

The same semantic can be expressed as:

```
<owl:ObjectProperty rdf:ID="hasPassportID">
  <rdfs:domain rdf:resource="#Tourist"/>
  <rdfs:range rdf:resource="#PassportID"/>
</owl:ObjectProperty>
<owl:FunctionalProperty rdf:about="#hasPassportID"/>
```

Common examples of functional properties include age, height, date of birth, sex, marital status, etc.

Properties may be stated to be inverse functional with the element owl:InverseFunctionalProperty. If a property is inverse functional then the inverse of the property is functional and the inverse functional property defines a property for which two different objects cannot have the same value. The inverse of the property has at most one value. The following example states that the property isThePassportIDof is to be inverse functional:

```
<owl:InverseFunctionalProperty
                    rdf:ID="isThePassportIDof">
  <rdfs:domain rdf:resource="#PassportID"/>
  <rdfs:range rdf:resource="#Tourist"/>
</owl:InverseFunctionalProperty>
```

Therefore, there can only be one passport ID for a tourist. The inverse property of isThePassportIDof, i.e. the functional property hasPassportID has at most one value.

A reasoning engine can infer that no two tourists can have the same passport ID and that if two tourists have the same passport number, then they refer to the same individual.

FunctionalProperty and InverseFunctionalProperty can be used to relate resources to resources, or resources to an RDF Schema Literal or an XML Schema datatype.

Properties may be also stated to be symmetric. The symmetric property (owl:SymmetricProperty) is interpreted as follows: if the pair (x, y) is an instance of A, then the pair (y, x) is also an instance of A.

For example, the property b2bLink of the class Hotel of our e-tourism ontology may be stated to be a symmetric property:

```
<owl:ObjectProperty rdf:ID="b2bLink">
  <rdf:type rdf:resource="&owl;SymmetricProperty"/>
  <rdfs:domain rdf:resource="#Hotel"/>
  <rdfs:range rdf:resource="#LeisureOrganization"/>
</owl:ObjectProperty>
```

This expresses the fact that a Hotel can establish B2B (Business-to-Business) links with several leisure organizations from the tourism industry. For example, a Hotel can establish a B2B link with a Golf course and a SPA. When a reasoner is given the fact that a Hotel A has established a B2B link with a Golf course B, the reasoner can infer that the Golf course B has also a B2B link with the Hotel A.

When a property is stated to be transitive with the element owl:TransitiveProperty, then if the pair (x, y) is an instance of the transitive property P, and the pair (y, z) is an instance of P, we can infer the pair (x, z) is also an instance of P

For example, if busTour is stated to be transitive, and if there is a bus tour from Funchal to Porto Moniz and there is a bus tour from Porto Moniz to São Vicente, then a reasoner can infer that there is a bus tour from Funchal to São Vicente. Funchal, Porto Moniz, and São Vicente are individuals of the class Where. This is expressed in OWL in the following way:

```
<owl:TransitiveProperty rdf:ID="busTour">
  <rdfs:domain rdf:resource="#Where"/>
  <rdfs:range rdf:resource="#Where"/>
</owl:TransitiveProperty>
```

Or equivalently:

```
<owl:ObjectProperty rdf:ID="busTour">
  <rdf:type rdf:resource="&owl;TransitiveProperty"/>
  <rdfs:domain rdf:resource="#Where"/>
  <rdfs:range rdf:resource="#Where"/>
</owl:ObjectProperty>
```

Both the owl:SymmetricProperty and owl:TransitiveProperty properties are used to relate resources to resources.

5.6   Property Restrictions

Restrictions differ from characteristics since restrictions apply to properties with specific values. Property restrictions allow specifying a class for which its instances satisfy a condition. A restriction is achieved through the owl:Restriction element which contains an owl:onProperty element and one or more restriction declarations. Examples of restrictions include owl:allValuesFrom (specifies universal quantification), owl:hasValue (specifies a specific value), and owl:someValuesFrom (specifies existential quantification).

The owl:allValuesFrom element is stated on a property with respect to a class. A class may have a property P restricted to have all the values from the class C, i.e. the constraint demands that all values of P should be of type C (if no such values exist, the constraint is trivially true). Let us see an example to better understand this concept:

```
<owl:Class rdf:ID="TouristOutdoorSportPlayer">
  <rdfs:subClassOf>
    <owl:Restriction>
      <owl:onProperty rdf:resource="#plays"/>
      <owl:allValuesFrom
                rdf:resource="#OutdoorSport"/>
    </owl:Restriction>
  </rdfs:subClassOf>
</owl:Class>
```

The individuals that are members of the class TouristOutdoorSportPlayer are those such that if there is an object that is related to them via the #plays property, then it must be #OutdoorSport. No assertion about the existence of the relationship #plays is made, but if the relationship holds then the related object must be of the class #OutdoorSport.

Using the owl:hasValue element, a property can be required to have a specific value. For example, individuals of the class FunchalSiteSeeing can be characterized as those places that have 9000 as a value of their zip code. This is expressed with the following statements:

```
<owl:Class rdf:ID="FunchalSiteSeeing">
```

```
    <rdfs:subClassOf>
      <owl:Restriction>
        <owl:onProperty rdf:resource="#hasZipCode"/>
        <owl:hasValue rdf:datatype="&xsd;string">
          9000
        </owl:hasValue>
      </owl:Restriction>
    </rdfs:subClassOf>
  </owl:Class>
```

In terms of logic, the owl:someValuesFrom element allows expression of existential quantification. This element describes those individuals that have a relationship with other individuals of a particular class. Unlike owl:allValuesFrom, owl:someValuesFrom does not restrict all the values of the property to be individuals of the same class. When owl:someValuesFrom is stated on a property P with respect to a class C, it specifies that at least one value for that property is of a certain type.

For example, the class TouristGolfPlayer may have a owl:someValuesFrom restriction on the #plays property that states that some value for the plays property should be an instance of the class Golf. This expresses the fact that any tourist can play multiple sports (e.g. Golf, PaintBall, Tennis, etc.) as long as one or more is an instance of the class Golf.

```
  <owl:Class rdf:ID="TouristGolfPlayer">
    <owl:intersectionOf rdf:parseType="Collection">
      <owl:Class rdf:about="#Tourist"/>
      <owl:Restriction>
        <owl:onProperty rdf:resource="#plays"/>
        <owl:someValuesFrom rdf:resource="#Golf"/>
      </owl:Restriction>
    </owl:intersectionOf>
  </owl:Class>
```

The individuals that are members of the class TouristGolfPlayer are those that are related via the #plays property to at least one instance of the Golf class. The owl:someValuesFrom element makes no restriction about other relationships that may be present. Therefore, an individual of the class TouristGolfPlayer may play other sports.

5.7 Cardinality Restrictions

Cardinality restrictions are also property restrictions. In OWL, three different cardinality restrictions exist:
- owl:maxCardinality – specifies the maximum number of individuals,
- owl:minCardinality – specifies the minimum number of individuals, and
- owl:cardinality – specifies the exact number of individuals.

The element owl:maxCardinality: is stated on a property P with respect to a particular class C. If a owl:maxCardinality with the value n is stated on a property with respect to a class, then any instance of that class will be related to at most n individuals by property P. The variable n should be a non-negative integer.

For example, the property #visitLocal of the class SiteSeeingPackage may have a maximum cardinality of 10 since it is considered that a site seeing package should not include more than 10 places to visit.

```
<owl:Class rdf:ID="SiteSeeingPackage">
...
  <rdfs:subClassOf>
    <owl:Restriction>
      <owl:onProperty rdf:resource="#visitLocal"/>
      <owl:maxCardinality rdf:datatype=
                      "&xsd;nonNegativeInteger"> 10
      </owl:maxCardinality>
    </owl:Restriction>
  </rdfs:subClassOf>
</owl:Class>
```

The element owl:minCardinality is very similar to the element owl:maxCardinality. As the name suggests, the only difference lies in the fact that it specified a lower boundary for the cardinality of a property P of a class C. The following example shows that the property visitLocal of the class SiteSeeingPackage has a minimum cardinality of 2. It expressed that a site seeing package should include the visit to at least 2 site seeing locals.

```
<owl:Class rdf:ID="SiteSeeingPackage">
...
  <rdfs:subClassOf>
    <owl:Restriction>
      <owl:onProperty rdf:resource="#visitLocal"/>
    <owl:minCardinality
```

```
            rdf:datatype="&xsd;nonNegativeInteger"> 2
      </owl:minCardinality>
      </owl:Restriction>
    </rdfs:subClassOf>
  </owl:Class>
```

The owl:cardinality, the last cardinality restriction statement, is a useful element when it is necessary to express that a property has a minimum cardinality which is equal to the maximum cardinality. This is a convenience element.

It should be noticed that when using OWL Lite the cardinality elements, owl:maxCardinality, owl:minCardinality, and owl:cardinality, can only specify the values 0 and 1. On the other hand, OWL Full allows cardinality statements for arbitrary non-negative integers. Furthermore, when using OWL DL, no cardinality restrictions may be placed on transitive properties

6.   PUTTING ALL TOGETHER: THE E-TOURISM ONTOLOGY

The following example describes the e-tourism ontology. This ontology can be use to integrate tourist information systems or simply serve as a schema to carry out inferencing.

```
<!DOCTYPE rdf:RDF [
  <!ENTITY xsd "http://www.w3.org/2001/XMLSchema#">
  <!ENTITY owl "http://www.w3.org/2002/07/owl#">
]>

<rdf:RDF
  xmlns:owl="http://www.w3.org/2002/07/owl#"
  xmlns:rdf="http://www.w3.org/1999/02/22-rdf-syntax-
ns#"
  xmlns:rdfs="http://www.w3.org/2000/01/rdf-schema#"
  xmlns:xsd="http://www.w3.org/2001/XMLSchema#"
  xmlns ="http://dme.uma.pt/jcardoso/owl/e-tourism#"
  xml:base="http://dme.uma.pt/jcardoso/owl/e-
tourism#">

<owl:Ontology rdf:about="">
  <rdfs:comment>E-Tourism OWL Ontology
  </rdfs:comment>
```

```
    <owl:versionInfo> v.1 2005-10-25
    </owl:versionInfo>
    <owl:priorVersion>
    <owl:Ontology rdf:about=
    "http://dme.uma.pt/jcardoso/owl/tourism.owl"/>
    </owl:priorVersion>
    <owl:backwardCompatibleWith rdf:resource=
        "http://dme.uma.pt/jcardoso/owl/tourism.owl"/>
    <rdfs:label>E-Tourism Ontology</rdfs:label>
</owl:Ontology>

<owl:Class rdf:ID="When">
    <rdfs:comment> Describes when a tourist can carry
                    out a particular activity
    </rdfs:comment>
</owl:Class>

<owl:Class rdf:ID="Place"/>
<owl:Class rdf:ID="Where">
    <rdfs:comment> Describes where a tourist can carry
                    out a particular activity or stay
                    overnight
    </rdfs:comment>
    <owl:equivalentClass rdf:resource="#Place"/>
</owl:Class>

<owl:Class rdf:ID="Activity"/>
<owl:Class rdf:ID="What">
    <rdfs:comment> Describes an activity a tourist
                    can carry out
    </rdfs:comment>
    <owl:equivalentClass rdf:resource="#Activity"/>
</owl:Class>

<owl:Class rdf:ID="Tourist">
    <rdfs:comment> Describes a tourist. Every tourist
                    is a person
    </rdfs:comment>
    <rdfs:subClassOf rdf:resource="#Person"/>
</owl:Class>

<owl:Class rdf:ID="EUTourist">
```

```
    <rdfs:subClassOf rdf:resource="#Tourist"/>
  </owl:Class>

  <owl:Class rdf:ID="NonEUTourist">
    <rdfs:subClassOf rdf:resource="#Tourist"/>
    <owl:complementOf rdf:resource="#EUTourist" />
  </owl:Class>

  <owl:Class rdf:ID="PassportID">
    <rdfs:comment> Tourists have passports with an ID
    </rdfs:comment>
  </owl:Class>

  <owl:Class rdf:ID="Hotel">
    <rdfs:comment> Hotel is a place where a tourist
                    can stay overnight
    </rdfs:comment>
    <rdfs:subClassOf rdf:resource="#Where"/>
  </owl:Class>

  <owl:Class rdf:ID="HotelRoomView">
    <rdfs:comment> Enumerates the views a hotel room
                    can have
    </rdfs:comment>
    <owl:oneOf rdf:parseType="Collection">
      <owl:Thing rdf:about="#Sea"/>
      <owl:Thing rdf:about="#Mountain"/>
      <owl:Thing rdf:about="#City"/>
    </owl:oneOf>
  </owl:Class>

  <owl:Class rdf:ID="LeisureOrganization">
    <rdfs:comment> A leisure organization provides
                    activities that tourists can carry out
    </rdfs:comment>
    <rdfs:subClassOf rdf:resource="#Where"/>
  </owl:Class>

  <owl:Class rdf:ID="Squash">
    <rdfs:comment> Squash is an activity a tourist
                    can carry out
    </rdfs:comment>
```

```
    <rdfs:subClassOf rdf:resource="#What"/>
  </owl:Class>

  <owl:Class rdf:ID="Paintball">
    <rdfs:comment> Paintball is also an activity
                   a tourist can carry out
    </rdfs:comment>
    <rdfs:subClassOf rdf:resource="#What"/>
  </owl:Class>

  <owl:Class rdf:ID="Golf">
    <rdfs:comment> Golf is an activity a tourist
                   can carry out
    </rdfs:comment>
    <rdfs:subClassOf rdf:resource="#What"/>
    <owl:disjointWith rdf:resource="#Squash"/>
    <owl:disjointWith rdf:resource="#Paintball"/>
  </owl:Class>

  <owl:DatatypeProperty rdf:ID="ageYear">
    <rdfs:comment> The year a tourist was born
    </rdfs:comment>
    <rdfs:range rdf:resource= "&xsd;positiveInteger"/>
    <rdfs:domain rdf:resource="#Tourist"/>
  </owl:DatatypeProperty>

  <owl:DatatypeProperty rdf:ID="category">
    <rdfs:comment> The category of a tourist (e.g.
                   Junior, Young, Senior)
    </rdfs:comment>
    <rdfs:domain rdf:resource="#Tourist"/>
  </owl:DatatypeProperty>

  <owl:ObjectProperty rdf:ID="hasActivity">
    <rdfs:comment> Describes an activity that can be
                   carried out a certain place
    </rdfs:comment>
    <rdfs:domain rdf:resource="#Where"/>
    <rdfs:range rdf:resource="#What"/>
  </owl:ObjectProperty>

  <owl:DatatypeProperty rdf:ID="hasZipCode">
```

```
      <rdfs:comment> Each place has a zip code
      </rdfs:comment>
      <rdfs:domain rdf:resource="#Where"/>
      <rdfs:range rdf:resource="&xsd;string"/>
    </owl:DatatypeProperty>

  <owl:ObjectProperty rdf:ID="plays">
      <rdfs:comment> The activity that a person
                     carries out
      </rdfs:comment>
      <rdfs:domain rdf:resource="#Person"/>
      <rdfs:range>
        <owl:Class>
          <owl:unionOf rdf:parseType="Collection">
            <owl:Class rdf:about="#Squash"/>
            <owl:Class rdf:about="#Golf"/>
            <owl:Class rdf:about="#Paintball"/>
            </owl:unionOf>
        </owl:Class>
      </rdfs:range>
      <owl:equivalentProperty rdf:resource="#engages"/>
    </owl:ObjectProperty>

  <owl:ObjectProperty rdf:ID="isPlayedBy">
      <owl:inverseOf rdf:resource="#plays"/>
    </owl:ObjectProperty>

  <owl:ObjectProperty rdf:ID="hasPassportID">
      <rdfs:comment> Carrying out an activity or engaging
                     in an activity are two equivalent
                     properties
      </rdfs:comment>
      <rdf:type rdf:resource="&owl;FunctionalProperty"/>
      <rdfs:domain rdf:resource="#Tourist"/>
      <rdfs:range rdf:resource="#PassportID"/>
    </owl:ObjectProperty>

  <owl:InverseFunctionalProperty
                          rdf:ID="isthePassportIDof">
      <rdfs:domain rdf:resource="#PassportID"/>
      <rdfs:range rdf:resource="#Tourist"/>
    </owl:InverseFunctionalProperty>
```

```
<owl:ObjectProperty rdf:ID="b2bLink">
  <rdfs:comment> Hotels establish B2B links with
                 leisure organizations
  </rdfs:comment>
  <rdf:type rdf:resource="&owl;SymmetricProperty"/>
  <rdfs:domain rdf:resource="#Hotel"/>
  <rdfs:range rdf:resource="#LeisureOrganization"/>
</owl:ObjectProperty>

<owl:TransitiveProperty rdf:ID="busTour">
  <rdfs:comment> Bus tours are offered from place A
                 to place B
  </rdfs:comment>
  <rdfs:domain rdf:resource="#Where"/>
  <rdfs:range rdf:resource="#Where"/>
</owl:TransitiveProperty>

<owl:Class rdf:ID="GoodWeather"/>
<owl:Class rdf:ID="BadWeather"/>
<owl:Class rdf:ID="AverageWeather"/>

<owl:ObjectProperty rdf:ID="hasWeather">
  <rdfs:comment> Describes the weather at a
                 particular place
  </rdfs:comment>
  <rdfs:domain rdf:resource="#Where"/>
</owl:ObjectProperty>

<owl:Class rdf:ID="PlacesWithGoodWeather">
  <rdfs:comment> Describes the tourist places with a
                 good weather
  </rdfs:comment>
  <rdfs:subClassOf>
    <owl:Restriction>
      <owl:onProperty rdf:resource="#hasWeather"/>
      <owl:allValuesFrom rdf:resource="#GoodWeather"/>
    </owl:Restriction>
  </rdfs:subClassOf>
</owl:Class>

<owl:Class rdf:ID="FunchalSiteSeeing">
```

```
    <rdfs:comment> Describes the places that tourist can
see in Funchal. These places have the zip code 9000,
i.e. the city of Funchal.
    </rdfs:comment>
    <rdfs:subClassOf>
      <owl:Restriction>
        <owl:onProperty rdf:resource="#hasZipCode"/>
        <owl:hasValue rdf:datatype="&xsd;string"> 9000
        </owl:hasValue>
      </owl:Restriction>
    </rdfs:subClassOf>
</owl:Class>

<owl:Class rdf:about="SiteSeeingPackage">
    <rdfs:comment> A site seeing package should include
at least 2 places to visit, but no more than 10.
    </rdfs:comment>
    <rdfs:subClassOf rdf:resource="#Where"/>
    <rdfs:subClassOf>
      <owl:Restriction>
        <owl:onProperty rdf:resource="#hasZipCode"/>
        <owl:minCardinality
              rdf:datatype="&xsd;nonNegativeInteger"> 2
        </owl:minCardinality>
      </owl:Restriction>
    </rdfs:subClassOf>
    <rdfs:subClassOf>
      <owl:Restriction>
        <owl:onProperty rdf:resource="#hasZipCode"/>
        <owl:maxCardinality
              rdf:datatype="&xsd;nonNegativeInteger"> 10
        </owl:maxCardinality>
      </owl:Restriction>
    </rdfs:subClassOf>
</owl:Class>

<owl:Class rdf:ID="TouristGolfPlayer">
    <owl:intersectionOf rdf:parseType="Collection">
      <owl:Class rdf:about="#Tourist"/>
      <owl:Restriction>
        <owl:onProperty rdf:resource="#engages"/>
        <owl:someValuesFrom rdf:resource="#Golf"/>
```

```
    </owl:Restriction>
  </owl:intersectionOf>
</owl:Class>

<owl:Class rdf:ID="TouristOutdoorSportPlayer">
  <rdfs:comment> Describes the tourist places with a
                 good weather
  </rdfs:comment>
  <rdfs:subClassOf>
    <owl:Restriction>
      <owl:onProperty rdf:resource="#engages"/>
      <owl:allValuesFrom
                        rdf:resource="#OutdoorSport"/>
    </owl:Restriction>
  </rdfs:subClassOf>
</owl:Class>

<owl:Class rdf:ID="OutdoorSport">
  <owl:unionOf rdf:parseType="Collection">
    <owl:Class rdf:about="#Golf"/>
    <owl:Class rdf:about="#Paintball"/>
  </owl:unionOf>
</owl:Class>

</rdf:RDF>
```

7.   QUESTIONS FOR DISCUSSION

Beginner:
1. RDF, RDFS, and OWL are languages that correspond to layers of the semantic Web stack and are built on top of XML. Why is XML not itself a semantic language?
2. What are the limitations of RDFS that make it not sufficiently expressive to describe the semantics of Web resources?

Intermediate:
1. Two instance with a different rdf:ID can actually represent the same individual. With OWL, how can you make it explicit that the two instances are different?

2. Use the XMLSchema to define a complex data type to model a student record (e.g. name, degree, ID, etc.) and reference this data type within an OWL ontology.

Advanced:
1. OWL is based on the open world assumption. Identify the characteristics that do not make OWL follow the closed world assumption.
2. Describe a scenario that illustrates how reasoning engines can use the owl:unionOf and owl:intersectionOf elements to carry out inference.

Practical Exercises:
1. Select a Web site, such as www.amazon.com, and develop an OWL ontology to model the information present on its main page.
2. Validate the OWL ontology developed with an OWL validator (e.g. http://owl.bbn.com/validator/)
3. Use a reasoning engine, such as JESS (herzberg.ca.sandia.gov/jess/) to infer knowledge from the developed ontology.

8.   SUGGESTED ADDITIONAL READING

- Antoniou, G. and van Harmelen, F. *A semantic Web primer*. Cambridge, MA: MIT Press, 2004. pp. 238: This book is a good introduction to Semantic Web languages.
- Shelley Powers, *Practical RDF*, O'Reilly, 2003, pp. 331: This book covers RDF, RDFS, and OWL. It provides a good source of information for those interested in programming with RDF with Perl, PHP, Java, and Python.
- Seffen Staab, *Ontology Handbook*, Springer, 2003, pp. 499: This book covers provides a good introduction to Description Logics and OWL.
- OWL Overview – http://www.w3.org/TR/owl-features/
- OWL Reference – http://www.w3.org/TR/owl-ref/
- OWL Guide – http://www.w3.org/TR/owl-guide/

9.   REFERENCES

Berners-Lee, T., J. Hendler, et al. (2001). The Semantic Web. Scientific American. **May 2001**.

Berners-Lee, T., J. Hendler, et al. (2001). The Semantic Web: A new form of Web content that is meaningful to computers will unleash a revolution of new possibilities. Scientific American.

DAML (2001). DAML+OIL, http://www.daml.org/language/.

Decker, S., S. Melnik, et al. (2000). "The Semantic Web: The Roles of XML and RDF." Internet Computing **4**(5): 63-74.

Horrocks, I., F. v. Harmelen, et al. (2001). DAML+OIL, DAML.

Jasper, R. and M. Uschold (1999). A framework for understanding and classifying ontology applications. IJCAI99 Workshop on Ontologies and Problem-Solving Methods.Vol: pp.

OWL (2004). OWL Web Ontology Language Reference, W3C Recommendation, World Wide Web Consortium, http://www.w3.org/TR/owl-ref/. **2004**.

RDF (2002). Resource Description Framework (RDF), http://www.w3.org/RDF/.

RDFS (2004). RDF Vocabulary Description Language 1.0: RDF Schema, W3C, http://www.w3.org/TR/rdf-schema/.

Chapter 11

SEMANTIC TECHNOLOGY FOR E-GOVERNMENT

Ralph Hodgson and Dean Allemang
TopQuadrant, Inc. – rhodgson@topquadrant.com, dallemang@topquadrant.com

1. INTRODUCTION

In the last five years a number of significant developments have occurred that motivate the use of Semantic Technology in e-Government. In 2001, the US President announced 24 e-Government initiatives (US President's E-Government Initiatives, 2001).

In 2004 the Federal Enterprise Architecture (FEA) was first published (Federal Enterprise Architecture, 2004). It is well-known that Semantic technology is an enabler for federation, mediation, aggregation and inferencing over information from diverse sources. Why then, not advocate its use for helping solve interoperability, integration, capability reuse, accountability and policy governance in agencies, across agencies and even across governments?

With this vision, TopQuadrant set out in 2002 to bring Semantic Technology to the attention of the emerging technology work-groups of the US Government at their *"Open Collaboration"* Workshop meetings in Washington DC (Collaborative Expedition Workshops). What followed is a success story of growing awareness and advocacy of semantic technology in e-Government.

In this paper we gave an account of one of the pilot projects that happened within the, now-called, Semantic Interoperability Community of Practice (SICoP, 2005). This group, under the leadership of Brand Niemann, was established for the purpose of achieving "semantic interoperability" and "semantic data integration" in the government sector, seeking, through pilots, to demonstrate the power of semantic technology (Niemann, B.,

2005). The SICoP group is also producing in a series of White Papers[1] (SICoP Module 1, 2005, SICoP Module 2, 2006).

We will describe the "*eGOV FEA-Based Capabilities and Partnering Advisor*", referred to in-short as the "*FEA Capabilities Advisor*", some reference will be made to the Federal Enterprise Architecture Reference Model Ontology (FEA-RMO). First, as necessary background, the FEA Reference Model (FEA-RM) is briefly described.

2. THE FEDERAL ENTERPRISE ARCHITECTURE REFERENCE MODEL (FEA-RM)

In response to the US President's identification of e-government as a key component of his management agenda, the US Federal Enterprise Architecture Program Management Office has proposed five reference models for the architecture of e-government. These reference models were conceived by researching and assembling current practices of the various government agencies. The goals of the reference models include:

- Elimination of investments in redundant IT capabilities, business processes, or other capital assets
- Saving time and money by leveraging reusable business processes, data, and IT-components across agencies
- Providing a simpler way for agencies to determine whether IT investments they are considering are not duplicative with other agencies' efforts
- Identification of common business functions across agencies
- Providing means to agencies to evolve FEA business reference model in response to their changing situation and needs

The FEA models are illustrated in Figure 11-1, from the FEA Program Management Office Web-Site (Federal Enterprise Architecture, 2004). The FEA was established by US Government's Office of Management Budget (OMB), with support from the Federal CIO Council.

---

[1] As an indication of worldwide interest, we note that one module of the series has been translated into Japanese (SICoP Module 1, Japanese, 2005).

Federal Enterprise Architecture (FEA)

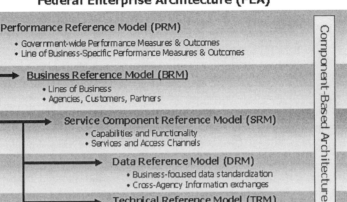

Figure 11-1. The 5 Federal Enterprise Architecture (FEA) Models

The FEA has five models:

1. Performance Reference Model (PRM),
2. Business Reference Model (BRM),
3. Service Component Reference Model (SRM),
4. Technology Reference Model (TRM) and
5. Data Reference Model (DRM).

Each of these is, at its core, a taxonomic structure of Enterprise Architecture constructs as indicated in the figure above. Like other reference models, this is not enterprise architecture itself, but a model to guide enterprise architects in government agencies as they create their own, agency-specific, enterprise architectures. Like other reference models, it provides design guidance, and allows for latitude for specific agencies to tailor and/or map to their specific Enterprise Architectures.

The first full version of the FEA Reference Model (FEA RM) was released in 2004. The work reported in this paper made use of the first four models. At the time of our work, the DRM was under revision.

3.   THE FEDERAL ENTERPRISE ARCHITECTURE REFERENCE MODEL ONTOLOGY (FEA-RMO)

Reference models are typically written in natural language, and are presented as some form of human-readable document. The reference models of the FEA are no exception. This form of presentation has the advantage that the reference models can be read by anyone who can read PDF files; but it has the disadvantage that the process of reusing the reference model ("alignment") can only be verified by an interpretation process whereby an enterprise architect (or whoever has the job of making the alignment) determines what the reference architecture means, and argues for the particular alignment of their architecture to the model. This is a highly ambiguous and subjective task, and is prone to errors and even misuse.

A formal representation of a reference model addresses this problem by providing an unambiguous (or at least, less ambiguous) representation of the reference model, and allows for the definition of objective criteria for whether an architecture is actually conformant.

By representing the reference models in a semantic-rich language like RDF/S and OWL, much of the interpretation and enforcement of the reference model can be automated. Consider, for example, a *"Service Architecture Advisor"*, which would check proposed service implementations for compliance to the reference architecture. Such an advisor could make recommendations about how the architecture could achieve greater compliance with the reference architecture or with other services that are already available. As a second example, in fact the subject of this paper, consider a *"Capabilities Advisor"* that uses the reference model to advise on capabilities that are available or are being built to support particular services and lines-of-business. By having an ontology of the FEA, a system can *"make connections"* between requirements and capabilities and give advise based on inferences.

Figure 11-2 illustrates how ontological relationships can answer questions about aspects of an Enterprise. An executive, manager or employee can discover how the activities of the business support business goals, how capabilities support those activities, and what systems enable the capabilities.

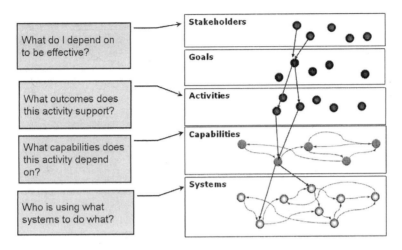

Figure 11-2. Some questions that can be answered by a Semantic Model of an Enterprise

An ontology-based system can answer questions such as:

- Who is using what business systems to do what?
- Who is using what technologies and products to do what?
- What systems and business processes will be affected if we upgrade a software package?
- What technologies are supporting a given business process?
- Where components are being re-used or could be re-used?
- How is our agency architecture aligned with the FEA?

An example of inferencing over properties is shown in Figure 11-3. Using RDF/OWL transitive and sub-properties enables new information to be inferred.

These, and other motivations, led to the development of the FEA Reference Model Ontologies, FEA-RMO, in 2004. FEA-RMO is open source and available at the General Services Administration (GSA)'s OSERA web-site (FEA-RMO, 2005).

FEA-RMO is a number of ontologies built using the W3C standard Web Ontology Language OWL. The FEA Reference Model Ontology architecture mirrors that of the FEA RM itself, that is, the Performance Reference Model (PRM) organizes the overall architecture, making reference to the other models as needed. The Business Reference Model (BRM) draws upon the Service Reference Model (SRM), the Data Reference Model (DRM) and the Technical Reference Model (TRM). In representing these models a recurring design pattern which we named the *"Class-instance Mirror Pattern"* was found to be essential for representing the reference models.

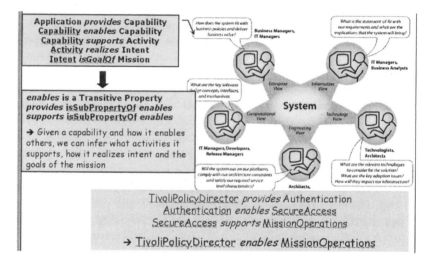

Figure 11-3. An example of Inferencing in an Enterprise Architecture

The table below indicates some of the concepts used in the FEA-RMO. Note that, because of changes that were underway, the DRM was not modeled at the time of this work.

Table 11-1. FEA-RMO Ontologies

Model	Ontology	Example Concepts
Performance Reference Model	PRM	Measurement Area Measurement Category Generic Indicator
Business Reference Model	BRM	Business Area Line of Business Sub-function
Service Component Reference Model	SRM	Service Domains Service Type Component
Technology Reference	TRM	Service Area Service Category

Model		Service Standard
		Service
		Specification
Data	DRM	*Out of Scope*
Reference		
Model		

FEA-RMO also includes a model, the FEA Core Ontology that is not explicitly called out in the FEA RM, where concepts and properties common to all the reference models are defined. This provides modularity to the ontology design that allows for simplified maintenance and integration of the models.

More information on FEA-RMO can be found on the web (Allemang et al., 2005a), and also in a technical paper published in the International Semantic Web Conference (ISWC) 2005 Proceedings (Allemang et al., 2005b).

4. THE E-GOV ONTOLOGY

A candidate application of the FEA-RMO is a system that can advise agencies on who has or intends to have what capabilities in support of services within lines of business. Such a system needs the FEA-RMO but also an ontology about agencies, initiatives, programs and capabilities. This was the motivation for the E-Gov Ontology, referred to in short as EGOV.

The starting point for EGOV was a model of US Agencies and their bureaus and offices. Finding a current list of all the US Agencies and their bureaus and offices was not easy. At the time of the project the best source turned out to be a site at Louisiana State University (LSU Libraries, 2003).

A small RDF graph, with about 3 concepts and 4 properties placed at each agency, would have solved this problem. The remark "*A little RDF goes a long way*", attributed to Professor Jim Hendler, is very apt and in fact was a motivation to see this as an ideal application of RDF. Placed on a server at each agency, the small RFD graph could be populated with instance triples. Aggregating these triples using an RDF crawler would then produce the bigger picture of all offices of all agencies of government.

Getting all the agencies to adopt RDF is of course no easy matter. Nonetheless, this graph is at the heart of the eGOV ontology and is ready to be deployed to realize this vision.

The ontology model goes beyond this simple graph and Figure 11-4 shows an overview of some of the main concepts that drive the *FEA Capabilities Advisor*. Some relationships have been simplified to simple "*has*" links. In the real model, relationship naming and relationship qualification (in particular, inverse, transitive and sub-property qualifiers) is very important to support inferencing.

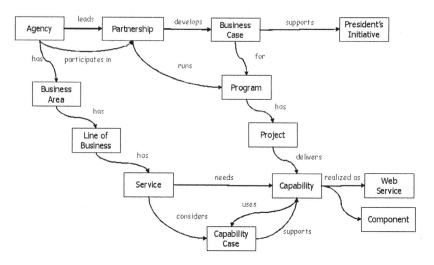

Figure 11-4. Some Classes in the Capabilities Advisor Ontology Model

It is rarely a good idea to have one large ontology. A number of OWL ontologies are involved in the *FEA Capability Advisor* system. Some dependencies of the Ontology Architecture are depicted in Figure 11-5.

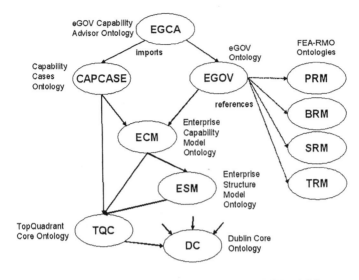

Figure 11-5. Ontology Architecture of the FEA Capabilities Advisor

Dependencies to other ontologies are also listed in Table 11-2. The *eGOV Capability Advisor Ontology*, EGCA, is an application-level ontology whose main purpose is to import the EGOV Ontology and the *Capability Cases* Ontology.

Table 11-2. FEA Capabilities Advisor Ontologies

Domain	Ontologies	Example Concepts (*properties*)
e-GOV Ontology	EGOV	Agency, Bureau, Partnership
Capability Case Ontology	CAPCASE	Capability Case, Solution Story
Enterprise Capability Model	ECM	Capability, Challenge, Force, Goal, Initiative, Measure, Mission, Objective, Strategy
Enterprise Structure	ESM	Association, BusinessArea, Company, Consortium, Department, Division, GovernmentBody,

Domain	Ontologies	Example Concepts *(properties)*
Model		Institution.
TopQuadrant Core	TQC	Artifact, Activity, Organization, Resource
Dublin Core	DC	*contributor, coverage, creator, date, description, format, identifier, language, publisher, relation, rights, source, subject, title, type*

A common pattern in the modeling has been to make use of OWL restrictions to enable the OWL Reasoner to do efficient classification. In many cases, the reasoning required is graph traversal. An example of graph traversal is shown in Figure 11-6, where the so-called *"Line-Of-Sight"* between entities of the Enterprise can be inferred from the ontology models.

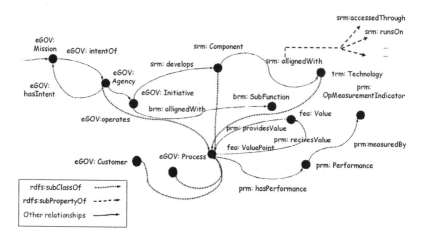

Figure 11-6. How "Line-Of-Sight" is enabled by the FEA and eGOV Ontologies

5.   EGOV FEA-BASED CAPABILITIES AND PARTNERING ADVISOR

The *FEA Capabilities Advisor* uses a semantic engine driven by Ontologies to advise different stake-holders on the capabilities that are available or are being developed to support the Federal Enterprise Architecture and the President's e-Government initiatives.

The system was envisioned as a set of capabilities accessible through WEB Services that would allow agencies, other governments, businesses, and citizens to make queries about the FEA model, to find capabilities that support agency services, to be advised of relevant partnerships, and to assess compliance of their agency business models and architectures with FEA models.

5.1   Motivating User Scenario

One proposed use of the *FEA Capability Advisor* is a *"Business Case Constructor"*. This idea is well aligned to government imperatives to have more effective business cases from agencies and better system support for business case decision support. Through such a system, redundancy, compliance, overlaps and opportunities for synergies across business cases could then be assessed.

In FY04, agencies' capital asset plans and business cases required a demonstrated capacity for collaboration across agencies. In support of this requirement the *Capabilities Advisor* focused on improving quality of agencies' business cases (Exhibit 300).

For the Office of Management Budget (OMB) the *Capabilities Advisor* provides business management insights. For example, the system could provide insights into how the OMB process was being followed, the reasons and patterns of conformance issues and how different projects may relate to each other. In this way, the system focuses on improving the quality of agencies' business cases[2] by providing them with:

- Project-specific guidance for completing forms (Exhibit 300 and Exhibit 53)
- Information on how their project must comply with the FEA
- Knowledge of what related initiatives exist, and candidate federal, state and local partners for their project

For the Office of Management Budget (OMB), the system provides business management insights such as how OMB process is being followed, the reasons and patterns of conformance issues and how different projects may relate to each other.

For business case authors, the system helps with questions such as:

- Who can be candidate federal, state and local partners for my project?

---

[2] In the US, an agency's business case for budget allocation is submitted on an "Exhibit 300" form.

- How do agencies integrate their business cases with FEA?
- How do agencies develop the credible commitments, risk mitigation, and foresight in contracting needed to develop successful business cases?
- What are the new roles and relationships that central agencies, such as GSA, must explore to leverage government wide progress?

5.2   Design of the FEA Capabilities Advisor

The system uses *Capability Cases* as a way to communicate the value of potential IT Capabilities (Polikoff et al., 2005). A *Capability Case* is a way to express aspects of a solution through stories of real (or envisioned) use within a business context. Capability Cases are a way to do requirements that allows business people, technical people and other stakeholders to identify with the emerging solution. Upstream from Use Cases they support the conversation about *"what the system should be"* as opposed to *"how the system will work"*.

Figure 11-7 shows the US President's eGOV initiatives as depicted in the *Capabilities Advisor*. The system is ontology-driven and uses a Datalog engine, RDF Gateway from Intellidimension[3], to drive the web screens and to reason over user actions. On the left is a browser that shows those concepts in the ontology that have been tagged as *"browsable"*. The figures in parenthesis are the number of instances of each class in the system.

Clicking on a class displays a list of instances. Clicking on an instance provides a detailed view as illustrated in Figure 11-8. The *Business Gateway* Initiative is described along with links to enabling capabilities and to the IT program that is realizing the initiative.

---

[3] RDF Gateway is a platform for the Semantic Web from Intellidimension, on the web at www.intellidimension.com.

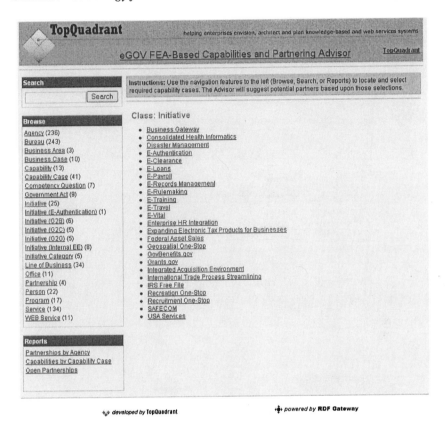

Figure 11-7. The 24 President Initiatives in the Capability Advisor

Initiative (G2B): Business Gateway

Property	Value(s)
capabilities:	Policy Engine, Permit Manager, Eligibility Advisor
description:	The Business Gateway ("BG"), business.gov, will provide the Nation's businesses with a single, internet-based access point to government services and information to help businesses with their operations.
managing agency:	Small Business Administration
organizational unit(s):	Office of Management and Budget
program(s):	Business Gateway Program
is initiative of:	Government to Business
URL	http://www.whitehouse.gov/omb/egov/c-3-5-bg.html

Figure 11-8. The Business Gateway Initiative

By following the link to the *"Eligibility Advisor"* Capability, the details of that capability appear, along with links to where else the capability is applicable, see Figure 11-9. These are links inferred through the *"inverseOf"* property.

Capability Case: Eligibility Advisor

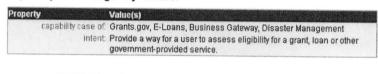

Property	Value(s)
capability case of:	Grants.gov, E-Loans, Business Gateway, Disaster Management
intent:	Provide a way for a user to assess eligibility for a grant, loan or other government-provided service.

> Add this Capability Case to my Requirements

Figure 11-9. The Capability Case "Eligibility Advisor"

The *"Add"* buttons acts in the metaphor of a shopping cart and allows the system to suggest potential partnerships. As each capability is added, the list of possible partnerships is updated, as illustrated below in Figure 11-10.

Selected Capability Cases

- Eligibility Advisor [remove]
- Alert Me [remove]
- Policy Engine [remove]
- Loan Locator [remove]
- Interactive Map [remove]

Suggested Partners

- Federal Asset Sales Partnership (for Policy Engine)
- Recreation One Stop (for Interactive Map)
- The GovBenefits.gov (for Alert Me)

Partnership: Recreation One Stop

Property	Value(s)
description:	Partnership includes supporting partners and data sharing partners
managing agency:	Department of the Interior
partnership mode:	Inviting Partners
participating body:	Smithsonian Institution, General Services Administration, Bureau of Land Management, Tennessee Valley Authority, Bureau of Reclamation, United States Geological Survey, Federal Highway Administration, National Oceanic and Atmospheric Administration, United States Fish and Wildlife Service, National Park Service
is owning partnership of:	Recreation One-Stop Program

Figure 11-10. Selected Capability Cases and Suggested Partners

The system finds partnerships by following relationships in the model. Given a *Capability Case,* the system can find *Capabilities* that it enables. Each *Capability* is implemented by some IT *Program.* Each *Program* in turn is performed by a *Partnership.* Many of these links are the *inverse* of properties found in the model.

We can express a rule of this sort in a straightforward way using a query language for RDF, in which patterns of nodes and links can be expressed in an abstract form. The query engine finds matches in the graph for the abstract triples.

We give an example of such a rule using the RDFQL query language of RDF Gateway (a working draft for a standard query language SPARQL (Prud'hommeaux et al, 2005) has recently become available).

In RDFQL, a pattern for a triple is expressed as three elements set off in {braces}; the first element corresponds to the *predicate* of a triple; the second to the *subject,* and the third to the *object,* so each pattern is of the form {predicate subject object}. Entities in the triples can either be literals corresponding to nodes in the graph, or variables, which can match any node. Variables are indicated with a question-mark (?) as the first character of the name.

The rule for discovering partnerships shown above appears in Figure 11-11.

```
select ?a  ?b ?c  ?d
     using #ds, fea_full
     where {[rdf:type] ?a [CapabilityCase]}
     and {[enables] ?a  ?b}
          and {[rdf:type] ?b [Capability]}
     and {[isImplementedBy] ?b  ?c}
          and {[rdf:type] ?c [Program]}
     and {[isPerformedBy] ?c  ?d}
          and {[rdf:type] ?d [Partnership]} ;
```

Figure 11-11. Example of an RDF Gateway rule, 'getSuggestedPartners()'

Figure 11-11 can be transcribed into English in a straight-forward manner; "Find ?a of type CapabilityCase (i.e., ?a in a triple subject=?a, predicate=rdf:type, object=CapabilityCase), and a Capability ?b that ?a enables. From that ?b, find a Program ?c that is implemented by ?b. Finally, find a Partnership ?d that ?c is performed by." This query describes a graph structure that is matched against the model; every matching set of Capability Case, Capability, Program and Partnership is found. With a more involved query, further filtering can be done, e.g., to ensure that only the selected

Capability Case is considered, and that more information (e.g., the print name) is retrieved for each entity.

Class: WEB Service

- Find a Capability
- Find a Service
- Find an Agency
- Get Status of a Business Case
- Get Status of a Grant Application
- Get Status of a Loan Application
- Register for a Loan
- Submit a Business Case
- Subscribe to a Capability
- Unsubscribe to a Capability
- Verify Policy

Figure 11-12. Web Services listing in the eGOV Capability Advisor

Capability Cases are either realized as components or as Web Services. Some envisioned Web Services are listed in Figure 11-12.

By associating Web Services with the eGOV and FEA-RMO ontologies a much richer directory service can be implemented.

The FEA-RMO Ontologies have been used to build a prototype of an ontology-driven FEA Registry (TopQuadrant FEA Registry, 2005). A working prototype of the Capability Advisor can be accessed on the Web (TopQuadrant eGOV Capability Advisor, 2006).

6.   CONCLUSIONS

The entire development process for the ontologies of FEA-RMO and the *FEA Capability Advisor* took just about three months, from project inception to delivery, confirming that it is possible to deliver semantic technology solutions in short time frames. A key to this speedy development was a good starting point; the published FEA RM. Although it was developed and delivered as a natural language publication, FEA RM was highly structured and quite consistent. Along with the use of ontology design patterns, this allowed the modeling process to proceed smoothly and with minimal ambiguity.

RDF as a foundation technology provided a great deal of the functionality needed to support distribution of the models in a coherent and semantically consistent way. The role of OWL was more subtle. While the reasoning capabilities of OWL were essential in allowing the models to express the appropriate constraints between the elements, the actual reasoning capabilities required were considerably less than those specified in the OWL standard (Patel-Schneider, Hayes, Horrocks (ed), 2004).

Reasoning could be achieved with a simple reasoner for RDFS reasoning, combined with A-box reasoning on inverses, transitive properties, and *owl:hasValue* restrictions. This reasoning can be handled quite easily by technologies such as Rete (Forgy, C, 1982), Datalog (Ceri, S., Gottlob, G., Tanca, L., 1989), Prolog (K. L. Clark and F. G. McCabe, 1982), and need not make use of tableaux algorithms. This suggests that perhaps other reasoning strategies could have considerable applicability in the semantic web.

The FEA-RMO project suggests a whole area of applicability of semantic web technologies. Enterprise Architecture is by its very nature a distributed knowledge capturing problem and needs technologies that can support the aggregation of knowledge held in different locations. The features of the FEA Reference Model that made RDF/OWL so appropriate (distribution of modifications, the need for modifications to be able to specify just what part of the model is being modified) applies to reference models in general, not just the FEA RM.

The *FEA Capabilities Advisor* has demonstrated the power of inferencing in supporting portfolio management across agencies. In any reuse initiative that attempts to save money through collaboration, having timely and accurate information, is crucial for efficiency and effectiveness. The appeal of this pilot project is how the federation of simple OWL models can enable an up-to-date representation of the structure, services and IT capabilities of government agencies. Using semantic technology enables a federated approach to IT Portfolio Management.

7. QUESTIONS FOR DISCUSSION

Beginner:
1. What is an Enterprise Architecture?
2. How might an Enterprise Architecture help an organization be more efficient, effective and innovative?
3. Mention was made in the paper about the power of traversing graphs to make connections across concepts in the model. Consider what connections within and across enterprises would be interesting to make and discuss how they may be supported by EA ontologies.
4. What aspects of an Enterprise might you want to model? Which aspects of an Enterprise should be left out of a model and why?

Intermediate:

1. In a project involving multiple ontologies, what factors influence how you determine which concepts reside in which ontologies?
2. When ontologies need to be re-factored, how might concepts and properties from one ontology be migrated to another? In addition to the concepts, what other modeling constructs would need to be moved?
3. What are the alternative ways to model an Enterprise Architecture? How do they compare with the ontology approach?
4. How could a Federal Enterprise Architecture improve government services at the state (or provincial, or county, or regional) level? What role could the Semantic Web play?

Advanced:

1. Referring to Figure 11-6. Suppose that a component named Atlas is *alignedWith* technology "J2EE". What else can you say about Atlas and J2EE, based on the semantics of RDFS and OWL?
2. The Federal Enterprise Architecture has four *subfunctions* under the line of business "*education*", "*Cultural and Historic Exhibition*", "*Cultural and Historic Preservation*", "*Elementary, Secondary and Vocational Education*", and "*Higher Education*". The EPA has a charter to provide information to the population about environmental factors that affect their health and well-being. What extra sub-functions might the EPA want to add, under the line of business "*Education*"? What other agencies might also provide services that operate under that same sub-function?
3. Information modularity and reuse are good engineering practices. Why did the eGov initiative require a Presidential Order? What forces might have prevented the agencies from cooperating in the absence of the order? Which of these forces are particular to government, and which ones could be a factor in other semantic application areas?
4. What aspects of an Enterprise would need to have rules in addition to OWL?

Practical Exercises:

1. Explore the FEA-RMO Ontologies using an ontology editor (e.g., Protégé, or SWOOP).
2. Browse the FEA Capabilities Advisor prototype at http://www.solutionenvisioning.com/tq/prototype/eGOVAdvisor. Use the "*Capability Cases*" to look for partnerships.
3. Run the FEA Ontology-Based Registry demonstrator, FEA-RMO, at http://www.solutionenvisioning.com/tq/prototype/FEARMO.
4. Visit the US government official list of executive agencies at http://www.loc.gov/rr/news/fedgov.html. What capabilities can you think

of that could be shared between different agencies? Try the same thing with governments of other countries. Could capabilities be shared from one government to another?

8.   SUGGESTED ADDITIONAL READING

- Antoniou, G. and van Harmelen, F. *A semantic Web primer*. Cambridge, MA: MIT Press, 2004: An excellent introduction to Semantic Web languages.
- The FEA-RMO papers provide more insight into how the ontologies were modelled (Allemang et al., 2005a, 2005b).
- The FEA-RMO Ontologies themselves may make interesting reading. These are on the Web at the following URLs:

FEA - http://www.osera.gov/owl/2004/11/fea/FEA.owl
BRM2PRM - http://www.osera.gov/owl/2004/11/fea/BRM2PRM.owl
PRM - http://www.osera.gov/owl/2004/11/fea/prm.owl
BRM - http://www.osera.gov/owl/2004/11/fea/brm.owl
SRM - http://www.osera.gov/owl/2004/11/fea/srm.owl
TRM - http://www.osera.gov/owl/2004/11/fea/trm.owl
Merged Ontology - http://www.osera.gov/owl/2004/11/fea/feac.owl

- Munindar P. Singh, Michael N. Huhns, "Service-Oriented Computing: Semantics, Processes, Agents", John Wiley & Sons, 2005: Provides good coverage of Semantic Web Services standards and how semantics will influence Service-Oriented Architectures.
- Polikoff I. and Coyne R.F., *"Towards Executable Enterprise Models: Ontology and Semantic Web Meet Enterprise Architecture"*, Journal of Enterprise Architecture, Fawcette Publications, August 2005: gives a more detailed coverage of enterprise architecture models.
- Pollock, J. and Hodgson, R. *Adaptive Information: Improving Business Through Semantic Interoperability, Grid Computing, and Enterprise Integration*, Wiley-Interscience, September 2004.

9.   REFERENCES

Allemang et al (2005a), Federal Reference Model Ontologies (FEA-RMO), White Paper, http://www.topquadrant.com

Allemang et al. (2005b), "Enterprise Architecture Reference Modeling in OWL/RDF" in "The Semantic Web – ISWC 2005, 4th International Semantic Web Conference, ISWC 2005", Galway, Ireland, November 6-10, 2005, Proceedings, ISBN: 3-540-29754-5

Brickley, Guha (ed). RDF Vocabulary Description Language 1.0: RDF Schema http://www.w3.org/TR/rdf-schema/

Ceri, S., Gottlob, G., Tanca, L (1989), "What you always wanted to know about Datalog (and never dared to ask)", IEEE Transactions on Knowledge and Data Engineering 1(1) pps. 146-166

Collaborative Expedition Workshops, http://colab.cim3.net/cgi-bin/wiki.pl?ExpeditionWorkshop

FEA-RMO (2004), Federal Enterprise Architecture Reference Model Ontology, http://www.osera.gov/

Federal Enterprise Architecture (2004), http://www.feapmo.gov/

Forgy, C (1982) "Rete: A Fast Algorithm for the Many Pattern/Many Object Pattern Match Problem", pp 17-37, Vol 19, Artificial Intelligence

Jackson, Joab (2005), "GSA gets semantic with architecture reference models", Government Computer News, 2/07/05, Vol. 24, No. 3, http://www.gcn.com/24_3/enterprise-architecture/35004-1.html

K. L. Clark and F. G. McCabe, (1982), "PROLOG: A Language for Implementing Expert Systems", in J. E. Hayes, D. Michie, and Y.-H. Pao, editors, Machine Intelligence, volume 10, pages 455--470. Ellis Horwood, Chichester.

LSU Libraries (2003), Lousiana State University Libraries: Federal Agencies Directory, http://www.lib.lsu.edu/gov/fedgov.html

Niemann, B. (2005), Web-Services.gov, http://www.web-services.gov

Patel-Schneider, Hayes, Horrocks (ed), (2004), "OWL Web Ontology Language Semantics and Abstract Syntax", http://www.w3.org/TR/owl-semantics/

Polikoff, I, Coyne, R.F. and Hodgson, R., (2005), Capability Cases – A Solution Envisioning Approach, Addison-Wesley.

Polikoff I. and Coyne R.F (2005), "Towards Executable Enterprise Models: Ontology and Semantic Web Meet Enterprise Architecture", Journal of Enterprise Architecture, Fawcette Publications, August 2005

Pollock, J. and Hodgson, R. (2004) Adaptive Information: Improving Business Through Semantic Interoperability, Grid Computing, and Enterprise Integration, Wiley-Interscience

Prud'hommeaux, Eric and Seaborne, Andy, eds. (2005), "SPARQL Query Language for RDF", http://www.w3.org/TR/rdf-sparql-query/

Rector (2005), A. Representing Specified Values in OWL: "value partitions" and "value sets" (ed) http://www.w3.org/TR/swbp-specified-values/

SICoP (2005), Semantic Interoperability Community of Practice, http://web-services.gov/ and http://colab.cim3.net/cgi-bin/wiki.pl?SICoP

SICoP Module 1 (2005), "Introducing Semantic Technologies & the Semantic Web", http://colab.cim3.net/file/work/SICoP/WhitePaper/SICoP.WhitePaper.Module1.v5.4.kf.02 1605.doc

The SICoP Module 2 (2006), "The Business Case for Semantic Technologies", http://web-services.gov/SICOPsemwave2006v1.0.pdf and http://colab.cim3.net/file/work/SICoP/2005-09-14/BizValue050914.pdf

SICoP Module 1, Japanese (2005), "Introducing Semantic Technologies & the Semantic Web", http://www.semanticweb.jp/SICoP/SICoP%94%92%8F%91.pdf

TopQuadrant eGOV Capability Advisor (2006), http://www.solutionenvisioning.com/tq/prototype/eGOVAdvisor

TopQuadrant FEA Registry (2005), http://www.solutionenvisioning.com/tq/prototype/FEARMO

TopQuadrant, Enterprise Architecture, http://www.topquadrant.com/tq_ea_solutions.htm

US President's E-Government Initiatives (2001), Office of Management Budget, http://www.whitehouse.gov/omb/egov/c-presidential.html

Chapter 12

BIOINFORMATICS APPLICATIONS OF WEB SERVICES, WEB PROCESSES AND ROLE OF SEMANTICS

Satya Sanket Sahoo and Amit Sheth
Large Scale Distributed Information Systems (LSDIS) Lab, Department of Computer Science, University of Georgia, GA, USA. – {sahoo,amit}@cs.uga.edu

1.   INTRODUCTION

The Human Genome Project (HGP) started in 1990 and ended in 2003, with the aim of discovering the 20,000-25,000 human genes (Barbara R. Jasny et. al. 2003), was the progenitor of the discipline of bioinformatics (David S. Roos 2001). The use of computational tools to store the large amount of data generated by the HGP, to retrieve data and critically to share the data for further study led to development of web based tools and a nascent data management framework.

A biological experimental process consists of multiple stages from 'culture' (involving the growing or collection of sample that contains material of interest) to analysis of the output of a software application. As we see in Figure 12-1, data is generated at all the stages of the experimental lifecycle, in various formats, with different context of use and in extremely large volume. This experimental lifecycle (with various modifications in terms of implementation) with rapid increase in automation at each step is increasingly characterizing biology, from Genomics to Proteomics to Glycomics. This approach is also called 'High-Throughput Experiment' and is being aggressively adopted by the biological community to deal with the inherent complexity of biology.

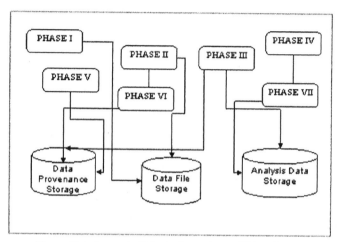

Figure 12-1. A generic biological experimental lifecycle

One of the early data management policy decisions in the HGP was making available the generated data to the community-wide research teams for further study. The World Wide Web played an important role in sharing of this data and making tools, using this data, available for use to biologists. Currently, a large number of applications like BLAST – for homology based search, GenScan – for *ab intio* gene prediction, CUBIC – for binding site prediction, microarray data analysis or ProDom – for protein domain partition are web based tools that use web accessible databases like PDB, KEGG, nr or SwissProt to provide a wide range of computational tools to biologists.

Web Service, with its attributes of platform – independence, web-based access is an ideal framework for ensuring the worldwide use of these bioinformatics resources. Hence, Web Services have been rapidly adopted by the community to enhance the accessibility and usability of their tools. Many bioinformatics tasks involve complex, multi-step processes. If the intermediate steps are implemented as Web Services, their integration to form a Web Process is a logical next step.

2.   SEMANTIC WEB SERVICES IN LIFE SCIENCE

The chapter focuses on a wide spectrum of disciplines in biological sciences and the application of Semantic Web Services, but there are multitudes of other fields in bioinformatics that are not covered. Hence, the readers are encouraged to use this chapter as a learning ground to understand the uses of Semantic Web Services and apply it in the context of other areas of biological sciences and related bioinformatics.

There are now more a thousand Web Services (Stevens's et. al. 2006) offering access to biological resources including, public sequence databases, sequence alignment tools and, format converters. Most of these resources are standalone computational tools with minimal interoperability amongst themselves. Often, the output of one Web Service has to be manually ported from one service to another by the user. For example, a BLAST (Altschul SF et. al. 1997) Web Service may require the input data to be in a standard format (like FASTA), and the users have their data in a local format. But, there is another Web Service that takes in data, in any comma separated format, and converts it into FASTA format. Thus the user has to physically move the output of the converter service to the BLAST Web Service as input.

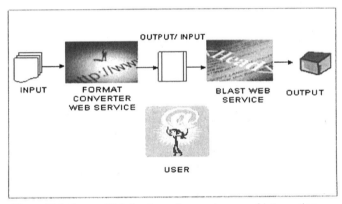

Figure 12-2. Current Web Services often require manual intervention

This form of manual intervention is not feasible in high throughput experimental framework that involves largely automated generation of extremely large amount of data. Hence, composition of Web Services into Web Processes is increasingly becoming a prerequisite in bioinformatics.

Search and discovery of relevant Web Services by researchers can be optimized by use of Semantic Web technology. Using semantic annotation of Web Services, using frameworks like WSDL-S (R. Akkiraju et. al. 2005), will enable semi-automated or automated discovery of Web Services. Moreover, semi-automated or automated composition of candidate Web Services into Web Processes, involving complex processes, mandates the use of Semantic Web technology to match input, output and data formats of constituent Web Services and their seamless integration.

3.   BIOINFORMATICS WEB SERVICES AND PROCESSES

In the following sections, we describe various fields of biological research and the application of Web Services and Web Processes in these areas. In the section, 'Case Study' we discuss in-depth the role of semantics in the search, discovery and integration of Web Services into Web Processes, with specific example in glycoproteomics. The three broad areas of life sciences research, we describe, are Computational Genomics, Computational Proteomics and Structural Bioinformatics.

3.1   Computational Genomics

The use of computational tools to analyze and interpret genomic data is a broad definition of computational genomics. We cover two specific sections of this vast and rapidly developing field namely, 'genomic sequence comparison' and 'finding potential genes' in a sequences organism.

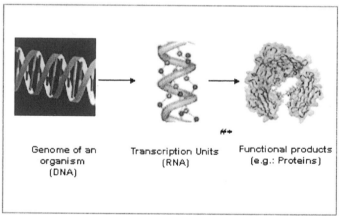

Genome of an   Transcription Units   Functional products
organism   (RNA)   (e.g.: Proteins)
(DNA)

Figure 12-3. The central dogma of biology[1]

[1] # RNA image source: <http://www.fhi-berlin.mpg.de>
* Protein image source: <http://glycam.ccrc.uga.edu/glycam_research.html>

The genome of an organism (constituted of the Deoxyribose Nucleic Acid i.e. DNA) contains the genetic information that is needed by an organism to manufacture needed biological substances to survive. Parts of this genome is *transcribed* into a biological substance called Ribose Nucleic Acid i.e. RNA. This RNA is, in turn, *translated* by other cellular units (ribosomes) that manufacture the corresponding protein or other needed substances. This is also called as the 'central dogma' in biology.

Using computational tools, in addition to traditional experimental approaches, the computational genomics field involves gene finding and sequence comparison among other steps. The use of Semantic Web Processes that integrate heterogeneous computational resources, implemented as semantic Web Services, will increasingly play a critical role in aiding genomic researchers.

3.1.1 Bio-sequence comparison

Background

The DNA and RNA biological entities in an organism are made up of linear sequences of biochemical substance called nucleotides. These nucleotides are represented by four 'bases' namely Adenine (A), Guanine (G), Cytosine (C) and Thymine (T) (which is replaced by Uracil (U) in RNA).

ATG GCC TTT AAA AAA AAA GGG CCC CTT TTT AAA A

Figure 12-4. An example of sequence of nucleotides

In case of proteins, the sequences are made of amino acids. There are 20 known amino acids and their combination (along with other biological entities like sugars) decides their biological functions. Each of the 20 amino acids is represented using a specific character, similar to the nucleotide sequences).

VAY WR QA GL SYIR YSQI CAK AVRDALKTEFKAN

Figure 12-5. An example of sequence of amino acids

In this section, we focus on the comparison of two or more nucleotide (DNA) or amino acid (protein) sequences. The main aim of aligning sequences is to understand or discover functional, structural and evolutionary similarities. The comparison is done; for example, between a newly sequenced genome of an organism against existing genomes to discover their functionality or identify gene sequences (contain the code for a given protein or other biological entity). The degree of similarity between sequences is a pointer to the gene functionality or identification of the unknown sequence. To compare these linear sequences, they are aligned using algorithmic approaches (that may also use various heuristics to reduce the search space). There are various types of alignments:

a) **Global vs. local alignment:** In case of global alignment, the sequences are compared in their entirety and gaps in the sequences are inserted, where needed, to make the compared sequences of same length. But, in case of local alignment, a particular portion of the sequence is compared against a portion of another sequence. The aim of local alignment is to look for the optimal alignment between the sub-regions.

b) **Gapped vs. ungapped alignment:** The alignment algorithm introduces gaps in the sequences to optimize the match, in case of gapped alignment. In case of ungapped alignment, gaps are not introduced in the sequences.

c) **Pairwise vs. multiple alignments:** Alignment involving two sequences is called pairwise alignment and that involving multiple sequences is called multiple alignment.

There may any permutation of the above types of alignment, for example, local pairwise ungapped alignment or global multiple ungapped alignment.

Role of Semantic Web Services

There are many web-based algorithms for alignment of sequences, with the Basic Linear Alignment Search Tool (BLAST) as the most popular tool. There are two variants of BLAST tool:

a) **NCBI BLAST:** http://ncbi.nlm.nih.gov/BLAST

b) **WUBLAST:** http://blast.wustl.edu

BLAST utility is available in form of Web Services. The Web Services have been developed by many research groups namely, European Bioinformatics Institute (EBI, www.ebi.ac.uk/Tools/webservices/WSWUBlast.html), IBM alphaWorks (http://www.alphaworks.ibm.com/tech/ws4LS) and are also available as parallel or distributed implementations. For example, the WSWUBlast, at EBI, is used to compare a novel sequence with those in a protein or nucleotide database (http://www.ebi.ac.uk/Tools/webservices/services.html).

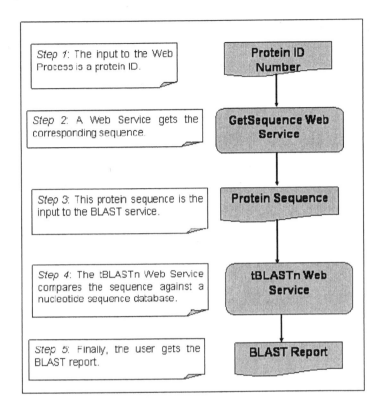

Figure 12-6. A bio-sequence comparator Web Process involving multiple Web Services in sequence

There has been a lot of progress on integrating these Web Services into Web Processes. Many of these initiatives use semantics in the composition of Web Processes using a combination of generic Web Service description and domain ontologies. The generic Web Service description ontologies such as WSDL-S, OWL-S (David Martin et. al. 2004) specify common Web Service concepts. The domain ontology specifies concepts that relate the Web Service to a domain, such as type of service. Workflow engines, namely Taverna (Tom Oinn et. al. 2004) and Pegasys (Sohrab P Shah et. al. 2004), are initialized with available BLAST related Web Services that can be configured and enacted as a workflow.

3.1.2   Computational gene finding

A gene in an organism's genome codes for a protein or other biological substances. Computational gene finding involves the identification of sections in the genome of an organism that encodes for relevant bioentity.

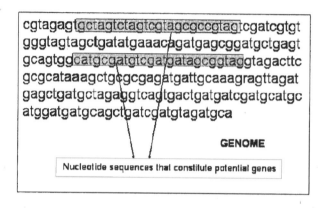

cgtagag gctagtctagtcgtagcgccgtag tcgatcgtgt
gggtagtagctgatatgaaacagatgagcggatgctgagt
gcagtgg catgcgatgtcgatgatagcggtag gtagacttc
gcgcataaagctgcgcgagatgattgcaaagragttagat
gagctgatgctagaggtcagtgactgatgatcgatgcatgc
atggatgatgcagctgatcgatgtagatgca

GENOME

Nucleotide sequences that constitute potential genes

Figure 12-7. Genes in a genome

There are two approaches for gene finding:

a) **Homology-based methods:** A newly sequenced genome, with unknown genes locations, is compared to homologs in sequence databases. By finding similar sequences, with known genes, to the newly sequenced genome, genes in the newly sequenced genome are predicted.

b) *Ab initio* **methods:** This method involves the prediction of genes in a genome using common distinguishing characteristics of known genes.

Some of the common distinguishing characteristics of genes are coding regions and boundaries of coding region.

Role of Semantic Web Services:

There are many computational gene prediction tools (using *ab initio* method) that use different algorithmic approaches using multiple modeling techniques. The main drawbacks of homology based technique are the required availability of homologous genomes to the newly sequenced genome (else, homology based prediction is not possible) and the, often, inaccurate prediction of gene boundaries. The following are some of the popular available tools using *ab initio* techniques:

a) **GRAIL:** (http://compbio.ornl.gov/Grail-1.3/) This is a gene finding program for eukaryotic genome, including human and mouse

b) **GeneScan:** (http://genes.mit.edu/GENSCAN.html) This tool is based on generalized hidden markov model (GHMM) which models both strands of the DNA. It is mainly used for eukaryotic genomes.

c) **Glimmer:** (http://cbcb.umd.edu/software/glimmer/) This tools is generally used for gene prediction in prokaryotic genomes.

Only GeneScan, out of the above listed tools, is also available as a Web Service. A scenario for the use of a Web Process would be for the comparison of results from similar tools (implemented as Web Services) to arrive at a common predicted gene list. This combined approach to *ab initio* gene prediction, using different algorithm and representational model, may be of interest to bioinformaticians.

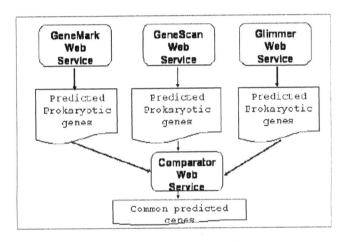

Figure 12-8. This Web Process involves parallel and sequential execution of multiple Web Services to predict genes in given genome.

3.2   Computational Proteomics

Proteomics is the study of complete set of proteins produced by a species. The main goal of proteomics is to identify and quantitate the proteins that are present in an organism, cell type, tissue or other cellular parts. We cover one sub area in the proteomics i.e. the prediction of the function of a protein. Other areas of computational proteomics involve the use of similar suite of computational tools, used independently or in combination, to study and analyze proteins.

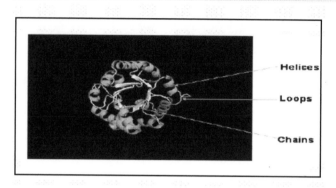

Figure 12-9. Secondary structure of Triose Phosphate Isomerase protein (1Chain)*

3.2.1   Functional prediction of proteins

Proteins may be classified according to their structure or their functions. These classification parameters are not mutually exclusive, but are interdependent. Proteins function is determined by many factors including its constituent sequence, its structure as well as other attached biological entities like sugars. The structure of a protein is also determined by its function, evolved over a period of time.

Protein function may be predicted at multiple levels of specificity:

a) **Generic function:** For example, a given protein is an enzyme

b) **Specific function:** The given protein is an enzyme involved in digesting other proteins.

Role of Semantic Web Services:

There are many different approaches to predict the function of a protein, including:

a) **Sequence comparison:** The new sequence is aligned to known genes in a sequence database and function of the new gene is derived from the known genes. One of the BLAST tools, PSI-BLAST, is used for sequence comparison.

b) **Phylogenetic profile analysis:** The phylogenetic profile of a protein is a string that encodes the presence or absence of protein in a sequenced

---

*protein image source: RCSB PDB (http://pdbbeta.rcsb.org/pdb) using PyMOL (http://pymol.sourceforge.net/) application

genome. The phylogenetic profile of proteins that participate in common functions are often 'similar'. An online tool that does phylogenetic profile analysis is Protein Link Explorer (PLEX) at http://bioinformatics.icmb.utexas.edu/plex/plex-new.html.

c) **Protein – protein interaction:** The interaction between two proteins is a useful way to predict the function of new protein. There are many public, web-based protein interaction databases like Protein Interaction Database (DIP) at http://dip.doe-mbi.ucla.edu/.

Similar to gene prediction method, these multiple approaches to function prediction in protein may be combined to arrive at a consensual result. This would involve the implementation of the above listed resources as Web Services. These Web Services may be composed, with a number of permutations, into a Web Process.

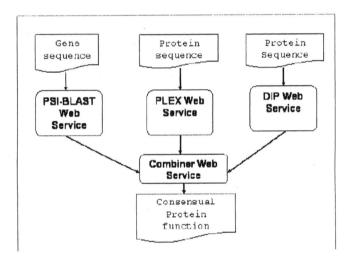

Figure 12-10. A Web Process combining multiple Web Services to output a consensual protein function

3.3 Structural Bioinformatics

The determination of structure of biological entities including proteins, RNA, and simulation of interactions between proteins are computationally intensive areas of research in bioinformatics. The structure of a biomolecule plays a critical role in determining its characteristics and functionality.

3.3.1   Molecular Dynamic simulation of proteins and interactions

The constituents of biological entities i.e. molecules are perpetually in motion, except at absolute zero temperature. As relevant biological activity do not take place at absolute zero temperature, the motion of the constituent molecules in biological substances determine their conformation. In flexible molecules, such as RNA, proteins or sugars, a single structure cannot describe their structure. Hence, the structure of such biological entities is a suite of individual conformations.

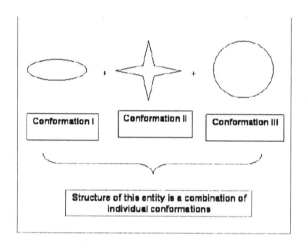

Figure 12-11. The suite of conformations, varying over a particular parameter (E.g. time)

Role of Semantic Web Services

The simulation of these individual conformations is calculated using the multitude of forces that act on an entity. There are many algorithmic approaches that take into consideration the various factors acting on an entity to determine the different conformations that fit.

The implementations of these algorithms are extremely expensive in terms of computational resources. There are multiple approaches to optimize the performance of these applications, including dedicated clusters and grid computing.

Grid based Web Services are an exciting area of current bioinformatics research. The notion behind this approach is to distribute the computation of a Web Service across a grid, perhaps transparently to the user, to enhance the time based performance parameters. [my]Grid (Carole Goble 2005) is a project involved in the use of grid based services (mostly Web Services) for data and application resource integration.

Web processes, composed of 'grid-aware' Web Services would be ideal to carry out molecular dynamics simulation computations. A potential Web Process may be a process involving the multiple services that simulate the conformation of a biomolecule under multiple conditions, namely temperature, pressure or time.

4.   CASE STUDY

The common thread in all the above discussed fields of bioinformatics is the implementation of available resources as Web Services and their integration into Web Processes to carry out complex, multi-step biologically relevant function. The discovery of candidate Web Services and their integration into Web Processes is possible only within a semantic framework. In this section, using a case study, we will expand on the application of semantics in the implementation of Web Services and composition of Web Processes in glycoproteomics.

Background

Proteins, the biological workhorse in an organism, have many modifications after their translation (refer to figure on 'The central dogma in biology') called post-translational modifications. These post-translational modifications play an important role in deciding the function of a protein. One of the post-translational modifications involves the attachment of glycans (modifications of sugars), this process is called glycosylation. Glycoproteomics involves the study of interactions between proteins and glycans. One of the main objectives of glycoproteomics is to identify glycoproteins and quantify their presence.

As part of the Integrated Technology Resource for biomedical glycomics, established by National Center for Research Resources, a team of biologists, biochemists at the Complex Carbohydrate Research Center (CCRC) and computer scientists at the Large Scale Distributed Information Systems (LSDIS) lab at the University of Georgia are working towards the standardization of experimental protocols for high-throughput glycoproteomics research. The different phases of a workflow involved in the glycoproteomics experiment are detailed in Figure 12-12.

The workflow involves both wet-lab experiments (involving experiments conducted by biologists) that cannot be completely automated using computational applications. But, there are many steps that can be automated and exposed as Web Services.

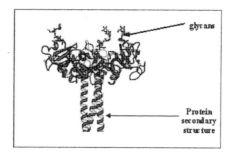

Figure 12-12. The result of a post-translational modification (glycosylation) in proteins (Glycoprotein image source: http://www.functionalglycomics.org/static/consortium/)

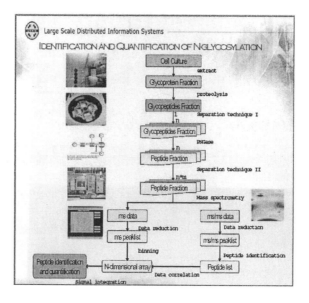

Figure 12-13. The workflow being developed as part of the biomedical glycomics project at the Complex Carbohydrate Research Center (CCRC) and the Large Scale Distributed Information Systems (LSDIS) Lab

```
<?xml version="1.0" encoding="UTF-8"?>
<wsdl:definitions targetNamespace="urn:ngp"
......
xmlns:
wssem="http://www.ibm.com/xmlns/WebServices/WSSem
antics"
 xmlns:
ProPreO="http://lsdis.cs.uga.edu/ontologies/ProPr
eO.owl" >

<wsdl:types>
  <schema targetNamespace="urn:ngp"
    xmlns="http://www.w3.org/2001/XMLSchema">
......
</complexType>
  </schema>
  </wsdl:types>
    <wsdl:message name="replaceCharacterRequest"
wssem:modelReference="ProPreO#peptide_sequence">
       <wsdl:part name="in0"
type="soapenc:string"/>
       <wsdl:part name="in1"
type="soapenc:string"/>
       <wsdl:part name="in2"
type="soapenc:string"/>
   </wsdl:message>
```

Figure 12-14. An example WSDL-S of a Web Service used in the glycomics workflow

Semantic annotation of these Web Services with concepts from domain ontology enables their search, discovery and integration using semantic techniques. The domain ontology, ProPreO (S. S. Sahoo et. al. 2005), is used in the semantic annotation of Web Services used in the glycomics workflow. ProPreO is an ontology to model the complete glycoproteomics experiment.

The semantic annotation of these Web Services is at two levels:

a) **Service level:** This annotation describes the Web Service as a monolithic entity. Hence, a user searching for a Web Service that can parse a protein FASTA file and output a list of protein sequences may search using keywords that describe the task implemented by the Web Service.

b) **Operation level:** The specific operations in a Web Service may also be annotated using relevant concepts from ProPreO. The annotation includes the description of the input and output of an operation.

Service level semantic annotation help in the search and discovery of individual Web Services, whereas, operation level semantic annotation enable the use of multiple Web Services (or their operations) to be integrated into a Web Process.

5. CONCLUSION

The use of Web Services is increasing at a rapid rate in bioinformatics. Web Services offer the ability of providing web-based access, platform-independent development and deployment. Web Processes, constituted of Web Services, enable automation of complex multi-step processes. The use of Web Services technology enables biologists to process and analyze data at equal pace with high-throughput experimental data generation. But, with increasing number of available Web Services, it is almost impossible to search for a suitable Web Service with specific input and output, by a researcher. Further, the composing of a Web Process using these candidate Web Services is a daunting task for any user.

Hence, use of semantics namely, ontology-based keywords to annotate Web Services enable application to search, discover and integrate Web Services seamlessly. We describe the use of WSDL-S as a method to semantically annotate Web Services. As the field of bioinformatics grows, with an attendant increase in number of available Web Services, the use of semantics is assuming a critical role in enabling their usage by biologists as part of their standard suite of research tools.

6. ACKNOWLEDGMENT

This work is part of the Integrated Technology Resource for Biomedical Glycomics (5 P41 RR18502-02), funded by the National Institutes of Health National Center for Research Resources.

The background content in section 3 is based on the contents of course BCMB 8210, offered by the Institute of Bioinformatics, University of Georgia. All involved teaching faculty (Dr. Ying Xu, Dr. Jessica Kissinger, Dr. PhuongAn Dam and Dr. Rob Woods) are acknowledged.

7.   QUESTIONS FOR DISCUSSION

Beginner:
1. Which project is widely believed to be the progenitor of the field of bioinformatics?
2. Why Web Services form an ideal framework for the development and deployment of bioinformatics computing resources?

Intermediate:
1. What are the two types of annotation of Web Services used in the biomedical glycomics project?
2. Name the different types of BLAST search listed at the NCBI BLAST website.

Advanced:
1. Make a list of bioinformatics Web Services registries. Also, list the approach implemented to search and discover Web Services in the Web Services registry.
2. Identify a Web Services, from the three areas of bioinformatics research areas (except structural bioinformatics), which may be implemented over a grid to optimize performance.
3. What are the two different types of ontologies used in the annotation of Web Services?
4. What are the advantages of using ontology based keywords in annotation of Web Services against the use of words from a simple controlled vocabulary?
5. A number of biological domain ontologies are listed at Open Biological Ontologies (OBO) at http://obo.sourceforge.net/. List all relevant Web Services for annotating a Web Service that compares gene sequences.

8.   SUGGESTED ADDITIONAL READING

*   "Current topics in computational molecular biology", T Jiang, Y Xu and MQ Zhang, MIT Press, 2002

9.   REFERENCES

Barbara R. Jasny and Leslie Roberts, Building on the DNA Revolution, Science Apr 11 2003: 277

David S. Roos, Bioinformatics--Trying to swim in a sea of data, Science Feb 16 2001: 1260-1261

Roberts Stevens, Olivier Bodenreider, and Yves A. Lussier, Semantic Webs for Life Science, PSB 2006, January 3-7, 2006, Grand Wailea, Wailea, Maui

Altschul SF, Madden TL, Schaffer AA, Zhang J, Zhang Z, Miller W, Lipman DJ., Gapped BLAST and PSI-BLAST: a new generation of protein database search programs, Nucleic Acids Res. 1997 Sep 1;25(17):3389-402.

R. Akkiraju, J. Farrell, J.Miller, M. Nagarajan, M. Schmidt, A. Sheth, K. Verma, "Web Service Semantics - WSDL-S (Position Paper for the W3C Workshop on Frameworks for Semantics in Web Services)

David Martin, Massimo Paolucci, Sheila McIlraith, Mark Burstein, Drew McDermott, Deborah McGuinness, Bijan Parsia, Terry Payne, Marta Sabou, Monika Solanki, Naveen Srinivasan, Katia Sycara, "Bringing Semantics to Web Services: The OWL-S Approach", Proceedings of the First International Workshop on Semantic Web Services and Web Process Composition (SWSWPC 2004), July 6-9, 2004, San Diego, California, USA

Tom Oinn, Matthew Addis, Justin Ferris, Darren Marvin, Martin Senger, Mark Greenwood, Tim Carver, Kevin Glover, Matthew R. Pocock, Anil Wipat and Peter Li. Taverna: A tool for the composition and enactment of bioinformatics workflows Bioinformatics Journal 20(17) pp 3045-3054, 2004, doi:10.1093/bioinformatics/bth361

Sohrab P Shah, David YM He, Jessica N Sawkins, Jeffrey C Druce, Gerald Quon, Drew Lett, Grace XY Zheng, Tao Xu, BF Francis Ouellette. Pegasys: software for executing and integrating analyses of biological sequences. BMC Bioinformatics 2004, 5:40

Scott Doubet and Peter Albersheim, CarbBank. Glycobiology, 2, 1992, 505

Sahoo, S. S.; Sheth, A. P.; York, W. S.; Miller, J. A. "Semantic Web Services for N-Glycosylation Process", International Symposium on Web Services for Computational Biology and Bioinformatics, VBI, Blacksburg, VA, May 26-27, 2005.

Jun Zhao, Carole Goble and Robert Stevens Semantic Web Applications to E-Science in silico Experiments In Thirteenth International World Wide Web Conference (WWW2004) pp. 284-285, New York, May 2004

Carole Goble Putting Semantics into e-Science and Grids in Proc E-Science 2005, 1st IEEE Intl Conf on e-Science and Grid Technologies, Melbourne, Australia, 5-8 December 2005

Chapter 13

BUILDING SEMANTIC BUSINESS SERVICES

Sanjay Chaudhary, Zakir Laliwala and Vikram Sorathia.
Dhirubhai Ambani Institute of Information and Communication Technology,Post Bag No. 4, Near Indroda Circle, Gandhinagar 382 007, Gujarat, India.- sanjay_chaudhary@da-iict.org, zakir_laliwala@da-iict.org, vikram_sorathia@da-iict.org.

1. INTRODUCTION

This chapter aims to provide comprehensive exposure to various issues involved in the development of Semantic Web services based Business Process Orchestration. Marketing of Agricultural Produce is selected as the problem domain. The present discussion covers various topics from understanding the problem up to the identification and resolution of the implementation issues. At each stage, an attempt is made to provide a brief background, current research trends, available techniques, selection of tools and details about implementation steps. As an outcome, the reader shall gain the required skills and sufficient level of familiarity of current standards and research in each area.

In section 1, the reader is introduced to the evolution of Agricultural Marketing in India, and the reforms that are planned for implementation. Section 2 discusses a trading use case in the future market followed by a section dedicated to explain the implementation challenges. A discussion on development lifecycle describes the implementation steps for the proposed system. In the subsequent sections, detailed and step-by-step development procedures are provided with comments on relevant standardization, research approaches and tool-sets.

Agricultural Marketing Marketing of agricultural produce is a complex task involving various stack holders, products and business scenarios. In a developing country like India, this activity is influenced by local, socio-economic and cultural characteristics. Evaluating the business processes at regional or national scale reveals diversity in products, terminology and processes involved to perform complete business activities. While other complex but well-defined business processes are experiencing benefits of services driven e-business; the 'marketing of agricultural produce' has remained untouched by this revolution. Government of India is now planning to introduce agricultural marketing reforms to streamline trading processes involved in all markets throughout the nation. The legal framework is being duly formulated, yet unavailability of proper underlying IT infrastructure will continue to inhibit the implementation and penetration of such technological advancement amongst the users. In absence of such capabilities, the conventional trading transactions will continue to provide meager benefits to a farmer who looses a better price in other potential market, or a wholesaler - who might have got the desired quality product at a lower cost directly from the farm. There is a need to develop affordable and reliable solution that links all the actors involved in the system and provide an environment for a competitive business.

Evolution of the Agricultural Marketing Process in India Beginning with the era of barter system, where goods were exchanged for goods, or goods were exchanged for services, through the weekly Bazaar, to more organized Mandi and market yards of the present and the trends towards realizing the reforms in the future markets. This way, the process has evolved to a very matured and complex level (Sreenivasulu V, et al 2001). An informal gathering of the people at a designated place and time has remained a valid model for quite a long time. Today, wholesale spot markets and derivative markets are emerging as hubs for agricultural marketing business (Thomas S, 2003). The trade in this market is heavily influenced by local, socio-economic and cultural characteristics. This is the reason why same product may have different prices at different market yards. Yet the producers have no choice to search for the best available price and forced to sell their products in the local market. Inhibitive transport and storage costs also play a vital role, apart from the urgency to sell the perishable products. Buyers and wholesalers on the other hand face difficulties to purchase desired quality of products at competitive prices. The Model Act (Ministry of Agriculture, Govt. of India, 2003) is formulated to bring reforms in the Agricultural Marketing Process. Additional responsibilities are assigned to the existing Agricultural Produce Market Committee (APMC) to realize the reforms having following objectives:

- To promote setting up of privately-owned markets
- To promote direct sale and contract farming
- To provide transparency in trading transactions
- To provide market-led extension

- To ensure payment on the same day
- To enable value addition in agricultural produce by promoting processing

2. TRADING USE CASES IN FUTURE MARKET

As indicated earlier, the Act, a typical trade can span across the markets located at various places. Privately owned markets will be allowed and food processing and other related industries will be encouraged to trade directly with the farmers. Contract farming will also be formalized according to the provisions of the Act. Hence the trading in such a competitive market will be more complex than that of in the existing scenario.

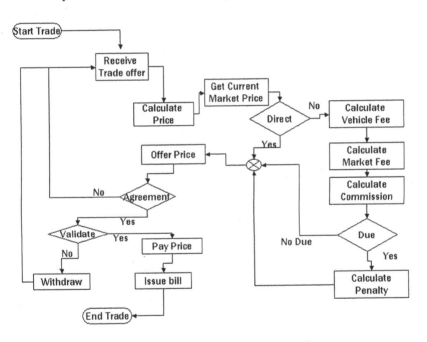

Figure 13-1. Workflow in the Trading Use Case

Execution of a Trade This section provides a brief account of a use case to sell an agricultural produce. A seller can come to the market place or in case of a direct marketing; a farmer can express his intention to start a trade of agricultural produce. An authorized market functionary carries out measurement and grading of the produce and collect fees in case a vehicle is used to transport the produce. Price of the produce can be set by tender bid, auction or any other transparent system. In case of direct sale, a seller is exempted to pay any market fee or commission; otherwise the market fee is imposed on the seller. Only license holders are allowed to carry out any trade in the market area. If they fail to pay any fees to the APMC or fail to pay the agreed-upon price of the purchased good, the APMC may cancel the license of the trader. If the trade is carried out by license holders in a manner explained above, the bill will be issued and the transaction will be recorded in the APMC database. Figure 13-1 represents a simplified workflow capturing few aspects of a typical trade. The trade starts with the intention of the trader to sell a particular agricultural produce. The price is set by the auction or any other transparent system as defined in the Act. Once the agreed upon price is received, it is published for the traders.

3.   IMPLEMENTATION CHALLENGES

After the implementation of the Act, it is being envisaged that the trading will span across the nationwide markets. To develop and deploy the services to support this vision comes with the challenge of its inherent heterogeneity. In the nation of diverse cultural values, the terminology used in trading varies from place to place. The software and hardware infrastructure at this scale also cannot be expected to be homogeneous throughout. The consequence of this scenario introduces many difficult challenges.

3.1   Understanding the Process

The reforms suggested by the Act consist of details regarding the trade in legal terms. The Act introduces many new concepts with comprehensive definitions and originates a new vocabulary in the domain. From the software development aspect, the developer must be familiar with the vocabulary to design and execute specific tasks in a prescribed manner. The challenge is to convert the statements of the Act to appropriate formal representation that can be utilized as a benchmark for the further software development effort. For this reason, the domain knowledge representation is a prerequisite with consideration from the following three aspects:

Terms Used in the Act To understand the problem, consider Definition 1, defining an Agriculturist in the context of the Model Act.

Definition 1 (Agriculturist) *means a person who is a resident of the notified area of the market and who is engaged in production of agricultural produce by himself or by hired labor or otherwise, but does not include any market functionary.*

This definition is made up of some concepts like: "Notified Area", "Agricultural Produce", "Market Functionary". These words are also properly defined in the act along with other provisions. Yet, the meaning of these terms may not be intuitively clear to the person responsible for the development. Hence, a proper methodology is required to represent all the concepts and relations among terms.

Terms Used by the Traders The act expresses various agricultural produces at a level of abstraction. In the real world, one specific agricultural produce is referred with various terms in various regions. The general terms for the produce are further attributed specific terms on the basis of the quality, type, processing and other parameters. While trade is underway, the persons involved in the process usually dwell upon such attributes that are not expressed in the act. One can also predict the change in the terms to attribute the specific crop changing from place to place. Hence a representation is required that covers all the *de facto* terms and concepts prevailing in the domain.

Terms Used by the Developers The developers responsible for generating services use specific terms for expressing the functionality of the methods and variables used in the discrete functionality. When, the trade is expected to span across many geographical locations, it is likely that different developers have followed different naming conventions for developing specific service blocks. Hence at the time of composing the services the same terms denoted with different symbols needs to be resolved.

3.2   Definition of Business Model

The Act represents only the regulatory aspect of the trading. The implementation details will vary based on the quality of the software development process being followed by the individual developers. Defining a commonly agreeable business model is a difficult problem in case of agricultural domain. For instance, the regulated and privately owned markets may differ in implementation details from Quality of Services point of view (Cardoso, J. and Sheth A 2004). The existing business models may prove insufficient or conflicting. Hence to arrive to a clear definition of a business model is a difficult challenge.

3.3   Making Business Web Enabled

It is relatively easy to expose business functionalities over the web with the help of Web services. Yet providing complete business functionality that utilizes several Web services is still a considerable challenge for a large-scale integration. Consistent availability of dependable ICT infrastructure across markets can be an issue especially in under-developed and remote regions of the country.

3.4　　Access to Information for the Functionaries

Most of the Functionaries of this e-trading system are dependent on timely and relevant information to carry out informed decisions (Chaudhary S, et al 2004). Current mechanisms for communicating the information include telephone calls, radio, black board and public address systems. Yet it is evident that the scope of all the above-mentioned information communication technology is limited to the local market and is insufficient to meet the information need of traders in future context.

3.5　　Access to Instruments for End-Users

Under a futuristic assumption, the end-users may range from a farmer possessing a PDA with a limited computing capability up to an export enterprise that might have implemented enterprise level information system. But in a proposed development cycle they all are clients to the business orchestration services. Hence it is a difficult challenge to cater the need of clients with varying computing capability.

3.6　　Negotiation Support

The biggest challenge is the terms used by the farmers and traders, which can be inhibitive in automating the negotiation process. With the advent of distributed e-business systems, interested parties can engage in real-time or near-real time negotiation process. Negotiation Support Systems are in place for more than twenty years, yet enabling the support for negotiation in e-trading will continue to be a difficult challenge.

4.　　DEVELOPMENT

With the identification of the implementation challenges, this section proposes a development lifecycle for realization of the system. It has been observed that many business services require certain common functionalities that might be implemented and hosted by a separate organization. If Service Orientation is followed for the development; it is likely that such business services are implemented as Web services. There is a possibility that other organizations can be enabled to utilize these loosely coupled services to meet their requirements. Hence, it is quite possible in today's scenario that for a complete business process, an enterprise can make the use of several of such open, reliable and interoperable services (Lu L, Zhu G, Chen J, 2004).

From the service provider's point of view, as these services can be joined together to constitute a complete business process, it has become essential to make provisions for efficient integration with heterogeneous client environments. See (Piccinelli G, Stammers E, 2002) for an impressive historical overview of merger of Business Services with IT services. As the pool of available service grow large, the selection of appropriate services becomes difficult due to heterogeneity at various levels. Semantic Web Process Lifecycle (Cardoso, J. and Sheth A 2004) is proposed to address these integration issues. The development approach being proposed here is based on similar philosophy but with more emphasis on implementation aspects of the Semantic Web services based Business Process. Figure 13-2 represents the lifecycle with eight steps described in the discussion.

4.1   Model Act

The legal acceptance of the proposed Act by the Government is the starting point of the lifecycle of this development. The provisions in the Act clearly define various entities involved in the trade. It specifies the role of each entity with specific attributes also including the flow of the trading process. Hence, the Act plays a crucial role in identifying the requirements and to derive business logic of the desired system.

4.2   Development of Business Objects

Based on the provisions in the Act, respective markets are expected to engage in the development of business objects to implement various business functionalities.

4.3   Exposing Discrete Functionality

While traders are expected to engage in trade over electronic media, there emerges an important requirement to access a small part of business process hosted by a node. To enable standards based uniform access of such small component; the developed business objects are exposed as Web services. With the help of this, trade will be enabled across the nation by giving access to services developed by individual markets.

4.4   Trading in Market

Once all the business functionalities in various markets are accessible, the trading in the market will take place. The Act has dealt with abstract terms like Functionaries, Agricultural Products and related terms but at the time of trading, the individual transactions will involve very specific terms used by the traders. Management of instance data will be required to be addressed. Here the methodology for the consideration of terms used in trading will be required to be defined formally.

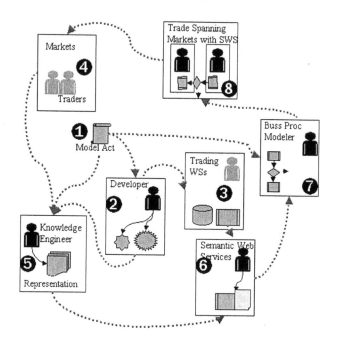

Figure 13-2. Development Lifecycle of Semantic Business Services

4.5 Post Compliance Development

After achieving successful compliance of Act in practice, next steps from 5 to 8 as indicated in the Figure 13-2 can be taken as follows:
- **Knowledge Engineering** The knowledge Engineer develops the formal representation of the terms and their relationship as used by traders and developers along with the provisions defined in the Act.
- **Semantic Web service** The formal representation will make it possible to annotate various Web services deployed at different markets. Hence, the concentration will be on semantically enriching the developed Web services to enable appropriate integration.

- **Business Process Modeler** The annotated Web services are utilized by the Business Modeler to design complete business process according to the provisions of the act.
- **Business Process Orchestration Service** The Business Process Orchestration server will accept the requests directly from the traders to initiate and execute the trade (Sorathia V, et al 2005).

5. DEVELOPING AGRICULTURAL MARKETING ONTOLOGY

To enable e-trading, one of the important challenges is the utilization of uniform terms across the market. In this section, the development of an ontology that covers all the terms, relations among them and the logical expression of the legal provision are discussed. First the discussion starts with the theoretical aspects covering a methodology to create ontology. This is followed by the current standardization to create the ontology. Next section provides a brief introduction to the W3C standard that has been followed in developing the ontology. An approach is provided for the purpose followed by a step-by-step development of the ontology with the help of selected tool.

5.1 Approach

According to the definition of the Agriculturist in the act, any person resident of the notified area, engaged in the production of Agricultural Produce is considered Agriculturist, only if he is not a Market Functionary. This definition uses few terms that also need to be defined clearly. The logical equivalent of the definition can be written as:

```
Agriculturist(X) ←
is_resident_of(X, notified_area) and
is_producing(X, agricultural_produce) and
{not(market_functionary(X))}
```

In the similar manner, the details related to the regulation of marketing of notified agricultural produce can be converted into logical representation. The following list contains few entries for evaluation of a trading instance.

```
selling(seller,X)
buying(buyer,X)
```

```
quantity(X,Q)
is_transported_by(X,head load)
is_less_than(Q,4)
price(X,p)
is_settled_by(P,transparent_system)
is_a(seller, pretty_trader)
is_kind_of(seller, esse_comm_dist_agency)
is_a(seller, auth_fair_price_shop_dealer)
is_a(seller,licensee)
is kind_of(X,notified_agri_produce)
is_covered_under(X,contract_farming)
is_brought_by(X, licensee)
is_a(current_trade, direct_sale)
is_a(current_trade, ordinary_sale)
```

Once the logical representation is completed, it is converted into standard based representation so that it can be uniformly accessed across the system. There are many standards proposed over a period of time. One of the recent significant standards is OWL and the same is selected for the present experiment.

5.2   Step-by-Step Development

There are many tools available to build ontology according to the OWL Standard. Some tools are equipped with the facility of validating the ontology and the reasoning capability to infer new facts from the represented concepts. Some of the leading tools for developing Ontology include Protégé, OilEd, KAON, OntoEdit and OntoStudio. We have selected Protégé as the Ontology builder tool for this experiment. Now we will see the step-by-step instruction to build ontology using Protégé. To design ontology using Protégé the only required prerequisite is the recent version of Protégé with Protégé OWL Plug-in. The recent version of Protégé can be downloaded from the Protégé Web Page[1]. The setup installation program is packaged with the OWL Plug-in, and user can select the installation of this plug-in during the setup. For recent version of the OWL-Plug-in, user can check for the updates at CO-ODE Web Page[2].

1. **Adding Class** Each class or concept in OWL is considered as a set of individuals. An ontology starts with defining set under the set

---

[1] Protégé Download Page http://protege.stanford.edu/download/download.html
[2] OWL Plug-in for Protégé Download Page: http://www.co-ode.org/downloads/

owl:Thing. The present chapter deals with agricultural marketing therefore the concepts in this domain can be appropriately added as subclass of the owl:Thing. In introducing terms as new concepts, the Protégé allows to select different types of classes for appropriate representation. A primitive class is the simplest expression of the domain concept. If not specified, every class being added is added as a primitive class. According to the definition of an Agriculturist, along with other requirements; one specific restriction is that the person should not be a market functionary. This kind of restriction can be covered in OWL representation as follows:

```
<owl:Class rdf:ID="Agriculturist">
<owl:disjointWith>
<owl:Class rdf:about="#market_functionary" />
</owl:disjointWith>
<rdfs:subClassOf
      rdf:resource="#Agriculture_Market" />
</owl:Class>
```

2. **Adding Property** Each concept generally exhibits a specific functionality. Concepts also possess relationships with other concepts. This feature can be expressed by defining the Property in the ontology. Depending on the context such property can exhibit functional, inverse, transitive or symmetrical relationship.
3. **Adding Restrictions** Many terms in the act are defined using additional terms of the domain. Sometimes definition includes certain constraints to be met to classify the given term. To realize such concepts defined with specific restrictions the OWL has mechanism to define restrictions. The restrictions can be defined with concepts like Universal Existential Quantifiers, cardinality restrictions on the value etc.
4. **Adding Instances** Once classes and the relationships among them are defined with appropriate restrictions, the instance of the class can be added. By opening the *Individuals* tab, the specific class can be selected. The Individual Editor will display all the relevant slots that can be filled to complete the task of adding the individual instance.

For detailed account on step-by-step development of OWL Ontologies, reader is recommended the Practical Guide (Horridge M. et al (2004).

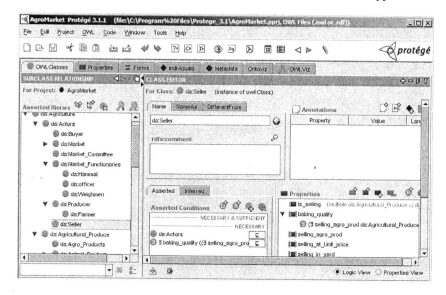

Figure 13-3. Building Ontology

6.   BUILDING WEB SERVICES

In this section, discussion is focused on creation of Web services that will enable semantic query on the ontology developed in previous section. The following definition of Web services given by (Stencil Group 2001) clarifies the important qualities of Web services that makes it appropriate approach for the given problem.

Definition 2 (Web Service) *Loosely coupled, reusable, software component that semantically encapsulate discrete functionality and are distributed and programmatically accessible over standard Internet protocols.*

6.1   Step-by-Step Development of Web Services

Following section will guide the reader to build Web services to access the ontology stored in a repository.

Prerequisites This exercise requires the reader to be familiar with working knowledge of Java and XML programming. Eclipse is used as a primary IDE for the development in this experiment. User is expected to get basic familiarity with the Eclipse development philosophy.

Hosting Ontology Repository The Ontology developed in the previous section will be used for annotation of Web service descriptions. Apart from service annotation, it will also help in resolving any ambiguity or in identifying relationship with other terms used by the traders. Ontology Repository is deployed to host the developed ontology that can later be accessible programmatically by various services over standard Internet protocols. Considerable amount of tool is freely and commercially available for hosting the ontology repository. A good repository supports standard ontology formats, standard query languages and capability of persistent storage in popular database products. Sesame is selected to host ontology repository for this experiment. Recent version of Sesame can be obtained from the OpenRDF download page[3]. Configuration of the repository is relatively easy and readers are advised to refer to the product documentation for their system specific configuration steps.

Building Java Client As indicated in the discussion of development lifecycle, generation of Business Object is an important step and can safely be considered to be intuitive to most developers. Yet this section provides an example implementation of a client developed in Eclipse to clarify its role in overall development lifecycle. The program discussed here acts as a client to the Ontology Repository. A java program is displayed in Figure 13-4; that takes the input string from the user, creates a valid SeRQL query expression; connects to the server with required credentials and retrieves the response from the repository.

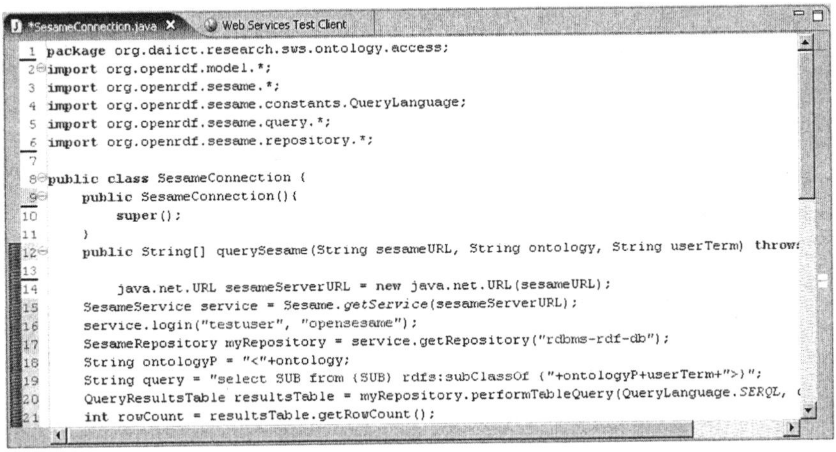

```
    *SesameConnection.java  X      Web Services Test Client
 1  package org.daiict.research.sws.ontology.access;
 2  import org.openrdf.model.*;
 3  import org.openrdf.sesame.*;
 4  import org.openrdf.sesame.constants.QueryLanguage;
 5  import org.openrdf.sesame.query.*;
 6  import org.openrdf.sesame.repository.*;
 7
 8  public class SesameConnection {
 9      public SesameConnection(){
10          super();
11      }
12      public String[] querySesame(String sesameURL, String ontology, String userTerm) throws
13
14          java.net.URL sesameServerURL = new java.net.URL(sesameURL);
15          SesameService service = Sesame.getService(sesameServerURL);
16          service.login("testuser", "opensesame");
17          SesameRepository myRepository = service.getRepository("rdbms-rdf-db");
18          String ontologyP = "<"+ontology;
19          String query = "select SUB from {SUB} rdfs:subClassOf {"+ontologyP+userTerm+"">)";
20          QueryResultsTable resultsTable = myRepository.performTableQuery(QueryLanguage.SERQL,
21          int rowCount = resultsTable.getRowCount();
```

Figure 13-4. Java Client for Connecting Sesame Repository

---

[3] Sesame Download Page: http://www.openrdf.org/download.jsp

Figure 13-5 displays successful realization of two of the required functionalities of the development lifecycle. One is the utilization of the ontology and another requirement of exposing the business object as a Web service. As evident in the Figure 13-5, the Eclipse Package Explorer contains list of java files, each encapsulating discrete business functionality. In the middle pane, the methods of the deployed Web service are visible. The querySesame method is based on the java file as displayed in the code snippet above. As evident, both the java program and the Web service accept a user input. The code displays the generation of query to retrieve all the concepts that has rdfs:subClassOf relationship with the term provided by the user. As displayed in Figure 13-5, the list of sub class of Mango is listed as a result of query prepared based on the term entered by the user, i.e. "Mango".

Building Web Service For quite a long time, building Web services has been a difficult task as it involves many technologies, tools and the know-how. Eclipse WTP[4] project is devoted towards making this process relatively easy and therefore selected for the current experiment. Stable Build 1.0 M8 used for the development can be downloaded from the M8 Page [5]. The page also enumerates the requirements for the installation of this version that should be strictly followed.

Once installation is done properly, the following steps to build the required Web service can be followed. Open newly installed Eclipse and select the J2EE prospective. Create new project by following *File →New →Project →Dynamic Web Project.* Along with other trivial requirements, the new project creation wizard requires to select the *Target Runtime.* Click on new button and provide the local Tomcat installation details. The present experimentation was done using *Apache Tomcat v5.0* and *j2sdk1.4.2_03*. If done properly, the wizard will result in creation of project directory structure that can be explored in the *Project Explorer*. Locate *Java Source* folder to define the source files that will be used for developing the Web services. Reader can create the java programs in the same workspace or import it from the existing project that was discussed in previous section. The program containing the querySesame method created to access the ontology repository can be imported into existing workspace.

To build the Web service, select the java file and press right-click to open *New →Other →Web services →Web service.* In the newly opened wizard, select *Bottom up Java bean Web service* and check *Generate Proxy, Test the Web service, Monitor the Web service* and *Overwrite files without*

---

[4] Eclipse Web Tools Platform (WTP) project: http://www.eclipse.org/webtools/
[5] http://download.eclipse.org/webtools/downloads/drops/S-1.0M8-200509230840/

warning options and press *Next*. The next object selection page will prompt for the *Bean* to be selected. In next *Service* Deployment Configuration page, appropriate Web service *Runtime, server* and *J2EE* versions can be selected. The next page will display Web services Java Bean Identity with the details of Web service *URI, WSDL Folder, WSDL File.* The available methods, style and usage can also be chosen on the page. Clicking on finish will execute the required tasks and if done successfully, user will prompted to start the **Server**. The Web service Client Test page will display options for testing the generated proxy. In the next page of the wizard the reader can select options for publishing the Web service to Public UDDI Registry. Clicking on finish will result in execution of the Web service. Web service Test client will be opened where user can select from available methods. Clicking on the querySesame method will result in test client same as indicated in Figure 13-5. User will be prompted for Sesame repository URL, Ontology hosted on it and the user term. Clicking *Invoke* button will display the outcome of the method in the *Result* section.

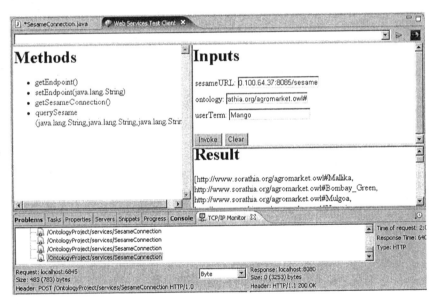

Figure 13-5. Java Client for Connecting Sesame Repository

7.   SEMANTIC WEB SERVICES

The discussion just dealt with the steps to expose business objects as Web services. By publishing in public registry these components can be discovered and accessed over the Internet. It is evident from the scale at which Web services based business process integration is being addressed here, that discovery of appropriate services is a critical challenge for a conventional search. Augmentation of Web services with enhanced service description is therefore a prerequisite to any efforts towards automation in discovery, invocation, binding or composition of the developed Web services. It is claimed (Cabral, L., Domingue, J, et al 2004) that there are three different approaches prevailing in the research community to achieve the goal of Semantic Web services. By making sure that services meet the functional requirements, by providing components that fulfills the desired activities or by aggregating vocabulary in service description.

7.1   Relevant Standards

Among important standards OWL-S is derived from DAML-S. It is based on Description Logic. It provides Profile, Process Model and Grounding Ontologies to facilitate Description and Reasoning of the service description files. Web service Modeling Framework (WSMF) is based on a model describing Web service from different aspects. To support scalable communication among the services, this approach recommend emphasizing mediation at syntactic, business logic, message exchange and dynamic invocation levels. As a part of WSMF, the Semantic Web enabled Web services (SWWS) Project is planned to provide framework to support description, discovery and mediation. Another project under WSMF is Web service Modeling Ontology (WSMO), which provides formal service ontology and language. Based on UPML (Unified Problem Solving Method Development) the Internet Reasoning Server (IRS II) is another important framework for Semantic Web services. It consists of Task Models, Problem Solving Methods (PSM), Domain Models and Bridges. While these approaches introduce specific solutions for respective philosophy, the METEOR-S (Patil, Oundhakar et al. 2004) is offered to resolve the issues by leveraging advantage of semantics with the existing standards. It provides complete lifecycle of Semantic Web Processes including development, annotation, discovery, composition and orchestration.

7.2   Approach

These research approaches have their own unique merits but to expect a large-scale penetration of any one approach in real life implementation (Cardoso, J., Miller, J., et al. 2004) is too early to predict. Adding semantics to the service description may seem to be an easy alternative. Here, the requirement for the developer is to be able to use the "Concepts" of the domain for which the services are being developed. This is typically realized by selecting and using the relevant ontology. Easy access to the ontology therefore should be integrated with the annotation process. Penetration of concepts of ontology and decent tool support has resulted in development of large ontologies in various domains. Manual annotation using these large ontologies may turn out to be tedious job. Need was felt for a mechanism that enables the user to use and manage specific ontologies for describing the Web services that are being developed. To reduce the manual effort the mechanism can be designed to support automatic or semi-automatic matching process with little user intervention. One such approach (Patil, Oundhakar et al. 2004) was proposed to enable semi-automated annotation of the existing service descriptions with ontology by employing machine learning techniques. In the case of Agricultural Marketing, the ontology covering all the concepts and relations can be utilized uniformly across all the markets to avoid any ambiguity related to the expressed terms. We have adopted the METEOR-S Web service Annotation Framework to annotate WSDL files with known vocabulary. In this approach semi automatic annotation of services is made possible by adopting the schema-matching technique.

7.3   Step-by-Step Development

This section explains how a process of Semantic Web service Annotation is carried out. For semantically annotating the existing Web services, the method is explained in detail with the tool named *METEOR-S Web service Annotation Framework* (MWSAF). MWSAF is Eclipse based tool and can be downloaded from LSDIS tool downloads page[6].

Before starting with the MWSAF, the ontology and all the involved Web services should be assessable to the developer. In this experimentation Agricultural Marketing Ontology will be used for annotation. In current discussion, the business objects developed based on the defined use case and were exposed as Web services. After making provisions of the prerequisites,

---

[6] MWSAF Download Page: http://lsdis.cs.uga.edu/projects/meteor-s/mwsaf/

extract the downloaded package to a convenient place. Open the Eclipse IDE and click on *File →Import →Existing Project into Workspace.* When prompted for selection of the root directory, click on browse to locate the place where the archive was extracted. If the project is successfully imported in the workspace, the *Package Explorer* will display project files under the root folder named *MWSAF.* In the directory tree, locate the mwsaf.resource folder to explore the content. Open mwsaf.properties file to edit the entries to suit the installation. Appropriate changes in MWSAF HOME, NegativeDictionary and other properties should be made. To run the program, locate MWSAF.java file in mwsaf package from the package explorer, right click and select *Run as - Java Application.* In a user-friendly graphical interface, user is provided many options in **File** and **Tools** menu. To begin with the annotation exercise, click on *File →Open →Open WSDL From.* Here one can choose to select either File or URL option. In this experiment, the ReceiveTradeOff-er.wsdl is selected. As we want to use the Agricultural ontology to annotate the WSDL file, we will now select *File →Open Ontology From File* and locate AgroMarket.owl as developed earlier. In the left side of the GUI, the WSDL can be explored. Similarly in the right pane, the ontology file can be traversed. Next step is to select *Tools → Match Web Service.* MWSAF matches the terms used in the WSDL with the concepts given in the ontology. The middle pane displays the concept mappings and other statistics as displayed in Figure 13-6. Developer can select the acceptable matches out of the offered ones by clicking on the radio button of each offered mapping. These selected mappings can be accepted by clicking on the *Accept Mapping* button. Once the mapping is over, the WSDL file is ready to be annotated. This can be done by clicking on *File → Write WSDL.* The result of this option annotated WSDL file ReceiveTradeOff-erAnnotated.wsdl will be stored in *AnnotatedWSDL* sub-directory of the root. For detailed account on step-by-step development, the reader is recommended to read the User Guide (LSDIS Lab 2004) available on the tool Web Page.

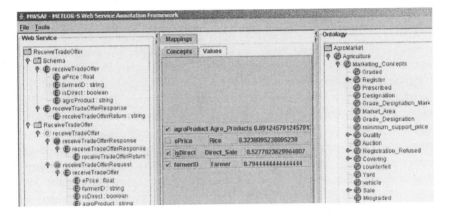

Figure 13-6. Annotating WSDL File

8. BUILDING BUSINESS PROCESS MODEL

To employ Web services as Business Services, there are many issues needed to be resolved. Apart from general issues identified earlier in the chapter, specific problems in management of communication, handling of data, handling exceptions and support for transaction among collaborating Web services are very critical.

8.1 Relevant Standards

One straight solution for addressing these critical issues is to achieve consensus based standardization in the process. XLANG, BPML, WSFL, BPSS, WSCL, WSCI, BPEL4WS and WS-Choreography enlist the result of a standardization process that prevailed in last five years (XML Cover Pages 2004). These disjoint and parallel standardization efforts have resulted in the problem of heterogeneous and sometimes conflicting specifications (Parastatidis S, Webber J, (2004). Subsequently, the very objective of Web service, i.e. interoperability, is clearly defeated. Composition of Web service is also affected by this problem. Initially, to achieve the composition amongst the Web services, Microsoft introduced a structural construct based XLANG and in parallel IBM brought graph-oriented processes based WSFL. BPEL4WS has emerged as a business process definition standard as a result of consensus among the organizations that initially promoted different standards for the same. In its next version, the popularly known BPEL4WS 1.1 will be renamed as WS-BPEL 2.0. BPEL4WS allows proper management of messages being exchanged betweens involved in carrying out a complete business process (Andrews T, et al 2003). BPEL relies on WSDL for its known capability of describing incoming and outgoing message for a given Web service. This helps in designing and implementation of Web services based business process management functionality. Business processes deployed on BPEL engine are Web service Interfaces that can be accessed platform in-dependently. By correlating the messages, BPEL4WS provides mechanism to preserve Web service state. This also helps in long running transactions, which may have several situations where certain completed tasks should be undone due to some erratic condition. To achieve this task BPEL4WS supports structured programming constructs like conditional branching, loop, sequence and flow. BPEL4WS also supports fault handling and compensation mechanism. BPEL4WS employs various constructs like Variables, Partners, Partner links, Flow, Sequences etc, some of them will be elaborated the coming section.

8.2   Approach

For developing model for business process the trading use case described in section 2.1 is utilized. The approach here is to derive a business workflow based on the flow chart depicted in Figure 13-1. The next important step is to select appropriate tool to realize the design and execute the business process. Readers can choose from a vast amount of tools supporting the workflow. Oracle BPEL Process Manager, Biztalk Server, IBM WebSphere Business Integration Server Foundation and Cape Clear Orchestrator provide support with their commercial application packages. Among a few noteworthy open source tools: ActiveBPEL, JBoss jBPM, MidOffice BPEL Editor (MOBE), Bexee BPEL Execution Engine and IBM BPWS4J available as Alphaworks software can be considered.

8.3   Step-by-Step Development

Development and deployment of a business process requires two separate tasks. The first is to create the model of the process from available business logic and the collaborating Web services. The second step is to host the process on a BPEL execution engine. Many commercial and open source tools allow both of these facilities in a single package. Here separate discussion is provided for each step.

Business Process Modeler. IBM BPWS4J Editor is used for designing the business process. BPWS4J is successfully tested on JDK version 1.4.1

and Tomcat version 4.1.24[7]. The system used for designing business service therefore must be configured with these prerequisites. The selected editor can be downloaded as bpws4j-editor-2.1.zip file from the tool web page[8]. Next step is to extract the downloaded zip file from download directory to Eclipse root directory. This will result in creation of a sub-directory com.ibm.cs.bpws.tools.bpwsbuilder under the Plug-ins directory of Eclipse installation. The installation can be verified by starting the Eclipse instance. Open Window→Open Prospective→ Others. In Select Prospective window, select BPWS and press OK. A new file can be created by opening File→New→Other. In New window, from the given list of Wizards, click on the *BPWS* folder to select BPWS File and follow the steps.

Now the actual business process modeling begins. The Figure 13-7 displays the building of a new process in the BPWS prospective. To make the decision about what is to be added, now the focus of attention will switch between the BPEL modeler and the problem workflow. In a typical scenario of a business process, a process can span across various existing systems hosting many Web services. Mapping this to our application, a trade process requires interactions of various Web services hosted by APMC and partner organizations. WSDL of respective Web services explains the service invocation and other details.

---

[7] Tomcat: http://archive.apache.org/dist/jakarta/tomcat-4/archive/v4.1.24/

[8] BPWS4J Editor: http://www.alphaworks.ibm.com/tech/bpws4j/download

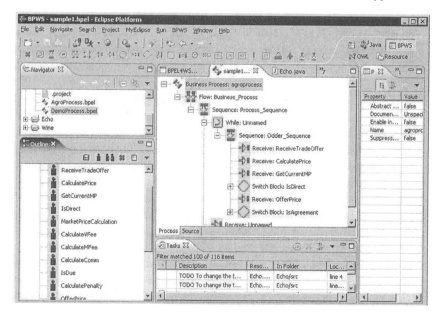

Figure 13-7. BPWS Editor

The discovery of appropriate services here can be enhanced with semantic annotation as described in the previous section. Here, according to the BPEL4WS specification, the message conversation amongst the partners is defined in Partner Link Types. It also defines the role played by individual Web services in the whole transaction. The portType role dictates the allocation of messages to appropriate receivers. For a quick overview on step-by-step development of BPEL4WS document using BPWS4J Editor, reader is recommended the Reference Guide (Mukhi N. 2002) and for detail reference see (Stemkovski V et al 2003). The code snippet contains a part of Marketing.bpel that indicates the Partner links, role and portTypes in our experiment.

```
<partnerLinks>
    <partnerLink name="CalculatePrice"
    xmlns:ns1="http://10.100.64.38:8080/FirstWS/services/CalculatePrice"
        partnerLinkType="ns1:CalculatePricePLT" myRole="CalculatePriceService"/>
    <partnerLink name="IsDirect"
    xmlns:ns2="http://10.100.64.38:8080/FirstWS/services/IsDirect"
        partnerLinkType="ns2:IsDirectPLT"/>
```

Stateful interactions among the Web services in a given business process is achieved by message exchange. Content of these messages include data vital to the application. Variables are the artifacts that hold the data in the messages. The code snippet contains variables defined in the marketing application.

```
<variables>
    <variable name="agroProduct"
    xmlns:ns15="http://10.100.64.38:8080/FirstWS/services/ReceiveTradeOffer"
    messageType="ns15:agroProduct"/>
    <variable name="price"
    xmlns:ns16="http://10.100.64.38:8080/FirstWS/services/CalculatePrice"
    messageType="ns16:price"/>
    <variable name= ......
```

It can be noted that the declaration of a variable consists of a unique name and message type, which is a XML Schema simpleType. While variables are used to store intermediate state data in messages between partners, it also warrants the need to exchange the data between variables. BPEL4WS specification introduces the notion of *assign* activity to copy data amongst variables. It also supports construction and insertion of new data using expressions. In agricultural trade scenario, calculating price requires this activity to extract market prices and add market fees. The code snippet displays an activity that copies end point references between partner links.

```
<flow name="AgroMarket"> <sequence name="AgroProcess_Sequence">
<receive name="CalculatePrice"  partnerLink="CalculatePrice"
    xmlns:ns20="http://10.100.64.38:8080/FirstWS/services/CalculatePrice"
    portType="ns20:CalculatePrice" operation="calculatePrice" >
    </receive>
<reply name="CalculatePrice" partnerLink="CalculatePrice"
    xmlns:ns21="http://10.100.64.38:8080/FirstWS/services/CalculatePrice"
    portType="ns21:CalculatePrice" operation="calculatePrice"
    variable="price">
    </reply>
```

Code snippet given above depicts one of the most vital elements in BPEL specification instrumental to achieve concurrency and synchronization amongst the partners. The *Flow* construct enables the grouping of activities. Depending upon the conditions defined, it is possible to execute all or selected activities within the scope of the Flow. This is critical to achieve concurrency in real-life business scenarios. Invoking partner service is one of the most common activities for any business process. Depending upon the business logic, these invocations can be synchronous or asynchronous. Synchronous invocation can possibly result in error condition that returns as WSDL fault. It is necessary therefore to make provisions for efficient fault handling while using the invoke operation.

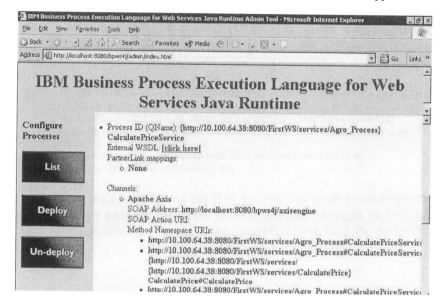

Figure 13-8. Business Process Hosted on BPEL Engine

BPEL Engine BPWS4J Engine Version 2.1 is selected as the BPEL Engine for this experiment. The tool can be downloaded from BPWS4J page[9] on IBM AlphaWorks Site. To install the Engine simply copy the bpws4j.war file into Tomcat's webapps directory. The installation can be verified by accessing http://localhost:port/bpws4j using any standard web browser. The hostname and port can be replaced according to the case, for example http://10.100.64.-38:8080/bpws4j. As depicted in the Figure 13-8, the BPWS4J Engine can be managed by accessing the administrator interface available at http://localhost:port/bpws4j/admin/index.html. Three basic operations are allowed namely List, Deploy and Un-deploy the services, can be accessed by clicking on any of respective button in the left pane. To deploy the services, the ***Deploy*** option can be accessed by clicking on the deploy button. Two inputs are required to deploy the process. The BPEL file generated by the modeler and WSDL file that describes the process are to be deployed. After providing all the required inputs, the process can be deployed by clicking Start Serving the Process button. The deployed service can be accessed by pointing the web browser to http://localhost:8080/bpws4j. The page represents the services

---

[9] BPWS4J Engine http://www.alphaworks.ibm.com/tech/bpws4j/download

hosted on the BPEL Engine. Figure 13-8 represents the services hosted on the BPEL Engine.

9. CONCLUSION

This chapter has demonstrated the complete development cycle of semantic Web services based Business Process Orchestration for Agricultural Marketing. In this chapter, challenging real-life business problem, which is considered for implementation at a large scale is explained. Basic complexities involved in the problem are revealed from diverse aspects. The business process integration in such a challenging environment was addressed by the adding semantics into the service description. Various aspects and phases involved to develop semantic business services are discussed with many example implementations of related concepts, tools and techniques to achieve over all goal to demonstrate a full lifecycle of the development process for e-trading of agricultural produce.

10. QUESTIONS FOR DISCUSSION

Beginner:
1. Why simple Web services are not sufficient for all complex real-life applications? Evaluate Semantic approach as one of the solutions of this problem.
2. Are existing UDDI registry systems capable to support publishing and discovery of Semantic Web services?

Intermediate:
1. Explain the ways in which properties can be characterized in OWL. Explain each property type by taking proper examples.
2. What is the purpose of developing Standard Upper Ontology? What role it is expected to play in interoperability?

Advanced:
1. Explore how rule based knowledge representation can be developed on the top of the developed ontology. Find out the major recommendations in this direction including standards, models and architectures

Practical Exercises:
1. Explore protégé SWRL plug-in to build rules for the developed ontology.
2. Build the rules according to RuleML and provide a comparative note on the capabilities of SWRL and RuleML.

11. SUGGESTED ADDITIONAL READING

- Stuckenschmidt, Heiner & Harmelen, Frank Van: *Information Sharing On The Semantic Web*. New York. Springer Verlag, 2005. 3-540-20594-2.: This book tries to provide insight in applying semantics to enable information sharing by providing sound insight of theory, standards, tools and techniques for developing Ontologies to realize the goal of semantic web.
- Gomez-Perez, Asuncion, Fernandez-Lopez, Mariano & Corcho, Oscar: *Ontological Engineering: With Examples From The Areas Of Knowledge Management, E-Commerce And The Semantic Web*. London. Springer, 2004. 1-85233-551-3: This book provides excellent account of practical aspects to develop Ontologies along with discussion on application in different domains.
- Fensel, Dieter: *Ontologies: A Silver Bullet for Knowledge Management and Electronic Commerce*, 2nd ed.. (2nd ed.) Berlin. Springer-Verlag, 2004. 3-540-00302-9: Provides effective overview of current state-of-the-art in Ontology related topics.
- Singh Munindar P. & Huhns, Michael N.: *Service-Oriented Computing: Semantics, Processes, Agents*. England. John Wiley and Sons, 2005. 0-470-09148-7: Apart from introduction to Web services and Semantic Web related standards, this book covers a wider prospective including topics on Enterprise Architectures, Service Oriented Computing (SOA), Execution Models, Transactions and Coordination Frameworks. It also includes discussion on advance research topics like multi-agent systems, service selection, security and related issues.
- Zimmermann, Olaf, Tomlinson, Mark & Peuser, Stefan: *Perspectives on Web services: Applying SOAP, WSDL and UDDI to Real-World Projects*. New York. Springer, 2003. 3-540-00914-0: This is an excellent reference book for professionals as well as students planning to concentrate on the emerging areas of Web services and SOA. Case studies given in the book provide professional approach to develop Web services.

12. REFERENCES

Patil, A., S. Oundhakar, et al. (2004) MWSAF - METEOR-S Web Service Annotation Framework. 13th Conference on World Wide Web, New York City, USA.

Andrews T, et al, (2003), Business Process Execution Language for Web Services, Version 1.1.

Cabral, L., Domingue, J., et al (2004) Approaches to Semantic Web Services: An Overview and Comparisons. In: First European Semantic Web Symposium (ESWS2004), Heraklion, Crete, Greece (2004)

Cardoso, J. and Sheth A (2004) "Introduction to Semantic Web Services and Web Process Composition", First International Workshop on Semantic Web Services and Web Processes Composition (SWSWPC 2004), "Semantic Web Process: powering next generation of processes with Semantics and Web services", Revised Selected Papers, LNCS, Springer-Verlag Heidelberg, Vol. 3387, pp.1-13, 2005. ISBN: 3-540-24328-3.

Cardoso, J., Miller, J., et al. (2004) "Academic and Industrial Research: Do their Approaches Differ in Adding Semantics to Web Services", First International Workshop on Semantic Web Services and Web Processes Composition (SWSWPC 2004), "Semantic Web Process: powering next generation of processes with Semantics and Web services", Revised Selected Papers, LNCS, Springer-Verlag Heidelberg, Vol. 3387, pp.14-21. 2005. ISBN: 3-540-24328-3.

Chaudhary S, Sorathia V, Laliwala Z, (2004) Architecture of Sensor Based Agricultural Information System for Effective Planning of Farm Activities. IEEE International Conference on Services Computing, 2004 (SCC'04), Conference Proceedings, pp. 93-100

Horridge M. et al (2004) A Practical Guide To Building OWL Ontologies With The Protégé-OWL Plug-in Edition 1.0. http:/www.co-ode.org/resources/tutorials/-Protégé-OWL-Tutorial.pdf

LSDIS Lab (2004) MWSAF User Guide, http://lsdis.cs.uga.edu/projects/meteors/-mwsaf/downloads/mwsaf-users-guide.pdf

Lu L, Zhu G, Chen J, (2004) "An Infrastructure for E- Government Based on Semantic Web Services" SCC'04, Conference Proceedings, pp . 483-486

Mukhi N.(2002) :Reference guide for creating BPEL4WS documents Quick reference for the BPWS4J editor. http://www-128.ibm.com/developerworks/web-services/library/ws-bpws4jed/

Parastatidis S, Webber J, (2004) Assessing the Risk and Value of Adopting Emerging and Unstable Web Services Specifications, SCC'04, Conference Proceedings, pp. 65-72.

Piccinelli G, Stammers E, (2002) "From E-Processes to E- Networks: an E-Service oriented Approach", International Conference on Internet Computing,

Sorathia V, Laliwala Z and Chaudhary S, (2005) Towards Agricultural Marketing Reforms: Web Services Orchestration Approach, '2005 IEEE International Conference on Services Computing (SCC 2005).

Sreenivasulu V, Nandwana H, (2001) Networking of Agricultural Information Systems And Services in India, INSPEL 35(2001) 4, pp 226-235

Stemkovski V, Tihankov A,Razumovsky K, (2003) Implementation of the BPEL4WS demo: http://www-128.ibm.com/developerworks/edu/ws-dw-ws-bpelws-i.html

The Stencil Group (2001) Defining Web Services, http://www.perfectxml.com/X-analysis/TSG/WebServices.asp

Ministry of Agriculture, Government of India (2003). The draft model legislation: The State Agricultural Produce Marketing (Development and Regulation) Act.

Thomas S, (2003): Agricultural Commodity Markets in India: Policy Issues for Growth, Technical report, IGIDR, Bombay, India.

XML Cover Pages (2004) Standards for Business Process Modeling, Collaboration, and Choreography http://xml.coverpages.org/bpm.html

Chapter 14

PROGRAMMING THE SEMANTIC WEB

Jorge Cardoso
Department of Mathematics and Engineering, University of Madeira, 9000-390, Funchal, Portugal – jcardoso@uma.pt

1. INTRODUCTION

Many researchers believe that a new Web will emerge in the next few years based on the large-scale ongoing research and developments in the semantic Web. Nevertheless, the industry and its main players are adopting a "wait-and-see" approach to see how real-world applications can benefit from semantic Web technologies (Cardoso, Miller et al. 2005). The success of the semantic Web vision (Berners-Lee, Hendler et al. 2001) is dependant on the development of practical and useful semantic Web-based applications.

While the semantic Web has reached considerable stability from the technological point of view with the development of languages to represent knowledge (such as OWL (OWL 2004)), to query knowledge bases (RQL (Karvounarakis, Alexaki et al. 2002) and RDQL (RDQL 2005)), and to describe business rules (such as SWRL (Ian Horrocks, Peter F. Patel-Schneider et al. 2003)), the industry is still skeptical about its potential. For the semantic Web to gain considerable acceptance from the industry it is indispensable to develop real-world semantic Web-based applications to validate and explore the full potential of the semantic Web (Lassila and McGuinness 2001). The success of the semantic Web depends on its capability of supporting applications in commercial settings (Cardoso, Miller et al. 2005).

In several fields, the technologies associated with the semantic Web have been implemented with considerable success. Examples include semantic Web services (OWL-S 2004), tourism information systems (Cardoso 2004), semantic digital libraries, (Shum, Motta et al. 2000), semantic Grid (Roure,

Jennings et al. 2001), semantic Web search (Swoogle 2005), and bioinformatics (Kumar and Smith 2004).

To increase the development of semantic Web systems and solutions, in this chapter we will show how semantic Web applications can be developed using the Jena framework.

2.   THE SEMANTIC WEB STACK

The semantic Web identifies a set of technologies, tools, and standards which form the basic building blocks of an infrastructure to support the vision of the Web associated with meaning. The semantic Web architecture is composed of a series of standards organized into a certain structure that is an expression of their interrelationships. This architecture is often represented using a diagram first proposed by Tim Berners-Lee (Berners-Lee, Hendler et al. 2001). Figure 14-1 illustrates the different parts of the semantic Web architecture. It starts with the foundation of URIs and Unicode. On top of that we can find the syntactic interoperability layer in the form of XML, which in turn underlies RDF and RDF Schema (RDFS). Web ontology languages are built on top of RDF(S). The three last layers are the logic, proof, and trust, which have not been significantly explored. Some of the layers rely on the digital signature component to ensure security.

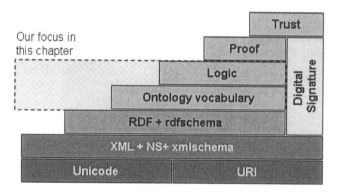

Figure 14-1. Semantic Web stack (Berners-Lee, Hendler et al. 2001)

In the following sections we will briefly describe these layers. While the notions presented have been simplified, they provide a reasonable conceptualization of the various components of the semantic Web.

URI and Unicode. A Universal Resource Identifier (URI) is a formatted string that serves as a means of identifying abstract or physical resource. A

URI can be further classified as a Uniform Resource Locator (URL) or a Uniform Resource Name (URN). A URL identifies resources via a representation of their primary access mechanism. A URN remains globally unique and persistent even when the resource ceases to exist or becomes unavailable.

Unicode provides a unique number for every character, independently of the underlying platform or program. Before the creation of unicode, there were various different encoding systems making the manipulation of data complex and required computers to support many different encodings.

XML. XML is accepted as a standard for data interchange on the Web allowing the structuring of data but without communicating the meaning of the data. It is a language for semi-structured data and has been proposed as a solution for data integration problems, because it allows a flexible coding and display of data, by using metadata to describe the structure of data. While XML has gained much of the world's attention it is important to recognize that XML is simply a way of standardizing data formats. But from the point of view of semantic interoperability, XML has limitations. One significant aspect is that there is no way to recognize the semantics of a particular domain because XML aims at document structure and imposes no common interpretation of the data (Decker, Melnik et al. 2000). Even though XML is simply a data-format standard, it is part of the set of technologies that constitute the foundations of the semantic Web.

RDF. At the top of XML, the World Wide Web Consortium (W3C) has developed the Resource Description Framework (RDF) (RDF 2002) language to standardize the definition and use of metadata. RDF uses XML and it is at the base of the semantic Web, so that all the other languages corresponding to the upper layers are built on top of it. RDF is a simple general-purpose metadata language for representing information in the Web and provides a model for describing and creating relationships between resources. RDF defines a resource as any object that is uniquely identifiable by a URI. Resources have properties associated with them. Properties are identified by property-types, and property-types have corresponding values. Property-types express the relationships of values associated with resources. The basic structure of RDF is very simple and basically uses RDF triples in the form of (subject, predicate, object). RDF has a very limited set of syntactic constructs and no other constructs except for triples is allowed.

RDF Schema. The RDF Schema (RDFS 2004) provides a type system for RDF. Briefly, the RDF Schema (RDFS) allows users to define resources (rdfs:Resource) with classes, properties, and values. The concept of RDFS class (rdfs:Class) is similar to the concept of class in object-oriented programming languages such as Java and C++. A class is a structure of similar things and inheritance is allowed. This allows resources to be defined as instances of classes. An RDFS property (rdf:Property) can be viewed as an attribute of a class. RDFS properties may inherit from other properties (rdfs:subPropertyOf), and domain (rdfs:domain) and range (rdfs:range) constraints can be applied to focus their use. For example, a domain constraint is used to limit what class or classes a specific property may have and a range constraint is used to limit its possible values. With these extensions, RDFS comes closer to existing ontology languages.

Ontologies. An ontology is an agreed vocabulary that provides a set of well-founded constructs to build meaningful higher level knowledge for specifying the semantics of terminology systems in a well defined and unambiguous manner. Ontologies can be used to assist in communication between humans, to achieve interoperability and communication among software systems, and to improve the design and the quality of software systems (Jasper and Uschold 1999).

In the previous sections, we have established that RDF and RDFS were the base models and syntax for the semantic Web. On the top of the RDF/S layer it is possible to define more powerful languages to describe semantics. The most prominent markup language for publishing and sharing data using ontologies on the Internet is the Web Ontology Language (OWL 2004). OWL adds a layer of expressive power to RDF/S, providing powerful mechanisms for defining complex conceptual structures, and formally describes the semantics of classes and properties used in Web resources using, most commonly, a logical formalism known as Description Logic (DL 2005).

Logic, Proof, and Trust. The purpose of this layer is to provide similar features to the ones that can be found in First Order Logic (FOL). The idea is to state any logical principle and allow the computer to reason by inference using these principles. For example, a university may decide that if a student has a GPA higher than 3.8, then he will receive a merit scholarship. A logic program can use this rule to make a simple deduction: "David has a GPA of 3.9, therefore he will be a recipient of a merit scholarship."

The use of inference engines in the semantic Web allows applications to inquire why a particular conclusion has been reached (inference engines, also called reasoners, are software applications that derive new facts or associations from existing information.). Semantic applications can give proof of their conclusions. Proof traces or explains the steps involved in logical reasoning.

Trust is the top layer of the Semantic Web architecture. This layer provides authentication of identity and evidence of the trustworthiness of data and services. While the other layers of the semantic Web stack have received a fair amount of attention, no significant research has been carried out in the context of this layer.

3. SEMANTIC WEB DEVELOPMENT ENVIRONMENTS

Several frameworks supporting OWL ontologies are available. We will briefly discuss the ones that are used the most by the developer community, namely the Jena framework, Protégé-OWL API and the WonderWeb OWL API, which are all available for Java language. These three APIs are open-source and thus interested people can carry out an in-depth study of their architecture. This is very important for the current stage of semantic Web development since it is difficult to know what the application's scope of the semantic Web will be in the near future. Therefore, open frameworks will allow for an easier integration of semantic Web components into new projects.

Jena (Jena 2002; Jena 2005) is a Java framework for building semantic Web applications developed by the HP Labs Semantic Web Programme. It provides a programmatic environment for RDF, RDFS and OWL, including a rule-based inference engine and a query language for RDF called RDQL (RDQL 2005). Since we are mostly interested in ontology support, in subsequent sections we will discuss the Jena 2 Ontology API included in the Jena toolkit. This API supports several ontology description languages such as DAML, DAML+OIL and OWL. However building ontologies in OWL W3C's language is strongly recommended because DAML and DAML+OIL support may be removed in future releases of Jena. Because Jena 2 Ontology API is language-neutral, it should be easy to update existing projects using Jena and other ontology languages to support OWL. Jena OWL API supports all three OWL sublanguages, namely OWL Lite, OWL DL and OWL Full. Specifying an URI to an OWL ontology, Jena parses the ontology and creates a model for it. With this model it is possible to manipulate the ontology, create new OWL classes, properties or individuals (instances). The parsing of OWL documents can be highly resource consuming, especially for documents describing large ontologies. To address this particularity, Jena provides a persistence mechanism to store and retrieve ontology models from databases efficiently. As stated before, Jena includes an inference engine which gives reasoning capabilities. Jena provides three different reasoners that can be attached to an ontology model, each of them providing a different degree of reasoning capability. More capable reasoners require substantially more time to answer queries. Therefore, developers should be very careful when choosing a reasoner. Of course, it is possible to create a model with no reasoner defined. An interesting aspect of Jena is that its inference engine is written in a very generic way so that it allows developers to write their own inference rules to better address their needs. This generic implementation also allows for attaching any reasoner that is compliant with the DIG interface, which is a standard providing access to reasoners, such as Racer, FaCT, and Pellet. Another important aspect is that it is very easy to find documentation and practical programming examples for Jena.

Protégé (Protégé 2005) is a free, open-source platform that provides a growing user community with a suite of tools to construct domain models and knowledge-based applications with ontologies. It was developed by the Stanford Medical Informatics Labs of the Stanford School of Medicine. The Protégé-OWL API is an open-source Java library for OWL and RDF(S). The API provides classes and methods to load and store OWL files, to query and manipulate OWL data models, and to perform reasoning (Protégé-API 2006). This API, which is part of the Protégé-OWL plug-in, extends the Protégé Core System based on frames so that it can support OWL ontologies and allows users to develop OWL plug-ins for Protégé or even to create standalone applications. Protégé-OWL API uses Jena framework for the parsing and reasoning over OWL ontologies and provides additional support for programming graphical user interfaces based on Java Swing library. The Protégé-OWL API architecture follows the model-view pattern, enabling users to write GUIs (the "view") to manipulate the internal representation of ontologies (the "model"). This architecture, together with the event mechanism also provided, allows programmers to build interactive user interfaces in an efficient and clean way. A community even stronger than Jena's one has grown around Protégé, making it very easy to find good documentation, examples and support for this API.

WonderWeb OWL API (OWLAPI 2006) is another API providing programmatic services to manipulate OWL ontologies. It can also infer new knowledge once a reasoner is attached to the ontology model. Pellet is one of the reasoners that is currently supported. One should note that the current release of this API is still in working progress. Consequently, there are some issues that need to be corrected. Nevertheless, WonderWeb OWL API was successfully used in several projects such as Swoop (SWOOP 2006) and Smore (SMORE 2006), respectively, an ontology editor and a semantic annotation tool, from the MIND LAB at the University of Maryland Institute for Advanced Computer Studies. This demonstrates that this API is mature enough to be considered when developing semantic Web applications. One major drawback of the WonderWeb OWL API is lack of documentation. Currently, Javadoc documentation and some open-source applications that use this API, is what can be found about it. It is very difficult to find practical examples. This fact may lead developers to choose to discard this API.

4.   OUR RUNNING ONTOLOGY

Our recent work has involved the development of a Semantic Course Management System (S-CMS). Course management systems (CMS) are becoming increasingly popular. Well-known CMSs include Blackboard.com and WebCT.com whose focus has centered on distance education opportunities. Typically, a CMS include a variety of functionalities, such as class project management, registration tool for students, examinations, enrolment management, test administration, assessment tools, and online discussion boards (Meinel, Sack et al. 2002).

The S-CMS system that we have developed is part of the Strawberry project[1] and explores the use of semantic Web technologies to develop an innovative CMS. The S-CMS provides a complete information and management solution for students and faculty members. Our focus and main objective was to automate the different procedures involved when students enroll or register for class projects. Managing a large course and its class projects is a complex undertaking. Many factors may contribute to this complexity, such as a large number of students, the variety of rules that allow students to register for a particular project, students' background, and student's grades.

The development of a semantic Web application typically starts with the creation of one or more ontology schema. For simplicity reasons, in this chapter we will only present one ontology, the University ontology. This ontology will be used in all the programming examples that we will show. As with any ontology, our ontology contains the definition of the various classes, attributes, and relationships that encapsulate the business objects that model a university domain. The class hierarchy of our simple ontology is shown in Figure 14-1 using the OWL Viz Protégé plug-in (OWLViz 2006).

---

[1] http://dme.uma.pt/jcardoso/Research/Projects/Strawberry/

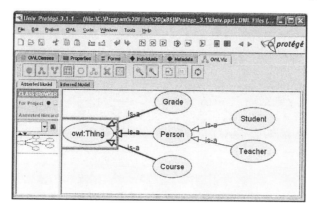

Figure 14-2. Class hierarchy

Some of the properties of our ontology are shown in Figure 14-2 using Protégé (Protégé 2005).

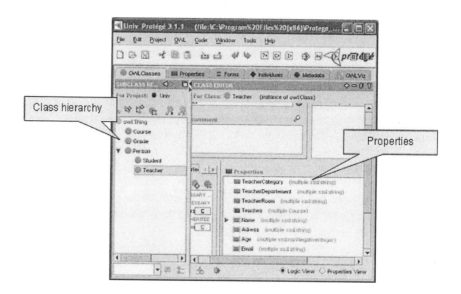

Figure 14-3. Classes and properties

5. USING JENA

Jena is a framework for building Semantic Web applications. It provides a programmatic environment for RDF, RDFS and OWL. It also includes a rule-based inference engine. Jena is open source and is a development effort of the HP Labs Semantic Web Research program. HP Labs have made considerable investments in Semantic Web research since 2000 which lead to the development of standards (such as RDF and OWL) and semantic applications (such as Jena).

The Jena toolbox includes a Java programming API that gives a framework to program semantic Web applications. The API is divided into five sets of functions that deal with the processing of ontologies, namely:

- Processing and manipulation of RDF data models
- Processing and manipulation of ontologies
- SPARQL query support
- Inference on OWL and RDFS data models
- Persistence of ontologies to databases

In this chapter we will focus primarily on the API responsible for the processing and manipulation of OWL ontologies.

5.1 Installing Jena

To install Jena the first step is to download Jena API from http://jena.sourceforge.net. The version used for the examples shown in this chapter was Jena 2.3. Once you have downloaded Jena (in our case the package was named Jena 2.3.zip), you need to extract the zip file.

You will find in the /lib directory all the libraries needed to use the Jena API. To develop semantic applications with Java you will need to update your CLASSPATH to include the following libraries:

- `antlr-2.7.5.jar`
- `arq.jar`
- `commons-logging.jar`
- `concurrent.jar`
- `icu4j_3_4.jar`
- `jakarta-oro-2.0.8.jar`
- `jena.jar`
- `jenatest.jar`
- `junit.jar`
- `log4j-1.2.12.jar`

- `stax-1.1.1-dev.jar`
- `stax-api-1.0.jar`
- `xercesImpl.jar`
- `xml-apis.jar`

5.2   Creating an Ontology Model

The main Java class that represents an ontology in memory is the OntModel.

```
OntModel model;
```

In Jena, ontology models are created using the `ModelFactory` class. A model can be dynamically created by calling the `createOntologyModel()` method.

```
OntModel m = ModelFactory.createOntologyModel();
```

When creating an ontology it is possible to describe its characteristics, such as the ontology language used to model the ontology, the storage scheme and the reasoner.

To describe specific characteristics of an ontology, the method `createOntologyModel(OntModelSpec o)` needs to be called and accepts a parameter of the type `OntModelSpec`. For example, `OntModelSpec.OWL_DL_MEM` determines that the ontology to be created will have an OWL DL model and will be stored in memory with no support for reasoning. Various other values are available. Table 14-1 illustrates some of the possibilities.

Table 14-1. Types of ontology models with Jena

Field	Description
`DAML_MEM`	A simple DAML model stored in memory with no support for reasoning
`DAML_MEM_RDFS_INF`	A DAML model stored in memory with support for RDFS inference
`OWL_LITE_MEM`	A simple OWL Lite model stored in memory with no support for reasoning
`OWL_MEM_RULE_INF`	A OWL Lite model stored in memory with support for OWL rules inference
`RDFS_MEM`	A simple OWL Lite model stored in memory with no support for reasoning

More than 20 different ontology models can be created. The following segment of code illustrates how to create an OWL ontology model, stored in memory, with no support for reasoning.

```
import com.hp.hpl.jena.ontology.OntModel;
import com.hp.hpl.jena.ontology.OntModelSpec;
import com.hp.hpl.jena.rdf.model.ModelFactory;

public class CreateModel{
  public static void main(String[] args) {
    OntModel model = ModelFactory.createOntologyModel(
                              OntModelSpec.OWL_MEM);

  }
}
```

5.3   Reading an Ontology Model

Once we have an ontology model, we can load an ontology. Ontologies can be loaded using the `read` method which can read an ontology from an URL or directly from an input stream.

```
read(String url)
read(InputStream reader, String base)
```

In the following example, we show a segment of code that creates an OWL ontology model in memory and loads the University ontology from the URL `http://dme.uma.pt/jcardoso/owl/University.owl`.

```
OntModel model = ModelFactory.createOntologyModel(
                          OntModelSpec.OWL_MEM);
model.read("http://dme.uma.pt/jcardoso/owl/University.owl");
```

For performance reasons, it is possible to cache ontology models locally. To cache a model, it is necessary to use a helper class that manages documents (`OntDocumentManager`), allowing subsequent accesses to an ontology to be made locally. The following example illustrates how to add an entry for an alternative copy of an OWL file with the given OWL URI. An alternative copy can be added by calling the method `addAltEntry`.

```
import com.hp.hpl.jena.ontology.OntDocumentManager;
import com.hp.hpl.jena.ontology.OntModel;
import com.hp.hpl.jena.ontology.OntModelSpec;
```

```
import com.hp.hpl.jena.rdf.model.ModelFactory;

public class CacheOntology {
  public static void main(String[] args) {
    OntModel m = ModelFactory.createOntologyModel(
                          OntModelSpec.OWL_MEM);
    OntDocumentManager dm = m.getDocumentManager();
    dm.addAltEntry(
            "http://dme.uma.pt/jcardoso/owl/University.owl",
            "file:///c:/University.OWL");
    m.read("http://dme.uma.pt/jcardoso/owl/University.owl");
  }
}
```

Since we specify that a local copy of our University ontology exists in file:///c:/University.OWL, Jena can load the ontology from the local copy instead of loading it from the URL.

5.4   Manipulating Classes

OWL ontology classes are described using the OntClass Java class. To retrieve a particular class from an ontology we can simply use the method getOntClass(URI) from the OntModel or, alternatively, it is possible to use the listClasses() method to obtain a list of all the classes of an ontology. The class OntClass allows us to retrieve all the subclasses of a class using the method listSubClasses(). For example, the following segment of code allows listing of all the subclasses of the class #Person of our University ontology.

```
String baseURI=
          "http://dme.uma.pt/jcardoso/owl/University.owl#";

OntModel model = ModelFactory.createOntologyModel(
                          OntModelSpec.OWL_MEM);

model.read("http://dme.uma.pt/jcardoso/owl/University.owl");
OntClass p = model.getOntClass(baseURI+"Person");
for(ExtendedIterator i=p.listSubClasses(); i.hasNext();)
{
    OntClass Class=(OntClass)i.next();
    System.out.println(Class.getURI());
}
```

In our scenario the output of this example is:

```
http://dme.uma.pt/jcardoso/owl/University.owl#Student
http://dme.uma.pt/jcardoso/owl/University.owl#Teacher
```

The `createClass` method can be used to create a new class. For example we can create the new class `#Researcher` and set as superclass the class `#Person` from the previous example,

```
OntClass p = model.getOntClass(baseURI+"Person");
OntClass r = model.createClass(baseURI+"Researcher");
r.addSuperClass(p)
```

The class `OntClass` has several methods available to check the characteristics of a class. All these methods return a Boolean parameter. Some of these methods are illustrated in table 14-2.

Table 14-2. Methods to check the characteristics of an OntClass object

`isIntersectionClass()`	`isComplementClass()`
`isRestriction()`	`hasSuperClass()`

5.5   Manipulating Properties

With Jena, properties are represented using the class `OntProperty`. Two types of OWL properties exist:

- Datatype Properties are attributes of a class. These types of properties link individuals to data values and can be used to restrict an individual member of a class to RDF literals and XML Schema datatypes.
- Object Properties are relationships between classes. They link individuals to individuals. They relate an instance of one class to an instance of another class.

It is possible to dynamically create new properties. The `OntModel` class includes the method `createXXX()` to create properties (and classes as we have already seen previously). As an example, the following code creates a new class named `#Project` and an `ObjectProperty` named `#ProjectOwner`. Using the `setRange` and `setDomain` methods of the class `ObjectProperty` we set the domain of the new property to `#Project` and its range to `#Person`.

```
...
OntClass p=model.createClass(BaseUri +"#Project");
ObjectProperty po=
         model.createObjectProperty(BaseUri+"#ProjectOwner");
po.setRange(model.getResource(BaseUri+"#Person"));
po.setDomain(p);
...
```

A DatatypeProperty can be created in the same way, but using the `createDatatypeProperty` method, i.e.

```
DatatypeProperty p=
  model.createDatatypeProperty(BaseUri+"#ProjectDate");
```

The class `OntProperty` has several methods available to check the characteristics of a Property. All these methods return a Boolean parameter. For example,

Table 14-3. Methods to check the characteristics of an OntProperty object

isTransitiveProperty()	isSymmetricProperty()
isDatatypeProperty()	isObjectProperty()

The following segment of code can be used to list the properties of a class. Basically the `listDeclaredProperties()` from the class `OntClass` needs to be called.

```
import com.hp.hpl.jena.ontology.OntClass;
import com.hp.hpl.jena.ontology.OntModel;
import com.hp.hpl.jena.ontology.OntModelSpec;
import com.hp.hpl.jena.rdf.model.ModelFactory;
import com.hp.hpl.jena.util.iterator.ExtendedIterator;

public class ListProperties {
  public static void main(String[] args) {
    String baseURI=
            "http://dme.uma.pt/jcardoso/owl/University.owl#";

    OntModel model = ModelFactory.createOntologyModel(
                                 OntModelSpec.OWL_MEM);

    model.read(
            "http://dme.uma.pt/jcardoso/owl/University.owl");
```

```
OntClass cls = model.getOntClass(baseURI+"Person");
System.out.println("Class:");
System.out.println("   "+cls.getURI());
System.out.println("Properties:");
for(ExtendedIterator j=cls.listDeclaredProperties();
                                         .hasNext();)
  {
      System.out.println("   "+(OntProperty)j.next());
  }
 }
}
```

The output of executing this example is:

```
Class:
   http://dme.uma.pt/jcardoso/owl/University.owl#Person
Properties:
   http://dme.uma.pt/jcardoso/owl/University.owl#Age
   http://dme.uma.pt/jcardoso/owl/University.owl#Address
   http://dme.uma.pt/jcardoso/owl/University.owl#Email
   http://dme.uma.pt/jcardoso/owl/University.owl#Name
```

#Age, #Address, #Email, and #Name are properties of the class #Person.

5.6   Manipulating Instances

Instances, also known as individuals of classes, are represented through the class Instance. Having a class OntClass it is possible to list all its instances using the method listInstances(). A similar method exists in the class OntModel but is named listIndividuals(). For example, the following segment of code lists all the individuals of the University ontology,

```
import com.hp.hpl.jena.ontology.Individual;
import com.hp.hpl.jena.ontology.OntModel;
import com.hp.hpl.jena.ontology.OntModelSpec;
import com.hp.hpl.jena.rdf.model.ModelFactory;
import com.hp.hpl.jena.util.iterator.ExtendedIterator;

public class ListInstances {
```

```
public static void main(String[] args) {
   OntModel model = ModelFactory.createOntologyModel(
                                    OntModelSpec.OWL_MEM);

   model.read(
            "http://dme.uma.pt/jcardoso/owl/University.owl");
   for(ExtendedIterator i= model.listIndividuals();
                                       .hasNext();)
   {
      System.out.println(((Individual)i.next()).toString());
   }
 }
}
```

The output of executing this example is:

```
http://dme.uma.pt/jcardoso/owl/University.owl#Adelia
http://dme.uma.pt/jcardoso/owl/University.owl#Fatima
http://dme.uma.pt/jcardoso/owl/University.owl#Carolina
http://dme.uma.pt/jcardoso/owl/University.owl#ASP
http://dme.uma.pt/jcardoso/owl/University.owl#SD
http://dme.uma.pt/jcardoso/owl/University.owl#CF
http://dme.uma.pt/jcardoso/owl/University.owl#Grade_1
http://dme.uma.pt/jcardoso/owl/University.owl#Grade_3
http://dme.uma.pt/jcardoso/owl/University.owl#Grade_2
http://dme.uma.pt/jcardoso/owl/University.owl#IC
http://dme.uma.pt/jcardoso/owl/University.owl#JC
http://dme.uma.pt/jcardoso/owl/University.owl#RF
```

To list all the individuals of the class #Student, we can add the following lines of code to the previous example:

```
OntClass Student = model.getOntClass(
     "http://dme.uma.pt/jcardoso/owl/University.owl#Student");
for(ExtendedIterator  i= Student.listInstances();i.hasNext();)
{
    System.out.println(((Individual)i.next()).toString());
}
```

Now we can create instances dynamically. The following example creates an instance #Jorge of type #Teacher and set the name and e-mail of the instance #Jorge to "Jorge Cardoso" and jcardoso@uma.pt, respectively.

```
Resource tClass=model.getResource(baseURI+"#Teacher");
Individual teacher=
            model.createIndividual(baseURI+"#Jorge",tClass);
DatatypeProperty name =
            model.getDatatypeProperty(baseURI+"#Name");
teacher.addProperty(name,"Jorge Cardoso");
DatatypeProperty email =
            model.getDatatypeProperty(baseURI+"#Email");
teacher.addProperty(email,"jcardoso@uma.pt");
```

5.7 Queries with Jena

One task that is particularly useful once an ontology is available, is to query its data. An OWL knowledge base can be queried using API function calls or using RDQL (RDF Data Query Language). Jena's built-in query language is RDQL, a query language for RDF. While not yet a formally established standard, (it was submitted in January 2004), RDQL is commonly used by many RDF applications. RDQL has been designed to execute queries in RDF models, but it can be used to query OWL models since their underlying representation is RDF. It is a very effective way of retrieving data from an RDF model.

5.7.1 RDQL Syntax

RDQL's syntax is very similar to SQL's syntax. Some of their concepts are comparable and will be well-known to people that have previously worked with relational database queries. A simple example of a RDQL query structure is,

```
SELECT variables
WHERE conditions
```

Variables are represented with a question mark followed by the variable name (for example: ?a, ?b). Conditions are written as triples (Subject Property Value) and delimited with "<" and ">". RDQL allows us to search within a RDF graph to find subgraphs that match some patterns of RDF node triples.

Using our University ontology, we can inquire about the direct subclasses of the class #Person. This can be achieved with the following RDQL query:

```
SELECT ?x WHERE (?x <rdfs:subClassOf> <univ:Person>)
USING rdfs FOR <http://www.w3.org/2000/01/rdf-schema#>
     univ FOR
               http://dme.uma.pt/jcardoso/owl/University.owl#>
```

The ?x in this query is a variable representing something that we want of the query. The query engine will try to substitute a URI value for ?x when it finds a subclass of #Person. The "rdfs" and "univ" prefixes make the URIs in the query shorter and more understandable. Executing the above query to the University ontology illustrated in Figure 14-1 we expected to retrieve two URIs. One corresponding to the #Student concept and the other to the concept #Teacher, i.e.

```
<http://dme.uma.pt/jcardoso/owl/University.owl#Student>
<http://dme.uma.pt/jcardoso/owl/University.owl#Teacher>
```

RDQL allows complex queries to be expressed succinctly, with a query engine performing the hard work of accessing the data model. Sometimes, not every part of the ontology structure is known. For example, if we wish to inquire about the list of courses that a student has enrolled for. Since we do not know all the URIs, we have to use variables to represent the unknown items in the query. For instance, "Show me all Y where Y is a "Course", X is a "Student", X is named "Adelia Gouveia", and X studies Y." The response will list all the possible values for Y that would match the desired properties. The query for this question would be,

```
SELECT ?y
WHERE (?x <univ:Name> "Adelia Gouveia"^^xsd:string),
      (?x <univ:Studies> ?y)
USING univ FOR
               <http://dme.uma.pt/jcardoso/owl/University.owl#>
```

We can also ask for all the students that have passed courses with a grade higher than 12,

```
SELECT ?x,?c
WHERE (?x <univ:HasGrade> ?y),
      (?x <univ:Studies> ?c),
      (?y <univ:Value> ?z) AND ?z>12
USING univ FOR
               <http://dme.uma.pt/jcardoso/owl/University.owl#>
```

5.7.2   RDQL and Jena

Jena's `com.hp.hpl.jena.rdql` package contains all of the classes and interfaces needed to use RDQL in a Java application.

```
import com.hp.hpl.jena.rdql;
```

Jena's RDQL is implemented as an object called `Query`. To create a query it is sufficient to put the RDQL query in a `String` object, and pass it to the constructor of `Query`,

```
String queryString ="...";
Query query = new Query(queryString);
```

The method `setSource` of the object `Query` must be called to explicitly set the ontology model to be used as the source for the query (the model can alternatively be specified with a FROM clause in the RDQL query.)

```
query.setSource(model);
```

Once a `Query` is prepared, a `QueryEngine` must be created and the query can be executed using the `exec()` method. The `Query` needs to be passed to the `QueryEngine` object, i.e.

```
QueryEngine qe = new QueryEngine(query);
```

The results of a query are stored in a `QueryResult` object.

```
QueryResults results = qe.exec();
```

Once we have the results of a RDQL query, a practical object that can be used to display the results in a convenient way is to use the `QueryResultsFormatter` object.

```
QueryResultsFormatter formatter =
          new QueryResultsFormatter((QueryResults) results );
formatter.printAll(new PrintWriter(System.out));
```

An alternative to using the `QueryResultsFormatter` object is to iterate through the data retrieved using an iterator. For example,

```
QueryResults result = new QueryEngine(query).exec();
```

```
for (Iterator i = result; i.hasNext();) {
    System.out.println(i.next());
}
```

With RDQL it is possible to inquire about the values that satisfy a triple with a specific subject and property. To run this query in Jena, the University ontology is loaded into memory. The query is executed using the static `exec` method of Jena's `Query` class and the results are processed. For example, the following segment of code retrieves all the RDF triples of an ontology.

```
import java.util.Iterator;

import com.hp.hpl.jena.ontology.OntModel;
import com.hp.hpl.jena.ontology.OntModelSpec;
import com.hp.hpl.jena.rdf.model.ModelFactory;
import com.hp.hpl.jena.rdql.Query;
import com.hp.hpl.jena.rdql.QueryEngine;
import com.hp.hpl.jena.rdql.QueryResults;

public class RDQL {
    public static void main(String[] args) {
        OntModel model = ModelFactory.createOntologyModel(
                                    OntModelSpec.OWL_MEM);
        model.read(
                "http://dme.uma.pt/jcardoso/owl/University.owl");

        String sql= "SELECT ?x,?y,?z WHERE (?x ?y ?z)";
        Query query=new Query(sql);
        query.setSource(model);
        QueryResults result = new QueryEngine(query).exec();
        for (Iterator i = result; i.hasNext();) {
            System.out.println(i.next());
        }
    }
}
```

5.8   Inference and Reasoning

Inference engines, also called reasoners, are software applications that derive new facts or associations from existing information. Inference and inference rules allow for deriving new data from data that is already known. Thus, new pieces of knowledge can be added based on previous ones. By creating a model of the information and relationships, we enable reasoners to draw logical conclusions based on the model. For example, with OWL it is possible to make inferences based on the associations represented in the models, which primarily means inferring transitive relationships. Nowadays, many inference engines are available.

- Jena reasoner – Jena includes a generic rule based inference engine together with configured rule sets for RDFS and for OWL.
- Jess – Using Jess (Gandon and Sadeh 2003) it is possible to build Java software that has the capacity to "reason" using knowledge supplied in the form of declarative rules. Jess has a small footprint and it is one of the fastest rule engines available. It was developed at Carnegie Melon University.
- SWI-Prolog Semantic Web Library – Prolog is a natural language for working with RDF and OWL. The developers of SWI-Prolog have created a toolkit for creating and editing RDF and OWL applications, as well as a reasoning package (Wielemaker 2005).
- FaCT++ – This system is a Description Logic reasoner, which is a re-implementation of the FaCT reasoner. It allows reasoning with the OWL language (FaCT 2005).

In the following sections we will concentrate our attention on using the Jena rule based inference engine programmatically.

5.8.1 Jena Reasoners

The Jena architecture is designed to allow several inference engines to be used with Jena. The current version of Jena includes five predefined reasoners that can be invoked, namely:

- **Transitive reasoner**: A very simple reasoner which implements only the transitive and symmetric properties of `rdfs:subPropertyOf` and `rdfs:subClassOf`.
- **DAML micro reasoner**: A DAML reasoner which provides an engine to legacy applications that use the DAML language.
- **RDFS rule reasoner**: A RDFS reasoner that supports most of the RDFS language.
- **Generic rule reasoner**: A generic reasoner that is the basis for the RDFS and OWL reasoners.
- **OWL reasoners**: OWL rule reasoners are an extension of the RDFS reasoner. They exploit a rule-based engine for reasoning. OWL reasoners supports OWL Lite plus some of the constructs of OWL Full.

In this section we will study how to develop Java applications using the OWL reasoning engines since OWL is becoming the most popular language on the semantic Web compared to DAML and RDFS.

5.8.2   Jena OWL Reasoners

Jena provides three internal reasoners of different complexity: OWL, OWL Mini, and OWL Micro reasoners. They range from the simple Micro reasoner with only domain-range and subclass inference, to a complete OWL Lite reasoner.

The current version of Jena (version 2.3) does not fully support OWL yet. It can understand all the syntax of OWL, but cannot reason in OWL Full. Jena supports OWL Lite plus some constructs of OWL DL and OWL Full, such as `owl:hasValue`. Some of the important constructs that are not supported in Jena include `owl:complementOf` and `owl:oneOf`. Table 14-4 illustrates the OWL constructs supported by the reasoning engines available.

Table 14-4. Jena reasoning support

OWL Construct	Reasoner
rdfs:subClassOf, rdfs:subPropertyOf, rdf:type	all
rdfs:domain, rdfs:range	all
owl:intersectionOf	all
owl:unionOf	all
owl:equivalentClass	all
owl:disjointWith	full, mini
owl:sameAs, owl:differentFrom, owl:distinctMembers	full, mini
owl:Thing	all
owl:equivalentProperty, owl:inverseOf	all
owl:FunctionalProperty, owl:InverseFunctionalProperty	all
owl:SymmeticProperty, owl:TransitiveProperty	all
owl:someValuesFrom	full, (mini)
owl:allValuesFrom	full, mini
owl:minCardinality, owl:maxCardinality, owl:cardinality	full, (mini)
owl:hasValue	all
owl:complementOf	none
owl:oneOf	none

For a complete OWL DL reasoning it is necessary to use an external DL reasoner. The Jena DIG interface makes it easy to connect to any reasoner that supports the DIG standard. By communicating with other ontology processing systems, such as RACER or FAcT, Jena can enhance its ability for reasoning in large and complex ontologies.

5.8.3   Programming Jena reasoners

Given an ontology model, Jena's reasoning engine can derive additional statements that the model does not express explicitly. Inference and inference rules allow for deriving new data from data that is already known. Thus, new pieces of knowledge can be added based on previous ones. By creating a model of the information and relationships, we enable reasoners to draw logical conclusions based on the model.

As we have already done previously, the first step to develop a semantic Web application with support for reasoning is to create an ontology model,

```
String baseURI=
            "http://dme.uma.pt/jcardoso/owl/University.owl#";

OntModel model = ModelFactory.createOntologyModel(
                            OntModelSpec.OWL_MEM);

model.read("http://dme.uma.pt/jcardoso/owl/University.owl");
```

The main class to carry our reasoning is the class `Reasoner`. This class allows us to extract knowledge from an ontology. Jena provides several reasoners to work with different types of ontology. Since in our example we want to use our OWL University ontology, we need to obtain an OWL reasoner. This reasoner can be accessed using the `ReasonerRegistery.getOWLReasoner()` method call, i.e.,

```
Reasoner reasoner = ReasonerRegistry.getOWLReasoner();
```

Other reasoners can be instantiated with a call to the methods `getOWLMicroReasoner()`, `getOWLMiniReasoner()`, `getRDFSReasoner()`, and `getTransitiveReasoner()`.

Once we have a reasoner, we need to bind it to the ontology model we have created. This is achieved with a call to the method `bindSchema`, i.e.,

```
reasoner = reasoner.bindSchema(model);
```

This invocation returns a reasoner which can infer new knowledge from the ontology's rules. The next step is to use the bound reasoner to create an `InfModel` from the University model,

```
InfModel infmodel=ModelFactory.createInfModel(reasoner,model);
```

Since several Java packages are needed to execute and run the examples that we have given, the following segment shows all the Java code needed to instantiate a reasoner.

```
import com.hp.hpl.jena.ontology.OntModel;
import com.hp.hpl.jena.ontology.OntModelSpec;
import com.hp.hpl.jena.rdf.model.InfModel;
import com.hp.hpl.jena.rdf.model.ModelFactory;
import com.hp.hpl.jena.reasoner.Reasoner;
import com.hp.hpl.jena.reasoner.ReasonerRegistry;

public class InstanciateReasoner {
  public static void main(String[] args) {
    OntModel model = ModelFactory.createOntologyModel(
                                OntModelSpec.OWL_MEM);

    String BaseUri=
              "http://dme.uma.pt/jcardoso/owl/University.owl";
    model.read(BaseUri);

    Reasoner reasoner = ReasonerRegistry.getOWLReasoner();
    reasoner=reasoner.bindSchema(model);
    InfModel infmodel
            = ModelFactory.createInfModel(reasoner,model);
  }
}
```

Once a reasoner is instantiated, one of the first tasks that we can execute is to check for inconsistencies within the ontology data by using the `validate()` method, i.e.,

```
ValidityReport vr = infmodel.validate();
if (vr.isValid()){
  System.out.println("Valid OWL");
}
else {
  System.out.println("Not a valid OWL!");
  for (Iterator i =  vr.getReports(); i.hasNext();){
    System.out.println(i.next());
  }
}
```

This example prints a report if the ontology data is found to be inconsistent. The following output shows the example of a report generated when trying to validate an inconsistent ontology,

```
Not a valid OWL
  - Error ("range check"): "Incorrectly typed literal due to range
(prop, value)"
Culprit=
        http://dme.uma.pt/jcardoso/owl/University.owl#Carolina
Implicated node:
            http://dme.uma.pt/jcardoso/owl/University.owl#Email
Implicated node: 'carolina@uma.pt'
```

The report indicates that the email address (#Email) of the individual #Carolina has an incorrect type.

One other interesting operation that we can carry out is to obtain information from the ontology. For example, we can retrieve all the pairs (property, resource) associated with the resource describing the course CS8050, which is defined with ID #CS8050.

```
String BaseUri=
                "http://dme.uma.pt/jcardoso/owl/University.owl";
. . .
Resource res = infmodel.getResource(BaseUri+"#CS");
System.out.println("CS8050 *:");

for (StmtIterator i =
    infmodel.listStatements(res,(Property)null,(Resource)null);
    i.hasNext(); )
{
  Statement stmt = i.nextStatement();
  System.out.println(PrintUtil.print(stmt));
}
```

The output of running the previous example is shown below. To make the output more readable we have replaced the URI http://dme.uma.pt/jcardoso/owl/University.owl with the symbol @ and the URI http://www.w3.org/2001/XMLSchema with the symbol §.

```
CS8050 *:
(@#CS8050 rdf:type @#Course)
```

```
(@#CS8050 @#IsStudiedBy @#Adelia)
(@#CS8050 @#CourseName 'Semantic Web'^^§#string)
(@#CS8050 @#IsStudiedBy @#Carolina)
(@#CS8050 @#IsTeachedBy @#IsabelCardoso)
(@#CS8050 rdf:type owl:Thing)
(@#CS8050 rdf:type rdfs:Resource)
. . .
(@#CS8050 owl:sameAs @#CS8050)
```

Instance recognition is another important operation in inference. Instance recognition tests if a particular individual belongs to a class. For example, in our University ontology, #Adelia is known to be an individual of the class #Student and the class #Student is a subclass of the class #Person. One question that can be asked is if #Adelia is recognized to be an instance or individual of the class #Person, in other words is Adelia a person? This can be asked of the inference model using the contains method, i.e.,

```
Resource r1 = infmodel.getResource(BaseUri+"#Adelia");
Resource r2 = infmodel.getResource(BaseUri+"#Person");

if (infmodel.contains(r1, RDF.type, r2)) {
    System.out.println("Adelia is a Person");
} else {
    System.out.println("Adelia is not a Person");
}
```

Other interesting examples of inference include the use of the transitivity, union, functional, and intersection properties.

5.9 Persistence

As we have seen above, Jena provides a set of methods to load ontologies from files containing information models and instances. Jena can also store and load ontologies from relational databases. Depending on the database management system used, it is possible to distribute stored metadata. While Jena itself is not distributed, by using a distributed database back end, an application may be distributed. Currently, Jena only supports MySQL, Oracle and PostgreSQL. To create a persistent model in a database we can use the ModelFactory object and invoke the createModelRDBMaker method. This method accepts a DBConnection connection object to the database. An object ModelMaker will be created and can subsequently be used to create the model in the database.

For example, to store an existing ontology model in a database we can execute the following segment of code,

```
Class.forName("com.mysql.jdbc.Driver");
String BaseURI=
          "http://dme.uma.pt/jcardoso/owl/University.owl";
DBConnection conn = new DBConnection(
                         "jdbc:mysql://localhost/UnivDB",
                         "mylogin",
                         "mypassword",
                         "MySQL");
ModelMaker maker=ModelFactory.createModelRDBMaker(conn);
Model db=maker.createModel(BaseURI,false);
db.begin();
db.read(BaseURI);
db.commit();
```

And to read a model from a database we can use the following program,

```
Class.forName("com.mysql.jdbc.Driver");
String BaseURI=
               "http://dme.uma.pt/jcardoso/owl/University.owl";
DBConnection conn = new DBConnection(
                         "jdbc:mysql://localhost/UnivDB",
                         "mylogin", "mypassword", "MySQL");
ModelMaker maker=ModelFactory.createModelRDBMaker(conn);
Model base=maker.createModel(BaseURI, false);
model=ModelFactory.createOntologyModel(
                         OntModelSpec.OWL_MEM,base);
```

6. QUESTIONS FOR DISCUSSION

Beginner:
1. Identify the main differences between XML and RDF.
2. Install Jena in your computer and create programmatically an OWL ontology describing painters and their paintings. The ontology should be able to represent the following statements: "Painter X has painted the painting Y", "Painter X was born in W", and "Painting Y was painted in year Z".
3. Create several individuals for the Painters ontology. For example: Paul Cezanne, born 1839, Aix-en-Provence, France, painted "Le paysan" and

"Le Vase Bleu"; Leonardo da Vinci, born 1452, Vinci, Florence, painted "Mona Lisa" and "The Last Supper"; Michelangelo Buonaroti, born 1475, Florence, painted "Sybille de Cummes" and "Delphes Sylphide".

Intermediate:
1. Identify the main differences between RDFS and OWL.
2. Write down an RDQL query which retrieves the names of all the painters born in Florence using the ontology created in the previous exercise.
3. Use Jena to execute the previous RDQL query and write down the results of executing the query on the ontology.
4. Make your ontology persistent in a database.

Advanced:
3. Write down and execute an RDQL query which retrieves the paintings Michelangelo Buonaroti painted in 1512 (note: The "Sybille de Cummes" was painted 1512).
4. Validate your model using Jena's inference engine.
5. Why is inference a time consuming operation?

7.   SUGGESTED ADDITIONAL READINGS

- Jena Documentation, http://jena.sourceforge.net/documentation.html. This is a fundamental source of information to start programming with the Jena Framework.
- Antoniou, G. and van Harmelen, F. *A semantic Web primer.* Cambridge, MA: MIT Press, 2004. 238 pp.: This book is a good introduction to Semantic Web languages.
- H. Peter Alesso and Craig F. Smith, *Developing Semantic Web Services*, AK Peters, Ltd, October, 2004, 445 pp.: The book presents a good overview of Semantic Tools in chapter thirteen.

8.   REFERENCES

Berners-Lee, T., J. Hendler, et al. (2001). The Semantic Web. Scientific American. **May 2001**.

Berners-Lee, T., J. Hendler, et al. (2001). The Semantic Web: A new form of Web content that is meaningful to computers will unleash a revolution of new possibilities. Scientific American.

Cardoso, J. (2004). Issues of Dynamic Travel Packaging using Web Process Technology. International Conference e-Commerce 2004, Lisbon, Portugal.

Cardoso, J., J. Miller, et al. (2005). Academic and Industrial Research: Do their Approaches Differ in Adding Semantics to Web Services. Semantic Web Process: powering next generation of processes with Semantics and Web services. J. Cardoso and S. A. Heidelberg, Germany, Springer-Verlag. **3387**: 14-21.

Decker, S., S. Melnik, et al. (2000). "The Semantic Web: The Roles of XML and RDF." Internet Computing **4**(5): 63-74.

DL (2005). Description Logics, http://www.dl.kr.org/.

FaCT (2005). FaCT++, http://owl.man.ac.uk/factplusplus/.

Gandon, F. L. and N. M. Sadeh (2003). OWL inference engine using XSLT and JESS, http://www-2.cs.cmu.edu/~sadeh/MyCampusMirror/OWLEngine.html.

Ian Horrocks, Peter F. Patel-Schneider, et al. (2003). SWRL: A Semantic Web Rule Language Combining OWL and RuleML, http://www.daml.org/2003/11/swrl/.

Jasper, R. and M. Uschold (1999). A framework for understanding and classifying ontology applications. IJCAI99 Workshop on Ontologies and Problem-Solving Methods.

Jena (2002). The jena semantic web toolkit, http://www.hpl.hp.com/semweb/jena-top.html, Hewlett-Packard Company.

Jena (2005). Jena - A Semantic Web Framework for Java, http://jena.sourceforge.net/,.

Karvounarakis, G., S. Alexaki, et al. (2002). RQL: a declarative query language for RDF. Eleventh International World Wide Web Conference, Honolulu, Hawaii, USA.

Kumar, A. and B. Smith (2004). On Controlled Vocabularies in Bioinformatics: A Case Study in Gene Ontology. Drug Discovery Today: BIOSILICO. **2**: 246-252.

Lassila, O. and D. McGuinness (2001). "The Role of Frame-Based Representation on the Semantic Web." Linköping Electronic Articles in Computer and Information Science **6**(5).

Meinel, C., H. Sack, et al. (2002). Course management in the twinkle of an eye - LCMS: a professional course management system. Proceedings of the 30th annual ACM SIGUCCS conference on User services, Providence, Rhode Island, USA, ACM Press.

OWL (2004). OWL Web Ontology Language Reference, W3C Recommendation, World Wide Web Consortium, http://www.w3.org/TR/owl-ref/. **2004**.

OWLAPI (2006). "The WonderWeb OLW API, http://sourceforge.net/projects/owlapi."

OWL-S (2004). OWL-based Web Service Ontology. **2004**.

OWLViz (2006). OWL Viz. [Online] Available at http://www.co-ode.org/downloads/owlviz/.

Protégé (2005). Protégé, Stanford Medical Informatics. **2005**.

Protégé-API (2006). The Protégé-OWL API - Programmer's Guide, http://protege.stanford.edu/plugins/owl/api/guide.html.

RDF (2002). Resource Description Framework (RDF), http://www.w3.org/RDF/.

RDFS (2004). RDF Vocabulary Description Language 1.0: RDF Schema, W3C, http://www.w3.org/TR/rdf-schema/.

RDQL (2005). Jena RDQL, http://jena.sourceforge.net/RDQL/.

Roure, D., N. Jennings, et al. (2001). Research Agenda for the Future Semantic Grid: A Future e-Science Infrastructure http://www.semanticgrid.org/v1.9/semgrid.pdf.

Shum, S. B., E. Motta, et al. (2000). "ScholOnto: an ontology-based digital library server for research documents and discourse." International Journal on Digital Libraries **3**(3): 237-248.

SMORE (2006). "SMORE - Create OWL Markup for HTML Web Pages, http://www.mindswap.org/2005/SMORE/."

Swoogle (2005). Search and Metadata for the Semantic Web - http://swoogle.umbc.edu/.

SWOOP (2006). "SWOOP - A Hypermedia-based Featherweight OWL Ontology Editor, www.mindswap.org/2004/SWOOP/."

Wielemaker, J. (2005). SWI-Prolog Semantic Web Library, http://www.swi-prolog.org/packages/semweb.html.

Index